INTRODUCTION TO
POLITICS

leonard robinson
taehyun nam

Kendall Hunt
publishing company

CONTENTS

THE DEFINITION OF POLITICS

Can we find a category within which we can put the following people together?

Barack H. Obama and George W. Bush. Obviously these people have been the occupants of the White House. Obama is the current incumbent who succeeded the 43rd President Bush. Thus, the category "the US presidents" include both individuals.

How about Nancy Pelosi and Dick Cheney? Well, it is not so obvious, but some may recall seeing these people side by side in the chamber of the House when George W. Bush gave speeches to the Congress during his presidency. Pelosi was there as the Speaker of the House and Cheney sat in the dual role as the Vice President who was the president of the Senate, thereby having the constitutional authority to break any tie votes in that body. What do their share? Pelosi and Cheney have or had a great amount of influence on the legislative bodies. So, why don't we say they belong to a category called "prime legislators of the US Congress" for now.

Can we find a common ground among these four people? Hmm . . . Not easy, but there seems to be something, right? They make important decisions and their effects are national and often go beyond our national boundary. Their noticeable decisions, of course not made all together, include the US invasion of Afghanistan (2001) and Iraq (2003), building the Guantánamo Bay Detention Camp (2002) and its closure (2008), providing federal money to revive companies such as the Bank of America and the General Motors (2009), and not helping out companies such as Lehman Brothers (2008). Because of their decisions, some people lost their jobs while others kept theirs. Some had to abandon their family and headed to foreign countries for war, never to return while some gained political and financial benefits. In turn, their family members and neighbors have been affected by these decisions.

Stop and Think[1]

Can you put them in a single category? There is not a right or wrong answer. But you must really stop reading to ponder a little. A category that can include Barack H. Obama, George W. Bush, Nancy Pelosi and Dick Cheney . . .

How about "human being"? Sure, they are all human beings like everybody else. Therefore, this category does not tell us any interesting aspects of these four people. Again, come up with a category that all of these four people belong to and at the same time more or less unique for these four people. How about "leaders"? Good but still too broad and thus not so informative, isn't it? Some of you may be cheer leaders, but do not see much common with these people. Let's try "the US national leaders" and it is more specific than the previous one.

To these US national leaders, let's add Saddam Hussein. He was the president of Iraq between 1979 and 2003[2] and exercised almost absolute leadership, allowing no rival. Under his watch, Iraq went to war with its neighbor, Iran (1980–1988), invaded another neighbor Kuwait (1990), and eventually confronted the US led international forces (2003). For sure many people from all over the globe lost their lives because of his ability to make important decisions. Among the categories that we just created, which one does he belong to? He doesn't belong to first category, "the US presidents." Nor does he belong to "prime legislators of the US Congress" or "the US national leaders." After all, He was Iraqi. We could drop the US, and a category "national leaders" might do the trick. So we can say Barack H. Obama, George W. Bush, Nancy Pelosi, Dick Cheney, and Saddam Hussein belong to the "national leaders" category.

By now, you must have a good idea where we are heading. Let's add one last figure. Your parents. Yes, your parents. Can there be a category to put Barack H. Obama, George W. Bush, Nancy Pelosi, Dick Cheney, Saddam Hussein, and your parents together?

Stop and Think

Take your time. Try to create a category for all of them.

Do your parents do anything similar to the "national leaders"? Even if your parents are employed in the government, focus on their functions at home, not at their work. At first, no similarity may be apparent. What do your parents do? They prepare meals, clean the house, work on the garden, watch TV, and read newspapers. Moreover, they make decisions: prepare chicken or salmon for dinner; clean the house today or tomorrow; buy an apartment or rent a house; plant roses or pine trees; watch football or soccer; read the New York Times or the Washington Post. Do these decisions affect you? Not always, but often they do. Let's say that you have had chicken dishes in the last three dinners in a row and want something else like salmon. Your mother emphasizes the fact that chicken is cheap and she has a stack of frozen chicken packs and demand you eat whatever she prepares. And you are very, very hungry and poor (well, in this scenario you're back to your parent's home after all) and then you are likely to follow her instruction. On the table you may hear her continuing advocacy of the virtue of frugality and your father may add some footnotes on the worst recession since the Great Depression and worsening job situations of the nation. This family is reacting to the economic problems by cutting costs and their decisions affect you in a great deal. You may have to eat more chickens, get no birthday gifts from your parents (let alone their help with your tuition), give up the TV at your room, or lose the family house. Notice that your parents make decisions and they affect your life. You are subjected to the consequences, often not so serious but sometimes very grave, ensuing from their decisions. In this sense, your parents have something in common with the national leaders at a family scale. So the new category better reflect this aspect. What would that be? How about "authorities"? This term is blind to the geographic boundaries (the US vs Iraq) or domain of influence (executive vs legislative), and at the same time, it points to the core of relationships that we are greatly interested, politics.

Now that we have this category called authorities, see if you can think of someone else who might fit to it. We may easily find a list of people. A mayor may come to your mind first, and of course, there are city councilors. Beyond the city boundary, there are people at the state level. State legislators and governors seem to well fit to this category. Along with them Senators represent your state while members of the Congress represent their districts. So far so good. Can you think of anybody else who could fit to this category? How about your older sister or your significant other? Don't they make decisions like "I want to play soccer, and you come out play with me," and make your life less enjoyable should you refuse to follow them? If so why don't we put them, too, into the category for now?

Let's think about what the "authorities" do. Since Bush started the war in Afghanistan in 2001, the US has spent about 870 billion dollars for the war in Afghanistan and Iraq (as of July 2009)[3] and the figure continues to rise. That's a lot of money. So much so that it's hard to have a real sense about the magnitude of this amount of money and how "authorities" could have used that money differently. So, let's do some math. In a small town called Salisbury, MD where we write this book mostly, taxpayers have been spending since 2001 43.5 million dollars for the wars and this money could have been used for 8,135 students (about 1,000 students more than the entire Salisbury University students) receiving Pell Grants of $5,350. In California, the figure is 114.9 billion dollars and that could have been paid for 1,650,766 elementary school teachers for one year.[4] These are estimates; however, very telling one for our discussion. The "authorities" decided to allocate a huge amount of resources to a sector (two wars in this case), which means that amount of resources cannot be used for other purposes (education, health care, foreign aids etc). In other words, the "authorities" prioritize goals of the society. They didn't say that health care is not important, but their rank of priorities makes certain things smaller recipients of resources than the others. For example, if you were pondering the idea of serving in the Army, you might find it attractive partly due to increased financial incentives thanks to the authorities' emphasis on war efforts. For example, in 2007 you could have picked up $20,000 "quick ship" bonus from the US Army if you had reported to basic training by the end of the fiscal year and many young men and women actually did so reversing the trend of underachievement of recruitment during the preceding months.[5] On the contrary, those who wanted to get higher education might have found it not so easy to secure funds for it due to, in part, "authorities" decided to channel the money away from higher education. In Pennsylvania, for example, resident college students experienced a drop of the maximum amount of state grant to $4,120 from about $4,700. In California, the state officials are considering the end of a state scholarship program.[6]

The "authorities" decisions are not limited to material interests, of course. Instead, realms of non-material world are also a major ballpark. Let's take a look at the fight against HIV/AIDS in Uganda. If you were in charge of this fight, what would you do? Uganda started the country's famous strategy known as "Abstinence, Be Faithful, use Condoms" or ABC early on in the 1990s. As the name suggest, this strategy emphasized three different aspects of sexual activities. On one hand, free sexual relationships were discouraged. On the other hand, protected sexual relationships were encouraged. This strategy was a huge success. A success may be quite an understatement since the prevalence of the disease dropped to 6% from 15%[7] when most of African countries have continued to suffer this disease's pandemics. This strategy's major element was widely available condoms stopping the diseases' spread in this polygamy society.[8] The fight looked promising. However, the fight took a weird turn when President Museveni of Uganda and the first lady began to reshape it beginning in 2003. Despite the scientific understanding that condoms do contribute to the successful fight, the government took on the rise of a new religion of the country, Protestantism. For many Christian leaders, including Mrs. Museveni, the promotion of condom use was against their teaching. In turn, the government and Christian groups, such as Glory of Virginity Movement, launched abstinence only programs.[9] Furthermore, public schools largely stopped educating the youth about safe sex and condom use.[10] To make the matter worse, the government let the flow of condoms dry. As a result, the country departed from the effective tactic, undermining its fight against the AIDS. This case shows that the "authorities" can switch a society's emphasis from one value (encouraging condoms use) to another (discouraging sex) even when such a switch contrasts common senses (condom works; discouraging sex in the polygamy society in which females depend on it for their welfare doesn't make sense). Did it have significant effects on Ugandan citizens? Of course. First of all, the AIDS became a moral issue, not medical or scientific one. Mrs. Museveni led a street march for virginity while tribal leaders pledged rewards to female virgins and banned miniskirts.[11] Second, there are gloomy signs of the pandemic's comeback.[12]

There is one thing we should notice: there are not much we can do about "authorities." Many viable options for you to alter their decisions do not exist even though the decisions affect you negatively. To be correct, there are some means available for us. For example, you can vote for your favorite presidential candidate, sue city councilors, or rally in front of your mayor's office. However, if you compare these options' availability (how often do you vote?) and user-friendliness (any one knows how to sue the government?) to what the "authorities" have (almost limitless) and how easy it is for them (it's their job!) you will realize the unbalanced nature of the relationship between "authorities" and you. Still not convinced? You cannot start a war, can you? Some can. You cannot lower taxes on yourself, can you? Some can. You cannot force others to follow a certain religion, can you? Some can. And so on.

As you have guessed, we were talking about the very meaning of our major topic, politics. What is politics?

Stop and Think

Now define politics. Do not just google it or open a dictionary. Try to come up with a definition of your own. You have heard the word many, many times. What does it mean?

Let us introduce a couple of definitions.

Definition A: "authoritative allocation of values"[13] and resources, which determines "who gets what, when and how"[14]

Definition B: "activities associated with the control of public decisions among a given people and in a given territory, where this control may be backed up by authoritative and coercive means"[15]

The first one is a combination of two old definitions of politics while the second one is much more recent one. Between them, about a half century has passed; however, the two have similar aspects. From the similarities, we can infer the definition of our own. First, both definitions address domain of the concept: decisions. Who will get the federal aid? When will the money be available? Will there be any criteria to be eligible for the fund? These are typical questions raised in political debates. And these are different from decisions that we usually make at home or school. As matter of fact, decisions are consistently being made by everyone in a society. But not all of them are necessarily associated with politics. Then, what make up the domain of politics? What differentiate these debates and the quarrel over chicken dish on the table? We can find a clue from Definition B: "public" decisions. Discussing politics, we are largely interested in decisions affecting many people in a society. The federal government is such an entity of which decisions affect significant part of the population. For example, in 2009 the Obama administration reversed the former president Bush's veto against the legislation raising federal tax on tobacco in order to fund the State Children's Health Insurance Program. By singing a similar legislation, the Obama government raised the tax from 4 cents to $1.01 a pack.[16] How public is this decision? 45 million adult smokers will have to pay more dollars for their smoking and 1 million of them will likely quit the habit.[17] There are nervous tobacco growers and factory workers who may worry about declining demands. Millions of adults will get healthier, which could save medical costs for the entire society. So, that's quite public. On the other hand, your decision to quit smoking is very private.

So, politics is about making such public decisions. But this is not enough to define politics. For example, Michael Jackson, a well known and popular singer died in 2009. The family decided to make the funeral public. As a result, 31.1 million Americans watched it on TV in 2009. That's public, but not really political. What is a difference? Political decisions have a special character: it is "authoritative" or "backed up by authoritative and coercive means." The government's decision to raise the federal tax on tobacco is authoritative because it is very difficult for others to challenge (if you were a smoker, think about what you can do about it except paying more money or quitting smoking). The government has all the necessary bureaucrats, lawyers, and law enforcement officers such as the police to make sure you follow the rule. This is basically different from MJ's case where you could decide to join in the event or not on your own.

This reveals the fundamental essence of politics: power. Most of the people do not have the power to raise the federal tax on anything and force you to follow the decision. Most citizens lack any authority to start a war and have thousands and thousands of men and women in the military to go to towns in the Middle East. But some do have such power. Therefore, when we talk about politics, we are largely discussing the unbalanced power relationships among various actors: the government vs the citizens; the president vs the DC mayor; the political party with majority seats vs the rest; USA vs Iraq during the Iraq War; lobbyists vs the public; industry vs the consumers; and so on. Therefore, the politics is about not only making public and authoritative decisions but also gaining the power.

Stop and Think

Now, let's try again. Reformulate your definition of politics reflecting what we have discussed so far.

Let us propose our definition of politics. When we say politics, we refer to *actions related to power in the realm of public affairs in which decisions are authoritative and coercive.*

THE RELEVANCE OF POLITICS TO YOUR DAILY LIFE

How relevant is the politics to your daily life? Is there anyone who met your mayor today? How about yesterday? The day before yesterday? No? How about the House representative of your electoral district? Have you ever met her or him? Most of you may lack any direct encounter with political leaders. Therefore, it might be natural to perceive politics as not so relevant to your daily life. Rather it seems happening far away mostly in state capitals or Washington DC. However, the fact that you do not see "authorities" or politicians often or the feeling that you are far away from political debate should not deceive you because the politics is relevant to everything you do. Hard to believe? Well, then why don't we look at realms of everyday life that appear to be apolitical?

Scene 1: Student X who is a daughter of Mexican immigrants is frustrated to see a rejection letter from a California state university to which she applied.

This scene may be very familiar to you, and you may see her situation in a personal light. For example, her failure may be attributed to her poor essay, low GPA, or meager SAT scores. There may be more reasons than these, but they can hardly be political, right? Well, as you are reading this book, you may belong to the generation who suffered the Great Recession of 2008–09 during the US economic substantially shrank. The range of its impact was international and it hurt countless people. Families lost houses, parents were fired, and grandparents painfully watched their retirement funds evaporating. The victims also included university students nationwide. Probably, however, none endured the consequences of the recession more than university students in California. In 2009 the state university system decided to raise student fee by 20 percent, shrink the enrollment size, and cut employees' paychecks.[18] This fee increase of $672 actually followed another fee increase already set in the early in the year, affecting about 450,000 students. This was especially painful to many because of the special benefits of the universities: its relatively low tuitions and high qualities. Due to these circumstances, California state universities attracted large numbers of students from low income family and ethnic minorities. Now their smaller enrollments along with high fees would limit or deny them necessary access to higher education for their social advance. Our Student X might be a victim of this unfortunate development of the state of California. But it still seems economic, not so political. Hang on. As said, the recession was a national disaster, causing problems all over the country. However, some states fared better than the others (California belonged to the latter). Then, this discrepancy begs questions, among which is why some states, such as California, suffered more than other states? There are various explanations, but regarding California, we cannot explain its troubles without looking at its politics. The trouble was that the state faced $24 billion deficit in 2009. With such a huge deficit, the state had two options: raising taxes or cutting services. If your concern were the higher education, you would think that raising taxes must be the solution. That could have easily happened especially given its political situation where Democrats who strongly advocated tax hikes controlled both houses of the Legislature. However, the state legislature dragged on and on. Why? Unlike most states, California requires a two-thirds majority to pass its budget. Therefore, even though Democrats had 49 seats (out of 80) in the house, they could not pass the budget. The Republicans learned a hard lesson when their colleagues were previously punished for their collaboration with Democrats who raised taxes. Therefore, this time the Republicans sat tight and resisted Democrats' appeal to increase taxes over and over again in order not to lose their reelection. As a result, the state failed to have a budget on time. The governor finally declared a fiscal state of emergency and the state issued i.o.u.'s to contractors and tax-payers. This crisis was over finally when Republicans controlling 29 seats forced Democrats to agree to deep cuts in state services so that they can look tough. They may achieve their political goal (looking tough against tax increase), but for that many had to pay a very steep price, including of course many university students of California.

Scene 2: Student Y just gained 6 pounds after he lost 4 pounds during his diet that lasted about one month, and this diet was his third one this year.

When we were young, yo-yo meant a round toy that goes up and down on a string attached to it. Now this term is more associated with body weights that go up and down on diet. Are you one of them experiencing yo-yo? This is a very personal issue. Or, is it really? According to David Kessler, the Harvard-trained doctor,

University of Chicago-studied lawyer, medical school dean and former commissioner of the Food and Drug Administration under two presidents, the answer is a definite no.[19] You may recall the crispy and attractive taste of egg rolls in a restaurant. Then, you might have consumed what a Kessler called a combination of salt, fat, and sugar, and they are widely available. According to Kessler, the foods that we typically eat out are "bathed in salt, fat and sugars"[20] and thus consuming such foods does not satisfy hunger. Instead, "the salt-fat-sugar combination will stimulate that diner's brain to crave more."[21] As people continue to consume such foods, their brains get chemically "wired" so that we are led to eat more and more of them.[22] Why can't the government come up with some regulations or simple but strong guidance for consumers? One answer is that "the content of [government] nutrition messages may have been compromised so much by input from various organized interests that the messages are too generic and non-directive to consumers to help them make health-promoting food choices."[23] As a seller of unhealthy foods, the food industry has strong incentives to discourage any governmental intervention against their profits, and they are in a good position to achieve that goal. Their lobbyists sit with governmental officials discussing policies and put pressures on governmental agencies to weaken regulations.[24] We are not only bathed in unhealthy foods but also flooded by commercials. "[E]ach year the food industry spends an estimated $10 billion to influence the eating behavior of children. The average child sees 10,000 food advertisements per year, 95 percent of them for fast food, soft drinks, candy and sugared cereals—all high-profit and nutrition-poor products."[25] The "authorities" have chosen not to act with this as well. Therefore, their decision to not act, or not as aggressive as they should, is a major part of reasons why Student Y repeatedly fail to lose his weight.[26] As you can see, the food industry has been politically successful in their efforts to keep the issue buried from the public. On the other hand, consumers have been politically unsuccessful in reigning in the greed of the food industry. Until some major political events happen, therefore, individual consumers like Student Y or you would continue to struggle with yo-yo.

Allow us to repeat saying that the politics is relevant to everything you do. Your college application, your struggle with weight, the quality of air you breathe in, marrying someone you love, things that you can carry on in airplane, community activities of your church, price of gas you pay, your neighborhood of the same race, and the list goes on. It is critical to understand the depth of relevance of politics in your daily life you are subjected to somebody else's political power. Without realizing this, individuals like us remain largely incapable of solving many problems that we encounter everyday.

Notes

1 Lave and March (1993) utilized this format for readers.
2 "Saddam Hussein profile" Retrieved July 15, 2009 from BBC News http://news.bbc.co.uk/2/hi/middle_east/1100529.stm
3 "The numbers include all of the approved funding for the wars to date as well as estimates of pending money based on the most recent war spending supplemental submitted by President Obama to Congress on April 9, 2009." Cost of War. Retrieved July 15, 2009 from National Priorities Project http://www.nationalpriorities.org/.
4 These calculations come from the formula of Federal Budget Trade-offs. Retrieved July 15, 2009 from National Priorities Project http://www.nationalpriorities.org/.
5 Thom Shanker, "Army, Shedding a Slump, Met July Recruiting Goal," *The New York Times*, August 11, 2007.
6 Jonathan D. Glater, "Scholarships for College Dwindle as Providers Pull Back Their Support," *The New York Times*, June 26, 2009.
7 Helen Epstein, "God and Fight Against AIDS," *New York Review of Books*, April 28, 2005, http://www.nybooks.com/articles/17963.
8 Human Rights Watch, "Uganda: 'Abstinence-Only' Programs Hijack AIDS Success Story," March 29, 2005. http://www.hrw.org/en/news/2005/03/29/uganda-abstinence-only-programs-hijack-aids-success-story?print (accessed July 16, 2009).
9 Uganda government and these groups sought and gained the US federal funds from the Bush administration that were given groups with no condom programs. See Helen Epstein, "God and Fight Against AIDS."
10 Human Rights Watch, "Uganda: 'Abstinence-Only' Programs Hijack AIDS Success Story."
11 Helen Epstein, "God and Fight Against AIDS."
12 Leigh Anne Shafer, Samuel Biraro, Jessica Nakiyingi-Miiro, Anatoli Kamali, Duncan Ssematimba, Joseph Ouma, Amato Ojwiya, Peter Hughes, Lieve Van der Paal, Jimmy Whitworth, Alex Opio, and Heiner Grosskurth, "HIV

prevalence and incidence are no longer falling in southwest Uganda: evidence from a rural population cohort 1989–2005," *AIDS* 22(August 2008) 1641–1649.

13 David Easton, "An Approach to the Analysis of Political Systems," *World Politics* 9, (1957): 393–400.

14 Harold D. Lasswell, *Politics: Who Gets What, When, How* (New York: McGraw-Hill, 1932).

15 Gabriel A. Almond, G. Bingham Powell, Jr., Kaare Strom, and Russell J. Dalton. *Comparative Politics: A Theoretical Framework, Third edition* (New York: Longman, 2001), 3.

16 Wendy Koch, "Biggest U.S. tax hike on tobacco takes effect," *USA Today*, April 3, 2009 http://www.usatoday.com/money/perfi/taxes/2009-03-31-cigarettetax_N.htm.

17 Ibid.

18 "Calif. University System OKs 20 Percent Fee Hike," *The New York Times*, July 21, 2009 http://www.nytimes.com/aponline/2009/07/21/us/AP-US-California-University-Cuts.html

19 Lyndsey Layton, "Crave Man: David Kessler Knew That Some Foods Are Hard to Resist; Now He Knows Why," *The Washington Post*, April 27, 2009, http://www.washingtonpost.com/wp-dyn/content/article/2009/04/26/AR2009042602711.html.

20 Ibid.

21 Ibid.

22 Ibid.

23 Laura S. Sims, *The Politics of Fat: Food and Nutrition in America*, (Armonk, NY: M.E. Sharpe, 1998), 272.

24 Kelly D. Brownell and David S. Ludwig, "Fighting Obesity And the Food Lobby," *The Washington Post*, June 9, 2002, B7 http://www.washingtonpost.com/ac2/wp-dyn?pagename=article&node=&contentId=A15232-2002Jun7&notFound=true.

25 Ibid.

26 For more discussions, see Barry Yeoman, "Unhappy Meals" *Mother Jones*, January/February 2003, 40–45; Marion Nestle, "Pushing Soft Drinks: 'Pouring Rights'" in *Food Politics: How the Food Industry Influences Nutrition and Health* (Berkeley: University of California Press, 2002), 197–218; Eric Schlosser, *Fast Food Nation: The Dark Side of the All-American Meal*, (New York: Houghton Mifflin Company, 2001).

Part I
BASIC CONCEPTS AND ISSUES

Part 1
BASIC CONCEPTS AND ISSUES

The Science and Art of Political Study

THE SOCIAL SCIENCE OF POLITICS: UNDERSTANDING THINGS AS THEY ARE

What is your major? Some of you must be thinking about political science (great!) or you have already decided to major in political science (fantastic!). By the way, have you thought about the name, political science? If you think about the name, it is atypical in its herd. Think about this. At many universities, Political Science is housed within college of liberal arts along with other majors such as philosophy, English, French, and arts. In the realm of humanities, arts, and social science that typically form the school of liberal arts, only political science has "science" in its name. Have you ever heard a major called, "philosophical science"? Neither have we. Why is that? What distinguishes political science from others? First of all, there is a topic issue. Political science differs from, for example, economics in that political scientists study politics while economists study, well, the economy. Major topics of political science will be discussed in the following chapters. For now, let's focus on the second factor: the way we look at the world. Political science, along with other disciplines of social science such as sociology, demands its students understand political phenomena critically and explain them effectively. The first step toward achieving this requirement is to be open-minded. Here, to have an open mind means more than just open to various ideas that you do not necessarily agree with. Let us explain what we mean by "open-minded." A political scientist "seeks to understand what different kinds of people define as truth and how that definition influences their lives and interactions with one another"[1] unlike classical thinkers, who looked for the truth. Classical thinkers such as Plato sought after the truth of politics and revealed them. According to Plato, "there can be no rest from troubles . . . for states . . . unless either philosophers become kings in their countries"[2] or kings become philosophers, and this is true "for all mankind."[3] Notice that this is a universal remedy for his ideal society. In other words, any state that adopts this solution will solve most problems regardless of the state's size, location, longevity, ethnic composition, format of the government, wealth, religion, and so on. Therefore, this, according to Plato, is the truth.

What political scientists look for is different because the truth that political scientists study is far from being universal. To illustrate this point, let us briefly consider a political truth, democracy. Democracy is the most popular form of government nowadays and regarded the best form created thus far, forging great political progress. If you look around it seems true that democracy is a political remedy for domestic problems. However, the virtue of democracy by no means enjoys the status of the universal truth, and it is, rather, the opposite. For example, how we see democracy is different from how democracy is understood by many in North Korea. Our idea of democracy is typically shaped by our Constitution that emphasizes the separation of power and electoral processes. From here, we have created separate branches within the federal government and continuous struggles and occasional collaborations among them ensued partly from this separation. The citizens of the United States have opportunities to vote and express their support or disapproval of these branches, especially the executive and the legislative, which determine the fate of political leaders. Political parties recruit leaders, educate them, and help with their elections in order to compete with other parties. This form of democracy is what we are mostly familiar with. However, democracy is radically different in North Korea, the formal name of which is the Democratic People's Republic of Korea. Its idea of democracy comes from their political history in which they fought a war against Japanese colonialism, the South Korean government, and the West led by the US. It has been the communist party that led the struggles to their victories and that has provided the country's safety and people's welfare. Therefore, their democracy has no competition between different branches of the government or among different political parties. Instead, the democracy guarantees the continuing dominance of the communist party and allows the citizens to express their support for the party with no real opportunity to show their disapproval. Nevertheless, they do have a democracy according to their definition, even though it is completely different from ours.

You may be rolling your eyes or laughing at this so-called democracy in North Korea. After all, North Korean citizens have suffered starvation, international isolation, brainwashing, and brutal repression. Therefore, if you say that North Korean democracy is just a hoax, you may not be too incorrect. But the problem for us as students of political science is, then, critical thinking largely stops there with only the verdict in your hand. This is not undesirable, but not so productive either. North Korean democracy is a joke. North Korea should adopt the democratic form of government. So what? What does it tell us? Not a lot, actually. Instead, such judgments will likely results in overwhelming supports (if your audience comprises Westerners) or angry rebukes (if your audience comprises North Koreans). Either way, it does not help us to understand North Korean politics. Instead, political scientists must give a critical look at the political happenings as they are, not as they should be. Is there any link between its famine in the early 1990s and the lack of competition embedded in North Korean political institutions? Or do we have to look into the passive and submissive political culture to explain the famine? Are the international sanctions to blame? If it is the lack of the competition that resulted in such catastrophes, what else did result from it? Do we see such undesirable social and economic consequences in other countries with similar political systems? How about Cuba or Zimbabwe? If the North Korean regime is so different from the Western democracy, why do they insist that they too have a democracy? If it is not a democracy, what makes the North Korean government so non-democratic? Can we find such non democratic elements in Western countries, too? How do we know country X is more democratic than country Y? Now, we have interesting questions to study. Notice that judgment-free curiosity produces more interesting questions and thus insights going much beyond value judgements. Therefore, it is critically important to look at political phenomena as they are, rather than as they should be.

HYPOTHESIS-BUILDING AND HYPOTHESIS-TESTING

One major difference, therefore, between classical thinkers and political scientists is whether they explain the world as they should be or as they are, and we advocate the latter approach because it is more productive than the other. Another major distinction between the two is their different emphasis on tests. Classical thinkers did not have their ideas exposed to rigorous tests. For example, Plato's Republic (see Chapter Two below) is filled with brilliant insights but it is hard to find parts where his arguments were tested. Therefore, the tests are left to the hands of readers. Individual readers may like some of his ideas while others may feel the same parts are not so relevant or even incorrect. Therefore, their evaluations of the same idea could widely vary. The readers will debate Plato's argument based on their own subjective interpretations from their previous readings, levels of education, personal experiences, emotions, political environment, and so on. Often, this kind of debates does not really produce an authoritative conclusion because there is not a productive way to reconcile contrasting personal, often emotional, evaluations.

To political scientists, tests are an important part of their mission so that they can minimize wasteful controversies on their works. Therefore, their works are usually structured so that their ideas can be put to test not only by the authors who would like to establish the validity of their explanations but also by their readers who would like to evaluate the authors' arguments. The more tests it passes, the more widely it gets accepted. The fewer tests it passes, the less credible it becomes. Let's say that Explanation X was proposed by Professor X who has been studying the Issue A in Country X. She puts her explanation to test and the result supported the explanation. Then, Professor X argues the Explanation X is valid, and her argument is credible because she has the proof. Professor Y who read this report was not convinced because he had his own explanation (Explanation Y) for the same issue. So, he wanted to see for himself. He repeats the test that Professor X conducted with his own data that he collective from Country Y. The result supported Professor X's explanation, to his great disappointment. Nevertheless, he realized that Explanation X is better and many more professors began to accept that explanation. As more and more scholars accept it, Explanation X became not the truth but a widely accepted fact regarding Issue A. Therefore, for many political scientists, it is imperative to base their studies on a comprehensible and clear structure, distinguishing political science from most other subjects in the field of liberal arts. Such a structure requires basic elements: concepts, definitions, variables, and hypothesis and its tests.

Let's begin with concepts. Do you support democracy? Oh, you do. Ok. Then, what is the thing that you just said that you supported?

Stop and Think

Why don't you list things that you think make democracy? Try to list at least four things.

You might have different things in your list, but here is our tentative list: competitive elections, free media, human rights, and rule of law. In other words, we are saying that if there is a state with these four elements, we would like to call its regime a democracy. If it lacks any of them, it is not a democracy. How about your list? What do you have in it? How different is it from our list? Your list may probably include election. How about free media? No? Well, do not worry. People have various ideas of democracy. One reason there is an absence of consensus is that democracy is not a concrete thing. You cannot touch, smell, hear, taste, or see it, can you? You may see politicians speaking on TV, but they are not democracy. Democracy is "an idea or mental construct that represents phenomena in the real world"[4] or a **concept**. Treat a concept as a label that you put on a toy box. Inside, there are things. We already played with a toy box with a label that says democracy. In that box, there were four things, remember? Competitive elections, free media, human rights, and rule of law were in our box. These are the contents of the box or the definition of a concept. In other words, components that we think make up a concept are the **definition**. Coming back to our toy box, therefore, our definition of a concept, democracy is a state with competitive elections, free media, human rights, and rule of law.

Concepts play major functions. First, well-defined concepts help scholars communicate better. For example, the definition of democracy reduces the amount of time and energy that could have been used to explain what he or she meant by democracy each time the word is used. Second, as political scientists, we study and analyze the concepts such as democracy or war, and thus concepts are the object of our discipline. Petrologists study rocks; Entomologists study insects; Oceanographists study oceans; political scientists study political concepts. Is North Korean democracy really a democracy according to our definition? Now, we can say no regardless of what North Koreans are saying about their proud democracy because North Korean polity completely lacks competitive elections and free media and because our definition includes elements that are more acceptable than the North Korean definition of democracy. Compare North Korean democracy to the American one. Is the latter better? Sure. How much better? How would you know? How about American democracy against the Mexican one? Can you tell if the former is better than the latter? Moreover, what led a country to have a better democracy than others? Answers to these questions will be discussed in the following chapters. For now, let's focus on concepts. As you can see, these questions address democracy—and more precisely—the levels of democracy. Which countries have higher levels of democracy than others? In order to answer any of these questions, we must able to measure the levels of democracy. We already have the concept defined and now let's try to measure it. There are four elements of democracy, and one of them is competitive election. To measure this element, we may want to ask a question "how many political parties genuinely competed in the previous presidential election?" or "how often does the country have a presidential election?" The next job must be gathering necessary data, such as the number of political parties or the frequency of presidential elections, to answer the questions. Then we have two measurements. Such an "empirical measurement of a characteristic"[5]—in this case the competitiveness of elections—is called a **variable**. Variables are useful in explaining and analyzing political phenomena.

Let's try to explain a problematic trend, the gap of political development in the world. We live in a stable democracy where elections are mostly competitive and the public can choose relatively free mass media for their information. Moreover, we have no real fear of extraconstitutional interventions such as *coup d'état* or imprisonment for political reasons. There are many countries sharing similar levels of democratic development. However, in many states, what we take for granted is unthinkable. For example, Somalia has been in the need of a functioning government, let alone competitive elections, since early 1990s, while its citizens have been subjected to civil wars, foreign interventions, one region's secession, and anarchy during that time. Somalia is only one member of the league of countries that lack the meaningful democratic stability. The members include Sudan (killing its own citizens), Zimbabwe (rigging elections), Belarus (allowing no competitive elections), Saudi Arabia (maintaining monarchy), North Korea (maintaining communist totalitarianism), Thailand (repeating *coup d'état*), and many more. What is causing this stark gap? There must be an explanation.

Stop and Think

Propose your explanation accounting for the causes of democratic development. It is only a proposal and, therefore, it can't be right or wrong, at least yet.

Have you made your proposal? If so, you are one of many scholars, including Lipset,[6] who linked a state's economic development to its political one. To test the proposal, it needs to be rewritten such as "rich countries are more likely to have a democracy". We already have some measurements of democracy and need to measure "rich countries." We could measure the size of the national economy, using the gross domestic product (GDP), or the quality of living standard, using life expectancy. Either way, now the concept is measurable. Let's say that we want to use the GDP. Finally, we have necessary elements of testing: one variable that we want to explain, another variable that we suspect as the cause, and a statement putting them together. Such a statement is called a hypothesis. In other words, a **hypothesis** is a "testable statement about the empirical relationship between cause and effect."[7] The effect, the variable to be explained is also called a **dependent variable**. It is often called as such because its values are expected to vary depending on the cause. In our example, the country's level of democracy is thought to go up and down depending on the country's wealth. The cause is often called as an **independent variable** because its variance is assumed to be independent. This is not entirely true since the amount of wealth, in our example, is also affected by many elements such as the size of natural resources, the education, industrialization, and so on. However, in the hypothesis, all the other elements are put on hold, and we treat the independent variable like a ball bouncing up and down on its own dynamics. Thereby, we can test the relationship between the two variables.

There are many ways to conduct tests. One way is to rely on data collected from many cases, typically in the form of numeric information, and this type of study is often called large *n* study (*n* referring to the number of cases). This type of data is so inundated with information that it is impossible for human intuition and intelligence to extract meaningful observation. Therefore, statistics is often imported to help researchers. This task is not easy, but rewarding because testing a hypothesis in multiple cases increases the study's credibility. Imagine a hypothesis was validated by a test in the US. The researcher would be delighted. Now imagine the hypothesis was confirmed not only in the US, but also in Canada, the UK, France, Germany, Belgium, Netherland, Luxemburg, Italy, Austria, Spain, Norway, Sweden, and Japan. The researcher must be thrilled for a good reason. Now her argument is applicable to almost all the developed states! A drawback of this type of study is that it does not reveal enough details, providing only a narrow picture of complicated problems.

*For example, MacCulloch[8] conducted a research addressing one of the most debated issues in the political science, revolution. Scholars have explored many aspects of revolutionary activities, and one of the most attractive questions has been why revolutions occur. MacCulloch's question was similar, but more specific: whether the poor are more likely to support revolutions.

Stop and Think

Write down his hypothesis. What is his dependent variable? What is the independent variable? What is the relationship between the two? Positive or negative?

Notice that his dependent variable is "support for revolutions" while his major independent variable is "wealth." How did he measure the support? He relied on data coming from "the Combined World Values Survey (asked in three waves between 1981 and 1995) and Euro-Barometer Survey Series (asked every year from 1976–1990) questions"[9] and these data come from "94,215 people who were randomly sampled over a cross-section of 61 nations."[10] In order to find the cause of "taste for revolt" he looked into the effects of several hypothesized independent variables including national economy, personal income, employment, age, marriage status, and education level, using a statistical model called probit regression. Analyzing data, he concludes that the level of economic development affects people's support for revolutions, finding an "increase in GDP per capita of $US 1,600 (in 2001 values) decreases the probability of supporting revolt by 2.4 percentage points, representing a 41% drop in support (i.e., from 5.9% to 3.5% of the European population) . . . For a person who jumps from the bottom to the top of the income distribution within their country, the probability of them having a taste for revolt declines by 2.5 percentage points."[11] His conclusion is empowered by the fact that his observation was validated not only in the case of Argentina or Uruguay, but also 61 countries in total, becoming a more general and applicable piece of knowledge. From this study, however, we do not learn much about the countries' economic situations in detail such as inflations, the dominance of upper class, land distribution, and so on. One might complain about this shortfall, but we must understand that the nature and purpose of large *n* studies is meant to serve a different goal. If the reader wish for an in-depth understanding on a subject, large *n* studies will not be appropriate for that purpose. Instead, small *n* studies would serve better.

Small *n* studies typically have a limited scope regarding the number of cases, such as three, two, or often one case. For example, Skocpol studied revolutions, largely focusing three cases: the French Revolution, the Russian Revolution, and the Chinese Revolution, explaining structural causes of social revolutions and providing rich details of them.[12] She called these events social revolutions for they are different from other form of revolutionary movement. According to her definition, social revolutions are "rapid, basic, transformations of a society's state and class structure: and they are accompanied and in part carried through by class-based revolt from below."[13] Looking into these social revolutions in detail (407 pages long) she revealed the common causes of social revolutions. The occurrence of revolutions (the dependent variable of this study) is explained by the collapse of the old regime. The collapse follows military and economic competition with much stronger states. The regime reacts to crises by launching reforms, and the success of this effort often depends on the class structure. If the landed upper class is strong enough to oppose reform, the ensuing conflicts between them and the regime is likely to incapacitate the state's ability to deal with problems. The state's capability also depends on the strength of domestic economy. The peasant revolts are another major independent variable explaining social revolutions, and it is in turn dependent on the presence of the well organized peasant community and weakened landlords. Skocpol combs through the histories of three countries, finding these elements in political

---

institution, economic situations, class structure, and foreign relations and providing detailed accounts of them. In her rich accounts one can find many interesting insights. For example, Kuomintang that ruled mainland China maintained its strong grip on urban areas on the East coast because this area was the economic and political center. No doubt, this control benefited the Kuomintang a great deal for its struggles against the Chinese Communist Party (CCP) that was isolated largely in the central rural areas. However, according to her, the Japanese invasion in 1937 changed the whole picture. The Japanese forces invaded largely lucrative urban areas, devastating the power base of the Kuomintang and, hence, helping the CCP and its eventual, successful Chinese Revolution.

The contrast is clear. On one hand we have a large *n* study providing a convincing view of a general pattern. It is convincing because a pattern is observable in many countries or the hypothesis passed multiple tests. However, this approach does not allow us to have an in-depth understanding of the cases. On the other hand, a small *n* study can fill such a void of details with a long narration of the rich history, social and economic background, important figures, and development of events of interest. Its drawback is that it is hard to know whether or not the researcher's insight is correct due to the limited tests. In other words, it is difficult to know if the researcher got the whole study wrong, for example, by identifying wrong independent variables or missing important ones.

Once a researcher chooses a methodology, it becomes his or her imperative to do it right. How can they improve the quality of their studies? There are many ways, such as case study, content analysis, experiments, computer simulation, and let us introduce just one of them, polling. Polling is a good way to collect data from a large number of observations. Remember that the previous example of MacCullochs used polling data and his data came from "94,215 people who were randomly sampled over a cross-section of 61 nations."[14] Polling is done by directly asking subjects a series of questions to measure specific concepts, especially regarding respondent's perception or feeling. Therefore, it is important to understand the link between a theoretical end, such as concepts that we already discussed, and a practical end, polling. For example, MacCulloch used a question asking "On this card are three basic kinds of attitudes *vis-a-vis* the society in which we live. Please choose the one which best describes your own opinion." The respondent could choose one of the following: "The entire way our society is organized must be radically changed by revolutionary action," "Our society must be gradually improved by reforms," and "Our present society must be valiantly defended against all subversive forces."[15] He used these answers to measure respondent's "taste for revolt." People who pick the first answer are assumed to have a high level of support for a revolution while their choice of third is thought to indicate a low level of the support. In this way, a concept, support for revolution, was measured. How about people's confidence in economic situations? How would you measure it? There are questions in Eurobarometer[16] such as "Are your expectations for the next 12 months better, worse, or the same, when it comes down to the economic situation in (OUR COUNTRY)?"; "Are your expectations for the next 12 months better, worse, or the same, when it comes down to the financial situation of your household?"; and "Are your expectations for the next 12 months better, worse, or the same, when it comes down to the employment situation in (OUR COUNTRY)?"[17] For a further understanding, let's work on another concept that is commonly used in our daily lives.

Stop and Think

Write questions so that you can measure the respondents' level of "love."

Love is such a subjective concept and often defies any attempts to define it. Nonetheless, it is also one of the most discussed concepts on so many occasions and formats if you think about love discussed by various people including William Shakespeare, Jesus, Brittney Spears, John Lennon, Leonardo DiCaprio, Leonardo da Vinci, your parents, your significant other, and so on. Therefore, it cannot be a bad idea to challenge this difficult task ourselves, especially for the sake of understanding conceptualization, measurement, and polling. Let's tentatively define it as a strong emotional desire toward another person and that we want to measure it (for the sake of convenience, we will limit our discussion to romantic love). What are those qualities of love that needed to be measured? First of all, the presence of the lover may be the most important. Second, the types of desire toward that person are another qualitative element of love according to the definition. Third, the intensity of love should be another element according to our definition. Your questionnaire should be able to measure these elements. The first question might be "Do you have a special person in your heart? 2) Yes; 1) No; or 0) Not applicable or available" or "Do you have a person that you have continued to date? 2) Yes; 1) No; or 0) Not applicable or available." Now you should measure the types of desire. You might ask "What do you want to do with that person? 6) Marriage with children; 5) Marriage with no children; 4) Living together with no marriage; 3) Dating from separated dwelling; 2) Occasional hang-out; 1) Nothing; or 0) Not applicable or available." To know intensity, we might want to ask a question like "How often does your desire occur to your mind? At least once 6) Every hour; 5) Every meal; 4) Every day; 3) Every week; 2) Every month; 1) Never or 0) Not applicable or available" or a question such as "How likely do you think you can find a replacement for your love? 6) Never; 5) Possibly, but I don't want to think about it; 4) Possibly; 3) Likely; 2) Easily; 1) Very easily; or 0) Not applicable or available" When we collect answers from respondents, we expect that responses from a person with strong love would give answers with high numbers. Inversely, people with a low level of love or no love will likely give answers with low numbers. Let's review hypothetical results of surveys of 100 people of Town X with population 100,000 who are 16 or older.

Result of Hypothetical Survey A of Town X Number of Responses			
Value	Presence of love	Desires	Intensity
6		6	37
5		4	23
4		10	15
3		60	11
2	70	10	6
1	20	5	5
0	10	5	3
Total	100	100	100

In this result, respondents mostly have their partners (70). However, their desires remain at relatively low levels while, interestingly the feeling is really intense. It is unusual to see such high levels of romantic love among the residents of a small town. Sensing a problem, the researcher decided to conduct another poll. A second poll was conducted and this is the result.

Result of Hypothetical Survey B of Town X Number of Responses			
Value	Presence of love	Desires	Intensity
6		0	60
5		0	0
4		0	0
3		0	0
2	10	10	10
1	70	60	5
0	20	30	25
Total	100	100	100

This result seems radically different from the previous example. Moreover, a significant number of respondents gave the answer, "Not applicable or available" and a great majority do not have their partners. Furthermore, they tend to have significantly low levels of desire while their love is mostly intense.

The previous examples illustrate how conceptualization leads to practical questions of measurability in surveys. At the same time, they raise an important issue of polling **sampling**. Conducting surveys is difficult and costly, preventing researchers from surveying the entire population. Instead, surveys are conducted on **samples** or "a number of cases or observations drawn from a population."[18] Selecting samples or sampling is, therefore, critically important. Imagine that the respondents of Survey A were largely college freshman, and the respondents of Survey B were mostly elderly in nursing homes, for unknown reasons (the researcher may be a freshman or have her father in the nursing home). Using either of these surveys, a researcher cannot produce a study analyzing Town X's trend of love because her study would be based on data overwhelmingly reflecting a particular group's trend when in fact the college freshmen or elderly are a tiny minority of the town. In other words, her data suffered the problem known as **selection bias**, an error occurring when "some members of the population are more likely to be included in the sample than are other members of the population."[19] As a result, her study would grossly overestimate the levels of romantic love (using Survey A) or underestimate it (using Survey B) than the actual level. How can she solve this problem of selection bias? The answer is **random sampling** giving every member of the population equal chance of being included in the sample. If samples can be randomly collected, the survey is expected to reflect the entire population. In order to do that, random numbers are generated using a computer program and given to each observation (each resident of Town X). After that, samples are picked, of course, randomly. Therefore, a freshman has only a chance equal to 100/100,000 or 1%, and so does an elderly lady in a nursing house, a middle age bus driver, a professor, or a baker. In this way, polling is expected to be free from selection bias and provide accurate information of the entire population.

Political science is different from other fields of study for its unique interests in politics and its emphasis on scientific approach of understanding. In order to improve our knowledge of politics, it is essential to come up with clear conceptualization and choose a right method of study.

Notes

1 Ruth Lane, *The Art of Comparative Politics* (Boston: Allyn and Bacon, 1997), 4.
2 Plato, "Republic," in *Great Political Thinkers: Plato to The Present*, eds. William Ebenstein and Alan O. Ebenstein (Forth Worth: Harcourt Brace College Publishers, 1991), 72.
3 Ibid., 72.

4 Philip H. Pollock III, *The Essentials of Political Analysis*, 2nd ed. (Washington DC: CQ Press, 2005), 7.

5 Pollock, *The Essentials of Political Analysis*, 2nd ed., 20.

6 Seymour M. Lipset, "Some Social Requisites of Democracy: Economic Development and Political Legitimacy," *The American Political Science Review* 53 (1959): 69–105.

7 Pollock, *The Essentials of Political Analysis*, 2nd ed., 29.

8 Robert MacCulloch, "The Impact of Income on the Taste for Revolt," *American Journal of Political Science* 48 (2004): 830–848.

9 Ibid., 832.

10 Ibid., 832.

11 Ibid., 843.

12 Theda Skocpol, *States and Social Revolutions* (New York: Cambridge University Press, 1979).

13 Ibid., 4.

14 MacCulloch, "The Impact of Income on the Taste for Revolt," 832.

15 Ibid., 832.

16 "Since 1973, the European Commission has been monitoring the evolution of public opinion in the Member States, thus helping the preparation of texts, decision-making and the evaluation of its work. Our surveys and studies address major topics concerning European citizenship: enlargement, social situation, health, culture, information technology, environment, the Euro, defence, etc." European Commission, *Eurobarometer Survey*, http://ec.europa .eu/public_opinion/index_en.htm.

17 European Commission, "Eurobarometer 61: First Results," March 2004, http://ec.europa.eu/public_opinion/ archives/eb/eb61/eb61_first_res_en.pdf.

18 Pollock III, *The Essentials of Political Analysis*, 2nd ed., 103.

19 Ibid., 104.

The Normative Study of Political Science

INTRODUCTION

As we discussed in Chapter 1, empirical research is designed to analyze, explain, and predict how political actors *actually* behave. As is the case with empirical analysis, the normative approach to political study is based on critical thinking. However, whereas empiricists aim to be value-free in their work (i.e., to avoid making moral judgments on the political phenomena they are studying), in the normative approach theorists and philosophers explicitly embed their arguments in ethical judgments of right and wrong. In doing so, they offer prescriptions for how political actors *should* behave, thereby providing a moral framework for politics.

The list of political philosophers who have endeavored throughout the centuries to create an ethical guidepost for political behavior is extremely long and quite distinguished. In this chapter we focus on several influential normative scholars, including Plato, Aristotle, Machiavelli, Hobbes, Locke, Rousseau, and Rawls. Some of the most crucial questions addressed by these authors include: Which form of government is superior? Is human nature predisposed toward conflict or toward cooperation? What do we mean when we speak of a social contract? And, what does a just system look like? Keep these questions in mind as you read and think about the philosophers and their theories discussed below.

PLATO (427–347 BC)

One of the most important early examples of the normative approach to political study is Plato's Allegory of the Cave, which is found in book VII of his classic work *The Republic*.[1] Plato uses the Allegory of the Cave to make the case for critical thinking in pursuit of knowledge and moral clarity. In doing so, he also describes the hazards faced by individuals who dare to question the received wisdom of the day in their search for the truth.

In the Allegory of the Cave Plato creates a fictional dialogue in which his mentor, Socrates, describes a society comprised of a dark cave populated by a number of individuals who are held in shackles. In this environment, in which the only light is that which is produced by a fire within the cave, "reality" is manufactured by individuals who purposely manipulate various statues and carvings in order to cast shadows on the wall facing the shackled population.[2] The implication here is clear: what individuals believe to be the truth can in fact be nothing more than an illusion manufactured by those with the power to create their chosen version of reality.

Plato, through Socrates, takes this lesson one step further. What happens when an individual, formerly shackled, manages to escape his bonds and to ascend the path out of the cave, thereby encountering for the first time the world as it actually exists? It would be reasonable to assume that this newly enlightened individual, after absorbing and contemplating the meaning of this shocking turn of events, might wish to return to his former home below in order to inform those still held in the cave of the truth that exists beyond their manufactured reality. However, upon descending back into the cave he finds that, rather than being greeted as a liberator, he is viewed with distrust, cynicism, and perhaps even murderous hatred by those who see him primarily as a threat to the world (and to the version of the truth) to which they have become accustomed.[3]

There are key lessons to be drawn from Plato's description of life inside (and outside) the cave. Most obviously, the Allegory of the Cave underscores the importance of the dogged search to discover the truth by those individuals with the skill and drive to undertake such an arduous task. Of course, Plato cautions that those who choose that path will almost surely encounter resistance and even outright hostility along the way.

The political prescriptions of the Allegory of the Cave, while perhaps less obvious, are nonetheless vitally important. By painting a picture of a world in which the masses are prone to gross misperceptions regarding the fundamental realities of society, and in which those with the power to do so all too often choose to manipulate the masses in order to secure their enslavement, the Allegory of the Cave can be seen as making a case against both democratic government and dictatorial rule. What, then, according to Plato, is the best form of government?

In *The Republic*, Plato describes, compares and contrasts five models of government. These include a Timocracy, which he defines as a state run by an upper-class selfishly obsessed with material considerations of wealth; an Oligarchy in which the wealthy preclude the lower classes from political life while at the same time contending with one another for an ever-larger share of riches and power; Democracy, a system that arises in the aftermath of mass revolt against the injustices of oligarchy, only to flounder on the rocks of the greed and self-interest of the democratic citizenry; Tyranny, which emerges as a backlash against the excessive liberties of democracy but which quickly devolves into harsh, dictatorial rule; and an Aristocracy, under which an enlightened ruler or small ruling class govern.[4]

The overlap between the lessons of the Allegory of the Cave and Plato's description and critique of the forms of government is clear. In the Allegory of the Cave, those who escape the darkness of the cave possess knowledge of the world that the masses in the cave lack. In the political world, the Philosopher-Kings (or "Guardians"), by dint of their education, moral training, and superior intellect, are uniquely qualified to lead the government and society out of the darkness and toward a brighter future. He refers to this form of rule as "government of the best," and believes that all others types of government are inferior.[5] Interestingly, Plato seems to make no assumption that the enlightened Aristocrats who govern the state meet the same type of resistance and hostility that is directed against the individuals who escape the allegorical cave.

Taken further, Plato's ideal model of government is closely linked to his conception of justice. Society in Plato's aristocracy is comprised of three general social classes: the guardians (rulers), the auxiliaries (military class), and the laborers.[6] So long as each individual in society both meets the responsibilities that come with being a member of the class to which he or she naturally belongs and resists the impulse to improve his or her lot in life by attempting to move up the sociopolitical ladder (for example, from laborer to auxiliary or auxiliary to ruling guardian class), the system is perfectly balanced, and thereby just. Those who are born to rule must rule; those who are born to protect must protect; those who are born to be workers must work. According to Plato, this natural order guarantees a stable society, and a just and morally superior state.[7]

ARISTOTLE (384–322 BC)

Although both Plato and Aristotle are major figures in the pantheon of ancient Athenian philosophers, the two men take different views on the question of which form of government is superior. As we discussed in the previous section, Plato makes an eloquent case for the superiority of a system guided by enlightened philosopher-kings. For his part, Aristotle expresses much more sympathy for a form of rule by the masses.

Like Plato, Aristotle, in his work *The Politics*, creates a comparative typology of governments.[8] Interestingly, although Aristotle is firmly embedded within the normative school, it could be argued that he employs an empirical approach in order to identify the one "best" form of government. Specifically, Aristotle creates a framework of analysis in which forms of government are distinguished by two sets of variables: the number of rulers, and the interests rulers seek to serve through their control of the system (their own interests, or those of society).

TABLE 2.1 Aristotle's Forms of Government.

Number of Rulers	Rule in interest of society	Rule in self-interest of leader(s)
One	Monarchy	Tyranny
Few	Aristocracy	Oligarchy
Many	Polity	Democracy

Under Aristotle's model, the forms of government identified are: Monarchy, in which a single individual rules in the best interests of society; Tyranny, which Aristotle defines as a rule by a single, self-interested individual; Aristocracy, in which a few individuals rule in the best interests of society; Oligarchy, under which a few, self-interested individuals rule; Polity, in which many individuals rule in the best interests of society; Democracy, which features rule by the many in their own self-interests.[9]

Aristotle's model of governments is depicted in Table 2.1:

Aristotle distinguishes between those governments with "right constitutions," by which he means those designed to serve the common good (e.g., Monarchy, Aristocracy, and Polity), and those governments with "wrong constitutions" (e.g., Tyranny, Oligarchy, and Democracy), which aim solely to serve the interests of the ruling class.[10] It is striking that a definitive consensus is lacking among scholars on the question of which form of government Aristotle believes to be the best. In a discourse that stretches over Books III and IV of *The Politics*, Aristotle, at various points, lauds the virtues of Aristocracy, Democracy, and Polity. On balance, however, the evidence suggests that he supports the ideal of the polity as the best form of government.

Two primary explanations emerge that support this interpretation. First, while not dismissive of an Aristocracy in the abstract, Aristotle sees such a system as being largely unattainable in the real world.[11] At any rate, he argues, the most attractive elements of an aristocracy—the fact that the policies that the state pursues are policies based on virtue and equality—may be found in mass-based government as well. Aristotle reasons: "Each individually will be a worse judge than the experts, but when all work together, they are better, or at any rate, no worse."[12] By empowering individuals, the system benefits from the various, complimentary strengths of the many. Aristotle summarizes this point by observing: "For where there are many people, each has some share of goodness and intelligence, and when these are brought together, they become as it were one single man with many pairs of feet and hands and many minds."[13]

Second, in Book IV, Chapter 11 of *The Politics,* Aristotle argues that a virtuous system is one in which the middle class plays the dominant role. In his view, the rich are driven by their unquenchable thirst for wealth and power towards authoritarianism, and the poor are simply too degraded to take an effective leadership role in politics. By comparison, the middle class is "the steadiest element" in society, neither voracious for power nor shrinking from it: "And the fact that it is among the middle sections that you find least reluctance to hold office as well as the least eagerness to do so; and both these are detrimental to states."[14] Given the crucial role that Aristotle accords to the middle class in providing virtue and balance to society, it is not surprising that he sees participatory government, and in the ideal a polity, as the best form of government.

NICCOLO MACHIAVELLI (1469–1527)

Having served in a series of important posts in the Florentine republic, Niccolo Machiavelli brings a unique perspective to the normative study of politics. It was in the aftermath of being deposed, harassed, and blacklisted by the Medici family that Machiavelli produced his most famous work, *The Prince*.[15] In *The Prince*, Machiavelli combines a pragmatist's take on the hazards of political life with the philosopher's desire to chart the best path of leadership.

The Prince represents Machiavelli's attempt to provide a practical blueprint for action by state rulers. According to Machiavelli, ethical considerations mean little, and in fact can be counter-productive, in terms of increasing the security of the prince and his territory. Effective leaders abandon dreams of the world as it *could* exist in favor of basing their policies on the world as it *does* exist. In Machiavelli's words:

> And many have imagined republics and principalities for themselves which they have never seen or known to exist in reality, for the distance is so great between how we live and how we ought to live that he who abandons what is done for what ought to be done learns his own ruin rather than preservation; because a man who wants to make a profession of goodness in everything is bound to come to ruin among so many who are not good.[16]

Machiavelli extends his harsh view of the world to his prescription for how a leader should relate to others. In the real world of political intrigue, a prince must be willing to lie, cheat, and use violence to protect his authority. For example, on the question of whether a prince should strive to be loved or feared, Machiavelli makes a forceful argument in favor of fear. Although he recognizes that in a perfect setting a rational leader would prefer to be both loved and feared, Machiavelli believes that this ideal combination is rarely achievable in the real world of politics. Once a prince recognizes that he must ground his rule in either fear or love, the logical choice is fear. Machiavelli basis this argument on his assumption that love in the hearts of the population is a fickle emotion that is by-and-large beyond the control of a leader to nurture, whereas fear is a state of mind that can be manufactured, manipulated, and sustained by the ruler.[17]

According to Machiavelli, the underlying challenge for a prince in these circumstances is to use enough force to instill fear, without using so much force as to engender a backlash of opposition from the prince's subjects. A leader who engages in selective acts of cruelty without going so far as to undertake a campaign of perpetual violence fosters fear-based acquiescence to his rule. In order to preserve his rule, a rational prince must "learn how not to be good, and to use his knowledge and not use it as necessity dictates." Summing up his argument on this point, Machiavelli bluntly states: "I conclude . . . that since men love at their own will and fear at the will of the prince, a wise prince must build his own foundation on what is his own and not on what belongs to others; he must only contrive to escape hatred, as was said."[18]

Furthermore, a rational prince must know when to keep his word and when to lie. Machiavelli evokes the image of a fox as an animal which, through cunning, can successfully defend itself by avoiding traps that have been laid to ensnare him. A successful ruler is one who "cannot, must not, keep his word, when keeping his word would work against him, and when the reasons which made him promise it have been removed."[19]

In *The Prince* Machiavelli makes the case for strong, dictatorial rule. He advocates a monarchy in which power is vested solely in the hands of a cunning, self-interested prince. Interestingly, Machiavelli was not consistent on the question of which form of government is superior. For example, in *The Discourses*, which he completed a couple of years after *The Prince*, Machiavelli expresses a greater faith in ability of the masses to rule effectively than in a monarch to do so. "But as for prudence and stability," says Machiavelli, "I say the people are more prudent, more stable, and better judges than a prince."[20]

The question of why Machiavelli expresses such seemingly incompatible arguments regarding the best form of government is open to debate. One can surmise that a couple of factors may have played a crucial role in his shifting views on the subject. First, Machiavelli hoped that *The Prince* might provide him with renewed access to the halls of political power; thus, he tailored his argument to reflect the worldview of those with the authority to grant him that access. Second, Machiavelli may have believed that only an authoritarian leader such as that described in *The Prince* could in fact unite the disparate territorial units in the region into a single Italian state.[21]

Machiavelli's mixed messages regarding the best form of government notwithstanding, the blunt and forceful views which he expresses in *The Prince* have carried much greater weight over the centuries than the claims he puts forth in *The Discourses*. Specifically, in a world in which greed, violence, and duplicity are the norm, a leader's primary concern must focus on enhancing his authority and security. This goal justifies dictatorial rule under which the prince is free to do whatever he deems necessary to protect his interests and survival. By securing his own interests, Machiavelli assumes that the prince also provides stable rule from which all citizens benefit.

THOMAS HOBBES (1588–1679)

Perhaps no political theorist in history has painted as stark a picture of human nature as Thomas Hobbes. Beginning with the assumption that humans in their natural state are characterized by greed, insecurity, and violence, Hobbes builds the case for a Leviathan—an all-powerful state with the capacity and will to tame man's fiercest tendencies, thereby providing order out of what would otherwise be chaos.[22] As shall be shown in the following discussion, Hobbes' theory, while designed explicitly to deal with the challenge of achieving stability within the state, has important implications for relations between states as well.

Hobbes believes that the relationships between individuals in society are characterized by mistrust and envy. Because humans are, generally speaking, equal both in their ability to desire that which others possess and to calculate how to seize that which they desire, it is natural that people view one another with great suspicion. In Hobbes' view, "men have no pleasure (but on the contrary a great deal of grief) in keeping company, where there is no power to over-awe them." More generally, in the absence of a powerful central authority, there exists "that condition which is called war; and such a war, as is of every man, against every man." In summary, Hobbes surmises that life for the average person is "solitary, poor, nasty, brutish, and short."[23]

Despite the dire picture which Hobbes presents us, his prescription is relatively simple: an all-powerful state must exist, one with the ability to apply overwhelming force in order to bring order out of chaos. Hobbes proposes that a social contract be forged, one that requires each citizen to recognize the authority of the "Leviathan" (monarch) to "use the strength and means . . . as he shall think expedient, for their peace and common defense."[24] The state upholds its part of the social contract insofar as it provides both internal order and security from external threats.

Although he holds a worldview that by modern standards seems extremely conservative, it is important to note that Hobbes's argument represents important theoretical progress on the issue of sovereignty. Writing at a time when monarchs were assumed to derive their right to rule from God, Hobbes links the Leviathan's rule to popular consent.[25] The leader in Hobbes' theory is vested with full authority to use whatever force he deems necessary not because his sovereignty is preordained by God, but because the citizens determine that such an arrangement is necessary to produce an orderly society.

Clearly, Hobbes' argument is designed as a prescription for how to organize power within the state in order to construct a stable domestic system. However, it is important to note that Hobbes's analysis of domestic politics also carries crucial implications for international relations. Specifically, although it is possible (and particularly so during Hobbes' lifetime) to imagine an all-powerful domestic state such as that which is described in *Leviathan*, it is much less plausible to imagine that the international system can be organized in such a way that the most important actors that make up that system (i.e., states) voluntarily surrender their sovereignty to a global Leviathan (i.e., an international authoritarian governing structure).

Later, in Chapter 12, we shall discuss the concept of anarchy, as that concept is used in the international relations literature. In that literature, anarchy refers to the absence of an overarching governing structure in the international system. To be sure, the United Nations (UN) is an important global actor, but the UN falls far short of the mark in terms of operating as a global government. Instead, it is an intergovernmental organization (IGO), whose member states often value the UN primarily as an arena through which they can promote and protect their own narrow self-interests.

Given Hobbes' view of human nature and the state of relations between actors in a system lacking a Leviathan, his lessons when applied to the international system are potentially catastrophic. If war is the natural consequence of humans living in a domestic system that is not governed by a Leviathan, is it not logical to assume that war would be the natural, perpetual state of things in the international system, given that it lacks an overarching, all-powerful governing authority? As we shall see in Chapter 11, this dilemma—how to achieve stability and order in a system that is dominated by self-interested actors—persists as an enduring challenge within the state-dominated international system.

JOHN LOCKE (1632–1704)

Like Hobbes before him, John Locke's argument regarding the best form of government, as well as the nature of the relationship between the state and society, rests on the concept of a social contract. However, Locke's view of human nature, as described in his *Second Treatise on Government*, is fundamentally different from that which is held by Hobbes.[26] Most importantly, whereas Hobbes believes that humans are naturally greedy and violent, Locke assumes that we are by nature cooperative and peaceful. Thus, while Hobbes argues that sovereignty for the ruler rests on the recognition by the state's subjects of the need to vest all necessary power and authority in the hands of the Leviathan, Locke believes that the primary purpose of the contract between the state and society is to maximize individual freedom and to constrain as much as possible the power of the state.

Locke believes that all individuals possess natural rights, which include life, liberty, and property. Furthermore, he asserts that, while all deserve equality of opportunity, inequality of outcome—the fact that some will possess more things of value than others—is fully justified. The moral justification for inequality of wealth is linked to the establishment of a monetary system. Prior to the creation of money as currency, the over-accumulation of resources such as agricultural products and other foodstuffs in the hands of an individual was irrational (and thus immoral), given the fact that such products were subject to spoilage after a period of time. However, under the monetary system, unlimited wealth, as constituted by gold and silver, could be hoarded indefinitely by any single individual without fear of loss of value due to spoilage.[27]

To the extent that the state has a role to play in exercising its authority over the behavior of individuals, it can only do so with the consent of the people. Specifically, Locke asserts that because we are rational we come to understand that a government, albeit one whose powers are sharply limited, is necessary in order to provide a legal framework for the protection of our natural rights.[28] This, then, is the basis for a social contract between citizens and the state: citizens agree to recognize the authority of the state to make and enforce those laws that are necessary for the protection of natural rights; the state agrees to restrict its power to make and enforce rules to those laws that are essential to the protection of natural rights.

In Locke's view, government is a necessary evil. Ideally, citizens might prefer to live in a true state of nature. However, given the fact that in the otherwise legitimate pursuit of our own self-interests we are likely to infringe at times upon the rights of others, the state has an important role to play in mediating the disputes that arise from such instances.[29] What happens, however, when the state begins to overstep its bounds—to accrue an amount of authority that is beyond that which it legitimately requires in order to protect the natural rights of its citizens? Locke's answer to this question is clear and unequivocal: if the state attempts to seize too much power for itself, the citizens have a right to revoke their consent to govern, thereby removing the state's legitimacy to rule and setting the stage for a possible revolution.[30]

The core elements of Locke's philosophical approach—his faith in the ability of individuals to make rational decisions about their own lives, his emphasis on equality of opportunity, and his argument for limited government—provide the basis for what has come to be known as the classical liberal school (*see* Chapter 5). In turn, the central tenets of the classical liberal school—suspicion of placing too much power in the hands of the government, support for free markets, and adherence to the principle negative freedom—provide the ideological roots for modern conservatism. Of course, Locke's views have met with criticism, much of it focused on his assumption that a natural harmony exists between the desires and interests of self-motivated individuals in a market system on the one hand, and a productive and stable community on the other hand. As is described below, among those who take this opposing view is the Swiss philosopher Jean-Jacques Rousseau.

JEAN-JACQUES ROUSSEAU (1712–1778)

At the beginning of his book *The Social Contract*, Rousseau simply but powerfully observes: "Man was born free, and (yet) he is everywhere in chains."[31] In that sense—his belief that humans lived in a state of nature which existed prior to the rise of more complex social units and before the creation of governments—Rousseau is on common ground with Hobbes and Locke. What distinguishes Rousseau from other social contract theorists is his claim—contrary to Hobbes—that man can live peacefully in a free society, as well as his view—contrary to Locke—that humans find freedom not through the expansion of the right to pursue their self-interests, but rather through their willingness to submit to the general will of the community.

Rousseau devotes the early stages of *The Social Contract* to the subject of slavery, broadly defined. In his view, the social order does not emerge naturally, but rather from a covenant freely entered into by the members of society. By that definition, any society based on slavery and inequality is illegitimate, insofar as it is logical to assume that no individual or group of people would freely enter into a covenant in which their equality is permanently denied. Rousseau observes that enslavement can take the literal form of being held as an individual in bondage by members of the wealthier classes. It can also result from the type of social contract that is promoted by Hobbes (see above) under which all of society must submit to the authority of an all-powerful state. In either instance, Rousseau argues that the ability of an individual or class to exercise authority over another individual or class reflects the power advantage the oppressor enjoys over the oppressed (an advantage that is facilitated by the unequal distribution of property), and thus is not based in any conception of moral duty on the part of the weaker party or parties to submit to a permanent status of inequality.[32]

Specifically in regards to Hobbes' promotion of a Leviathan state, Rousseau rejects the assumption that the security benefits that a brutal authoritarian state is intended to provide outweigh the costs. He warns that the policies that are implemented by a despot—wars against neighboring territories and oppression at home—might cause more problems than they resolve. "What do the people gain," asks Rousseau, "if their very condition of civil tranquility is one of their hardships?"[33]

Is the solution to strive for a return to the state of nature? Although Rousseau believes that during the pre-society state of nature period relations between individuals were peaceful, humans were nevertheless politically unfulfilled and the community morally underdeveloped. And yet Rousseau also believes that, whereas individuals living on their own in the state of nature were largely passive, society—and in particular the existence of private property within a community—creates material inequality between individuals, thereby fueling conflict, violence, and warfare.[34]

The challenge, then, is how to construct a community that maximizes the benefits and limits (or ideally eliminates) the costs of living in a social environment. Rousseau makes the case that perfecting human society requires that people view themselves as citizens who undertake to forge a social contract based on a commitment to an organic society, one in which individuals voluntarily surrender their obsession with their own self-interests for the greater interests of the community. As a result of this arrangement, "each citizen shall be at the same time perfectly independent of all his fellow citizens and excessively dependent on the republic—this result is always achieved by the same means, since it is the power of the state alone which makes the freedom of its members."[35]

Rousseau labels the collective expression of the interests of the community "the general will" and it is this alone which "can direct the forces of the state in accordance with that end which the state has been established to achieve—the common good . . . ."[36] Any individual who acts contrary to the will of the community may be forced by that community to abide by the general will. In Rousseau's view, the application of coercion by the community against a wayward individual is fully justified by his belief that individuals gain true freedom only by acting in concert through the general will.[37]

Rousseau's emphasis on community interests over individual rights raises the question of whether Rousseau is a democrat, as we understand that term today. In much of the Western world, and in particular in the United States, democracy has been inextricably linked to the political and civil rights of individuals, and more broadly to the concept of negative freedom, by which is meant the right of individuals to be free from unnecessary intervention by the state in their personal lives. Individuals who subscribe to this worldview are likely to be dubious of Rousseau's democratic credentials, focusing in particular on his emphasis on the general will of the community, on Rousseau's promotion of the right of the community to force individuals to abide by that will, and on the general suspicion that Rousseau expresses regarding private property. Some scholars have gone so far as to suggest that a philosophical line can be traced through history from Rousseau to totalitarian ideologies on the left and right.[38]

On the other hand, there are many people who are drawn to Rousseau's vision of a society in which an individual citizen finds the fullest degree of justice and freedom through his or her participation in the life of the community. They agree with Rousseau's argument that submitting to the community is an expression of freedom, and that the general will as expressed through the community promotes freedom. Those who look with favor upon Rousseau's model society may support the concept of positive freedom, under which it is argued that the state has a legitimate role to play in leveling political, economic, social, and cultural barriers in an effort to move towards genuine equality. In addition, scholars who are sympathetic to Rousseau's views reject outright the attempt to claim a causal linkage between his writing and the totalitarian states of the twentieth century, arguing that Rousseau's ideal vision of a small, self-governing community characterized by direct participation by citizens stands in stark contrast to the despotism of modern totalitarian regimes.[39] The fact that contemporary scholars still debate the meaning and implications of Rousseau's work is ample evidence of his continuing influence in the field of normative political study.

JOHN RAWLS (1921–2002)

As our discussion thus far illustrates, a great amount of space has been devoted in political theory literature to the concepts of social contract and equality. John Rawls provides a unique perspective on both of these concepts individually, while also framing an argument for how they come together to forge a particular version of justice within society.

Rawls' links his version of the social contract to a hypothetical "original position."[40] Under the original position, all individuals operate behind a "veil of ignorance" that makes it impossible for any individual to know his or her status within society. For example, if you were placed behind Rawls' veil you would be completely ignorant of your social standing, level of education and income, degree of intelligence, age, etc. Nor would you be aware of the circumstances of your society, including its political and economic conditions.[41]

Assuming that all individuals are rational and self-interested, Rawls poses the following question: what principles of justice would be rationally preferred by those who live behind the veil? Again, placing yourself in this context, would it be most rational for you to choose a system in which justice is linked to equality of opportunity and negative freedom, thereby creating conditions under which you might do very well if you happen to possess those characteristics and circumstances that contribute to success, but very poorly if you lack those characteristics and circumstances? Or, on the other hand, would it be more rational for you to link justice with equality of outcome and positive freedom, a system which might constrain the level of success you can attain (and in fact could lower the overall wealth and resources within society), while also cushioning the possibility that you might suffer from social and economic inequalities?

Rawls concludes that rational individuals would choose to define "justice as fairness."[42] Specifically, Rawls argues that it would be irrational for a person to gamble on a system in which inequality is supposed to be accepted as a necessary function of maximizing the total amount of wealth and satisfaction within society. In Rawls' view, no rational individual would prefer a system in which, if potentially stuck in a position of disadvantage, he or she will perpetually suffer while others reap the benefits of the opportunities that are afforded to them by the built-in advantages they enjoy in terms of education, class, race, etc. Instead, Rawls believes that individuals in this position will select a system based on equality of rights and duties, one that focuses on the goal of addressing the unfair position in which the disadvantaged are placed in a society that is characterized by unfettered social and economic inequalities.[43] In other words, they will construct a system that defines justice as fairness, resting on full equality of opportunity, an effort to obtain a degree of equality of outcome, and positive freedom.

The assumptions and arguments put forth by Rawls in *A Theory of Justice* have sparked much criticism and significant debate. One of the most interesting criticisms focuses on Rawls' assumption that individuals behind the veil of ignorance will logically choose the path of risk minimization. Rawls believes that it is more rational for an individual behind the veil of ignorance to choose a system that guards against the negative impact of socioeconomic inequality than it is for that same individual to gamble that he or she will benefit from a system that is not focused on reducing the effects of social and economic inequality. Without wading too deeply into what can be a very dense theoretical debate, critics reply that, even given the presence of the veil of ignorance, it is entirely plausible that an individual, based on his or her "full knowledge of general facts and scientific laws," may very well rationally calculate that he or she is likely to be in an advantageous position when the veil is removed.[44] According to this scenario, the individual is more likely to support a system that permits inequality in the name of negative freedom, based on the supposition that his or her benefits will be maximized within a system characterized by inequality of outcome.

Furthermore, many conservatives are uncomfortable with the policy implications of Rawls' theoretical findings. Rawls seeks to embed social justice within a particular form of democracy. As Rawls comments in his book *Justice as Fairness*, "one practical aim of justice as fairness is to provide an acceptable philosophical and moral basis for democratic institutions, and thus to address the question of how the claims of liberty and equality are to be understood."[45]

In Rawls' view, achieving justice as fairness requires a robust welfare state. Rawls favors taxation policies that are designed to improve the lot of those at the bottom of the ladder. For example, he supports taxes on inheritances and gifts as being necessary to "gradually and continually . . . correct the distribution of wealth and to prevent concentrations of power detrimental to the fair value of political liberty and fair equality of opportunity." In addition, the government must set overall tax rates with an eye toward generating the revenues required to pay for programs that move society toward greater levels of equality.[46] Clearly, then, Rawls' stance on these questions places him on the liberal side of the political spectrum, as the term "liberal" is used in contemporary political discussions in the United States.

REVISITING THE KEY QUESTIONS

At the beginning of our discussion on political theory we identified several key questions as being at the center of the normative study of politics. These questions include: Which form of government is superior? Is human nature predisposed toward conflict or toward cooperation? What do we mean when we speak of a social contract? And, what does a just system look like? With the obvious caveat that not every philosopher discussed here directly addresses each one of these issues, let us now return to these questions to see where the theorists we discussed stand.

Which Form of Government is Superior?

One of the most crucial questions addressed in the normative literature centers on which form of government is superior. Each one of the theorists discussed in this chapter has something important to say about this critical issue. Their responses can be divided in modern parlance into two general categories: those who favor democratic rule, and those who favor non-democratic rule.

Among the theorists examined in this chapter, Aristotle, Locke, Rousseau, and Rawls each favor some form of democratic government. We have previously discussed above in some detail the debate over Rousseau's democratic credentials. Ultimately, however, the fact that Rousseau clearly favors the creation of an ideal political system based on direct participation by citizens highlights the democratic underpinnings of his theory.

The philosophers who come closest to describing democracy as it is actually structured and operates in the United States and other developed democracies are Aristotle, Locke and Rawls. While the inclusion of Locke appears obvious given his emphasis on individual rights and freedoms, situating Aristotle and Rawls in this category may seem somewhat less so. However, Aristotle's faith in the rationality of the masses and his emphasis on the importance of the middle class mirrors key assumptions and elements that serve as the basis for organizing political life in modern democracies. As for Rawls, although he admits that his "veil of ignorance" is a completely artificial concept, the fact that Rawls uses the lessons drawn from the veil of ignorance exercise to make the case for the modern welfare state places his model of governance squarely in the contemporary democratic category.

On the other hand, Plato, Hobbes, and Machiavelli each argue against democracy and in favor of some form of authoritarian rule. Having said that, there are important differences among these philosophers on the issue of precisely what form of authoritarian government they support. Plato makes the case for an enlightened Aristocracy, under which a small ruling class governs with the best interests of all the state's citizens in mind.

For their part, both Hobbes and Machiavelli favor a harsher brand of dictatorial rule than that which is envisioned by Plato. In the view of Hobbes, an authoritarian government, often brutal in its treatment of its enemies, is required in order to bring order to a society that otherwise would be characterized by anarchy. Machiavelli argues that a ruler must be willing to use cunning and coercion in defense of his own security as well as that of the state. In the world of contemporary politics, these types of arguments—that the centralization of power and the denial of personal freedoms are necessary in order to provide for a more orderly society—are put forward time and again by authoritarian dictators as justifications for their repressive regimes.

Is Human Nature Predisposed Toward Conflict or Cooperation?

Many of the theorists we have discussed in this chapter incorporate basic assumptions regarding human nature into their philosophical frameworks. With the exception of Machiavelli and Hobbes, the general consensus in the normative literature tilts towards the view that humans, particularly in their "natural state," are by nature cooperative. For example, Plato assumes that a natural balance exists in society, a balance that is pegged to the harmonious relationship between individuals as members of one of the three main classes (ruling class, auxiliary class, or labor class) in Plato's model.

Aristotle places faith in the masses, and in particular in the members of the middle class, to make rational decisions in cooperation with one another on what is best for society. Rousseau makes a strong case for the ability of individuals as members of a community to come together in the name of forging effective governance. Locke is a passionate advocate of the idea that individuals are naturally peaceful in their relations with one another.

The views held by Machiavelli and Hobbes stand in stark contrast to those summarized in the previous two paragraphs. Both assume that humans are by their nature greedy, envious, and insecure, and that therefore human relations are naturally conflictual. Returning to the issue of which form of government is best, these assumptions on the part of Machiavelli and Hobbes regarding human nature serve as critical elements in shaping the view held by both men that authoritarian rule in which power is centered in the hands of a single leader is morally desirable because it is a necessary strategy for securing the state, the society, and ruler himself. In other words, the ends of stability and security often justify brutal means.

What Do We Mean When We Speak of a Social Contract?

The notion that a social contract exists that shapes the rights and duties of citizens and the government, and under which society and the state exchange commitments of mutual reciprocity, is a central one in the political theory literature. Although Hobbes, Locke, Rousseau and Rawls incorporate the social contract into their theories, each author provides a unique definition of the concept. Thus, while there is broad agreement that social contracts are critical elements that bind citizens to one another, and the society to the state, no consensus exists as to the nature of that contract. To a significant degree, this disagreement over the precise meaning of the social contract is linked to conflicting assumptions regarding human nature.

According to Hobbes, the social contract rests on the requirement that citizens surrender their personal liberties to an all-powerful state—the "Leviathan." In return, the state tames human conflict and provides security and stability. Assuming that the state meets its end of the bargain—the provision of peace and security—members of society must accept the necessity of dictatorial rule.

At the other end of the philosophical spectrum we find Locke. He assumes that individuals are inherently peaceful and cooperative, and believes that the biggest threat to peace and stability comes from vesting too much power in the hands of the state. Thus, whereas according to Hobbes the social contract was necessary as a tool for giving the state the power it needs to curb and control the inherently violent nature of its citizens, Locke argues that the social contract is desirable because it gives citizens a check against unfettered government power. Given Locke's suspicion regarding the power of the state, it is not surprising that he believes that only the citizens have the right to break the social contract, a right they can legitimately exercise when the state begins to overstep its authority.

Rousseau's conceptualization of the social contract differs from the views held by Hobbes and Locke. As was noted previously, Rousseau disagrees with Hobbes' argument that for individuals the state of nature is characterized by insecurity and violence; he also stands in opposition to Locke's emphasis on the interests and rights of individuals. Furthermore, Rousseau's version of the social contract rests on the assumption that individuals in society will surrender their narrow self-interests to the interests of the broader community, or "general will." By coming together in this manner, citizens forge a contract in support of the general will; it is this general will that then serves to direct the state to foster the common good.

Finally, Rawls adopts the concept of a social contract as an "original position" behind "the veil of ignorance." Unlike the other social contract theorists discussed here, Rawls sees the social contract not as something that exists in the real world, but rather as an artificial device for exploring the meaning of a just society. Rawls' argument regarding just society is reviewed below.

What Does a Just Society Look Like?

Although there is a great deal of focus in the normative literature on the desire to build a just society, political philosophers have long debated exactly what we mean by the concept of "just society." Most importantly, there is a lack of consensus centered on the following basic question: when we speak of justice, we mean to speak of justice for whom? For example, Plato equates justice with the interests of society, and most importantly with the goal of social stability. Plato believes that justice as stability is the product of a harmonious balance among the three main social classes; social balance is achieved when each citizen accepts his or her social status as determined by birthright.

For Machiavelli and Hobbes, the state has the right and responsibility to determine the meaning of justice for all its citizens. Nevertheless, subtle differences exist between the two on this issue. Specifically, whereas for Machiavelli justice is linked to the self-interests of the ruler, for Hobbes justice is shaped by the state's responsibility to provide security for its citizens.

In Locke's view justice is pegged to justice for the private citizens and in particular to negative freedom: the right of individuals to be free from unnecessary intervention by the state. Under Locke's model, a just society is one in which citizens enjoy the fullest degree of individual liberties. On the other hand, Rousseau believes that a truly just society is one in which citizens find their richest fulfillment in the act of coming together as an organic community.

For Rawls, a just society is one in which, contrary to Locke, the state takes an active role in the provision of positive freedom—the right of all individuals in society to enjoy a basic standard of the economic, political, social and cultural fruits of life. Guided by his principle of "justice as fairness," Rawls makes the case that the fairest system is one that tends to the needs and rights of those who are disadvantaged. Thus, Rawls defines a just society as one in which the state, while not necessarily achieving perfect equality, effectively redistributes economic resources and political opportunities towards those who are less well off within society.

PUZZLE: MUST WE CHOOSE BETWEEN LIBERTY AND SECURITY?

One of the most appealing characteristics of developed democracies is the perception that they have achieved a stable balance between individual liberties such as freedom of speech, freedom of assembly, and right to vote on the one hand, and the provision of security for the state and society on the other hand. This has reinforced the belief, widely held in the developed democratic states, that liberty and security are understood correctly as being mutually reinforcing, rather than mutually exclusive, conditions. In other words, not only is it unnecessary to make a choice between liberty and security, it may be counter-productive—and even dangerous—to do so.

This point of view is summarized by Benjamin Franklin: "Those who would give up essential liberty, to obtain a little temporary safety, deserve neither liberty nor safety."[47] The British philosopher John Stuart Mill adopts a similar stance, warning that coercion in the name of stability ultimately weakens the state. In his treatise *On Liberty*, he observes that "a State which dwarfs its men, in order that they may be more docile instruments in its hands even for beneficial purposes—will find that with small men no great thing can really be accomplished."[48]

It seems relatively easy to accept such arguments in societies with an established history of respect for the rule of law and the democratic rights of citizens, although, as we shall discuss shortly, this assumption is problematic even in developed democracies. On the other hand, in states without a tradition of democratic rule the idea that a country need not have to choose between liberty and security may seem far-fetched indeed. Many such states are plagued by weak and corrupt governments, low levels of development and/or high rates of socioeconomic inequality, and ethnic or religious divisions. These circumstances create conditions that may seem ripe for the type of unceasing violence that led Hobbes to advocate the creation of a Leviathan state. Leaders in these settings use the fear of instability to justify cracking down on the political and civil liberties of their citizens in the name of maintaining security.

Let us briefly consider two examples that appear at first glance to lend credence to the claim that, at least in certain countries that lack a sustained record of democratic governance and the rule of law, it may be necessary to prize security over liberty. In the case of Yugoslavia, despite its diverse religious and ethnic population the country experienced decades of relative tranquility under the stewardship of the communist leader, Marshall Tito. It was only in the aftermath of Tito's death and the collapse of the Yugoslav communist state that relations between Serbs, Muslims, and Croats deteriorated, leading not just to warfare, but also to a campaign of massive ethnic cleansing led by the Serbian president Slobodan Milosevic.[49] Thus, the lesson that one might draw from this case is that Yugoslav society enjoyed security only so long as the authoritarian state enforced stability within the country's multinational setting. As soon as Serbs, Muslims, and Croats were free to choose their future paths, society collapsed into chaos. We will return to reconsider this case shortly.

Our second example is that of Iraq. In the aftermath of the overthrow of Saddam Hussein's dictatorship, Baghdad was swept by a massive wave of civil unrest and looting. Then Secretary of Defense Donald Rumsfeld tried to brush off the unrest by commenting that Iraqis were simply coming to grips with their newly-won liberty. "And here is a country that is being liberated," lectured Rumsfeld at a press conference, "here is a people going from being repressed and held under the thumb of a vicious dictator, and they're free."[50]

Despite Rumsfeld's dismissive comments, the instability that erupted in Iraq shortly after Saddam's fall left many Iraqis with a declining sense of security under US occupation. The unease among Iraqis regarding the deteriorating security situation in their country is reflected in polling data gathered from 2005–2007. That data reveals that the percentage of respondents who rated the security conditions in their neighborhood or village as either "quite bad" or "very bad" rose from 38% in 2005 to 56% in 2007.[51]

Meanwhile, with Saddam's brutal, Sunni-based regime out of power a multi-faceted military conflict erupted inside Iraq. On various levels, the conflict inside Iraq pitted Sunni and Shiite militants against one another, while at the same time the US and its Iraqi government allies faced stubborn opposition separately from both Sunni and Shiite militias. In addition, the country's long-suffering Kurdish population was occasionally targeted by forces seeking to undermine the Kurds' influence in the new Iraq. Ultimately, the failure of the US to provide a basic level of security inside Iraq created an authority gap, and led many Iraqis to question America's role in Iraq.[52]

At first glance, then, it would seem that both Yugoslavia and Iraq serve as classic examples of formerly stable societies collapsing into internal chaos once personal liberties were extended to the citizens of these states. As dictatorial regimes were replaced by young, uncertain democracies, conditions emerged that were ripe for domestic conflict. Turning Franklin's argument inside-out, in both cases security appears to have been sacrificed for liberty, with the result being the provision of neither security nor liberty.

However, the assumption that a cause-and-effect relationship exists between the collapse of authoritarian rule and the subsequent expansion of democratic freedoms in Yugoslavia and Iraq on the one hand, and reduced levels of security on the other hand, represents an oversimplification. For example, there is ample evidence to support the theory that the brutal violence that erupted in the former Yugoslavia during the 1990s was not the natural by-product of Serbs, Croats, and Muslims choosing all at once to exercise their newly-found freedoms by going at each other's throats, but rather was sparked purposely by Slobodan Milosevic, a Serbian elite who won the presidency and then sought to consolidate his popularity within his Serbian base power by manipulating inter-communal tensions inside the country.[53] The collapse of security in post-communist Yugoslavia was not caused by the expansion of liberty to average citizens per se, but rather by the fact that an ethnic entrepreneur, Slobodan Milosevic, came to power who was willing to mutilate the liberty and security of large segments of the country's population in the name of his fellow Serbs, and in defense of his own political security.[54]

In Iraq, there is no denying that the country has been plagued by violence, much of it inter-communal fighting between the Sunnis, Shiites, and Kurds, since the overthrow of Saddam. However, it is also the case that under Saddam the state used its power advantage inside the country to brutally oppress Iraq's restive Kurdish and Shiite communities.[55] The most infamous case of Saddam's oppression of these communities occurred in 1988, when he ordered the use of chemical weapons against Iraqi Kurds. The gas attacks terrorized the Kurdish population and triggered a mass exodus, with over 70,000 Kurds fleeing their homes.[56]

Throughout much of Saddam's rule, the large majority of Iraq's population (Shiites and Kurds together comprise a substantial majority of Iraq's population) enjoyed neither liberty nor security. This sense of insecurity, with its roots in Saddam's dictatorial regime, has persisted under the post-Saddam regime, which has begun to expand basic freedoms. Clearly, far from being a product of the extension of personal liberty, the internal instability that characterized Iraq following Saddam's overthrow was simply the latest example of a state that has long been plagued by domestic insecurity.

The cases of Yugoslavia and Iraq illustrate that the relationship between liberty and security in states experiencing political transitions from authoritarianism toward democratic rule is fraught with complexities and potential complications. Turning back to the developed democracies, it may be tempting for citizens in countries such as the United States to assume that the balance struck between liberty and security in their own societies is constant and unchanging. This belief takes hold most clearly during periods of relative peace and prosperity, when the perceived threats to security are comparatively small. When the large majority of citizens believe themselves to be physically and economically secure, the question of how much liberty is too much rarely garners much sustained attention.

However, a much different picture emerges during periods of crisis, when rising fear may motivate certain political leaders as well as significant portions of the general population to reconsider the relative balance between liberty and security. The history of democratic societies is replete with examples of "backlashes" against liberty during times of heightened insecurity. The fear and uncertainty that are sparked during such crises create conditions under which public sentiment might emerge in favor of the curtailment of certain liberties in the name of increased security.

For example, during the early stage of the American Civil War, President Abraham Lincoln suspended the writ of *habeas corpus*, the constitutional guarantee to due process for all suspects arrested and detained. In conveying the suspension of *habeas corpus* to Union General Winfield Scott, Lincoln gave Scott the right to "arrest, and detain, without resort to the ordinary processes and forms of law, such individuals as he might deem dangerous to public safety."[57] It should be noted that Lincoln believed that his decision was not only necessary, it was also constitutional, given the fact that the US Constitution lists rebellion as one of two conditions under which *habeas corpus* may be temporarily suspended (the other being foreign invasion).[58] Not surprisingly, despite some public criticism that Lincoln was overstepping his authority, and in the face of an effort by Chief Justice Roger Taney to overturn his order, Lincoln's proclamation suspending *habeas corpus* stayed in place until the war's end.

More recently, as American military forces struck back in Afghanistan following the terrorist attacks of September 11, 2001, President George W. Bush enacted a policy under which individuals taken prisoner on the battlefield could be held as "unlawful enemy combatants" under military law. As was the case with Lincoln, the Bush administration held firmly to its claim that its treatment of wartime prisoners was both necessary and constitutional.[59]

Bush's stance was not without controversy. Civil libertarians and those on the left of the political spectrum charged that the treatment of foreign enemy combatants amounted to an illegal infringement on the constitution. The Bush administration came under further scrutiny after the passage of the Patriot Act, which gave the government broad powers to gather personal information about US citizens in secret. For example, the American Civil Liberties Union complained that the Patriot Act "threatens . . . fundamental freedoms" because it permits the government to access the private records of citizens "without telling (them) for weeks, months, or indefinitely."[60] In summary, critics believe that, in responding to the events of 9/11, Bush sacrificed too much liberty in the pursuit of enhanced security.

On the other hand, many people, including most conservatives, support the policies instituted by the Bush administration as being a necessary response to the threats faced by the United States following 9/11.[61]

Advocates of Bush's approach argue that limiting certain freedoms is as an effective tactic for achieving the strategic goal of defeating global terrorism. This point of view is grounded philosophically in the belief that a basic level of security is a necessary pre-condition for the full exercise of liberty.

Clearly, even in an established democracy such as the United States the debate over how to reconcile the civil liberties of individuals with the security requirements of the state and society has not been fully resolved. Periods of relative tranquility, during which a broad consensus seems to exist regarding the appropriate mix between liberty and security are punctuated by periods of intense debate and disagreement on the issue during times of crisis. On the question of whether we must choose between liberty and security, where do you stand?

Notes

1   Plato, *The Republic*, trans. Paul Shorey (Cambridge, MA: Harvard University Press, 1963), 119–129.
2   Ibid., 119–121.
3   Ibid., 123–129.
4   Ibid., Book VIII.
5   Ibid., 241.
6   Ibid., Book IV.
7   Ibid., 367–373.
8   Aristotle, *The Politics*, trans. T.A. Sinclair (Middlesex: Penguin Books, 1972).
9   Ibid., Book III, Chapter 7.
10 Ibid., 115.
11 Ibid., 171.
12 Ibid., 125.
13 Ibid., 171.
14 Ibid., 172.
15 Niccolo Machiavelli, "The Prince," in *The Prince and Other Writings*, trans. Wayne A. Rebhorn (New York: Barnes and Noble Classics, 2003).
16 Ibid., 66.
17 Ibid., 71–72.
18 Ibid., 66; 73.
19 Ibid., 75.
20 Machiavelli, "The Discourses," in *The Prince and Other Writings*, 182.
21 Wayne A. Rebhorn, "Introduction," in *The Prince and Other Writings*, xxxi.
22 Thomas Hobbes, *Leviathan* (New York: Barnes and Noble, 2004).
23 Ibid., 76–77.
24 Ibid., 108.
25 Leon P. Baradat, *Political Ideologies: Their Origins and Impact*, 8th ed. (Upper Saddle River, NJ: Prentice Hall, 2003), 10.
26 John Locke, *Two Treatises of Government* (London: Dent Dutton, 1978).
27 Ibid., 139–141.
28 Ibid., 180.
29 Ibid., 180.
30 Ibid., 224–242.
31 Jean-Jacques Rousseau, *The Social Contract*, trans. Maurice Cranston (London: Penguin Books, 1968), 49.
32 Ibid., 52–55.
33 Ibid., 54.
34 Maurice Cranston, "Introduction," in *The Social Contract*, 21.
35 Rousseau, *The Social Contract*, 99.
36 Ibid., 69.
37 Ibid., 64.
38 Baradat, *Political Ideologies: Their Origins and Impact*, 8th ed., 82–83.
39 Cranston, "Introduction," 34–35.
40 John Rawls, *A Theory of Justice*, rev. ed. (Cambridge, MA: Belknap Press of Harvard University Press, 1999), 11.
41 Ibid., 11; 118–119.
42 Ibid., 10.

43 Ibid., 13.

44 David Lyons, "Nature and Soundness of the Contract and Coherence Arguments," in *Reading Rawls*, ed. Norman Daniels (New York: Basic Books, N.Y.), 160–161.

45 John Rawls, *Justice as Fairness: A Restatement*, ed. Erin Kelly (Cambridge MA: Belknap Press of Harvard University Press, 2001), 5.

46 Rawls, *A Theory of Justice*, 245–247.

47 Bob Herbert, "Who Will Stand Up for the Constitution?" *New York Times*, January 19, 2006, 23. http://www.lexisnexis.com.proxy-su.researchport.umd.edu/us/lnacademic/auth/checkbrowser.do?ipcounter=1&cookieState=0&rand=0.028877812894674615&bhcp=1 (accessed June 26, 2009).

48 John S. Mill, *On Liberty* (Indianapolis, IN: The Bobbs-Merrill Co., Inc., 1956), 141.

49 Christopher Layne, "Blunder in the Balkans," *Policy Analysis* 345 (1999): 2–3. http://ciaonet.org.proxy-su.researchport.umd.edu/wps/lac01/lac01.pdf (accessed June 26, 2009).

50 Bob Woodward, *State of Denial: Bush at War, Part III* (New York: Simon & Schuster, 2006), 164.

51 British Broadcasting Corporation, "Iraq Poll February 2009," http://news.bbc.co.uk/2/shared/bsp/hi/pdfs/13_03_09_iraqpollfeb2009.pdf (accessed June 26, 2009).

52 Ibid.

53 V.P. Gagnon, Jr., "Ethnic Nationalism and International Conflict: The Case of Serbia," *International Security* 19 (1994–1995): 132. http://www.jstor.org (accessed June 27, 2009).

54 For a more general discussion of this phenomenon, see David A. Lake and Donald Rothschild, "Containing Fear: The Origins and Management of Ethnic Conflict," *International Security* 21 (1996): 41–75. http://www.jstor.org.proxy-su.researchport.umd.edu/stable/pdfplus/2539070.pdf (accessed June 27, 2009). See also Rogers Brubaker and David D. Laitin, "Ethnic and Nationalist Violence," *Annual Review of Sociology* 24 (1998): 440. http://web.ebscohost.com.proxy-su.researchport.umd.edu/ehost/pdf?vid=9&hid=107&sid=4e0f53ca-965f-4049-bd9b-7d4d38edcd70%40sessionmgr102 (accessed June 27, 2009).

55 Jason Brownlee, "Political Crisis and Restabilization: Iraq, Libya, Syria, and Tunisia," in *Authoritarianism in the Middle East: Regimes and Resistance*, eds. Marsha P. Posusney and Michele P. Angrist (Boulder: Lynne Rienner, 2005), 52–55.

56 Alan Cowell, "Fleeing Assault by Iraqis, Kurds Tell of Poison Gas and Lives Lost," *The New York Times*, September 5, 1988. http://proquest.umi.com.proxy-su.researchport.umd.edu/pqdweb?index=0&did=115504658&SrchMode=1&sid=1&Fmt=10&VInst=PROD&VType=PQD&RQT=309&VName=HNP&TS=1246141140&clientId=11426 (accessed June 26, 2009).

57 Doris K. Goodwin, *Team of Rivals* (New York: Simon & Schuster, 2005), 354–355.

58 Ibid., 524.

59 Council on Foreign Relations, "Military Commissions Made Legal," http://www.cfr.org/publication/11761 (accessed June 27, 2009).

60 American Civil Liberties Union, "USA Patriot Act," *Safe and Free: Restore Our Constitutional Rights*, http://www.aclu.org/safefree/resources/17343res20031114.html (accessed June 27, 2009).

61 James P. Terry, "Habeas Corpus and the Detention of Enemy Combatants in the War on Terror," *Joint Forces Quarterly* 48 (2008): 18. http://www.ndu.edu/inss/Press/jfq_pages/editions/i48/8.pdf (accessed June 27, 2009).

Power: The Core of Politics

INTRODUCTION

It is often argued that power is the central element in politics. In the words of 19th century British politician Benjamin Disraeli: "Real politics are the possession and distribution of power."[1] According to Richard Nixon, power is a positive force in political life: "Power," he explained, "is the opportunity to build, to create, to nudge history in a different direction."[2]

On the other hand, there are those who believe that power is a negative political element. Andrew Bard Schmookler sees power as an inescapable, if necessary, evil. As summarized by Schmookler: "No one is free to choose peace, but anyone can impose upon all the necessity for power . . . . The continuous selection for power has thus continually closed off many humane cultural options that people might otherwise have preferred. Power therefore rules human destiny."[3]

Given the core role that many accord to power in political life, understanding power is vital to making sense of the world of politics. In this chapter we will define power, discuss its role as both a cause and effect of politics, examine the sources of power, the techniques by which it can be employed, the instruments of power, and the characteristics of power. The chapter concludes with a consideration of the relationship between power and morality.

DEFINING POWER

At first glance, defining the concept of power may seem a straightforward task. Consider the following basic definition: power is the ability of one actor to get a second actor to do something the first actor desires. Is this a sufficient definition of the concept of power?

Think about the following example. If your classroom catches fire, and your professor tells you to leave immediately, and you do so, has he or she exercised power over you? According to the definition provided above the answer is yes, because you carried out the action that was ordered by your professor. In reality, however, assuming you are rational and wish to avoid the risk of death or injury, you would have chosen on your own to leave the room anyway. In fact, under this scenario the successful use of power by your professor would require that he or she order that you stay in the classroom despite the flames, and that you abide by that command.

The preceding example highlights the shortcomings of a definition of power that focuses solely on the interests of the actor attempting to exercise power. A richer definition of power requires that we also incorporate the interests and behavior of the actor targeted by the exercise of power. With this in mind, in this book we define power as the ability of one actor (either an individual or group) to get another actor (again, either an individual or group) to do something that the first actor desires, *and* which the second actor would not otherwise choose to do.[4]

POWER AS A CAUSE AND EFFECT OF POLITICS

Power is both a cause and effect of politics. It is a cause of politics in that the distribution of power among the relevant actors in a political system is a key determinant of political outcomes within that system. Power is an effect of politics insofar as political decisions that are taken by important actors such as the state can reshape the distribution of power in profound ways.

Most of the discussion in this chapter situates power within the context of states (i.e., countries) as they operate and relate to one another in the international system. However, it is important to keep in mind that power is also a critical variable within the domestic systems of countries. Power helps to determine both the ability of the state to exercise its will *vis-à-vis* society, as well as the extent to which actors within society can force the state to accede to their demands. Thus, it would be useful to examine briefly an example that illustrates power as both a cause and effect of domestic politics.

The Civil Rights Act of 1964 illustrates the dynamic relationship between power and politics in the domestic arena. Research shows that a crucial factor in explaining the adoption in the United States of the landmark Civil Rights Act of 1964 was the emerging consensus, across racial boundaries, in favor of equal rights and integration. In the words of one report: "Major legislation rarely occurs unless there are social pressures encouraging action. The Civil Rights Act of 1964 certainly was no exception."[5] Thus, a shift in public opinion provided civil rights advocates with the political muscle needed to achieve their goals; in other words, power (in this case, the power of public opinion) helped to cause a change in policy.

Power is also an effect of politics. The Civil Rights Act was designed specifically to empower African-American voters, mainly in the American South, who—for nearly a century after the US Civil War—often faced nearly insurmountable roadblocks in attempting to exercise their constitutional right to vote. Thus, a political decision, in the form of a new law, was used to increase the power of black voters to make their preferences heard.[6]

The political empowerment of African-Americans reached its zenith in 2008, when a dramatic surge in the number of African-Americans voters (nearly 2 million more blacks voted in 2008 compared to 2004) helped Barack Obama to capture the presidency. The impact of the increased turnout among blacks and other minority groups in 2008 was accompanied by a sharp uptick in voting for the Democratic presidential candidate among African-American voters: 95% of black voters cast their ballots for Barack Obama in 2008, compared to 88% who voted for Democrat John Kerry in 2004. At the same time, participation among white voters actually declined slightly between 2004 and 2008.[7] It is not too far-fetched, then, to trace the roots of the election of the first African-American president in the United States to the Civil Rights Act of 1964.

The Civil Rights Act highlights the role of power as both a cause and effect of domestic politics. A shift in public opinion, always a powerful force in democratic political systems, was a key element in causing the federal government in the United States to adopt legislation in the area of minority voting rights. In turn, the adoption of that legislation empowered African-American voters, thereby helping to produce a dramatic political development—the election of Barack Obama to the presidency in 2008.

UNDERSTANDING POWER: SOURCES, TECHNIQUES, INSTRUMENTS, AND CHARACTERISTICS

In order to fully grasp the meaning and importance of power in political life, it is essential that we disaggregate the concept—that we "pry power open" in an effort to gain a better understanding of the factors that shape power and its effects on politics. The bulk of the rest of this chapter is devoted to this task. We will examine the sources of power, the techniques by which power is exercised, the instruments or categories of power, and the characteristics of power, focusing primarily on how power shapes, and is shaped by, the capabilities, interests, and behavior of states, particularly within the international system.[8] Focusing on power and politics as those elements relate to states is particularly useful, given the widely-held recognition of states as the most important actors in political life.

Sources of Power

All political actors, including states, seek power as a way of protecting their interests and pursuing their objectives. We shall discuss the concept of the state in detail in Chapter 4. To clarify for now, a state is a political unit featuring a government that exercises sovereign authority over a specified territory and the population living within that territory. Unless otherwise indicated, in this book the term state is synonymous with what is commonly referred to in everyday language as a "country."

In the contemporary political world, states are recognized as possessing the legal authority to exercise power. As such, the state's legal authority is not a variable; by definition, all states are recognized as having the authority to employ power within limits prescribed by domestic and international law. The amount of state power possessed by a state, however, does vary significantly from state to state. State power initially derives from the sources of power available to a state. Three sets of sources shape power capabilities, and thus help to explain the differences in power between states: *natural sources of power, tangible sources of power, and intangible sources of power.*[9]

Natural Sources of Power

Some states enjoy a built-in advantage in terms of power capabilities, based on natural sources of power. Crucial natural sources of power include geography, resources, and population.[10] Geographic factors that can bolster power include size (large territorial space makes it harder for an outside aggressor to invade and occupy a country), natural boundaries (aggressors can find it difficult to traverse geographic features such as vast bodies of water and large mountain ranges), and climate (extreme cold or extreme heat can complicate the ability of a foe to carry out a sustained attack on a state's territory, while a temperate climate can promote domestic agricultural production).

Like geographic factors, natural resources are found naturally in a territory's environment. Natural sources such as fresh water, fertile soil, and reserves of precious minerals serve as the basis for power by sustaining the population and providing the underlying basis for economic development. For example, resources such as oil, diamonds, and copper are prized because of the wealth they generate through their sale on global markets. Such resources can be a valuable source of wealth for states that are fortunate enough to possess them.

It is important to note, however, that while high-value resources can empower a state, they also can increase the vulnerability of a state by making it an attractive target for others who wish to seize those resources. The example of the Gulf War is a classic case of this phenomenon. In that conflict, the very resource that increased Kuwait's power and wealth (oil) provided the incentive for Iraq's invasion and occupation of Kuwait in August 1990, particularly given the decline in Iraq's relative power status, a slide that began in the late 1980s and persisted into 1990.[11]

The competition to control valuable resources can also contribute to instability within a state. Several states in sub-Saharan Africa, including Nigeria, Sierra Leone, Angola, and Liberia, are plagued by conflicts that pit domestic actors against one another as they vie for control of high-demand resources. In the words of Nigerian journalist Sunday Dare, while a number of African states are blessed with rich deposits of natural resources, "From such blessings ... much sorrow has flowed." Domestic competition for control of valuable resources has "degenerated into conflicts and internecine wars. Retarded in their development, unbridled in their lust for power, steeped in official corruption, chaotic in their political engineering, many (African) states are now sprinting toward total collapse."[12]

A large population increases the power potential of a state. Ideally, a large population serves as the basis for economic growth and military development. In reality, however, in a country where population growth outpaces natural resources and educational and employment opportunities, a large population can be a source of weakness rather than strength. Under such circumstances citizens may begin to blame the government for deteriorating economic, social, health, and environmental conditions inside the country, triggering domestic instability, civil unrest, and in extreme cases the possibility of a revolution against the state.

Tangible Sources of Power

Natural elements such as geography, resources, and population are important sources of potential power. However, those natural elements must be converted into tangible sources in order for their full power value to begin to be realized. Tangible sources of power include technological modernization and socioeconomic development.[13] It is through the process of converting natural advantages in areas such as resources and population into tangible elements of power that a state begins to maximize its economic and military potential.

Tangible sources of power produce conditions that we can use to measure the relative level of power and development of a state. Later in this book we will examine several tools for measuring levels of socioeconomic development within states and comparing levels of socioeconomic development across states. One such tool is the *Human Development Index* (HDI), which uses factors such as life expectancy, adult literacy rates, combined levels of educational attainment, and per capita income to measure a state's success in converting its resources into an improving quality of life for its citizens. As depicted in Table 3.1, countries in the "developed" world—mainly Western and Northern Europe, North America, Japan, Australia, New Zealand, and Iceland—typically have the highest HDI scores, while states in certain lesser-developed regions—in particular in Sub-Saharan Africa—tend to have much lower scores.[14]

Interestingly, the states that score at the top of the 2008 HDI are not typically thought of as great military powers. This would indicate that the relationship between economic wealth and military power is a fairly complex one, and that economic power translates into military power only insofar as a state's leadership makes the choice to invest the country's wealth heavily in developing the state's military capabilities. As a country's economy develops, the state, if it chooses to do so, has more wealth at its disposal to lavish on the purchase of weapons produced abroad. Or, leaders may decide to increase investments in the domestic development of new weapons.

Furthermore, for those states with the resources and know-how to produce sophisticated weaponry at home, advanced military technologies can also be useful in generating wealth through the process of arms sales. North Korea is an example of a state that seeks both military and economic benefits from investing a large portion of the country's meager wealth into a weapons' program. Not only does the North Korean government feel it is enhancing the country's security through its program of weapons development, the missiles and other technologies that are produced through that program and can be sold abroad are a vital source of income for the cash-strapped state.[15]

Intangible Sources of Power

Ideally, states are able to maximize their power by converting their natural power sources to tangible sources of power. However, objective sources of power are only part of the story. While it is undoubtedly true that natural and tangible sources are a core determinant of power, one must not overlook the importance of intangible sources of power.[16]

One key intangible source of power is an actor's image and reputation. In certain circumstances, image of power is largely beyond the ability of an actor to control. For example, in the United States presidents can have

TABLE 3.1 Human Development Index Rankings, 2008.

Top Five Countries (1–5)	Bottom Five Countries (175–179)
Iceland	Mozambique
Norway	Liberia
Canada	Democratic Republic of Congo
Australia	Central African Republic
Ireland	Sierra Leone

Source: United Nations Development Programme, Human Development Reports, http://hdr.undp.org/en/statistics/

a difficult time achieving their legislative goals during their second-term in office because they are perceived of as being "lame-ducks."[17] The fact that an individual will be out of the White House within a couple of years may reduce his or her leverage within the political system. Looking down the road, members of Congress and other participants in the political process know that the current president will no longer be around, and thus may feel less constrained by the wishes and demands of that individual.

On the other hand, there are circumstances in which actors have the opportunity to manipulate to their advantage the perception that others hold about their power. If successful in this effort, they manage to produce an image of power that far exceeds the objective amount of power they actually possess. For example, during the American Civil War many Confederate commanders became masters at the art of power image manipulation. The ability of the Confederates to deceive Northern generals may have reached its zenith during the Union's Peninsula Campaign in the spring of 1862. As Confederate forces faced overwhelming odds, Southern generals developed some ingenious methods for manipulating the enemy's perception of the rebel army's power. In one famous example, the Confederates erected hundreds of wooden logs, dubbed "Quaker Guns," to give the appearance that they possessed a huge artillery force. Believing that he faced overwhelming firepower, Union General George McClelland brought his army to a halt. Unbeknownst to McClellan, his Army of the Potomac was actually more than six times larger than the Confederate force that faced him at the time.

Later during the same campaign, Confederate General John Magruder resorted to a grand theatrical ploy on the battlefield in order to shape his foe's perception of the size of Magruder's army. Magruder ordered his 15,000 troops to march through a wooded area into a clearing where they could be viewed by Northern troops, back into the woods, then back once more out into the clearing—and so forth—for an entire day. Magruder's ruse was designed to give the appearance that a never-ending stream of Confederates awaited George McClellan's army. Once more, McClellan, with 90,000 troops under his command, was fooled. Convinced yet again that he faced an enemy much larger than his own army, McClellan took up defensive positions, thereby foregoing an assault against the far smaller Confederate force.[18] Given the objective imbalance of power in favor of the North, such tactics were vital tools that permitted the South to at least somewhat even that balance through an enhanced image of power.

The case of Iraq's program of weapons of mass destruction (WMD) under Saddam Hussein serves as another example of the attempt to use the perception of power to shape the behavior of others. Beginning in the last half of the 1990s and continuing into the early part of the 21st century, Saddam Hussein played a cat-and-mouse game with the international community over Iraq's WMD program. We now know that Saddam's erratic behavior was designed not to hide outlawed weapon's (which the bulk of the evidence suggests Iraq did not have by that time), but rather was meant to plant the thought in the minds of foreign enemies such as Iran and the United States, as well as his enemies at home, that he still possessed WMDs. Saddam calculated—incorrectly it turned out—that the fear that he might have such weapons would deter a military assault against Iraq. He paid for the miscalculation with the destruction of his regime by American forces, and then with his own life at the hands of the Iraqi justice system.

Both of the examples cited above underscore another crucial intangible aspect of power: good leadership. In the case of the Confederacy, during the first two-plus years of the Civil War Southern military commanders proved time and again that their brilliant and imaginative leadership could more than offset the objective advantage the Union possessed in military might and economic power. In fact, it was not until the Union had in place determined and skilled military leaders (i.e., Ulysses S. Grant and William T. Sherman), and the South lost a key commander (Thomas "Stonewall" Jackson) that the tide of the war finally began to turn in favor of the North.

In Iraq, it is indisputable that during Saddam's rule Iraq possessed many of the natural and tangible prerequisites of power, including oil, water, arable land, a large and fairly well-educated population, and a massive, well-armed military force. Unfortunately for the citizens of Iraq, Saddam Hussein squandered these advantages through a series of poor policy choices, including Iraq's attack on Iran in 1980, his decision a decade later to invade Kuwait, and his failure to predict with accuracy the way the international community would respond to his refusal to cooperate consistently with weapons inspectors.

The case of Iraq under Saddam also highlights a third important intangible element of power: *national cohesion*. As we shall discuss in greater detail in Chapter 4, a state that possesses high levels of national cohesion features a population with a strong sense of shared identity and purpose. Furthermore, national cohesion is related strongly to the belief on the part of the large majority of the population of a country that the political leaders who hold power have a legitimate right to rule.

Issues surrounding national cohesion, both at home and abroad, were a major factor in explaining many of the blunders that plagued Saddam's regime. For example, Saddam miscalculated the degree of national cohesion in Iran when he attacked that country in 1980. Assuming that Iran's population was deeply divided in the aftermath of the Islamic revolution, Saddam believed that a short-term opportunity existed for addressing Iraq's long-term vulnerability *vis-à-vis* Iran, which was a substantially larger country in terms of its population and GDP than Iraq.[19]

In turn, one of the reasons Saddam feared that Iraq was vulnerable to Iran can be traced to questions surrounding national cohesion inside Iraq. Iran's population is predominantly Shi'a Muslim, and Shi'a Muslims comprise the majority of the population in Iraq as well. However, Saddam was a Sunni Muslim. In fact, the Sunnis may be just the third largest community in Iraq, following the Shiites and the Kurds. The fact that the Sunnis in Iraq exercised an amount of power that was disproportionate to their percentage of the population, while by comparison the larger Shi'a Muslim and Kurdish communities suffered violence and oppression at the hands of the Sunni-dominated regime, exacerbated Iraq's lack of national cohesion.

Saddam believed that in the long-run Iran might be enticed by Iraq's low levels of cohesion to launch a military offensive, the primary goals of which would be to protect Iraqi Shiites and to overthrow his regime. Thus, Saddam's miscalculation regarding strains in the national cohesion inside Iran combined with his concern over problems of national cohesion inside his own country, motivating him to launch his ill-advised war on Iran. That conflict ended in a bloody stalemate, having cost Iraq hundreds of thousands of lives and leaving the country's economy devastated.

TECHNIQUES OF POWER

Previously, we defined power as the ability of one actor to get a second actor to do something the second actor would not otherwise have chosen to do. One logical follow-up question in response to this definition would be to ask how power is exercised. In other words, what are the techniques that actors employ to get other actors to shape the behavior of other actors?

Coercion

We can distinguish between two techniques of power. The first technique is *coercion*. Coercion relies on the threat or use of force to bring about a desired change in the behavior of an actor. Under a strategy of coercion, one actor tells another actor: "do what I demand of you, or you will experience a pain or loss."

The policy that was employed by President George HW Bush in response to Iraq's invasion of Kuwait in August 1990 stands as a classic example of power as coercion. US strategy unfolded in two stages, both of which represented a resort to coercion in an effort to force a change in Iraq's behavior. In the first stage, which was dubbed "Operation Desert Shield," the Bush administration put together a broad military coalition, designed both to convince Saddam Hussein of the world's commitment to reverse his aggression against Kuwait and to deter Iraq from using Kuwait as a launching pad for an invasion of Saudi Arabia.[20] This stage relied on the threat of the use of force in an effort to bring about the desired change in Iraq's policy.

When Saddam Hussein failed to abide by a United Nations Security Council Resolution that demanded that Iraq withdraw its forces from Kuwait by January 15, 1991, the US strategy of coercion shifted from the threat of the use of force to the actual use of force. The United States and its allies launched "Operation Desert Storm," which began with a punishing air campaign, followed up by the use of ground forces against the battered Iraqi army[21]. The US-led offensive routed the Iraqis, many of whom simply surrendered or fled in terror back to Iraq. In the case of the Gulf War, then, coercion requiring the use of military power proved successful in achieving the objectives of the anti-Iraq coalition, albeit only after an effort to rely on coercion via the threat of force proved ineffective.

Persuasion

Power is often so strongly linked to coercive force that it may seem that coercion is the sole technique of power. This, however, is not the case. The second technique of power is *persuasion*. Under this technique, positive incentives are offered in an effort to change an actor's behavior. When power is used as persuasion, one actor signals to another actor: "do what I tell you to do and you will experience pleasure or a gain." For example, the Federal Government in the United States uses tax credits as an incentive to convince citizens to undertake actions they may not otherwise undertake (e.g., the tax credit program that was implemented by the Obama administration to entice Americans to purchase a home during the recession that struck the United States and the rest of the world toward the end of the first decade of the 21ˢᵗ century).

Returning to the example of the Gulf War, the United States utilized a combination of coercion and persuasion in organizing the military campaign. We have already discussed the manner in which America and it allies employed coercion against Iraq. In addition, the US administration used persuasion to bring Arab states into the anti-Iraq military coalition. One obvious example of this strategy occurred within the context of the US relationship with Egypt. The United States forgave a $7 billion debt owed by the Egyptian government for arms purchased from the US in the 1970s, and rescheduled the remainder of Egypt's debt to America. In return, the Egyptians gave military and political support to the American-led war effort.[22]

America also used incentives to gain Syria's support for the war against Iraq. Specifically, the US gave tacit approval to Syria's military crackdown in Lebanon in the fall of 1990.[23] In addition, the Bush administration promised Syrian President Hafez al-Asad that the United States would undertake a sustained effort to achieve a breakthrough in the Arab-Israeli peace process once the Iraqi army was defeated and driven from Iraq.[24] These political enticements were sufficient to convince the Syrians to condemn Iraq's invasion and to contribute a military contingent to the anti-Iraq coalition.

It is interesting to briefly consider the question of whether, given a choice, a rational actor should prefer to exercise power as coercion or power as persuasion. Recall Machiavelli's argument (*see* Chapter 2) that it is necessary for a leader to employ power as coercion, at least on occasion, in order to reinforce subservience to his or her rule. In Machiavelli's view, then, the use of force is rational, based on calculations of princely self-interest.

On the other hand, a strong case can be made that a rational leader, when he or she deems it necessary to use coercion, should seek to rely as much as possible on the threat, rather than the actual use, of force. Not only does resorting too frequently to the use of force risk creating more fierce opposition from the actors who are the target of the application of force (a fact, which as we noted in Chapter 2, Machiavelli himself recognized), employing forces involves the consumption of power. When actually utilized, sources of power such as economic wealth and military resources are depleted and must be replaced. On balance, therefore, it is clear that a rational leader would be well advised to use coercion quite selectively and judiciously, understanding that he or she must seek to replenish military, economic, and political instruments of power as they are used up.

INSTRUMENTS OF POWER

We have discussed the techniques of power available to states and other actors in pursuit of their interests. As noted in the previous section, actors must select between employing power as persuasion or power as coercion (and in the case of the latter technique, they must choose between coercion as the threat of the use of force or coercion as the actual use of force). These techniques of power draw from three *instruments of power*: military power, economic power, and political power.

Military Power

Military power is most often thought of as being exercised through coercion. In such instances the use of military power involves the threat or use of armed force to change the behavior of another actor. As described in our discussion of power as coercion, US strategy during the Persian Gulf Crisis—Desert Shield followed by Desert Storm—is an example of military power through coercion.

In addition to skilled leadership, the successful use of military coercion is shaped by the *balance of military capabilities* that exists between the actors involved in a dispute, as well as the *will* that each actor possesses to fully commit to making the sacrifices necessary to achieve victory. Military capability refers to objective indicators such as the number of personnel in uniform, and the size and technological sophistication of a country's arsenal. A state's military capability is shaped by the types of factors that were discussed in the preceding section on power sources, including natural sources of power (large territory, ample domestic resources, defendable borders, and a population size that is sufficient to support economic and military development without overwhelming the resources of the state); tangible sources (advanced levels of economic development and technological sophistication); and intangible sources (image and leadership).

In considering power relations in the military realm, it seems obvious that an actor who enjoys a military capability advantage relative to a potential enemy should be favored to win any armed conflict that might erupt between them. However, it is crucial that we also consider the role of will in the use of coercive military power. A state may enjoy an advantage based on its military capabilities when compared to those of an enemy; however, that advantage can be at least partially neutralized by the relative will of the two actors involved.

The Vietnam War is a dramatic example of the importance of will. The overwhelming advantage in military capability that the United States enjoyed during the Vietnam War *vis-à-vis* the North Vietnamese and their Viet Cong allies was at least partially negated by the simple fact that the North Vietnamese and Viet Cong never seriously believed that the US would resort to the use of nuclear weapons to win that conflict. In addition to the military support that the North Vietnamese and Viet Cong received from external actors such as the Soviet Union (USSR) and China, the absence of will on the part of the United States to use its full arsenal of weapons helped to balance out the military equation in Vietnam.

Furthermore, the North Vietnamese and Viet Cong communists displayed an overwhelming commitment to winning, a will that the South Vietnamese, in general, lacked.[25] For the North Vietnamese and Viet Cong, victory meant the reunification of Vietnam under the nationalist Marxist banner. By comparison, South Vietnamese soldiers were fighting for a corrupt authoritarian government in Saigon, and in a larger sense to maintain the artificial separation of Vietnam into two separate countries. Under these circumstances, it is not surprising that, on balance, the communist forces displayed a more vigorous desire to carry the fight to the bitter end in pursuit of victory than did the South Vietnamese. Ultimately, the North Vietnamese and Viet Cong triumphed in 1975 when they routed South Vietnamese forces and the country was reunited under the guidance of North Vietnamese leader Ho Chi Minh.

Military power may also be used as persuasion. Examples of military power as persuasion include strategies such as the offering of a mutual defense pact or the delivery of military equipment to another actor in exchange for a desired change in the behavior of that actor. During the Cold War, for example, the United States and the Soviet Union competed with each other for influence by offering military support to states in Europe, Africa, Asia, Latin America, and the Middle East. Because many of these states were plagued by military weakness, economic underdevelopment, and political instability their leaders were more than happy to accept the offer of assistance in exchange for aligning themselves with one superpower or the other.

While it may seem to be a straightforward proposition to use positive military incentives as an instrument of power, in the real world of politics this strategy can prove to be highly complicated, and even counterproductive. The *Iran-Contra Scandal* of the 1980s represents a classic example of the failure of military power as persuasion. In that case, the US administration of President Ronald Reagan linked three goals: support for anti-Marxist forces (the Contras) in Nicaragua, the release of American hostages in Lebanon, and the fostering of better relations with moderate elements inside Iran. Knowing that the Islamic Republic of Iran was desperate for military supplies as its war with Iraq dragged on, the Reagan administration offered to sell weapons to the regime of Ayatollah Khomeini, in return for which the Iranians would use their influence in Lebanon to secure the release of American hostages being held there. Congress having outlawed US aid to the Contra forces in Nicaragua, the Reagan administration intended to secretly funnel the cash from the Iranian arms sales to the Contras. The entire scheme eventually collapsed, leaving US hostages in Lebanon (although two Americans were released, three more were seized by Lebanese militants), the Contras still short on supplies, relations with Iran soured even further, and the Reagan administration to deal with a huge domestic scandal once the details of the plan became public knowledge.[26]

Economic Power

Economic power as coercion can take the form of sanctions, embargoes, the withholding or reduction of aid, and a general strategy of economic isolation toward a targeted actor. The oil embargo that was initiated in 1973 by the Organization of Petroleum Exporting Countries (OPEC) against several Western countries, including the United States, stands as a classic example of economic coercion. In that case, the Arab oil producing states sought to force a change in the policies of the US and Europe toward the Arab-Israeli conflict by resorting to the strongest weapon in the oil producers' power arsenal—control over much of the world's petroleum supply. In fact, after the embargo was implemented the US became more active in pushing for a breakthrough in the negotiations between Egypt and Israel, although that was a position that America probably would have favored anyway. More telling is the fact that, as the negative impact of the embargo began to be felt, many European countries became much more vocal in their criticism of Israel's occupation of Arab lands and in their defense of Palestinian rights.[27]

On the other hand, although coercive economic tactics are employed fairly often as a preferred option to the use of military power, their record of success is mixed at best. For example, economic sanctions against Fidel Castro's Cuba and Saddam Hussein's Iraq failed to achieve the core political objectives for which they were employed. In both cases, the underlying goal behind sanctions was to spark internal opposition inside the target countries, leading to the overthrow of the existing government. However, in neither case did the ruling regimes collapse as a result of sanctions.

What factors undermine the effectiveness of sanctions as tools for achieving the goal of regime change in target countries? Research indicates that the failure of sanctions to bring about fundamental political changes could be linked to *issue salience*. Specifically, given the fundamental interests that rulers have in maintaining their positions of power, they are highly likely to put up fierce resistance when their regimes are targeted for destabilization by outside actors through the application of sanctions.[28] In addition, it could be that, much as citizens tend to "rally around the flag" when their country faces a foreign military threat, so the effective application of sanctions is complicated by a tendency in most situations for domestic actors to set aside the grievances they may have against their own government in the face of external efforts at coercion through sanctions.[29]

Exercising economic power as persuasion involves the offering of incentives such as aid, debt forgiveness, and improved trade relations in exchange for which the target state agrees to change its behavior. In general, the use of positive economic incentives has a better track record of success than does the application of coercive techniques such as sanctions. For example, America's offer of debt forgiveness to Egypt in exchange for its support during the Gulf War (see above) is a classic case of the effectiveness of economic incentives. Another example of this approach is the effort, launched by the United States during mid-1990s, to convince North Korea to drop its nuclear program in exchange for economic aid. This arrangement appeared to be working until the North Koreans, frustrated over American foot-dragging in proving the aid that had been promised by the administration of President Bill Clinton, re-launched their nuclear program at the end of the 1990s.[30]

Political Power

As is the case with the other two instruments of power, *political power* may be employed using either coercion or persuasion. Political coercion typically involves isolating a target actor diplomatically, thereby seeking to achieve changes in the target. For example, despite the fact that the communists came to power in China in 1949, the United States refused to grant official diplomatic recognition to the People's Republic of China (Communist China) until 1979.[31] In choosing instead to treat the nationalist government on the tiny island of Taiwan as the official representative of China, the US attempted (unsuccessfully) to hasten the collapse of communist rule in China.

The evolution in the early 1970s of America's diplomatic policy toward the two major communist powers, the Soviet Union and China, stands as an example of the application of political power as persuasion. During this period, President Richard Nixon sought improved political relations simultaneously with both Communist China and the USSR. Under Nixon's diplomatic approach, which was dubbed détente, the promise of friendlier political relations, including official diplomatic recognition of the People's Republic of China, was used to

TABLE 3.2 Instruments and Techniques of Power.

	Coercion	**Persuasion**
Military Power	Threat or use of armed force (e.g., Gulf War)	Offer of military incentives such as arms transfers (e.g., Iran-Contra)
Economic Power	Threat or use of economic force such as sanctions and embargoes (e.g., OPEC embargo)	Offer of economic incentives such as aid and debt relief (e.g., Debt relief to Egypt during Gulf War)
Political Power	Threat or use of political force such as diplomatic isolation (e.g., Political isolation of "rogue" states such as Iran)	Offer of political incentives such as improved relations (e.g., Nixon's policy of détente *vis-à-vis* the Soviet Union and China)

draw each of the two great communist powers closer to the United States. This benefited America's strategic position in the world, not least because the warming of America's relations with the Soviet Union and China occurred against a backdrop of increasingly frosty relations between the Soviets and Chinese.

Our discussion of the instruments of power illustrates the point that each of these instruments may be employed using both coercive and persuasive techniques. Table 3.2 summarizes the relationship between the instruments of power and the techniques of power.

CHARACTERISTICS OF POWER

It is tempting to view power as simply the composite of an actor's capabilities, derived from the various types of sources discussed earlier in this chapter. This conceptualization of power, however, is too static. Ultimately, power's ability to shape political outcomes is linked to its several core characteristics: power is relative; power is situational; and power is dynamic.

Power is Relative

In this chapter, we have warned against equating power solely with capabilities. One reason it is dangerous to define power in this way is that it encourages us to assume that the power of any one actor can be determined in isolation from all other actors. Under this approach to understanding power, if we know the standard unilateral measures of power for a state—GDP, HDI, the size of military forces, etc.—we "know" the power of a state.

The problem with measuring power in this way is that it ignores the very basic yet essential fact that power matters precisely because some actors have more of it than others. It is the distribution of power among the relevant actors in a political context that grants an advantage to some of those actors, while placing other actors at a disadvantage. Power is most meaningful, therefore, when it is understood as *relative power*.

Consider the following scenario: you live completely alone on a deserted island, where you happen to have at your disposal a weapon of tremendous destructive force. Does your possession of that weapon make you powerful? Keeping in mind that power is the ability to change the behavior of others to meet your will, the answer is no. Because you live alone, and therefore have no other actor against whom you can threaten or actually employ the weapon, it is useless as an instrument of power.

Now imagine that you live on an island whose population consists of yourself and at least one other person. Moreover, you are the only person on the island who possesses the powerful weapon mentioned above. Assuming that you could use the weapon in such a way that you can do harm to others without harming yourself, your control of the weapon increases your power relative to others. It is the fact that you exist in a society with other individuals that creates the opportunity to exercise power.

The case of Iraq provides ample evidence of the relative nature of power. Iraq was able to invade and occupy Kuwait in 1990, encountering virtually no resistance from the Kuwaiti army. This outcome was not at all surprising, given the huge power differential in military capabilities between Iraq and Kuwait. Moreover, the fact that Iraq's power was declining relative to Arab states such as Saudi Arabia provided an added incentive for the Iraqis to occupy Kuwait as a way to increase their regional power.[32] Iraq, however, lost its military power advantage during the Persian Gulf Crisis when the United States and other actors formed a military coalition to come to the defense of Kuwait.

The relative power gap between the US and Iraq was even bigger by the time of the American invasion of Iraq in 2003. Researchers have dubbed this type of conflict a "war of inequality." At the time of the invasion, the tremendous power advantage the United States enjoyed over Iraq—America's GDP was over 100 times larger than Iraq's, its population was more than 10 times larger than that of Iraq, and it possessed a military capability unmatched in the history of the world, whereas Iraq's military was still greatly weakened in the aftermath of the Iran-Iraq War and the Gulf War—meant that the outcome of the war was never really in doubt.[33] Because the Bush administration recognized America's power advantage *vis-à-vis* Iraq, it calculated that there was a high likelihood that the United States could go to war and achieve its core strategic objectives (regime change and destruction of the WMDs that the US assumed Iraq possessed) at a relatively low cost in terms of lives lost and resources spent.[34]

Why then, given the overwhelming advantage in relative power enjoyed by the United States, did the US encounter major difficulties in Iraq following Saddam's overthrow? The mounting challenges that confronted the United States in Iraq following Saddam's fall can be traced primarily to a combination of poor strategic planning by American decision-makers (recall that leadership is an intangible source of power), along with determined opposition to the US occupation by a variety of actors in Iraq and elsewhere in the Middle East, including loyal supporters of Saddam Hussein and his Ba'th Party, Shiite factions seeking to seize control of Iraq in the aftermath of the collapse of Saddam's Sunni-dominated regime, and Al Qaeda-affiliated Islamists from around the region. As in Vietnam, anti-American forces in Iraq relied on their commitment to their cause to at least partially offset their material power disadvantages. These factors combined to shift the relative balance of power in a way that greatly complicated US operations in Iraq. It was not until the United States implemented the surge policy—the introduction of dramatically larger numbers of American troops into key areas of the country—complimented by a successful effort to co-opt previously anti-American Sunni tribal leaders, that the balance of power shifted once more in favor of the US and against anti-American forces inside Iraq.[35] In short, shifting patterns in the relative distribution of power explain the evolving conditions in Iraq since the overthrow of Saddam.

Power is Situational

Previously, we identified three main instruments or categories of power: military power, economic power, or political power. The United States is fortunate in that it possesses overwhelming amounts of power in each of these categories. Few other countries enjoy such a luxury. This means that for the majority of countries, their ability to exercise power in any given situation is determined not just by the relative distribution of power between themselves and other relevant actors, but also whether the instrument of power in which a state might have an advantage is relevant to that situation. That is, by their *situational power*.

If we think back to the example of the OPEC oil embargo, the oil producing states used power in a rational fashion because they recognized that the economic instrument was the one category in which they wielded significant power over the Western states. Specifically, choking off the supply of oil would cause substantial economic harm to the West, and therefore increase the likelihood that the US and other Western democracies might reconsider their support for Israel. By comparison, resorting to the threat of military attack, or attempting to isolate the US and its allies politically in the United Nations, would have had a negligible impact, given the weakness of the oil producing states in the military and political instruments of power. Nor would the use of the political or military instruments of power have helped major OPEC players such as Saudi Arabia to have achieved their more narrow national goals, which for the Saudis included using their oil wealth to increase their influence over the major Arab military powers (Egypt and Syria).[36] Thus, given the circumstances, the oil embargo was the perfect weapon for the oil producing states to employ.

On the other hand, the failure to understand the situational nature of power can have disastrous consequences. During the 1920s and 1930s, a consensus emerged, particularly in Europe and the United States, that political persuasion, as represented by diplomacy and public opinion, and practiced in the halls of the newly-minted League of Nations, was the most powerful force for peace and prosperity in the system. Thus, in September 1938 British Neville Chamberlain sought to avert war with Adolf Hitler by negotiating the Munich Agreement, under which Germany was permitted to occupy the region of Czechoslovakia known as the Sudetenland. As late as April 1939, US Secretary of State Cordell Hull expressed with confidence his belief that "a public opinion, the most potent of all forces for peace, is more strongly developing throughout the world."[37]

The faith that Hull and many other leaders of his era placed in the power of public opinion proved ill-founded. Throughout the 1930s, the fascist powers resorted time and again to brute military force in pursuit of their objectives, with seeming impunity. In the words of Winston Churchill, the dogged faith that many Western members of the League of Nations maintained in diplomacy and public opinion represented nothing more than "long-suffering and inexhaustible gullibility."[38] Beginning with Japan's occupation of Manchuria in 1932, continuing with Italy's invasion of Ethiopia in 1935, and culminating in the decade of the 1930s with Nazi Germany's attack on Poland in September 1939, the actions taken by the fascist states drove home the point that political power, exercised through diplomacy and a reliance on public opinion, was no match for well-armed, aggressive states bent on military conquest. Quite simply, the Western democracies attempted to employ an instrument of power (political persuasion) that was inappropriate and insufficient, given the nature of the threat posed by the coercive military actions of Germany, Japan, and Italy.

Power is Dynamic

An actor who is "strong" today may be "weak" tomorrow. This means that the power of a state is bound to wax and wane over time. In fact, the history of the world is the tale of *dynamic power*, as a series of empires or great power states, each of whom were once dominant, experience an inevitable decrease in power.

Consider the case of the former Soviet Union. During the latter half of the 1970s, it became a broadly held view in much of the world that the Soviet Union had emerged as the dominant military power in the global system.[39] One study released by the US-based Rand Corporation in 1980 concluded that a dramatic shift in military power capabilities had taken place during the decade of the 1970s, one that clearly favored the USSR. The report traced the increase in Soviet capabilities mainly to a pattern of robust growth in the Soviet state's investment in the military sector.[40]

The extent to which it was assumed that the US was losing ground to the Soviet Union is underscored in documents that have been declassified since the end of the Cold War. For example, in one 1980 report a Hungarian communist official informed his superiors that during a meeting he held with US diplomats in January of that year, the Americans had admitted that their estimates revealed that by 1979 the military balance clearly favored the Soviets. In fact, the Americans pressed the Hungarian on the question of Soviet intentions: specifically, did the Soviet Union intend to use its military advantage to threaten US interests around the world?[41]

Fast forward now a mere 3 years. In 1983, Yuri Andropov was named to replace Leonid Brezhnev, who had just died, as head of the Soviet Union. During his first speech as Soviet leader, Andropov described the decade of the 1970s as one "of further growth and influence of the socialist commonwealth." At the same time, Andropov admitted that it had become increasingly difficult for the USSR to match the military build-up of the United States under Ronald Reagan: "Probably, the Soviet Union feels the burden of (the) arms race into which we are being pulled, more than anybody else does."[42] Andropov also spoke of the growing unrest inside of Poland, a socialist state that was allied with the Soviet Union.[43]

Interestingly, the Soviet leader chose to ignore in his speech the war in Afghanistan, which by then represented a strategic quagmire that was draining Soviet coffers of billions of dollars. Nor did he address the building economic crisis in the Soviet system. Nevertheless, in retrospect it is clear that by the time Andropov came to power in 1983 the Soviet Union was on the precipice of a steep military, political, and economic decline.

By 1991, the Soviet Union was barely a shell of its former self. During the Gulf War in early 1991, the Soviets stood aside as the United States attacked and defeated Iraq, once an important Soviet ally in the Middle East. One by one the *Warsaw Pact* states (the socialist states of Eastern Europe) collapsed in the face of pro-democracy protests at home. Meanwhile, as we will discuss in detail in Chapter 12, inside the Soviet Union itself the effort by President Mikhail Gorbachev to salvage the Soviet system through reform had failed. Faced with the choice of moving forward toward radical change, or back toward the old Soviet model, the majority of forces in Soviet society came down on the side of moving forward. On December 25, 1991, the Soviet Union, which just 11 years earlier had been seen by American officials as being the most powerful state on the face of the earth, disbanded. The power of the Soviet Union, which had once waxed so highly, waned into nothingness.

CONCLUSION

Clearly, practitioners and scholars of politics have long recognized the important role that power plays in political life. "Politics," the EH Carr, "are . . . in one sense always power politics. Common usage applies the term 'political' not to all activities of the state, but to issues involving a conflict of power."[44] Thus, political outcomes are substantially shaped, if not largely determined, by the sources, techniques, instruments, and characteristics of power that have been described in this chapter.

PUZZLE: CAN POWER AND MORALITY CO-EXIST?

Those who study politics have long pondered the nature of the relationship between power and morality. Are power and morality completely distinct and separate approaches to politics? Or, are they related to one another, and if so, which causes the other? Does power determine our definition of morality, or does morality determine the use of power? Can power and morality coexist?

In theory, power and morality can operate as alternative approaches to politics. In his book *The Twenty Years' Crisis*, EH Carr uses the terms "utopia and reality" to describe these competing "methods of approach." According to Carr, the central elements of utopianism include individual free will, the application of ideals in politics, the role of the intellectual in political life, and the primacy of ethics in making policy. Thus, utopianists believe that policymaking involves the rational application of power to achieve moral ends.

Realism, on the other hand, assumes that the ability of humans to shape history is limited, asserts the importance of political practice over political theory, emphasizes the role of the bureaucrat in politics, and stipulates that policy is shaped in response to empirical reality. Realists, then, believe that policy is shaped by the desire to possess power, both as an end in and of itself, and as a tool for protecting one's self-interests.[45] Morality, understood as some set of universal ethical principles, has no legitimate role to play in the realists' version of political life.

Interestingly, after conceptualizing ethics and politics as competing schools of thought, Carr admits most political actors most of the time attempt to link power and morality. Thus, while they are theoretically separate, in practice power and morality do not operate in completely distinct and separate spheres. Having said that, Carr argues that it is common in politics for actors to seek to use power in such a way that their self-interests and the interests of the broader community are treated as one and the same. Carr refers to this as the "harmony of interest," according to which a state equates its self-interests with the universal good.[46] How we define morality, then, may be based on shifting calculations of self-interest, rather than on ethically grounded, long-standing, and universal ideals.

If Carr is correct in his claim that morality is a product of individual interests, then we must ask whose interests serve as the source of the definition of morality in a political system. A long line of scholars have concluded that, like it or not, the strongest actor in a political community determines what is moral and what is immoral within that community. This view is summarized vividly by Thucydides' in his account of the dialogue between the Athenians and Melians during the Peloponnesian War. Thucydides quotes the Athenians as telling the Melians: "the standard of justice depends on the equality of power to compel and in fact the strong do what they have the power to do and the weak suffer what they have to accept."[47] In other words, the strong get to decide what is "moral," and the weak must accept that decision, lest they risk their own destruction. Might makes right.

During the 20th century, the assumption that morality could be equated solely with the interests of the strong was a central element of fascist thought. Building on Darwin's theory of Survival of the Fittest, the fascists' viewed history as an unceasing struggle to conquer or be conquered. In 1926, Adolf Hitler stated the case for Darwinism applied to relations between national communities in stark terms:

It is evident that the stronger has the right before God and the world to enforce his will. History shows that the right as such does not mean a thing, unless it is backed up by great power. If one does not have the power to enforce his right, that right alone will profit him absolutely nothing. The stronger have always been victorious. The whole of nature is a continuous struggle between strength and weakness, an eternal victory of the strong over the weak. All nature would be full decay if it were otherwise.[48]

The example of Nazi Germany illustrates with shocking clarity that the naked pursuit of power, unchecked by ethical standards, can produce horrifically immoral results. Writing in 1943, WR Inge observed: "The biological doctrine of survival of the fittest may be interpreted to mean that power is the true aim of human endeavor." Inge summarizes the fascists' view of the world as "We dined as a rule on each other. What matter? The toughest survived."[49]

For obvious reasons, the example of 20th century fascism seems to delegitimize power as a positive element in political life. If power can result in an event such as the Holocaust, can we ever fully trust any political leader who wields it to do so justly? Power, it would seem, all too often leads to outcomes that privilege the material interests and physical security of the individual or group who possesses it at the expense of others.

On the other hand, it is at least theoretically possible that the strongest actor in a political system will use its power in pursuit of the common good. Thus, for example, in the aftermath of the 9/11 attacks, many political elites and commentators in the United States argued that the application of American power around the world within the context of the War on Terror would produce results from which people around the world would benefit, including the defeat of Islamist militancy, respect for human rights, and the spread of political and economic freedoms. Because the administration of George W Bush argued that the ends it sought were universally just, it also believed that the use of military coercion to achieve those ends was fully justified.[50]

Of course, this view of the Bush administration's post-9/11 policy was hotly disputed by many people. Critics charged that the decision by the United States to use armed force, particularly in the form of the invasion of Iraq, was driven by American self-interest, cloaked in the mantle of universal morality. The "moral" claims made by the US in explaining the decision to invade—for example, the desire to overthrow an evil dictator, the wish to introduce democracy and human rights to the Arab world—were window dressing, designed to hide America's interest in securing Iraqi oil and establishing a large military presence on the ground in the Middle East. If this critique is accurate, the US invasion of Iraq fits neatly into a pattern that has endured throughout history: powerful actors often create a "just" rationale for employing force in pursuit of goals that really serve their own self-interests.[51] Once more, we find that what is "right" becomes synonymous with the interests of the most powerful actor in the political system.

What, if anything, can be done to reshape the relationship between power and morality in such a way that power serves truly altruistic ends? Because power, as typically defined, seems to imply that morality is based on the evolving interests of some rather than the enduring rights of all, a necessary first step would be to identify a set of eternal ethnical principles that are applicable everywhere and always. Mohandas Gandhi, who led the nonviolent struggle to achieve India's independence from Britain, criticized the tendency to treat morality as being a relative, subjective concept.[52] Much as Christianity, Judaism, and Islam teach that there are eternal moral principles that should be upheld, Gandhi believed that the substance of morality, as represented by values such as justice and equality, is universal and timeless.

If we accept the assertion that certain eternal moral ideals exist, the next question that must be addressed is how to pursue those ideals. It is important to note that Gandhi did not view morality as an alternative to power. He believed not only that morality and power could coexist, but in fact that they were (or at least should be) mutually reinforcing elements in life. According to this view, it is impossible to achieve moral ends (say, e.g., a nation's desire to be free from racist tyranny) using immoral ends (say, e.g., the resort to violence as a reaction against racism).

Contrary to Machiavelli's argument that power is best acquired and maintained through fear (*see* Chapter 2), Gandhi believed: "Power is of two kinds. One is obtained by the fear of punishment and the other by acts of love. Power based on love is a thousand times more effective and permanent then the one derived from fear of punishment."[53] Power, as expressed through love and nonviolence, is the only pathway to true morality, as represented by peace, justice, and understanding. One cannot be separated from the other.

Critics of Gandhi's moral formula might argue that while in the abstract a philosophy of nonviolence may be morally preferable, political actors who adhere to such a policy are placing themselves at a distinct disadvantage, and perhaps even in mortal danger. If Inge is right that politics, as actually practiced, is often about who dines on whom, blind obedience to a strict policy of morality is likely to lead, as Machiavelli predicted, to one's own destruction. According to this line of argument, the historical record seems heavily stacked in favor of the use of power in pursuit of one's narrow self-interests and against the successful application of morality in pursuit of some universal good. If this critique is accurate, the moral goals espoused and ethical techniques employed by leaders such as Mohandas Gandhi and Martin Luther King, Jr, while to be admired, are not to be copied, lest we bring about our own ruin at the hands of those who seek their own interests through the use of violent force.

Clearly, then, the debate regarding the legitimate roles of power and morality in politics persists. The central issue in this debate pivots on the nature of the relationship between power and morality as two compelling elements of political life. On the question of whether power and morality can coexist, where do you stand?

Notes

1 Thinkexist.com, "Power Politics Quotes," http://thinkexist.com/quotes/with/keyword/power_politics/ (accessed July 1, 2009).

2 National Defense University, "Leveraging Power and Politics," in *Strategic Leadership and Decision Making*, http://www.au.af.mil/au/awc/awcgate/ndu/strat-ldr-dm/pt4ch17.html (accessed July 28, 2009).

3 Andrew B. Schookler, *The Parable of the Tribes* (Berkeley: University of California Press, 1984), 21; 23.

4 As will be discussed in Chapter 4, in the contemporary study of politics we often focus on the state as the most important actor that wields power. However, it is important to note that many non-state actors attempt to exercise power in political life as well. For example, the 9/11 attacks on New York City and Washington, DC represented an effort by a non-state actor (the terrorist group *Al Qaeda*) to force the United States government to change certain policies that *Al Qaeda* opposed, including America's support for sanctions on Saddam Hussein's Iraq, the stationing of US forces in Saudi Arabia, and America's staunch alliance with Israel.

5 The Dirksen Congressional Center, "Congress Link: Major Features of the Civil Rights Act of 1964," http://www.congresslink.org/print_basics_histmats_civilrights64text.htm (accessed July 1, 2009).

6 Ibid.

7 CNN.com—Election 2004, "Vote by Race," http://www.cnn.com/ELECTION/2004/pages/results/states/US/P/00/epolls.0.html (accessed August 5, 2009); CNN.com Local Exit Polls—Election 2008, "Vote by Race," http://www.cnn.com/ELECTION/2008/results/polls/#USP00p1 (accessed August 5, 2009); Project Vote, "New Project Vote Analysis of U.S. Census Bureau Survey Finds that a More Diverse Electorate Voted in November 2008 than in 2004," http://www.projectvote.org/newsreleases/429.html (accessed August 5, 2009).

8 We will examine states in detail in Chapter 4. A state is defined as a political actor that exercises jurisdiction over a specific territory and the population living within that territory, and whose existence as a sovereign state is recognized by the international community.

9 Karen A. Mingst, *Essentials of International Relations*, 3rd ed. (New York: WW Norton & Company, 2004), 108–112.

10 Ibid., 108–110.

11 Andrew T. Parasiliti, "The Causes and Timing of Iraq's Wars: A Power Cycles Assessment," *International Political Science Review* 24 (2003): 157–158. www.jstor.org (accessed July 12, 2009).

12 Sunday Dare, "A Continent in Crisis: Africa and Globalization," in *Taking Sides: Clashing Views on Controversial African Issues*, ed. William G. Moseley (Guilford, CT: McGraw-Hill/Dushkin, 2004), 139.

13 Mingst, *Essentials of International Relations*, 110.

14 United Nations Development Programme, "Statistics of the Human Development Report," *Human Development Reports*, http://hdr.undp.org/en/statistics (accessed July 13, 2009).

15 Lucy Hornby Reuters, "Analysis—North Korea's Weak Trade, Currency, Hint at More Arms Sales," June 18, 2009. http://www.forbes.com.

16 Mingst, *Essentials of International Relations*, 110–112.

17 Andrew W. Barrett and Matthew Esbaugh-Soha, "Presidential Success and the Substance of Legislation," *Political Research Quarterly* 60 (2007): 108. www.jstor.org (accessed July 12, 2009).

18 Bruce Catton and James M. McPherson, *The American Heritage New History of the Civil War* (New York: Viking, 1996), 123–126.

19 Joshua S. Goldstein, *International Relations*, 5th ed. (New York: Pearson Longman, 2004), 75.

20 Congressional Quarterly, *The Middle East*, 9th ed. (Washington, DC: CQ Press, 2000), 133.

21 Ibid., 139–142.

22 Ibid., 229.

23 Ibid., 324.

24 Ian J. Bickerton and Carla L. Klausner, *A Concise History of the Arab-Israeli Conflict*, 5th ed. (Upper Saddle River, NJ: Prentice Hall, 2007), 239.

25 Tim Wiener, "Robert McNamara, Architect of Futile War, Dies," *The New York Times*, July 7, 2009, A1; B10–B11.

26 Congressional Quarterly, *The Middle East*, 105–106.

27 Bickerton and Klausner, *Arab-Israeli Conflict*, 171–172.

28 Adrian U-Jin Ang and Dursun Peksen, "When Do Economic Sanctions Work? Asymmetric Perceptions, Issue Salience, and Outcomes," *Political Research Quarterly* 60 (2007): 135. http://www.jstor.org (accessed July 12, 2009).

29 James M. Lindsay, "Trade Sanctions as Policy Instruments: a Re-Examination," *International Studies Quarterly* 30 (1986): 160–162. http://www.jstor.org (accessed July 13, 2009).

30 Richard Bernstein, "How Not to Deal with North Korea," *The New York Review of Books*, March 1, 2007. http://www.nybooks.com/articles/19923 (accessed July 13, 2009).

31 Goldstein, *International Relations*, 39–41.

32 Parasiliti, "The Causes and Timing of Iraq's War," 160.

33 Goldstein, *International Relations*, 75.

34 Gregory Cashman and Leonard C. Robinson, *An Introduction to the Causes of War: Patterns of Interstate Conflict from World War I to Iraq* (Lanham, MD: Rowman & Littlefield, 2007), 348–349.

35 Peter D. Feaver, "Anatomy of the Surge," *Commentary* 125 (2008): 24–28. http://web.ebscohost.com (accessed July 14, 2009).

36 John Galvani, Peter Johnson, Chris Paine, Joe Stork, Rene Theberge, and Fred Vallongo, "Saudi Arabia: Bullish on America," *Middle East Research and Information Project*, 26 (1974): 17. http://www.jstor.org (accessed July 14, 2009).

37 *The Times (London)*, April 18, 1939. Quoted in E.H. Carr, *The Twenty Years' Crisis*, rev. Michael Cox (New York: Palgrave, 2001), 36.

38 Ibid.

39 John Mearsheimer, *The Tragedy of Great Power Politics* (New York: WW Norton & Company, 2001), 85.

40 Lt. Col. Gregory G. Hildenbrandt, "Military Expenditure, Force Potential, and Relative Military Power," August 1980, http://www.rand.org/pubs/reports/2008/R2624.pdf (July 11, 2009).

41 Cold War International History Project, "Report on the Talks of Gyula Horn, Representative of the HSWP CC Foreign Department in The United States and Canada," http://www.wilsoncenter.org/index.cfm?topic_id=1409&fuseaction=va2.document&identifier=5034D58E-96B6-175C-9050ECCD1351D7F6&sort=Collection&item=Soviet%20Invasion%20of%20Afghanistan (accessed July 11, 2009).

42 National Security Archive, *Did NATO Win the Cold War?* "Speech of General Secretary Comrade YU V Andropov of the Central Committee of the Communist Party of the Soviet Union," http://www.gwu.edu/~nsarchiv/NSAEBB/NSAEBB14/doc19.htm (accessed July 11, 2009).

43 Eventually, the internal opposition to Communist Party rule in Poland would spread to the surrounding states of Eastern Europe, leading to a general collapse of socialism across the region.

44 E.H. Carr, *The Twenty Years' Crisis* (New York: Palgrave, 2001), 97.

45 Ibid., 12–19.

46 Ibid., 71.

47 Thucydides, "The Peloponnesian War and the Melian Debate," in *Classic Readings and Contemporary Debates in International Relations*, 3rd ed., eds. Phil Williams, Donald M. Goldstein, and Jay M. Shafritz (Belmont, CA: Thomson/Wadsworth, 2006), 43.

48 Leon P. Baradat, *Political Ideologies: Their Origins and Impact*, 7th ed. (Upper Saddle River, NJ: Prentice Hall, 2000), 250.

49 W.R. Inge, "The Philosophy of the Wolf State," *Philosophy* 18 (1943): 12–13.

50 Neta C. Crawford, "Principia Leviathan," *Naval War College Review* LVII (2004): 67.

51 Ibid., 68.

52 Rudolf C. Heredia, "Interpreting Gandhi's *Hind Swaraj*," *Economic and Political Weekly*, June 12, 1999. http://www.swaraj.org/interpreting.htm.

53 S.F. Heart, "Quotes from Mohandas K. Gandhi," http://www.sfheart.com/Gandhi.html.

Organizing Political Life: States and Nations

INTRODUCTION

For thousands of years, humans have organized themselves into communities. The advantages of living in a social group are substantial. As compared to a solitary existence, community life provides protection from threats, increases the opportunity to access resources and to generate wealth, and creates the opportunity for social bonds and an enriching cultural life.

History has been characterized by social groupings of varying sizes and levels of organizational sophistication—ranging from small hunter-gatherer groups to vast empires. In the modern world, the predominant form of political organization is the state. Emerging first in Europe following the 1648 Treaty of Westphalia (which ended the Thirty Years' War), and then exported around the world through the process of colonialism, the modern state has become the main focus of political life.[1] In the 21st century, the international system encompasses over 190 states.

In this chapter we examine several crucial conceptual and empirical issues surrounding the state. We will define the concept of the state, discuss the different ways in which states organize and distribute power within their systems, consider the various methods by which states seek to legitimize their rule, and analyze the ongoing debate over the meaning and application of state sovereignty in a world characterized by an increasing number of failing and failed states.

The second part of this chapter is devoted to a discussion of the nation. Specifically, we will define what we mean by the term "nation," distinguish the concepts of nation and state from each other, and then trace the relationship between nations and states in the actual political world. Finally, we will consider the question of whether or not America is a nation.

DEFINING THE STATE

A state is defined as a political unit that features a government that exercises jurisdiction over a specific territory and the population living within that territory, and whose existence as a sovereign state is recognized by the international community. It is important to note that, in the vernacular of political science, the term "state" is often used interchangeably with what is commonly labeled a "country." In this context, when we speak of a "state" we are referencing a country (e.g., Germany, China, Iran, etc.). Unless otherwise noted, in this book the term "state" is synonymous with "country" (and vice versa).

To summarize, a state is comprised of the following essential characteristics:

1. Jurisdiction over territory within explicit, recognized boundaries.
2. Jurisdiction over the population living within that territory.

3. Institutions of government designed to maintain domestic order and to provide security from external threats.
4. Recognition by the international community of the state's sovereign existence.

Two important observations are in order at the outset of our discussion of states. First, as shall be illustrated in more detail later in this chapter, the four pillars of statehood cited above reflect the assumptions of "negative sovereignty." For over a century, these elements of statehood, as defined under negative sovereignty, have been treated as given in the international system. In other words, once a territory achieves the status of a state, it is recognized as having automatic legal jurisdiction over its territory and population. To be sure, states do vary in their abilities to govern effectively, but at least in theory this is irrelevant because all states in the system are expected to respect the domestic sovereignty of every other state.

Second, it is crucial to note that, although states are the most influential actors in contemporary politics, other types of actors also play an important role.[2] These other actors help to shape and, at times, even constrain the power of states. They include:

1. Intergovernmental Organizations (IGOs), which are international institutions whose members are states. The UN is an example of an IGO. In some cases, such as the European Union (EU), state members actually choose to surrender a portion of their sovereignty to the intergovernmental organization. For the most part, however, IGOs supplement rather than supplant the power of states.
2. Nongovernmental Organizations (NGOs), a term that refers to political organizations whose memberships are comprised of private individuals from multiple countries. Amnesty International is an example of a NGO.
3. Transnational Corporations (TNCs), which are private firms with business operations in multiple countries. Wal-Mart, which operates in dozens of countries, is a contemporary example of a TNC.
4. Individuals can also shape political life in profound ways, for better (e.g., Mohandas Gandhi and Martin Luther King) or for worse (e.g., Adolf Hitler and Osama bin Laden).
5. Quasi-states, which are political units that possess some, but not all, of the basic characteristics of a state. For example, the Palestinian Authority exercises some jurisdiction over a portion of the population on the West Bank as well as all of the Gaza Strip, as spelled out in a series of agreements that the Palestinians have forged with Israel since the early 1990s. However, the Palestinian Authority does not possess all of the qualities of a state. Most importantly, although many actors—including a series of US presidents—have expressed public support for the concept of a future Palestinian state, the global community does not yet recognize "Palestine" as a sovereign state. What the Palestinians have, then, is control over an entity whose characteristics fall short of those required for statehood.

Clearly, while states continue to dominate political life, the roster of important political actors extends well beyond states. The growing importance of non-state actors can be traced at least partly to the process of *globalization*. Globalization involves the lowering of the barriers to the flow of goods, services, capital, people, technology, information, norms, and ideas across state boundaries. Non-state actors take advantage of the authority gaps that are created as state controls over these types of activities are reduced. Whether or not the global economic crisis that erupted in 2007—a crisis that some observers have blamed on the lack of state controls over financial and other types of economic activities—leads to a reassertion of state authority and a diminished role for non-state actors, remains to be seen.

APPROACHES TO THE ORGANIZATION AND DIVISION OF STATE POWER

Despite the fact that all states feature the characteristics discussed above, they also vary in important ways. One way in which states differ relates to the organization and division of power within their political systems. Specifically, the constitutions of some states vest a great deal of power in the national government. In other states, power is divided between the national government and sub-national units. In still other instances throughout history, power has been highly fragmented and decentralized, favoring the sub-national territorial units within a state's boundaries.

A unitary state is one in which the national government is granted the preponderance of power under the state's constitution. Although sub-national units (e.g., provinces, regions, municipal governments, etc.) usually exist in these states, the majority of the power rests with the central government in the national capital city. The national government "ultimately controls all layers of government below it, and can reform, reorganize, or abolish units of local or regional government without any special constitutional constraint."[3] In short, in a unitary system sub-national governmental units are expected to defer on most issues to the laws, policies, and commands of the national government. A number of states in Europe fit the unitary state model; in addition, Japan is considered to be the largest unitary state in the world.

By comparison, in a federal system power is divided both horizontally (i.e., among branches of government at the national level) and vertically (i.e., between the national government and sub-national governing units). The most important difference between unitary states and federal states is that, unlike unitary systems, "Federal systems contain mid-level territorial units of government (states, provinces, regions) which have a guaranteed status in the constitution that gives them a degree of independence and autonomy from the central government." Several of the largest states in the international system feature federal systems, including the United States, India, Brazil, and Mexico.[4]

Within the federal model, variations exist. One point of difference centers on the process by which federalism emerges within a state. In some cases, such as what occurred in America when the United States transitioned from a confederation (see below) to a federal state, federalism comes about as a result of the aggregation of formerly independent territories into a more centralized, yet still not unitary, system. On the other hand, in a state such as modern Belgium federalism is the product of the disaggregation of the system away from the unitary model, as power is increasingly delegated to sub-national units inside Belgium.[5]

A second important variation within the federal model has to do with the degree to which residual powers—powers that are not expressly delegated under the state's constitution to a specific level of government—reside with the national government. Some federal states reserve a substantial degree of authority for the national government; such is the case in Canada, where the national government in Ottawa enjoys a broad range of powers over Canada's sub-units (provinces), including the right to disallow any law that is passed by a provincial government.[6] We can refer to this arrangement as "centralized federalism." By comparison, the US Constitution seems designed to tilt residual powers away from the national government and toward the states. As expressed in the 10th Amendment: "The powers not delegated to the United States by the Constitution, nor prohibited by it to the States, are reserved to the States respectively, or to the people." This type of arrangement can be labeled "decentralized federalism."

Finally, some states, called confederations, feature a high degree of decentralization. In a confederation, substantial power is vested in the sub-national units that make up the state. The limited power that does rest at the level of the central government resides there by authority and agreement of the member units, who may nullify any national-level policy with which they disagree. In fact, members are free to exit a confederation arrangement at their own choosing. For these reasons, confederations are extremely unstable and prone to collapse. There are few real-world examples of confederations; famous examples of confederations in history include the American states under the Articles of Confederation, as well as the southern Confederate States of America during the US Civil War.[7]

THE CHALLENGE OF ACHIEVING STATE LEGITIMACY

Although technically all states wield the legal authority to make laws that are binding on their citizens, the actual ability of states to do so is shaped in profound ways by the degree of legitimacy they possess. For that reason, state leaders strive to achieve and maintain legitimacy. It is important to distinguish between authority and legitimacy. Whereas authority refers to the *legal* right to rule, both as designated by the constitution of a state and as recognized by other states in the international system, legitimacy refers to the acceptance on the part of citizens that the state, its government, and its political elites have the *moral* right to make decisions that are binding on the population of the state.

Legitimacy is vital to effective governance. Without it, the state may find that it is extremely difficult to enforce laws and carry out policies with consistent effectiveness. In the absence of legitimacy, the reaction of citizens to the effort of the state to govern may range from apathy to outright hostility, and the state may find that it must resort to brute coercion against citizens in order to achieve its goals and maintain order.

This leads us to ponder an important question: how do states obtain this precious political commodity, legitimacy? One of the most famous social science models of legitimacy was constructed by the German sociologist Max Weber. According to Weber, three possible sources of legitimacy exist: traditional legitimacy; charismatic legitimacy; and rational-legal legitimacy.[8]

Traditional legitimacy is based on custom. Where traditional legitimacy exists, it serves to preserve the political, economic, social, and cultural status quo. In the contemporary world, traditional legitimacy is exemplified in systems that feature dynastic monarchies, such as those that still operate in parts of the Middle East (e.g., Saudi Arabia, Kuwait, Jordan, etc.).

Charismatic legitimacy draws from the personal qualities of a leader. In addition, legitimacy based on charisma is linked very closely to context—that is, perceptions of charisma are shaped not only by a leader's personality, but also by the historical circumstances, cultural environment, and political, social, and economic conditions that exist within a particular society at a specific juncture in history. The circumstantial nature of charisma is underscored when we consider the fact that, despite their vast differences in temperament and vision, Hitler and Gandhi were both considered to be "charismatic" leaders within their respective societies.

The final form of legitimacy identified by Weber is rational-legal legitimacy. In a rational-legal system, legitimacy is delinked from both custom (as in traditional legitimacy, where the institutions, rules and laws and procedures of governance are steeped in the enduring customs of society) and individual personality traits (as in charismatic legitimacy, where a popular political leader is free to create, alter, and ignore governing institutions, rules, laws and procedures at his or her whim). By comparison, rational-legal legitimacy is built on a foundation of respect for core institutions, rules, norms, and procedures, such as the state's constitution, the rule of law, and the conduct of competitive elections. In addition, systems that rely on rational-legal legitimacy feature merit-based bureaucracies that utilize abstract standard operating procedures to guide policy decisions and implementation.

Which source of legitimacy is superior? Although each of these models can be useful in achieving legitimacy, on balance basing the state's rule on rational-legal legitimacy is probably superior to either traditional legitimacy or charismatic legitimacy. On the one hand, traditional legitimacy is subject to uncontrollable erosion by the forces of modernization and change. On the other hand, charismatic legitimacy is linked to personality traits that are peculiar to a particular leader and to the specific historical context within which they rule; thus, charismatic legitimacy persists only as long as the charismatic leader is in power.

By comparison, rational-legal legitimacy seems best suited to persist over an extended period of time, at least partially because the laws, rules, procedures, and principles that comprise rational-legal legitimacy can be adapted to reflect the evolving needs, interests, and ethical norms of society. In addition, rational-legal legitimacy facilitates controlled change within a state system—for example, the replacement of leaders through fair, free, open, and regularly scheduled elections. Thus, rational-legal legitimacy provides the basis for a state that is responsive to the needs of citizen and is capable of producing and managing change, while maintaining order and avoiding chaos.

STATE SOVEREIGNTY AND THE PROBLEM OF FAILED STATES

As we noted earlier during our discussion of the basic characteristics of states, all states are granted sovereignty. Moreover, only states enjoy the automatic status of sovereignty. By comparison to the current system, political authority in pre-modern Europe (i.e., in Europe prior to the emergence of the state-centered system following the Treaty of Westphalia in 1648) "was shared between a wide variety of secular and religious institutions—between emperors, kings, princes and nobility, bishops, abbots and papacy, guilds and cities, agrarian landlords, and 'bourgeois' merchants and artisans, to name but the most important ones."[9]

The emergence of the state marked a crucial turning point in the history of political development. State sovereignty "claimed the supremacy of the government of any state over the people, resources, and ultimately, over all other authorities within the territories it controlled."[10] Perhaps most importantly, linking sovereignty to the authority of the secular state over its specified territory and the population therein began the process in Europe of delegitimizing the role of religion as a source of political identity and military intervention. Over time, European states came to accept the notion that religion should no longer serve as a legitimate rationale for war on the continent.

In the contemporary world, sovereignty is typically understood to mean that states have the right to rule over their domestic territories and populations free from external intervention, a concept that has been labeled "negative sovereignty."[11] Under negative sovereignty, once a territory is recognized as a state by other states in the international community, its legal existence is guaranteed. "Non-intervention and sovereignty . . . are basically two sides of the same coin."[12]

Negative sovereignty is considered by many people to be a cornerstone of the modern system of states. If universally respected, negative sovereignty theoretically prevents wars between countries, since no state is ever supposed to infringe upon the territory or internal affairs of another state. Moreover, negative sovereignty creates a system of legal equality in which all states, regardless of their size and strength relative to other states, are supposed to enjoy the same right to exist.

Nevertheless, the exercise of negative sovereignty poses serious challenges. Most importantly, the assumption of the legal equality of all states means that the sovereignty of even the weakest states in the system is supposed to be fully respected. Bluntly put, negative sovereignty requires the preservation of states which, by any practical political measure, should probably not exist.[13]

Somalia is an example *par excellence* of a failed state—that is, a state that lacks the capacity to carry out basic government tasks, the most important of which is the provision of security to its citizens. Somalia has not had a functioning government since the early 1990s. Following the overthrow of President Mohammed Siad Barre in 1991, the country has been nearly destroyed by clan conflict, with rival warlords fighting one another in an effort to expand their power.[14] The collapse of the central government has also created the opportunity for pirates to use Somalia as base of operations. Nevertheless, Somalia maintains its seat as a "sovereign" state member of the United Nations.

Given the growing problem of weak states and failing states, some observers argue that it is time to move away from an exclusive reliance on negative sovereignty. A study co-authored in 2009 by *Foreign Policy* magazine and *The Fund for Peace* illustrates the breadth and depth of the failed state challenge.[15] According to the report, every state in sub-Saharan Africa is in critical condition in terms of state weakness, as are a number of states in Asia and the Middle East. Specifically, the five weakest states in the international system as of 2009 were: Somalia, Zimbabwe, Sudan, Chad, and Democratic Republic of the Congo. In an ominous sign, three states that are considered by experts to be vital in the battle against global terrorism were also considered to be critically weak—Iraq (the 6th weakest state), Afghanistan (the 7th weakest state), and Pakistan (the 10th weakest state)—while Yemen, where Al Qaeda and its affiliates have shown an emerging presence in recent years, is described as "dangerously weak," and ranked as the the 18th weakest state.

Critics charge that negative sovereignty consigns the citizens of a weak state to conditions of seemingly permanent insecurity. These critics propose an alternative to traditional notions of negative sovereignty. Dubbed "positive sovereignty," this alternative requires a state to possess "the wherewithal to provide political goods for its citizens."[16] According to this view, at a bare minimum it is fair to expect a state to maintain a basic level of security at home, and to protect its population and territory from threats abroad.[17] Under positive sovereignty, a failed state would not have its existence guaranteed. Instead, the sovereignty of the state is linked to the effective performance of its government institutions. If a state does not perform up to par on these basic measures, its sovereign right to exist could be called into question.

It is interesting to note that treating the survival of sovereign states as sacrosanct is a fairly recent phenomenon. In fact, throughout much of the history of the state system, attaining sovereign status did not necessarily guarantee the political survival of a supposedly sovereign entity. In the case of Europe, for example, the number of sovereign political units plummeted between 1500 and 1900. In 1500, approximately 500 or so autonomous political entities existed in Europe; by 1900, the number of sovereign states had declined to about twenty-five, before increasing again during the era of decolonization.[18] The explanation for the dramatic decrease in the number of independent territories is simple: an entity that lacked the capability to perform the basic functions of a state, including the provision of security for its citizens and territory, was fair game to be occupied and absorbed by a more capable state. Presumably, should positive sovereignty reemerge in the international system, we would return to an era in which the absorption of a failed state by another more capable state (or states) would become the norm.

Of course, critics of positive sovereignty have pushed back against the attempt to encroach upon traditional negative sovereignty. For example, there are those who charge that positive sovereignty is culturally biased because it is based on a Western definition of rights.[19] Unlike much of the rest of the world, Western cultural norms tend to privilege the rights of individuals over the interests of the community. This is important, because the Western definition of rights would provide, at least in theory, the rationale for intervening in another country's domestic system where human rights violations (as defined by Western standards) are occurring.

In addition, given the fact that power is distributed unequally between states, if external interference becomes the international legal norm it is far more likely to be exercised against small states than against large states. Thus, for example, despite the fact that much of the rest of the world considers the continued use of the death penalty in the United States to be immoral and a human rights violation, the likelihood that the international system will act in concert to intervene in the American domestic system is virtually nil. On the other hand, the United States and other powerful countries have the ability to use force when they choose to do so against another state's domestic system. Critics object that quite often such interventions are really driven by the self-interest of the intervening powers, cloaked in the defense of "universal" human rights principles.[20]

In summary, many lesser-developed states fear that any shift from negative sovereignty toward a system based on positive sovereignty will empower the stronger states in the system, while harming the interests of weaker states. At the same time, negative sovereignty still carries a great deal of support in many strong countries because the governments in those states continue to covet the principle that they should be able to conduct their political affairs free from external meddling. For the time being then, how to define state sovereignty, and the rights and responsibilities sovereignty entails, remains in dispute.

THE NATION

Earlier in this chapter we defined the state as a political unit that features a government that exercises jurisdiction over a specific territory and the population living within that territory, and whose existence as a sovereign state is recognized by the international community. At its core, the state is a legal and territorial entity. The existence of any state rests of its recognition as such by the international community of states; the state exists to exercise authority over the territory within its boundaries and the population living within those boundaries.

A state's existence is based on acceptance and recognition by other states in the international system. On the other hand, the nation springs forth from within the hearts and minds of its members. A nation's existence reflects a sense of common belonging among a group of individuals, a perception that binds them together into a distinct, cohesive community.

Historically, the most powerful characteristics of national identity have been traits such as language, religion, culture, race, and tribe. This "ethnic nationalism" creates a high degree of solidarity among members of the nation. It also fuels a tendency toward exclusion and even suspicion toward those who are not members of the nation. The bonds of ethnic nationalism are deeply held and strongly cohesive; they are anchored in shared experiences and a subjective sense of belonging, thereby making ethnic national identity strongly resistant to efforts at manipulation or elimination by outside actors.

Briefly consider the following cases from the 20th century, each of which exemplifies the impact of ethnic nationalism, both as a basis for exclusion, repression, and violence, and as a rallying point for resistance, survival, and national preservation. During the 1930s and 1940s, Adolf Hitler sought to "cleanse" Germany of Jews and other "inferior" nations of people. Hitler's campaign of genocide resulted in the slaughter of six million Jews at the hands of the Nazi regime during the Holocaust. Despite this horrific event, the Jewish people as a nation survived, and just 3 years after the end of World War Two the modern Jewish state of Israel was born.

Throughout much of the 20th century, the white apartheid regime in South Africa attempted to weaken black racial identity in that country through the implementation of a number of policies, including the denial of basic political rights to blacks, a policy of forced social segregation, and an effort to convince black South Africans that tribe rather than race (South Africa's black population is comprised of several main tribes) should be their major focus of identity. This policy represented a classic effort by the white minority to maintain their control through a policy of divide and rule. However the apartheid regime's efforts at manipulation of national identity among black South Africans failed, and eventually the country's white rulers were forced to negotiate themselves out of power in the early 1990s.

In the Middle East, the Kurds—whose population spills into the territories of four separate but adjoining states (Iraq, Turkey, Iran, and Syria)—share deeply rooted bonds of culture, history, language, and ethnicity. The Kurdish people have suffered brutal persecution throughout much of their history. Recent examples of the persecution suffered by the Kurds include Saddam Hussein's use of chemical weapons against portions of the Kurdish population in Iraq during the 1980s, and the dogged attempt by Turkey to undermine Kurdish identity, including the Turkish government's absurd insistence in the past that the proper label for its Kurdish population is "Mountain Turks." The persistence of the Kurdish people in the face of such efforts is a testament to the power of Kurdish ethnic nationalism.

Each of the three cases cited above highlight the perils and positives of ethnic nationalism. On the one hand, ethnic nationalism drove the Nazi regime in Germany, the Apartheid government in South Africa, and the modern Turkish state to enact policies that were designed to either destroy another nation of people (in the case of Nazi Germany), or to subjugate them (in the cases of South Africa and Turkey). On the other hand, deeply held, shared bonds of ethnic identity helped the communities that were targeted to persevere in the face of hatred and repression.

A second variant of nationalism is civic nationalism. This form of nationalism is based on a common set of rights, laws, and procedures that are inclusive of all the citizens of a territory, regardless of ethnicity, religion, or heritage. Under civic nationalism, ethnic factors recede as a source of common identity. Instead, the state plays a vital role in promoting laws, policies, procedures, and images that over time encourage citizens to come together in a shared national identity where it previously did not fully exist.

The civic form of nationalism is particularly relevant in multinational democratic states such as the United States, Canada, and Britain. States such as these have used the rule of law, respect for equal rights, and economic growth to construct a common national identity that otherwise would probably not exist in their multi-ethnic societies. As compared to ethnic nationalism, civic nationalism is seen as inclusive. It bridges the gaps and tensions that might otherwise divide peoples of different ethnic, racial, and religious backgrounds within a state's boundaries, and facilitates the construction of a common community, centered on universally accepted rights, values, beliefs, and institutions.

Are the binding effects of civic nationalism irreversible? The phenomenon of *globalization*—the lowering of barriers against the flow of peoples, wealth, and ideas across borders in the contemporary international system—has begun to create questions about standing civic national identities, even in long-established, developed democracies. This is particularly clear when it comes to the issue of immigration flows from lesser-developed regions to the developed states. The influx of large numbers of immigrants, many of whom differ religiously, culturally, and linguistically from the majority population in the countries to which they have immigrated can be a source of tension within those states.

Let us consider an example from Switzerland which illustrates this emerging phenomenon. In 2009, the Swiss people voted to ban the building of minarets in the country. In a shocking outcome in what is traditionally seen as one of Europe's most tolerant societies, a referendum in Switzerland in November 2009 on whether to outlaw the construction of minarets was approved by 57.5% of the voters.[21] At the time of the vote, there were a grand total of four minarets across the entire country, with two more being planned. Furthermore, relatively few Muslim immigrants to Switzerland adhere to traditional styles of dress and conservative Islamic cultural habits.[22] The perception, however, that the minarets were symbols of a cultural threat was enough to produce a majority vote in favor of the referendum.

The example of Switzerland shows that questions of national identity—of what it means to be Swiss—linger even in one of the most stable, modern, and economically advanced states in the world. Such questions are not limited in the developed world to Switzerland. As we shall discover at the end of this chapter when we consider the question of whether or not America is a nation, the tension between seemingly entrenched values of civic nationalism and a possible resurgence of ethnic nationalism poses a potential challenge to national identity in the United States.

THE TANGLED RELATIONSHIP BETWEEN THE NATION AND STATE

We have seen that states are the dominant political units in the contemporary political system. We have also discussed the growing concern over the phenomenon of weak and failing states. Such states are a major source of instability and violence, both within their own domestic realms, as well as across the international system.

One of the most important variables that fuels state instability and weakness is the "fit" (or the lack thereof) between nations and states. In theory, the ideal relationship between the nation and state is captured in the concept of the *nation-state*. The nation-state may be defined most simply as a state whose population is comprised of a single nation of people.

The concept of the nation-state first emerged in Europe several hundred years ago. Interestingly, most scholars who have examined Europe's experience with nation-states have concluded that, contrary to popular perception, state-building in Europe—the construction of large, organized, powerful governmental units with clearly defined borders—actually preceded the emergence of national identity within those states.[23] Once established, states used a variety of tools, ranging from violent coercion directed against their populations to manipulation of symbols to programs of education and socialization in promoting the ideal that the people living within the borders of a particular state constituted a single nation. Against this historical backdrop, the civic form of nationalism was a particularly prevalent catalyst for forging national identities in the developed world.

Gradually, beginning in England and Western Europe, the concept of the nation-state then spread across Europe. During the era of colonialism, the state as the dominant form of territorial and political organization, and the concept of the nation-state as the ideal form of relationship between the population within the territory and the state, were exported around the globe. However, in the lesser-developed world, those territories that were colonized often found that their boundaries were redrawn by the colonial powers with little thought given to historical patterns of relations between communities of people.[24] The seeds of internal instability were thereby sown by the colonial powers.

The artificial borders and haphazard way in which different groups of people were thrown together within the boundaries of states created major stumbling blocks to the goal of forging real nation-states in the post-colonial, lesser-developed countries. One of these was the challenge of *multi-nationalism*, which we can define simply as a situation in which the population of a state is comprised of multiple nations of people. Under such conditions, members of ethno-national communities within a state's boundaries identify more with their own particular ethnic group than they do with the broader "nation." They self-define themselves as members of their specific ethnic group first, while weakly identifying themselves as citizens of their state.

For example, the country of Iraq features three major national communities—Sunnis, Shiites, and Kurds—as well as a polyglot of smaller religious and ethnic groups, and deep historical divisions along tribal and clan lines. Because the Iraqi state has traditionally been used by one of those communities (the Sunnis) as a means to ensure their dominance at the expense of all other groups inside of the country, the members of those other groups never fully identified with the central Iraqi state. In the face of violence, oppression, and intimidation from Saddam Hussein's Sunni-dominated regime, the other communities in Iraq looked inward—within their own groups—or outward—to external patrons such as the United States and Iran—to ensure their security. Whether or not post-Saddam Iraq can permanently fracture the hold of multi-nationalism on Iraqi society remains an open question.

Multi-nationalism refers to a state whose population is comprised of multiple national communities. What happens, however, when a single nation of people is divided among multiple states? *Irredentism* refers to a situation in which a nation of people is divided among multiple states, and the desire exists to unite those people within a single state's boundaries. Specifically, the term is used to describe the "attempts by an existing state to annex territories of other states that their co-nationals inhabit"[25]

Of course, as we previously noted, many European states faced a similar challenge early in their histories. However, the conditions and context under which lesser-developed states undertook this task were fundamentally different, and much more challenging, than was the case for most European countries. To begin with, in Europe the development of the state and nation—and of the ideal form of nation-state—was a sequential process. Typically, states were well entrenched and had established their governing authority before taking on the arduous task of bringing the populations under their authority together as a single nation.

By comparison, the challenge in the lesser-developed, newly decolonized states was much more daunting. These states were expected to undertake the dual tasks of state-building and nation-building simultaneously, rather than sequentially, and in the shortest time possible. Whereas "The European national state as we know it today had a long and painful gestation period," lesser-developed states have faced the expectations from both the international community and the citizens of the lesser-developed states that they will create a stable state structure and cobble together a shared national identity in the shortest time possible.[26] In addition, human rights norms within the modern international system do not permit lesser-developed states to employ the type of brute force and coercion that marked the experience of European states in forging a common identity within their boundaries.[27] Taken together, these factors have made it extremely difficult for many lesser-developed states to evolve in any meaningful way toward the ideal nation-state. Instead, dozens of states in the international system suffer from internal, national divisions that weaken their domestic systems and expose them to heightened external threats.

PUZZLE: IS AMERICA A NATION?

Most Americans have long assumed that they constitute a nation. For example, one poll released in June 2008 showed that 84% of respondents believed that there is a national identity in America.[28] Through consciously promoting a common creed, principles, and symbolic expressions of allegiance, the United States has overcome racial, religious, ethnic, and geographic divisions, forging an inclusive conceptualization of national identity in America.[29]

For many Americans, the belief that they are part of a nation is perhaps most simply expressed in the words of the Pledge of Allegiance: "one nation, under God, indivisible, with liberty and justice for all." And yet, even this basic expression of American nationalism is fraught with potential traps and contradictions. Due to the multinational nature of American society, are those who do not profess to adhere to Judeo-Christian beliefs part of the "one nation"? If access to full liberty and justice are denied to some in America on the basis of their race, religion, or ethnicity, can America truly be called a "nation"? In short, is 21st century America a nation?

It is important to place the process of American national development in its proper historical context. Perhaps the single most critical event that shaped the character of the American nation was the Civil War (1861–1865). In theory at least, the defeat of the Confederacy, whose very logic of existence rested largely on the claim that the American South represented a separate nation with its own unique culture, economic institutions (i.e., slavery), and value system, marked a major turning point in the effort to create "one America." The belief that the Civil War had cleared the major roadblocks to forging a single national identity was expressed eloquently by Private Sam R. Watkins of the Confederate Army of Tennessee. After the war, Watkins opined: "America has no north, no south, no east, no west; the sun rises over the hills and sets over the mountains, the compass just points up and down, and we can laugh now at the absurd notion of there being a north and a south."[30] In the longer view, the preservation of the Union, the completion of the Trans-Continental Railway just 4 years after the end of the Civil War in 1869, and the emergence of America as an economic, diplomatic, and military power on the international stage all seemed to signal the full and effective integration of America as a nation.

In reality, however, deep fissures remained in the national fabric of the "American nation" following the Civil War. The blight of racism was a lasting legacy of the country's painful experience during the post-Civil War era. Black Americans faced institutionalized discrimination as exemplified by the infamous Jim Crow laws in the South, and the full and equal right to vote was denied to blacks until the passage of the Civil Rights Act of 1964. African-Americans were subjected to harassment, intimidation, and violence at the hands of the Ku Klux Klan (KKK). Appallingly, nearly 4,000 Black Americans were killed by lynch-mobs between 1889 and 1946.[31]

Clearly, tremendous progress on the issue of race relations has occurred in America, as exemplified most dramatically by the election of the country's first African-American president, Barack Obama, in 2008. Many analysts following Obama's election predicted a sea change in race relations in the US; it became fashionable to predict and discuss the implications of "The End of White America." As one pundit put it: "The Election of Barack Obama is just the most startling manifestation of a larger trend: the gradual erosion of 'whiteness' as the touchstone of what it means to be American."[32]

In the aforementioned survey in which 84% of respondents believed that America is a nation, the majority of those who expressed that belief pointed to elements of civil and political life—principally freedom, patriotism, and democracy—as being the most important factors that forge a shared sense of identity in America.[33] These findings illustrate that the effort to build national identity in contemporary America has been grounded in a foundation of civic nationalism. Race and ethnicity, it would seem, are rapidly losing ground as central elements of what is means to be an American, as shared values, rights, and experiences increasingly bind the nation together.

Interestingly, in contrast to these assumptions regarding the solidarity of the American nation, a growing number of voices are expressing concern over the possible deterioration of American national identity, or even whether America has ever truly been a nation. Writing in the 1970s, American political scientist Walker Connor bluntly stated: "Whatever the American people are . . . they are not a nation in the pristine sense of the word.[34] More recently, two events in particular—the huge influx of illegal immigrants (primarily from Mexico), and the 9/11 terrorist attacks, have reinvigorated the debate over national identity in America.

In 2008, 11.6 million illegal immigrants resided in the United States. In 2009, the number dropped to 10.8 million, due mainly to a deep economic recession that shrunk the number of job opportunities in America. Of that 10.8 million in 2009, 6.65 million were from Mexico.[35] Some opinion surveys show that the majority of Americans are generally speaking, not outright hostile to illegal immigrants (e.g., a 2006 poll in *Time* magazine showed broad majority support for a Guest Worker's Program that would permit illegal immigrants to stay in the US for a fixed period of time, and for creating a path to citizenship for illegal immigrants). At the same time, many if not most Americans, do favor tougher enforcement policies at the American-Mexican border (62% in the *Time* poll said that the US government should take "whatever steps are necessary" to combat the flow of illegal immigrants across the border from Mexico).[36] It is interesting to note that some polling data suggests a substantial gap between elites (e.g., members of the legislative and executive branches of the federal government, business executive, union leaders, journalists, academics, and religious leaders) on the one hand, and the broader public on the other hand, when it comes to the relative weight of the threat posed by illegal immigration. By a wide margin, the masses see illegal immigration as a much greater threat than do elites.[37]

Perhaps no scholar has been so tightly linked to the debate over the impact of illegal immigration on America than Samuel Huntington. In his article "The Hispanic Challenge," Huntington argues that "The persistent inflow of Hispanic immigrants threatens to divide the United States into two peoples, two cultures, and two languages."[38] In Huntington's view, while it is true that creed—a broadly inclusive set of core values and principles—is the dominant element in American national identity, the foundational content of the creed is reflective "of the distinct Anglo-Protestant culture of the founding settlers." In other words, Huntington believes that American's "civic nationalism" is actually rooted in a very specific cultural and religious heritage. According to Huntington, key elements of that foundation include the English language, Christianity (and in particular Protestantism), and respect for the rule of law.[39]

Huntington asserts that the influx of illegal immigrants from Mexico presents a serious challenge to American national identity. He worries that, given their large numbers and tendency to cluster together in certain geographic regions once they arrive in the United States, Mexican immigrants will feel little pressure to assimilate into mainstream American culture. In the long run, Huntington frets both that large sections of the country will become culturally and linguistically Hispanic and that more broadly America as a whole will become bicultural and bilingual. He views these developments as being negative because they would undermine what he believes to be the essential, core Anglo-Saxon Protestant cultural roots of the American nation.[40]

Clearly, in the United States, there has been growing concern expressed about the impact of immigration, much of it illegal, from Mexico into the United States. Some have even gone so far as to argue that English should be declared as the official language of the United States. In 2010, the state of Arizona passed one of the strictest immigration laws ever adopted in America. The law requires that immigrants carry papers with them at all times proving their legal status, and grants police officers broad powers to detain individuals whom they suspect of being illegal immigrants.[41] These laws reflect a concern regarding the supposedly negative economic and social impact of illegal immigration, and an uneasy sense among a percentage of the American population that the phenomenon of illegal immigration from Mexico may pose a threat to American national identity, as defined by the likes of Huntington.

On the other hand, there are persuasive reasons to question Huntington's assertions regarding the so-called "Hispanic Challenge." It should be noted that Huntington relies heavily on abstract theoretical propositions as well as anecdotes related to single, isolated events to support his theory (e.g., the case of Latino fans rooting for Mexico at a soccer match in the US is used by Huntington as evidence to support his argument that Hispanics as a group are not assimilating properly into the American nation). Generally speaking, Huntington offers rather scanty systematic, empirical evidence in support of his thesis.

By comparison, Jack Citrin, Amy Lerman, Michael Merakami, and Kathryn Pearson examined a wealth of data regarding contemporary Mexican immigration into the United States.[42] Their statistical analysis showed that on a wide variety of measures—including acquisition of English, work ethic, religious commitment, and patriotism—Hispanics in America are largely assimilating by the 3rd generation. In other words, they are basically right on pace to assimilate at the same speed as previous immigrant groups from non-English-speaking countries who entered the United States in large numbers.

Furthermore, it is important to recognize that this is far from the first time in the history of the United States that Americans have reacted negatively to large-scale immigration from a particular region of the world. In the mid-19th century Irish immigrants, and to some degree immigrants from Germany, were the targets of discrimination and violence. In fact, one national political party that came to prominence during this period— The Know-Nothings—based its platform and ideology on a deeply held suspicion of, and antagonism toward, immigrants.

Several decades later the focus of concern shifted to immigrants from Southern and Eastern Europe, including Italy. As had been the case during the mid-19th century, the charge was leveled, and widely accepted by large numbers of Americans, that the new immigrants represented a threat to the fabric of American society and the American nation, not to mention an economic threat by taking jobs away from citizens who were already in the country. Furthermore, as was the case with the immigrant tide in the mid-19th century (and as is true currently of immigrants from Mexico), the immigrants from Southern and Eastern Europe were almost exclusively Catholic, a fact that raised the specter of a threat to Anglo-Saxon, Protestant dominance in America. For a period of time stretching into the 20th century, Catholics in America were the target of suspicion across a swath of the Protestant population, and even harassment and violence by extremist groups such as the KKK. Nevertheless, in each instance concerns regarding those immigrant populations eventually evaporated. It is entirely possible that the same process of assimilation and acceptance will occur with the Mexican immigrants of the late 20th and early 21st centuries.

Clearly, the contemporary debate in America over the pros and cons of immigration has deep historical roots. Specifically, the issue of illegal immigration from Mexico and parts of Central America and its possible impact on American national identity has unfolded and evolved over a number of years. By comparison, the 9/11 terrorist attacks were shocking, unanticipated, and unprecedented. In a single day, terrorists from the Islamist militant group Al Qaeda used jet planes as missiles against targets that represented the economic (World Trade Centers) and military (Pentagon) institutions of America. A third plane, apparently aimed at Washington, DC fell well short of its target, crashing in a field in Pennsylvania after passengers on the flight launched a counter-assault on the terrorists who had seized control of the cockpit.

An event such as 9/11 typically has the effect of strengthening the sense of patriotism in the target state. It is true that a wave of national pride swept across America in the weeks and months after the terrorist attacks of

Editorial cartoon from The Mascot newspaper, New Orleans, September 7, 1888.

September 2001. In one survey taken after 9/11, municipal officials in cities across America cited "increased patriotism" and "a greater sense of community" as being the two most important developments in their cities in reaction to the 9/11 attacks. Businesses in a number of communities reported that they quickly sold out their supply of American flags in the immediate aftermath of the attacks.[43] It would seem that the 9/11 attacks brought the American people together in the face of an external foe.

On the issue of national identity, is there any possible downside to the reaction of the government and public to the 9/11 attacks? Two come to mind. First, the perception of a persistent hostile threat from abroad with the capability to strike at the US on American soil raises once more the issue of the appropriate balance between liberty and security (see the puzzle question at the end of Chapter 2 in the text). Insofar as the US government enacted policies through laws such as the Patriot Act that seem to privilege security over personal liberty, central principles of the creed that stands at the core of American national identity may have been sacrificed. As a number of critics of the Patriot Act and similar laws that were passed after 9/11 pointed out, is it not possible that by curtailing certain freedoms in the name of security we are sacrificing precisely those principles, beliefs, and rights that define us as a free "nation"?

A second concern regarding the impact of events such as 9/11 on America's self-definition of itself as a nation centers on whether such incidences may cause many Americans to gravitate toward a more ethnically-based, exclusionary definition of nationalism. Writing in the midst of World War I, American social critic and essayist Randolph Bourne bemoaned growing levels of criticism and threats that were being aimed at German-Americans, including demands that German and all other non-English immigrants assimilate fully and without question into the dominant Anglo-Saxon national culture in America. Bourne described this process as "the thinly disguised panic which calls itself 'patriotism.'"[44]

One of the darkest blots on America's historical ledger was the internment of Japanese-Americans following the Japanese attack on Pearl Harbor on December 7, 1941. Executive Order 9066, issued by President Franklin Roosevelt in February 1942, "affected 117,000 Japanese-Americans, two-thirds of whom were native born citizens of the United States." Although one of the standard official US government explanations for the internment policy was that it was being done to protect Japanese-Americans against threats by their fellow US citizens, as one interned prisoner noted afterward "If we were put there for our protection, why were the guns at the guard towers pointed inward, instead of outward?"[45]

To what extent has a similar pattern of exclusionary nationalism manifested itself following the 9/11 attacks? Research conducted following 9/11 shows that the average citizen's conceptualization of nationalism, including his or her tolerance for internal diversity within the national community, can be shaped by whether national identity is defined according to a common "essence" (i.e., characteristics such as shared ethnic, religious, and/or cultural background), or conversely is seen as a rational, cooperative response by a community in response to a set of commonly-faced challenges. If nationalism is defined as "essence," it will promote "intolerance of difference, either internal or external."[46] If it is defined as a rational response that promotes

From http://www.flickr.com/people/fredmikerudy by Fred M. Miller. Copyright © by Fred M. Miller. Reprinted by permission.

cooperation in addressing a problem, nationalism promotes internal cooperation across religious, ethnic, racial, and cultural barriers—all who are willing to join in the community's effort to address the problems its faces will be welcomed as members of the group.

The debate over ethnic and religious profiling of air passengers in the US seems to hint at a possible slide toward ethnic, or "essence" nationalism. Because that form of nationalism automatically excludes members of ethnic and religious groups in the US who do not fit the mainstream profile of what it means to be "American," to the extent that ethnic nationalism has gained traction in the US after 9/11 it may call into question the notion that America is a "nation," as that label has come to be defined previously in America. If nationalism in American is increasingly understood by the majority to mean that certain minority groups must be excluded from the American national community, is America really a nation anymore?

On the question of whether or not America is a nation, where do you stand?

Notes

1 Robert Axtmann, "The State of the State: The Model of the Modern State and Its Contemporary Transformation," *International Political Science Review* 25 (2004): 262. http://www.jstor.org (accessed June 5, 2009).

2 Ellen Grigsby, *Analyzing Politics: An Introduction to Political Science*, 4th ed. (Belmont, CA: Wadsworth, 2009), 59–62.

3 Ken Newton and Jan W. Van Deth, *Foundations of Comparative Politics* (Cambridge: Cambridge University Press, 2005), 51–52, 82.

4 Ibid., 76, 80.

5 Wilfried Swenden, Marleen Brans, and Lieven de Winter, "The Politics of Belgium: Institutions and Policy under Bipolar and Centrifugal Federalism," *West European Politics* 29 (2006): 864. http:/web.ebscochost.com (accessed July 15, 2009).

6 The Canadian Encyclopedia, "Federalism," http://www.thecanadianencyclopedia.com/index.cfm?PgNm=TCE& Params=A1SEC820358 (accessed August 18, 2009).

7 Jan-Erik Lane, *Constitutions and Political Theory* (Manchester: Manchester University Press, 1996), 105.

8 Max Weber, *Essays in Economic Sociology*, trans. Richard Swedberg (Princeton, NJ: Princeton University Press, 1999).

9 Axtmann, "The State of the State", 260.

10 Ibid.

11 Robert H. Jackson, *Quasi-States: Sovereignty, International Relations and the Third World* (Cambridge: Cambridge University Press, 1993), 27.

12 Ibid.

13 Marina Ottoway and Stefan Mair, "States at Risk and Failed States: Putting Security First," *Policy Outlook*, September 2004, 7. http://ciaonet.org (accessed August 15, 2009).

14 David Blair, "Somalia: Analysis of a Failed State," *Telegraph*, October 18, 2008, http://www.telegraph.co.uk/news/worldnews/africaandindianocean/somalia/3479010/Somalia-Analysis-of-a-failed-state.html (accessed August 15, 2009).

15 Foreign Policy, "The Failed State Index," http://www.foreignpolicy.com/articles/2009/06/22/2009_failed_states_index_interactive_map_and_rankings, (accessed August 19, 2009).

16 Robert H. Jackson, *Quasi-States: Sovereignty, International Relations, and the Third World*, 29.

17 Ottoway and Mair, "States at Risk", 3.

18 MohammedAyoob, *The Third World Security Predicament*, (Boulder, Co: Lynne Rienner, 1995), 80.

19 Shashi Tharoor, "Are Human Rights Universal?" *World Policy Journal* 16 (1999/2000) http://ciao.net.org (accessed June 8, 2010).

20 Jules Lobel, Michael Ratner, Martha Honey and Tom Barry, "Humanitarian Military Intervention," *Foreign Policy in Focus 5* (2000). http.//ciao.net.org (accessed June 8, 2010)

21 Nick C. Bruce and Steven Erlanger, "Swiss Ban Building of Minarets on Mosques," *New York Times*, November 29, 2009, http://www.nytimes.com/2009/11/30/world/europe/30swiss.html (accessed April 25, 2010).

22 Ibid.

23 Ayoob, *The Third World Security Predicament*, 24–25.

24 Ibid., 35.

25 Thomas Ambrosia, *Irredentism: Ethnic Conflict and International Politics* (Westport, CT: Praeger Publishers, 2001), 2.

26 Ibid., 30.

27 Ibid., 31.

28 The National Bradley Project on America's National Identity, "E Pluribus Unum: The Bradley Project on National Identity," http://www.bradleyproject.org/index.html (accessed June 12, 2010).

29 Noah Pickus, *True Faith and Allegiance: Immigration and American Civic Nationalism* (Princeton, NJ: Princeton University Press, 2005), ix–x.

30 Sam R. Watkins, Co. *Aytch: A Confederate Memoir of the Civil War* (New York: Touchstone/Simon & Schuster, Inc., 2003), 3.

31 Joel Williamson, *A Rage for Order: Black/White Relations in the American South Since Emancipation* (Oxford: Oxford University Press, 1986), http://books.google.com/books?id=PkPiP4IJTCoC&pg=PT94&lpg=PT94&dq=%22how+many+lynchings%22&source=bl&ots=vInNn9_Y_t&sig=sYKGLRvGdq3XiCCK2q70DwWz2VA&hl=en&ei=OFsRTKvgC8L6lweAuO36Bw&sa=X&oi=book_result&ct=result&resnum=7&ved=0CDMQ6AEwBg#v=onepage&q=%22how%20many%20lynchings%22&f=false (accessed June 10, 2010).

32 Hua Hsu, "The End of White America?" *The Atlantic Magazine*, January/February 2009, http://www.theatlantic.com/magazine/archive/2009/01/the-end-of-white-america/7208/ (accessed June 10, 2010).

33 The National Bradley Project on America's National Identity, "E Pluribus Unum: The Bradley Project on National Identity," http://www.bradleyproject.org/index.html (accessed June 12, 2010).

34 Walker Connor, "A Nation is a Nation, is a State, is an Ethnic Group, is a . . . ," in *Nationalism*, eds. John Hutchinson and Anthony. D. Smith (Oxford: Oxford University Press, 1994), 38.

35 CBS News Online, "Number of Illegal Immigrants Plunges by 1 M," February 11, 2010, http://www.cbsnews.com/stories/2010/02/11/national/main6197466.shtml (accessed June 14, 2010).

36 Jyioti Thottam, "New Poll: Americans Favor a Guest Worker Program," *Time*, March 31, 2006, http://www.time.com/time/nation/article/0,8599,1179117,00.html (accessed June 14, 2010).

37 Roy Beck and Stephen A. Camarota, "Elite vs. Public Opinion: An Examination of Divergent Views on Immigration," Center for Immigration Studies, December 2002, http://www.cis.org/articles/2002/back1402.html (accessed June 14, 2010).

38 Samuel P. Huntington, "The Hispanic Challenge," *Foreign Policy* 141 (2004): 30. http://www.jstor.org (accessed June 14, 2010).

39 Ibid., 31–32.

40 Ibid., 40.

41 Randal C. Archibold, "Arizona Enacts Stringent Law on Immigration," *New York Times*, April 23, 2010, http://www.nytimes.com/2010/04/24/us/politics/24immig.html (accessed April 27, 2010).

42 Jack Citrin, Amy Lerman, Michael Murakami, and Kathryn Pearson, "Testing Huntington: Is Hispanic Immigration a Threat to American Identity?" *Perspectives on Politics* 5 (2007): 31–48.

43 John Pionke, "NLC Poll: Patriotism Most Positive Results of 9/11," *Nation's Cities Weekly*, February 4, 2002, http://www.thefreelibrary.com/_/print/PrintArticle.aspx?id=83077373 (accessed June 14, 2010).

44 Randolph S. Bourne, "Trans-national America," *The Atlantic Online*, June 1916, http://www.theatlantic.com/past/docs/issues/16jul/bourne.htm (accessed June 14, 2010).

45 The National Archives, "Teaching With Documents: Documents and Photographs Related to Japanese Internment During World War II," http://www.archives.gov/education/lessons/japanese-relocation/ (June 14, 2010).

46 Qiong Li and Marylyn B. Brewer, "What Does It Mean to Be an American? Patriotism, Nationalism, and American Identity After 9/11," *Political Psychology* 5 (2004): 729. http://www.jstor.org (accessed June 14, 2010).

Political Culture: The Values and Beliefs that Shape Politics

CHAPTER

5

THE DEFINITION OF POLITICAL CULTURE

Do you support democracy? Do you see democracy as the foundation of the US government? Do you find that your colleagues or friends share your evaluation of democracy? If your answers to these questions are positive, then you may also agree to this assertion: there is something about America's political culture that supports democracy. The World Value Survey of 2006 has a question asking the respondents their views on the importance of democracy. Only about 11.4% of the US respondents said democracy is not really important while 49.9% of them indicated that it is "absolutely important."[1] The rest of the respondents also gave a high mark to the importance of democracy. The US public support for democracy seems not bound by the national boundary, either. It is often reflected in US foreign policies as well. For example, according to former President George W. Bush, the US invasion into Iraq in 2003 was not an ordinary war, but "an epic struggle between democracy and tyranny,"[2] and this view was widely shared by the American public. In 2004, as many as a half of the Americans believed that the US military should stay as long as it takes to create a stable democracy in Iraq.[3] So, it seems that the support for democracy is deeply rooted in, and a major part of, the American political culture. This statement may seem obvious, but we haven't addressed an important question. What is political culture?

Let's review a few definitions of political culture. Political culture is defined as "the traditions of a society, the spirit of its public institutions, the passions and the collective reasoning of its citizenry, and the style and operating codes of its leaders [that] are not just random products .. but fit together as a part of a meaningful whole."[4] Another definition says that political culture is "a system of attitudes, values, and knowledge [regarding politics] that is widely shared within a society and transmitted from generation to generation."[5] Geertz defined it as a "historically transmitted pattern of meaning embodied in symbols, a system of inherited conceptions expressed in symbolic forms by means of which men communicate, perpetuate, and develop their knowledge about and attitudes toward life."[6] There are many more definitions of political culture, but most of them are not radically different from these definitions. The definitions are not identical, but address similar aspects of the same concept. What are the common elements?

First of all, according to these definitions, political culture does not necessarily involve active rational thinking. For example, to buy a car, people typically spend a lot of time making a series of careful decisions: brands, types, price ranges, services, loans, colors, and so on. In each of these dimensions, there are options (Ford, Kia, or Volkswagen; sedan or hatchback; under $25,000 or over $25,000; 8 year warranty or 10 year warranty; 36 month loan with no interest or 60 month loan with 5% interest; black, red, or silver) and preferences (Volkswagen > Kia > Ford; sedan < hatchback; under $25,000 > over $25,000; 8 year warranty < 10 year warranty; 36 month loan with no interest > 60 month loan with 5% interest; black < red < silver) over these options. The potential consumer looks at them and compares them across the dimensions in order to maximize his or her benefit and satisfaction from the purchase ("OK, I really like a silver Volkswagen hatchback, but will settle for a red Kia because a 10 year warranty and 36 month loan with no interest are really important to me"). On the contrary, according to the definitions, political culture is largely constituted by a feeling or tendency regarding political events. For example, American citizens like the idea of democracy, they are not comfortable with racial discrimination, and they are likely to be anti-communist. These feelings and evaluative tendencies originate typically from a cumulative learning process in collective environments such as family, school, or peer groups. Few people spend much time pondering if it is desirable or acceptable to like democracy or to be a communist. How many people do you know who have read Karl Marx in order to dislike communism? How many people around you have read Lenin to conclude that international communist revolutions are highly unlikely? Has anyone lived in a communist country? It is not really easy to identify a specific source of the often observed uncomfortable or negative feelings toward communism or socialism. Likewise, many people often struggle when asked "what's democracy?"

Second, in these definitions of political culture we assert that political culture is a collective phenomenon and is shared by a group and passed along to the next generation of the group. So, according to this idea, American political culture is a certain feeling or evaluative orientation that is shared by most members of the US, and the members learn it in a collective manner, which promises its longevity. Let's stay with the example of democracy. Anywhere you go in the US, you will find that most people share the positive feeling toward democracy. Compare this to Russia. According to the World Value Survey, about 25% of respondents in Russia did not think democracy is important, and 6% of the respondents consider democracy not important at all. Love for democracy does not seem to be shared by Russians as enthusiastically as in the US. Therefore, we can say that Russian political culture is different from US political culture at least on this dimension. Of course, political culture is not simple in a country. Within the US, different groups have different cultures. For this point, let us use a not-so-political example. Here, in this area known as the Eastern Shore around the Chesapeake Bay, Maryland, it is popular and common among people to eat steamed blue crabs cooked with a seasoning as you might have seen on a TV series, such as "Homicide" or "the Wire." Here in the Eastern Shore, the young learn how to break the crab and collect the flesh, slowly get better with them, and later teach others. Since many people consume blue crabs, it is very likely for any newcomers to the area or visitors will have their first experience of eating blue crabs sooner or later. Repeated occurrences of such gatherings with crabs gives anyone many opportunities to get to like the taste of crab or at least the atmosphere of eating together. And people do like them. In other words, it is a culture of the Eastern Shore. Is it American culture? Not really. In Lawrence, Kansas, this practice is simply foreign as it is in many other parts of the US. So it is a collectively shared sentiment in Eastern Shore, not in the US as a whole. In a similar vein, the enthusiasm toward capital punishment might be considered a hallmark of the political culture of Texas, but less so in the rest of the country.

This collective nature of political culture carries an important implication in political science since many regard studying political culture as a meaningful alternative to other approaches. For example, one could argue that revolution occurs because certain people, typically those who were repressed, expect benefits from the chaotic situation and therefore it is rational to join the movement. Or, one could argue that revolution occurs because of a set of socioeconomic structures such as troubled old regime or increasing foreign threats. However, political culture scholars think that people make decisions based on more than just their calculation of cost/benefits or what's given to them by society. Instead, they argue that "people's responses to their situations are shaped by subjective orientations"[7] and therefore "action can *not* be interpreted as simply the result of external situations: Enduring differences in cultural learning also play an essential part in shaping what people think and do."[8] According to this tradition of political culture, people who share a culture act in a similar way. For example, Americans, who love democracy, may respond to authoritarian leaders differently from Russians who do not share the same culture. Hence, under this assumption, understanding cultural differences between two groups, often states, could be a key to understanding political differences between them.

COMPARING POLITICAL CULTURES IN DIFFERENT REGIONS

The major purpose of this study of political culture is to understand the link between political culture and political events. We often observe a group following a unique political pattern, compared to other groups. Many suspect this can be attributed to the group's cultural tradition and try to show the causal link between the culture and its behavior. The first step to do this is to identify the group and its culture. This can be done in many ways, and here we introduce a few of them according to the size of the cultural categorization. Let's begin with studies focusing on large cultural zones. One could identify the regional culture encompassing many countries and see if these countries of a similar culture share behavioral patterns. Probably, one of the most famous cultural works in this tradition must be Huntington's article, "Clash of Civilizations?"[9] Huntington identifies eight macro political cultures: Western, Confucian, Japanese, Islamic, Hindu, Slavic-orthodox, Latin American, and African civilizations. He asserts that "Civilizations are differentiated from each other by history, language, culture, tradition, and, most important, religion. The people of different civilizations have different views on the relations between God and man, the individual and the group, the citizen and the state, parents and children, husband and wife, as well as differing views of the relative importance of rights and responsibilities, liberty and authority, equality, and hierarchy."[10] This suggests that, most countries with the Western culture share a particular set of cultural heritage that differs from the others, such as Middle Eastern countries.

How do these civilizations explain political events? According to Huntington, civilizations replaced old political boundaries such as the rivalry between the communist countries and the capitalist counterparts. "Groups or states belonging to one civilization that become involved in war with people from a different civilization naturally try to rally support from other members of their own civilization."[11] For example, the conflict between two former republics of the Soviet Union, Azerbaijan and Armenia evoked a new tension between Turkey and Russia. Why? It is because of their cultural ties. Turkey and Azerbaijan have both religious and linguistic bonds. But Russian backs Armenia that shares linguistic and religious ties to Russia. More globally, the victory of the West over the East seems to be challenged by new foes. On the domestic front, there are growing tensions between the increasing number of Muslim immigrants and Western European countries, their new homes. France banned Muslim women wearing their headscarves in the public areas to honor its secular tradition while the Swiss imposed national ban on building minarets or the towers of mosques. Internationally, US-led Western military forces have been dragged into long wars in Afghanistan and Iraq while North Korea not only developed nuclear weapons but also smuggles sophisticated weapon or expertise to countries like Iran. These too can be explained by Huntington's theory. He points out that the West is confronting the "Confucian-Islamic Connection" that is trying to defy the peacemaking efforts of the West and pursues the WMD because the West is at the peak of its power.[12]

COMPARING POLITICAL CULTURES IN DIFFERENT COUNTRIES: CHINA AND KOREA

The global approach such as Huntington's is interesting, but leaves many ambiguities. For one, it is clear that not all countries in one civilization behave similarly. For example, even though Huntington asserts that the Confucian civilization will clash with the West, there seem to be a clear divergence. There is North Korea that is technically at war with the US while it is developing nuclear weapons, defying the West-led nuclear proliferation regime. However, the country that shares the Korean Peninsula, South Korea has a fundamentally different relationship with the West. South Korea is a major US ally, hosting the US troops and a member of Organization for Economic Cooperation and Development (OECD), a hallmark of the prosperity in the global economy. In between the two Koreas, there is China, an important trading partner with the West and a political competitor with the US in East Asia. From the cultural perspective, this variation poses an interesting question because it is true that Confucianism is deeply rooted in all these East Asian countries as Huntington argued. Then, one might wonder, from the cultural perspective, if his assumption that Confucian culture is equally shared by all these East Asian countries is really sound. In other words, it might be possible that cultural heterogeneity may exist within a supposedly homogeneous cultural zone, resulting in the different policies. If that is the case, Huntington's thesis will need more careful review.

The possibility that Confucianism may mean different things in different East Asian countries was explored by Lucian W. Pye. Pye observes that these countries "had their separate versions of Confucianism, which increasingly diverged as each country followed a different path to political modernization."[13] According to him, the Chinese version was a major contributor to the centralization of political authority in China. In Chinese culture, authority is a purpose itself and "power is used simply to set an example of moral rectitude so that the conduct of all individuals would be exemplary."[14] As a result, in Chinese culture, a harmonious society—one of the major virtues of the Confucianism—is emphasized and contentious politics are discouraged. "Discouraging" may be an understatement; Pye points out that the Chinese have the "fear of disunity—nearly a phobia"[15] that not only dampens dissenting voices but also reduces competition among cultural units. Political leaders tend to see themselves as omnipotent father figures and expect "total deference and no explicit criticism."[16] As a father figure who has absolute power and total responsibility, any "loss of face," or shame, is not only something to avoid at any cost but also something not to evoke even for your rival.

In Korea, Confucianism shaped Korean culture in a dramatically different way from China. Confucianism showed what an ideal society could look like and enhanced Koreans' expectation about politics, social status, and personal virtues. Hence, it created "aspirations for acceptance and anxiety about unworthiness which have made [Koreans] audacious in carrying out enterprises that test and prove their worth."[17] During the Yi dynasty that adopted Confucianism as the formal political and religious ideology, the members of the *yangban* or mandarin class, instead of being in a harmonious brotherhood pursuing Confucian virtues, continued to wage political and cultural battles in the name of Confucianism. In this cultural context, political leaders are expected to be all-powerful but at the same time there is a great deal of emphasis on being "sympathetic, nurturing, and sensitive to the wishes of his followers-family."[18] Therefore, according to Pye, two different political cultures have actually evolved from a single cultural tradition, and this difference still lingers on in the political culture of these countries today. For example, the CCP is infamous for its secrecy over the party's internal power struggle. With a few rare exceptions, such as the one after the death of Chairman Mao, nothing but the harmony with big grins on the faces of the leaders was shown outside of the *Zhongnanhai* or the compound where the Chinese leaders deal with day-to-day tasks and make most decisions. Any source of potential "loss of face" is discussed and sorted out behind the tall wall surrounding the compound long before anything is revealed to the public. Such cultural emphasis on the harmony and unity is a rarity in Korea. Political leadership in South Korea has demonstrated anything but unity. The first president, Lee Syngman, was ousted by street protests and the succeeding government collapsed due to a military coup. Park Junghee, the junta leader, was assassinated and two succeeding presidents served jail time after the end of their presidency. Most recently, Roh Moo-hyun, the former president, committed suicide due to political pressures from the incumbent president—hardly harmonious leadership.

COMPARING POLITICAL CULTURES IN DIFFERENT COUNTRIES: ALMOND AND VERBA'S TRADITION

Scholars often analyze political culture at the national level in part because of the seemingly oversimplification as in the case of Huntington. It was Almond and Verba who set the tradition of political culture study at the state level by analyzing political cultures of five democratic countries.[19] Through survey research, Almond and Verba gauged citizens' evaluative orientation toward their political system and its input and output processes. Depending on the responses of a country, they characterized the country's political culture as belonging to one of the three categories: participants, subjects, and parochial.[20] A parochial political culture is characterized, on the one hand, by the lack of difference between politics and religion at both leadership and citizenry levels, and, on the other hand, by the "absence of expectations of change initiated by the political system."[21] In other words, in this culture people largely ignore government.[22] A subject political culture is mainly oriented toward the outputs of government, such as specific policies. Citizens demonstrate interests, like policies, or dislike them. However, they remain passive regarding inserting their own inputs to government. The third political culture is the participant political culture, and it is made by citizens who take part in the political process.

Almond and Verba expected a shift of culture from parochial to subjects, and finally to participants, as the country develops.[23] However, their research shows that the composition of political culture is complex. For one, they noticed that countries have a mixture of these political cultures, rather than one type of political culture. Moreover, some of their research results were surprising because they were contrary to the authors' expectations. For example, The English and the Italians scored low in identifying their political leaders, disputing the perception that the British have the most advanced political system and thus English political culture must be the most participant. Mexicans, who were expected to share parochial culture, demonstrated a surprisingly high level of understanding of politics.[24]

A similar study was done by another scholar who analyzed political culture, but this time over a long period of time. Inglehart discussed cultural shift in Western European countries.[25] He assumed that people who grew up during the time of economic scarcity would share materialist values emphasizing the need for physical well-being and safety. However, a generation who grew up in a more prosperous society such as in the Western European countries share a different set of cultural values or "postmaterial values."[26] Postmaterialism is characterized by the emphasis on goals such as to "give people more say in the decisions of the government; protect freedom of speech; try to make cities and countryside more beautiful; move toward a friendlier, less impersonal society; and move toward a society where ideas count more than money."[27] He shows that most European countries actually experienced the rise of the postmaterialism since 1973 until 1988.[28] This cultural shift affected the politics of the countries, he asserts. For example, it contributed to the rise of new political parties such as the New Left, ecologists, and ethnic parties.[29] At the same time, it decreased the overall support for Marxists. Moreover, the cultural change even altered foreign relations, such as "declining support for the Atlantic Alliance . . . erosion of political support for NATO."[30]

COMPARING POLITICAL CULTURES IN A SINGLE COUNTRY: NORTHERN AND SOUTHERN ITALY

As demonstrated through the review of Pye, cultural divisions within a supposedly single cultural zone are not rare. In fact, there are many examples showing a great variety of political culture within a cultural zone such as Western Europe, the former Soviet bloc, South America, Middle East, as well as East Asia. Then, you might wonder if we can take an additional step in this direction by asking the question, "Do we see such cultural divisions within a single country?" Almond and Verba's study already addressed this issue by, unexpectedly, finding the coexistence of all three cultures within the countries they studied. Inglehart also noticed materialism and postmaterialism were shared by different generations of the same society. However, it was Putnam who directly focused on the difference of political culture in a single country, and its impact.[31]

Putnam compared the political cultures of Northern and Southern Italy and found stark cultural differences between the Northern and Southern states. In the north he found vibrant civic culture, while this was not the case in the South. Putnam's definition of civic culture is made of several components. First, participation in public affairs is a major one. Citizens are interested in politics and national economy and eager to act to improve their society. In the absence of such participation, citizens tend to care for private or parochial interests. The second element is political equality. A civic community is "bound together by horizontal relations of reciprocity and cooperation"[32] while "vertical relations of authority and dependency"[33] are the mark of the absence of civic culture. The abundance of solidarity, trust, and tolerance is another major part of civic culture. The people in a society lacking civic culture experience no such solidarity among the members, trust is limited among only the close members of the family or clan, and they do not tolerate others who do not share their core values.

Putnam measured these elements of civic culture and found evidence showing that cultural difference is obvious. All measures showed that the northern states of Italy had a strong tradition of civic culture. However, the southern states largely lack most of the elements of civic culture. Putnam observed that this cultural difference was paralleled with a political difference, the state governments' performances. Regional governments in the northern states were simply better in all areas such as writing reform legislations and legislative innovation; providing services such as day care centers, housing and urban development, information, and family clinics; and most of all, they remained stable.[34] In this index of institutional performance, southern states scored consistently and significantly lower than their northern counterparts. Is this correspondence between cultural difference and the gap in the regional government's performance a mere coincidence? No. Putnam attributes the difference in institutional performances to the cultural difference.

POLITICAL SOCIALIZATION: CONDUIT FOR VALUES

A major component of political culture is collectivity. It is shared by a group of people. The group could be an entire continent, a country, or a region. No matter the size of the group, it typically shares a certain set of values, evaluations, or attitudes. Therefore, a new member or the ones who desire to join would find it to his or her advantage to learn the political culture in order to be a legitimate part of the group. When a girl is born, she has no choice but to be baptized in a church if her parents desire to do so. Let's imagine her extended family lives relatively close to each other and they all go to the church together. Soon she will learn the Christian teaching and develop a political awareness that fits the political values of her family. By doing so, she will share an increasingly large part of the political ideas of the church and be recognized by others as a trustworthy member of the group, which, in turn, could help her to make friends and enjoy the sense of community. A similar process occurs to many newcomers in the American society. The first generation of immigrants may maintain their own political culture from their home country, but they quickly begin to lose it as their children grow up in the US. Not only do they lose their language—German, Swedish, French, Somali, Spanish, or Korean—but they also learn to respect the virtues of separation of power, the fiesta on the fourth of July, or the love of guns or baseball. Now they have something to talk about with their American colleagues ("Hey. Did you see the game last night?") and they will increasingly feel more like their "American" classmates, neighbors, or coworkers. The learning process is called political socialization in which individuals learn the political culture of the group, internalize them, and strengthen their group membership.

Let's review specific political functions of political socialization.[35] First, it connects individual and collective identities. By adopting a certain set of values, cultural connection renders certain actions as reasonable in the group while it eliminates others as possible alternatives. Individuals learn to understand certain actions will be approved or encouraged by the group members who share the same cultural identity. Therefore, a young Palestine child who grew up watching Palestine's economic and social devastation and learning the history of his country's struggles against the Israeli occupation will feel justified as a Palestinian when he throws rocks at the Israeli forces and brags about it to his peers. Individuals also gain the sense that a certain action could complicate their relationship within the cultural group, which could therefore discourage such behaviors. For Israeli settlers who created a narrow enclave for themselves in the land of Palestine, the settlement is not just a place for habitation but also a symbol for the identity of Jewish people with a long history. Therefore, to them, giving back their land to Palestinians is simply not an option. Any discussion of the dismantlement of the settlements by anyone typically confronts fierce, and sometimes violent, resistance from the settlers.

In addition, political socialization establishes legitimate authority. This is "a historical process for a community and psychological one for individuals, linking people through a sense of common fate captured in the historical accounts people in a community share."[36] In Thailand, the king has virtually no real power according to the Thai constitution. Nevertheless, Thai people see him as a major element of their society and have revered him since 1946, when he was enthroned. Thus, the majority of Thai people have been socialized to support him, and his popularity among the public has in fact legitimized his authority as the real political force to reckon with. One vivid example was the military coup that occurred in 2006. The incumbent Prime Minister Thaksin Shinawatra was not really popular among the urban elite, including the military and royal supporters. In September, the military rolled into the capital and took control of the government away from the prime minister who was visiting New York City. In their first national address the coup leaders quickly implied that they sided with the king. They revealed that "The Administrative Reform Council [the military leadership], which has his Majesty the King as its leader, seized administrative power from the caretaker government by ordering the dissolution of the House of Representatives, the Senate, the government and the Constitutional Court."[37] Moreover, the military visited the king prior to the coup and obtained his blessing, without which the coup might have been almost impossible. The king's blessing was even visible through the yellow—the color of the monarch—ribbon attached to every soldier who participated in the coup.[38]

AGENTS OF SOCIALIZATION: EDUCATIONAL INSTITUTIONS; RELIGIOUS INSTITUTIONS; MEDIA; FRIENDS AND FAMILY

Political socialization is complex: it takes places through multiple channels in any given moment, and it occurs repeatedly to an individual. There are various agents of political socialization. The most noticeable agents include family, schools, and religion. From your own experience, or from those of your friends, it may not be that difficult to notice the parents' impact on their children's political orientations. You might have learned about the government or presidents from your parents. Some of you may recall lengthy conversations with your parents about political events. Some of you might have had heated debates with them. The political impacts of parents on their children are well analyzed. For example, children who grew up in homes where political discussions are common or parents participated in political activities tend to be involved in political activities more than children who did not have such parents. They tend to volunteer or register to vote more than their peers.[39] Children are found to share the partisanship and various political values with their parents and maintain them over long periods. Moreover, spouses can influence each other's political values, and grandparents could pass on their political values to their grandchildren through the parents as the middlemen.[40] Empirical studies, however, often fail to find the evidence to support the importance of family as a major agent of political socialization. One reason may be that the impact of political socialization within the family is just outweighed by other factors as the children grow. Then what are the other agents?

Educational institutions are also important agents of political socialization. Universities often serve as important places for lively debates during times of uncertainty and chaos. South Korean universities were a beacon of anti-government movement during the 1980s, as were university campuses of the US in the 1970s, China in the 1980s, and Iran in the 2000s. Students learn not only knowledge. They often gain novel values from their colleagues and professors and internalize them. In their seminary work on political culture, Almond and Verba identify formal education as the major determinant of political attitudes.[41] In fact, college students are more liberal than the population and they become more liberal as years go on.[42] What they study in college also matters. For example, on average most social science major students demonstrate a liberal orientation and so were economics students.[43] Faculty members also tend to be more liberal, as do this liberal tendency among the faculty influences students' political orientation.[44] Teaching experiences could shape the teachers' political views.[45] Others are suspicious of the role of educational institutions as an agent of political socialization. They found that compared to elementary education, the secondary or higher education may not be so significant in shaping political values of students.

Religious institutions gained a renewed attention for their role as major agents of political socialization. As a member of a religious institution or as a person who knows such a member, it might not have occurred to you that religious institutions play such a political role. However, a series of recent events here in the US have demonstrated the political influence of religion and religious institutions. For example, Islamic preacher Anwar al-Awlaki is known to turn normal people into terrorists using religious teaching, emphasizing violence as a legitimate means to carry out religious duties. Those who have gained such extreme values from him include a group of Canadian Muslims who were charged with plotting attacks in Ontario in 2006, a plotter of attack on Fort Dix in New Jersey in 2007, a Somali Islamist group that attracted recruits among young Somali-Americans living in Minnesota, and Major Nidal Malik Hasan, the Army psychiatrist who killed 13 people at Fort Hood, Texas, in 2009.[46] Radical Islam is a term that became familiar here in the US after the 9-11 Attack, but the political role of religion is not limited to Islam. For the majority of the religious US population, Christian churches play a major role in political socialization. Repeated religious practices such as services or bibles studies have convinced many Christians that their faith cannot tolerate certain social practices such as abortion, gay marriage, or stem cell research, and many actually act upon it by, among others, developing conservative social values and supporting the Republican Party.[47] Some take the political role much further than others. Jon Hagee, a pastor of San Antonio, Texas, often preaches that the US should support the Israeli government's effort to strengthen its occupation of the West Bank. For this cause, he founded a group called the Christian United for Israel (CUFI) in 2006 and mobilized his followers into political action, such as rallying or visiting members of Congress, in order to pressure foreign policy makers.[48]

PUZZLE: DOES CULTURE IMPEDE THE FIGHT AGAINST AIDS?

The epidemic of AIDS is a serious global problem, but it is more catastrophic in some parts of the world than others. According to Union Nationale des Architectes d'Intérieur, Designers (UNAID) report, globally, 33.4 million people live with HIV and 2.7 million of them were newly infected with HIV in 2008. Two million people died of AIDS-related illness in 2008. However, it is in the poorest part of the world, sub-Saharan Africa, that the threat is most acute and concentrated. In this region, 22.4 million people live with the HIV and among them 1.9 million are newly infected with the virus in 2008. The number of death related to AIDS is 1.4 million. In other words, this region accounted for 67% of HIV infections worldwide, 68% of new HIV infections among adults and 91% of new HIV infections among children, and 72% of the world's AIDS-related deaths in 2008. This regional concentration of the epidemic hit some Southern countries with an especially devastating blow. Swaziland and Botswana recorded the highest adult HIV prevalence, 26% and 24% respectively. South Africa has the world's largest population of people with HIV.[49] What can explain this substantial concentration of the epidemic in this region? No doubt, the socioeconomic infrastructure of this region is the major contributor: a limited reach of medical facilities and poor equipment, a lack of medical supplies and personnel, and the prohibiting price of drugs, and so on. However, sub-Saharan Africa is not the only part where poverty and the lack of socioeconomic structure are serious. For example, countries in the Caribbean region have similar economic and social problems, but the threat from the disease is much lower—0.7% of population having HIV and 0.8% of new infections.[50] Then, there must be unique factors in the sub-Saharan African region, allowing this problem to grow so horrible with no comparison. One possible answer might be the culture.

We could find a cultural factor that worsens the problem of the spread of AIDS in the sub-Saharan Africa in its patriarchic tradition, especially regarding sexual interaction. Many engage in sexual activities early and actively. Moreover, polygamy is a widely practiced cultural tradition in the region. Thanks to this tradition, men are entitled to many wives, which functions as a rich ground for the spread of AIDS. In the cultural context of monogamy, the sexual activities are often limited to a single spouse; however, the practice of polygamy allows infected men to spread the disease to multiple spouses, increasing the intensity of the spreading virus.[51] In a mining town in South Africa researchers conducted an investigation on the spread of HIV. They suspected that migrant workers who fled their poverty from all over southern Africa were actively looking for sexual partners and that this combination of economic problems and cultural tradition could be the major cause. They were right. The most suspected segments of the people were most vulnerable to HIV. Eighty percent of the prostitutes were HIV-positive and 30% of the miners carried the virus. What really surprised them was, however, the finding that 60% of the young women in the township were HIV-positive. As it turned out, mining workers, knowing that the prostitutes carried the high risk of the HIV infection, preferred to have sexual relationships with long-term girlfriends, and when they do, condoms were used far less.[52]

Another cultural impediment in the fight against AIDS in the sub-Saharan Africa is sadly related to the cultural shift in the US. In the past, many Christian evangelical leaders saw the disease as a moral and cultural issue. Most noticeably, Jerry Falwell once called AIDS "God's judgment on promiscuity."[53] This cultural, not scientific, judgment gained prominence during the Bush administration. The administration changed the priorities, giving more emphasis on abstinence, and hence more money to abstinence-only education programs in developing countries. This shift was timely for the growing Christian movements in countries like Uganda. Around one third of the Ugandan population has been "born again" in the past decade, and new churches were springing up all over the country. These Christian groups denounced the previously effective strategy, the equally divided emphasis on abstinence and condoms. To them the two cannot reconcile each other. These groups cursed condom use and destroyed the network of condom distribution. Furthermore, Population Services International—or PSI—a secular organization that had been distributing condoms in Uganda for years, had recently received US government funding to carry out an abstinence program, eroding the country's hard-earned progress in the fight against AIDS.[54] These cultural aspects are hardly only the causes, but certainly major causes of the tragedy of AIDS in sub-Saharan Africa.

CRITICISM

Political culture is a major field of political science, widening our understanding of modern politics. As the contribution grows, efforts have been made to examine the arguments of political culture studies. A starting point should be the very concept, culture. What is it? As we discussed, there are many definitions and major elements that are commonly found among these definitions. However, this question is not necessarily addressing what the definition is. Rather, this question addresses the confusing nature of culture. First, as previously pointed out, a culture is shared by a group of people. We have American culture. When we say it is American culture, we imply that it is uniquely American. If not and if that is shared by Western Europeans all over the world, we may call it Western culture as Huntington does. Then, what is American culture? In other words, what is the culture shared exclusively by Americans? The public support for democracy is not because it is also common in Western Europe. How about American fashion toward American football? One could argue that it is truly unique in the US and let's just pretend that it is correct (check the website of Canadian Football League or Korean American Football Association). Then, this brings us another dimension of the confusing nature of culture. Is it really *American* culture? In other words, do most Americans love football? Remember that if the culture is shared only by a small segment of American public, we should call it, as in the case of enjoying blue crabs, not as American, but say the Eastern Shore culture. If you have grown up in a family with a father who greatly enjoys watching football games on Thanksgiving days, you may have the impression that is the case. However, there are still millions and millions of American families who do not watch even the Super Bowl games, and thus it is not American culture. Then, what is the culture that most Americans share? Whatever that is, it must be clear now that the content that the concept, culture, is trying to capture is not so clear. This confusing nature was reflected by those who have tried to measure the culture and reported that they were not able to. The study of political culture is in debt to Inglehart who refreshed the interest in the topic by observing a cultural shift toward postmaterialism in Western European countries.[55] However, critics raise the very issue of the definition of political culture and how to measure it. By reexamining Inglehart's postmaterialism, they assert the concept is discussed based on a poorly conducted measurement[56] or worse, the concept has no relevance.[57] Similarly, Putnam's measurement of civic culture was challenged too. Critics point out his measurement was arbitrary[58] or ineffective,[59] demonstrating the illusive nature of culture that we discussed.

In addition, the complex nature of political culture is also complicating the study of political culture. We often hear that Muslim countries have an inherent political challenge to their political development, Islam. They argue Islam is culturally not compatible with democracy because of its radical and authoritative nature. However, when critics say Islamic culture, what are they referring to? Are they talking about Shia's emphasis on martyrdom or Sunni Islam's moderation? Are they referring to the most famous terrorist, Osama Bin Laden's interpretation of Islam or peaceful and moderate interpretation of Islam shared by about a billion people on the earth? We are not so sure about which Islam there are talking about; however, it is clear that they have failed to understand that there is a variety of Islamic tradition that non-Muslims can hardly understand. So, let's turn to a more familiar religion tradition, Christianity. There is, of course, the Catholic Church, and it contains some variations: Assyrian Church, Eastern Orthodox, Roman Catholic, and so on. From there, we have a range of Protestant traditions, including Anglican, Jehovah's Witness, Lutheran, Methodists, Mormon, Pentecostal, Presbyterian, Quakers, and so on. And of course, within one tradition, there are many differences regarding all kinds of issues, such as gay marriage, abortion, depending on numerous elements such as the pastor's personality or local tradition. So, when people say Christian tradition, what are they talking about? It must be one of them, but not certainly all of them.

An additional dimension of the difficulty of studying political culture is that culture changes over time. Let's look at the modern Western culture, whatever that is. The Western culture has its long tradition such as going to church on Sundays, here in the US. However, new traditions have arrived and become part of Western culture. It was not long ago when people frowned upon the idea of eating raw fish. Now it is stylish to eat sushi. A physical meditation of Hindu yogis became popular yoga. Children go to tae kwon do studios after watching a Japanese animation on TV. Some go to Buddhist temples while others go to Mosques on Fridays. Thus, when Huntington argues that Western civilization acts fundamentally different from the rest because of its culture, he might not have considered that cultures consistently change and adjust and therefore, it is not a very reliable explanatory variable.

Political culture is both an important topic in the study of political science and an effective tool enhancing our understanding of political phenomena in this world. However, as we discussed, understanding political culture requires a cautious approach and careful research design. This emphasis on caution should be loudly echoed among students of political science, especially nowadays when political and military conflicts among cultural groups seem to be rising.

Notes

1 World Values Survey Association. *World Value Survey 1981–2008 Official Aggregate v.20090901*, Aggregate File Producer: ASEP/JDS, Madrid, 2009. http://www.worldvaluessurvey.org. (accessed November 6, 2011)

2 David Stout, "Bush Says Iraq War Is Part of a Larger Fight," *The New York Times*, August 31, 2006, http://www.nytimes.com/2006/08/31/washington/31cnd-bush.html?_r=1&pagewanted=print. (accessed November 6, 2011)

3 Richard W. Stevenson, Janet Elder, and Fred Backus, "The 2004 Campaign: The Poll; Support for War is Down Sharply, Poll Concludes," *The New York Times*, April 29, 2004, http://www.nytimes.com/2004/04/29/us/the-2004-campaign-the-poll-support-for-war-is-down-sharply-poll-concludes.html?pagewanted=2&pagewanted=print.

4 Lucian W. Pye, "Introduction: Political Culture and Political Development," in *Political Culture and Political Development*, eds. Lucian W. Pye and Sidney Verba (Princeton, NJ: Princeton University Press, 1965), 7.

5 Ronald Inglehart, *Culture Shift in Advanced Industrial Society* (Princeton, NJ: Princeton University Press, 1990), 18.

6 Clifford Geertz, *The Interpretation of Cultures* (New York: Basic Books Harper Torchbooks, 1973), 89.

7 Inglehart, *Culture Shift in Advanced Industrial Society* (Princeton, NJ: Princeton University Press, 1990), 19.

8 Ibid., 19.

9 Samuel P. Huntington, "Clash of Civilizations?" *Foreign Affairs* 72 (1993): 22–49.

10 Ibid., 28.

11 Ibid., 35.

12 Ibid., 45–48.

13 Lucian W. Pye, *Asian Power and Politics: The Cultural Dimensions of Authority* (Cambridge: Harvard University Press, 1985), 55.

14 Ibid., 56.

15 Ibid., 64.

16 Ibid., 66.

17 Ibid., 58.

18 Ibid., 67

19 Gabriel A. Almond, and Sidney Verba, *The Civic Culture; Political Attitudes and Democracy in Five Nations* (Princeton, N.J.: Princeton University Press, 1963).

20 Ibid., 16.

21 Ibid., 17.

22 Ruth Lane, *The Art of Comparative Politics* (Boston, MA: Allyn & Bacon, 1997), 30.

23 Almond, and Verba, *The Civic Culture*, 22–28.

24 Ruth Lane, *The Art of Comparative Politics*, 32.

25 Inglehart, *Culture Shift in Advanced Industrial Society*.

26 Inglehart, *Culture Shift in Advanced Industrial Society*, 68.

27 Inglehart, *Culture Shift in Advanced Industrial Society*, 74–75.

28 Inglehart, *Culture Shift in Advanced Industrial Society*, 93.

29 Inglehart, *Culture Shift in Advanced Industrial Society*, 377.

30 Inglehart, *Culture Shift in Advanced Industrial Society*, 420.

31 Robert D. Putnam, *Making Democracy Work: Civic Traditions in Modern Italy* (Princeton: Princeton University Press, 1993).

32 Ibid., 88.

33 Ibid., 88.

34 Ibid., 75.

35 For detailed and additional discussions on this point, see Marc H. Ross, "Culture and Identity in Comparative Political Analysis," in *Comparative Politics: Rationality, Culture, and Structure*, eds. by Mark I. Lichbach and Alan S. Zuckerman (New York: Cambridge University Press, 1997), 45–53.

36 Ibid., 47.

37 Thomas Fuller, "Leader of Coup in Thailand Sets Timetable," *The New York Times*, September 20, 2006, http://www.nytimes.com/2006/09/20/world/asia/20cnd-thailand.html?ei=5094&en=36fdb27c89711194&hp=&ex=11588 11200&partner=homepage&pagewanted=print. (accessed November 6, 2011)

38 Ibid.

39 Hugh McIntosh, Daniel Hart, and James Youniss "The Influence of Family Political Discussion on Youth Civic Development: Which Parent Qualities Matter?" *PS: Political Science & Politics* 40 (2007): 495.

40 Paul A. Beck and M. Kent Jennings, "Parents as "Middlepersons" in Political Socialization," *The Journal of Politics* 37 (1975): 83.

41 Almond and Verba, *The Civic Culture; Political Attitudes and Democracy in Five Nations*, 135–136.

42 Mack D. Mariani and Gordon J. Hewitt, "Indoctrination U.? Faculty Ideology and Changes in Student Political Orientation," *PS: Political Science & Politics* 41 (2008): 773.

43 Ibid., 774.

44 Ibid., 773.

45 For the following discussion, see Kenneth P. Langton and M. Kent Jennings, "Political socialization and The High School Civics Curriculum in the United States," *The American Political Science Review* 62 (1968): 862–867.

46 Scott Shane, "Born in US, a Radical Clergy Inspires Terror," *The New York Times*, November 19, 2009.

47 John C. Green, "Religion and the Presidential Vote: A Tale of Two Gaps," *The Pew Forum on Religion and Public Life*, August 21, 2007, http://pewforum.org/Politics-and-Elections/Religion-and-the-Presidential-Vote-A-Tale-of-Two-Gaps.aspx. (accessed November 6, 2011)

48 PBS, "Bill Moyers Journal," aired October 7, 2007. http://www.pbs.org/moyers/journal/10052007/profile.html. (accessed November 6, 2011)

49 UNAID, *2009 AIDS Epidemic Update*, November 2009, 21–27. http://data.unaids.org/pub/Report/2009/jc1700_epi_update_2009_en.pdf. (accessed November 6, 2011)

50 Ibid., 53.

51 Helen Epstein, "God and Fight Against AIDS," *New York Review of Books*, April 28, 2005, http://www.nybooks.com/articles/17963. (accessed November 6, 2011)

52 Helen Epstein, "Hidden Cause of AIDS," *New York Review of Books*, May 9, 2002, http://www.nybooks.com/articles/archives/2002/may/09/the-hidden-cause-of-aids/. (accessed November 6, 2011)

53 Epstein, "God and Fight Against AIDS".

54 Ibid.

55 Ronald Inglehart, "The Renaissance of Political Culture," *American Political Science Review* 82 (1988): 1203–1230.

56 Harold Clarke and Allan Kornberg (and the Assistance of Petra Bauer-Kaase and Chris McIntyre),"The Effects of Economic Priorities on the Measurement of Value Change: New Experimental Evidence", *American Political Science Review* 93 (1999): 637–648.

57 Darren W. Davis and Christian Davenport, "Assessing the Validity of the Postmaterialism Index," *American Political Science Review* 93 (1999): 649–664.

58 Amber L. Selingson, "Civic Association and Democratic Participation in Central America: A Test of the Putnam Thesis," *Comparative Political Studies* 32 (1999): 342–362.

59 Robert W. Jackson and Ross A. Miller, "Individual-Level Evidence for the Causes and Consequences of Social Capital," *American Journal of Political Science* 41 (1996): 999–1023.

Ideologies: Frameworks for Political Action

INTRODUCTION

In Chapter 2 of this book we discussed the normative study of political life. The political theorists we examined in that chapter—individuals such as Hobbes, Locke, and Rousseau—constructed philosophical systems that are all inclusive . . . (and which) explain every dimension of political reality—including making explicitly moral judgments about the range and scope of political power, the role of the state, and the meaning of liberty, justice, equality, and citizenship.[1] The philosophical arguments put forward by these great thinkers laid the intellectual groundwork for modern ideologies as we know them today.

While political philosophies offer timeless, theoretical perspectives on how social and political institutions *should* be organized and individuals *should* behave in their political settings, ideologies are designed to provide concrete prescriptions for solving problems in modern society. Ideological development is linked closely to the mobilization of the masses into political life. Because the inclusion of the average citizens in the political life of society is a fairly recent phenomenon, ideologies themselves are a recent phenomenon. As we shall discuss in this chapter, the origins of the earliest modern ideologies—liberalism and conservatism—can be traced to 17th and 18th centuries, a period of time that was characterized by seismic political and economic changes (particularly in Europe), and the expansion of political and economic opportunities to new classes of citizens.

Because the creation of new ideologies has been linked to mass political mobilization, and the expansion of opportunities for mass participation through the 19th century occurred primarily in parts of Europe as well as North America, it is fair to say that the origins of the most influential ideologies is linked to the Western experience with political and socioeconomic development. The most powerful ideologies in contemporary history—liberalism, conservatism, and Marxism in their various manifestations—were Western intellectual creations that were then exported to the rest of the world. This process of ideological export from the West to the rest of the world has often resulted in an ill-fit between the ideologies themselves and the societies to which they are applied in the lesser-developed world.

Consider briefly the example of Marxism. Given the woeful record of economic underdevelopment and the concentration of wealth in the hands of a few people in the societies of the lesser-developed world, it is not surprising that the masses—and radical political elites as well—were drawn to Marxism's prescription of class struggle, popular resistance, and redistribution of wealth and power away from the tiny elite (many of whom had links to Western capitalist states) and toward the impoverished, oppressed masses. From the 1950s through the 1980s, leftist movements such as Marxism were some of the most popular ideological vehicles for mobilizing mass political action in the lesser-developed world.

However, a central assumption of classical Marxist thought made it a difficult tool for mobilizing the masses in lesser-developed states. As we shall discover later in this chapter, Marx's prescription for curing the ills of society was very specific: revolution by the proletariat (urban working class) against the bourgeoisie (owners of the means of the production in the cities) within the context of an advanced, industrialized capitalist system. And yet, by definition no lesser-developed states had achieved the stage of advanced industrialized capitalism. Thus, while many people in the lesser-developed world may have felt that Marxism spoke to their general grievances regarding the unequal distribution of wealth, power, and resources in their societies, the practical prescription offered by Marxism for addressing those grievances—proletarian revolution—was not relevant to their societies. In fact, as we will discuss in this chapter, the disjuncture between the central assumptions of classical Marxism and the actual socioeconomic conditions in many states opened the door for the Chinese Maoist version of communism to gain a foothold in some lesser-developed countries, as a more viable alternative to classical Marxism.

IDEOLOGY DEFINED

Ideologies marry abstract theoretical thought to political action. They provide a practical blueprint for addressing a specific set of problems through the application of concrete policy prescriptions. All ideologies, regardless of where they fall on the ideological spectrum—from radical Marxism on the far-left to reactionary fascism on the far-right—share several basic characteristics:

1. They promote specific sets of political, economic, social, and cultural goals.
2. They identify the factors that must be altered or eliminated in order for the goals they promote to be achieved.
3. They offer specific guidelines of action for how to eliminate those factors and obtain their stated goals.
4. They are intended to appeal to a broad segment of the population, although, given the detailed nature of ideologies they tend to be more attractive to certain segments, groups, or classes within society than to others.

Because most ideologies are designed to resonate with average citizens, they tend to be presented for popular consumption in fairly straightforward language. As compared to the dense, highly philosophical nature of normative theories, ideologies are meant to be concise and pragmatic. They provide a practical framework through which adherents to the ideology make sense of the world around them and seek to change it.

To some degree, in its simplest form an ideology provides a basic formula or checklist for determining where those who subscribe to that ideology stands on specific issues. For example, in the United States contemporary conservatives support a legitimate role for the state in legislating on moral issues, while calling for the state to take a hands-off approach on economic issues. Thus, contemporary conservatives support laws banning or restricting abortion, which they define as a moral issue. Contemporary conservatives also tend to oppose gay marriage, which they believe to be an immoral affront to traditional notions of marriage and the family. At the same time, they tend to oppose increased government regulation over the economy, and in fact often advocate for the rollback of regulations that already exist. For example, after the huge oil spill that ravaged the Gulf Coast region of the United States in 2010, many contemporary conservatives expressed wariness regarding cracking down too hard on oil companies or implementing a moratorium on permits for new offshore drilling sites.

On the other side of the political aisle in the US, modern liberals generally oppose government intervention on issues of personal morality (often liberals frame such issues as a question of an individual's right to make decisions regarding his or her own life), while supporting a more activist role for the state in the socioeconomic realm. For example, modern liberals define abortion not as a moral issue, but rather as one that hinges on a woman's right to choose. As one popular pro-abortion slogan states: Her body, Her choice. And modern liberals tend to support the notion that gays should enjoy full and equal rights within society, including the right to marry. On the other hand, they press for an active role by the government in a number of socioeconomic areas, ranging from environmental and work-place safety to affirmative action to regulations on corporate behavior.

For those who identify strongly as conservative or liberal, their ideological perspective serves as a framework through which their political views are shaped, and to some degree, predetermined. Anyone who follows American politics and the mass media is familiar with the so-called "Ditto-Head" phenomenon. Some regular listeners of conservative radio talk-show host Rush Limbaugh proudly call themselves "Ditto-Heads" as an indication that they march in line with Limbaugh's conservative ideological views. Conservative ideology, as espoused by Limbaugh, provides an unambiguous prism through which his listeners view the political world.

Certainly, ideology does provide a simple, clear blueprint for understanding politics and identifying solutions to society's ills. On the other hand, ideology becomes more problematic when it acts as an intellectual straight-jacket—when individuals begin to accept without much independent consideration the core assumptions of an ideology. It is useful here to recall Plato's Allegory of the Cave (*see* Chapter 2), which touches on the necessity of breaking the shackles that otherwise lead us to take in what we observe and hear in the world around us without thoughtful, critical questioning and analysis. It is an essential part of the rational human experience to poke, prod, question, analyze, and critique. We surrender this central element of our nature when we simply absorb without reflection a single ideological framework. To be clear, the argument being made here is not that one should never identify himself or herself with a particular ideology, but rather that an individual should only arrive at a particular ideological identity after careful, critical examination of the issues that confront society, and the solutions that competing ideologies offer for resolving those issues.

One of the more interesting implications of the process of critical analysis of ideologies is that an individual may find that she or he does not fall neatly into any particular ideological category. Consider for example the issues of abortion and the death penalty. In the United States, conservatives typically oppose abortion and favor the death penalty, while liberals usually favor abortion rights and oppose the death penalty. Many, if not most, self-professed conservatives fit this preference profile on those two issues, as do many or most self-professed liberals.

And yet, one can imagine an individual who is willing to break the traditional ideological mold. For example, if an individual were to decide that, according to his or her personal ideological beliefs, preservation of life is the benchmark for determining policy, that individual might oppose abortion (assuming he or she accepts the argument that life begins at conception) AND oppose the death penalty (based on the belief that the state does not have the right to take any person's life, under any circumstance). These policy stances seem perfectly congruent with each other, and yet when taken together fit neither the typical liberal nor conservative ideological frameworks. Again, the point in illustrating this example is not to argue against ideologies *per se*, but rather to encourage you as a rational, thoughtful individual to be wary of accepting any ideology with an uncritical eye, and to be willing to break free from ideological shackles when you find that your own personal beliefs do not perfectly match those of any one ideology.

IDEOLOGICAL SPECTRUMS

Most societies feature a political spectrum—the breadth of legitimate, competing ideologies that exist within a society's political system. In general terms, political spectrums may be conceptualized as existing on a plane from the far-left, (e.g., Marxism) to the far-right (e.g., fascism). In between may lay a number of relatively more moderate or centrist ideologies, including modern liberalism and contemporary conservatism.

Three important observations are in order regarding this typical political spectrum. First, in totalitarian states (e.g., Marxist states such as the former Soviet Union and fascist states such as Hitler's Germany), only one legal party is permitted. The ruling party has a complete monopoly over political life, and the ideological spectrum is restricted to the ideology of the ruling party. Thus, despite the fact that the ruling parties in the former Soviet Union and Nazi Germany were on opposite ends of the political spectrum—the Soviet Communist Party on the far-left; the German National Socialist Party (the Nazi Party) on the far-right—their systems were similar in that both were totalitarian states in which no official ideological competition was permitted (although differences and disagreements did occasionally erupt *within* the ruling parties of each state).

Second, in comparing the ideological spectrums of multiple states it becomes clear that significant differences can exist, even among states that normally are lumped together as being in the same category of political system. For example, in comparing developed democracies, on balance the ideological spectrum in the US is narrower than in many other developed democracies around the world. Whereas the political spectrums of European democracies are often broad enough to include parties fairly far out on the left (socialists of various stripes) and the right (ultranationalists) of the spectrum, in the US the ideological spectrum is generally bracketed by modern liberalism to the left and contemporary conservatism to the right—ideologies and parties farther out on the spectrum tend to gain minimal traction in the American system. These differences between states may be pegged to a combination of factors: political culture (it is often argued that Americans have a particularly pragmatic streak—what we might call in the modern pop cultural parlance a "Git-r-Done" attitude that leaves little room for lofty ideological debates), and a two-party system in America that forces the Democrats and Republicans to move toward the center of the political spectrum in order to maximize their support among the voters.

A third observation highlights the dynamic nature of ideological spectrums. What it means to be a liberal or conservative in a society can change markedly over time as social norms and values change. For example, at one time in America it was not necessarily unacceptable for a self-professed liberal to support the concept of "separate but equal." Under this maxim, although it was a moral and legal imperative that blacks receive equal treatment, it was also thought to be both moral and legal to enforce laws that kept the races separate. No liberal—and for that matter thankfully few Americans—would make such an argument today.

On the other hand, for nearly a century and a half conservatives held steadfast in their argument that the government should not intervene in economic affairs. Even during economic crises—including the onset of the Great Depression in 1929—conservatives retained their core belief in nonintervention by the state in the economy. Conservatives assumed that a free market was naturally self-correcting. President Herbert Hoover, a conservative Republican, refused to budge from this sacred tenet of conservatism, even as tens of millions of Americas suffered from the impact of the Great Depression, The election of a liberal Democrat, Franklin D. Roosevelt (FDR), to the presidency in 1932 opened the door to Roosevelt's New Deal policies of big government programs and spending as a way to ease the pain of the Great Depression on average citizens. Some of the concrete policies that emerged during this time—including the Social Security program—became widely accepted positive examples of "Big Government" in action. Only very recently has a new conservative movement emerged—the Tea Party—whose members actively oppose government-funded mandates such as Social Security and Medicare.

The dynamism of ideology means that our definition of certain ideologies shifts over time. The path of development for ideologies is shaped not just by evolving conditions and the discourse among competing ideologies within society, but also by critiques from within an ideological school of thought. In the discussion that follows we shall examine the development and evolution of each of the major contemporary political ideologies, beginning with liberalism.

Liberal Ideology: Classical Liberalism

We have discussed the fact that ideologies emerge within a specific historical context. One of the key impulses that spark ideological development is the desire by a class or element within society to offer a critique of the *status quo* and a blueprint for a new set of political, economic, and social principles that serve the interests and goals of that class. So it is with the ideology of liberalism.

At its core, liberalism when first constructed represented a critical analysis of, and an alternative to, the systems of feudalism and monarchy in Europe. Under the feudal system, monarchs parceled out land to elite members of the noble class. These "lords of the manor" then created arrangements under which serfs (lower class peasants) were forced to work the land and to provide a form of security for the manor, in exchange for which the lord provided food and security for his peasants.

By its very nature, the feudal system privileged the interests of rural elites, not just at the expense of their surfs, but also at the expense of urban centers. However, by the 17th century trade and industry had accelerated in the cities to the point that important new urban classes were emerging whose interests were not served by the feudal system. Meanwhile, as new wealth was created in the cities, monarchs saw an opportunity to tap into expanding urban revenues.

The new urban class of merchants and traders chafed under the restrictions of feudalism. They desired greater economic freedoms, including the right of rural peasants to seek their economic livelihood in the cities. In truth, the demand that serfs be granted the right to choose their place and type of work was linked to the basic self-interest of urban elites to expand their potential labor pool. Moreover, urban merchants, traders, and industrialists began to demand political freedom—the right to representation—as a trade-off for the state siphoning off some of their revenues through the process of taxation. These two policy prescriptions—economic freedom for all, and representative government—became the touchstones of classical liberalism.

As with any ideology, the specific policy proposals that were set forth by classical liberals were framed within a set of philosophically-derived assumptions. As we discussed in Chapter 2, the most important early contributor to classical liberal thought was the British political philosopher John Locke. From Locke's writings flow the central tenets of classical liberalism:

1. The belief that the rights of individuals are natural and inalienable. The state is neither the source of rights nor does it have the legitimate authority to deny the rights of its citizens.
2. The concept of popular sovereignty, which refers to the belief that the state and its political leadership derive its right to rule from the consent of the governed, rather than from any divine source. Popular sovereignty is the conceptual wellspring of democratic government.
3. Because individual rights are natural and inalienable, and given the presumption of popular sovereignty, government powers are limited to those that are necessary to maintain the liberty and freedom of citizens.
4. All people are born rational and equal. They deserve equality of opportunity, which refers to the equal right of all members of society to pursue their self-interests and goals. Equality of opportunity is linked to the concept of negative freedom, which defines individual freedom as the right to be free from government intervention. It is important to note that while classical liberalism argues that all individuals have the equal right to pursue their interests and goals free from government interference, it does not argue for equality of outcome. Inequality of outcome between individuals across society is moral and just as long as equality of opportunity exists.[2]

Given the fact that classical liberalism is based on the assumption of the inalienable rights of rational individuals to pursue their self-defined interests with as little government intervention as possible, it not surprising that classical liberalism is inextricably linked in the economic realm to free market capitalism. The classical liberals' free market economic prescription is best summarized in the notion of *laissez faire*: a system in which the state takes a hands-off approach, permitting all economic actors to pursue their self-interests through free competition. The individual who is most closely associated with promoting the superiority of the free market model is the Scottish philosopher and political economist Adam Smith.

In his seminal 1776 treatise *The Wealth of Nations* Adam Smith made a forceful case for the superiority of an economic system based on competition, free markets, and self-interest. According to Smith, everyone benefits more from a system that prizes the self-centered pursuit of individual wealth than they do from a system that is purportedly designed explicitly with the goal of promoting the common good. In one of the most famous passages from *The Wealth of Nations*, Smith summarizes his argument regarding self-interest thusly: "It is not from the benevolence of the butcher, the brewer, or the baker that we expect our dinner, but from their regard to their own interest."[3]

What precisely is the process by which the self-interested behavior by all the actors in a free market results in a positive outcome for all of society? According to Smith, an "invisible hand" exists in a market system, an unperceived mechanism by which what is good for the individual's economic self-interest is also good for the community.[4] Consumers need and desire high quality goods and services at low prices; producers desire to maximize their individual wealth, and in order to do so have an incentive to produce the best quality goods at the lowest prices, thereby both increasing their own market share (which is the driving impulse for self-motivated producers and sellers) while serendipitously also meeting the self-interests of consumers. In this way, a sort of natural equilibrium is achieved in a free market system in which the self-interests of each actor contributes to the interests of a community as a whole.

It is important to recognize that, contrary to the assumptions and claims made by many modern-day proponents of Adam Smith's model, Smith himself was quite wary of the negative effects of unfettered free market capitalism. Specifically, Smith warned against the tendency among capitalist economic elites to conspire together to clamp down on labor costs, to set prices, or to maximize their control over markets to the point of achieving a monopoly over a particular economic activity. "People of the same trade seldom meet together even for merriment and diversion, but the conversation ends in a conspiracy against the public, or in some contrivance to raise prices." The state, then, must play a crucial role in mitigating the negative impact of free market activity."[5] "The road to the free market," observed the 20th century political economist Karl Polanyi "was kept open by an enormous increase in continuous, centrally organized and controlled interventionism (by the state)."[6]

Smith championed certain policies that would surprise and even unsettle modern advocates of free market capitalism—those contemporary conservatives who see themselves as his intellectual heirs. The gap between Adam Smith the man and Adam Smith the myth is perhaps most glaring on the subject of taxes. Smith was an early advocate of a progressive tax system, in which the amount of taxes paid by members of society is pegged to their wealth. According to Smith, "The subjects of every state ought to contribute toward the support of the government, as nearly as possible, in proportion to their respective abilities, that is, in proportion to the revenue which they respectively enjoy under the protection of the state." He goes on to argue "It is not very unreasonable that the rich should contribute to the public expense, not only in proportion to their revenue, but something more than in that proportion." More generally, Smith was of the view that taxes are a civic duty to be carried out with pride: "Every tax, however, is to the person who pays it a badge, not of slavery but of liberty."[7] Such statements of support for taxation do not at all correspond with the view of contemporary conservatives, who, as we shall see later in this chapter, are passionate critics of taxation as one manifestation of big government.

Liberal Ideology: Modern Liberalism

One negative condition of free market economics that Adam Smith did not fully anticipate was its impact on the distribution of wealth within society. As England industrialized and became a more developed, urban society the gap between the haves and the have-nots was growing. "To the bewilderment of thinking minds, unheard-of wealth turned out to be inseparable from unheard-of poverty."[8] As the plight of the poor, particularly in the cities, became more obvious, members of an ideological faction within the Liberal School pushed back against what they viewed as the destructive excesses of unrestrained capitalism. From this critique of *laissez faire* economics modern liberalism was born.

As early as the late 18th century, a radical element within classical liberalism was beginning to express some shockingly dismissive opinions regarding the growing number of poor in their midst. One such militant classical liberal was William Townsend. Voicing his support for repeal of the Poor Laws that were designed to assist the underprivileged in Britain, Townsend stated "Hunger will tame the fiercest animals, it will teach decency and civility, obedience and subjection, to the most perverse."[9] Townsend also darkly observed "Speculation apart, it is a fact, that in England, we have more than we can feed, and many more than we can profitably employ under the present system of law."[10] It would seem that Townsend's prescription for what to do with the burgeoning underclass in England was simple—workers should be paid whatever wage, and work under whatever conditions their employers deemed appropriate, and if they did not like it they should be left to starve.

The erosion of the system of Poor Laws opened the door to an era of unrestrained free market capitalism. Reform-minded activists feared that a society was emerging in which "the workers were physically dehumanized (and) the owning classes were morally degraded. The traditional unity of a Christian society was giving place to a denial of responsibility on the part of the well-to-do for the conditions of their fellows."[11]

Prominent among those who expressed concern over the potential negative impact of unfettered free market economics was the British philosopher Thomas Hill Green. In his writings, Green took particular aim at the classical liberals' attachment to "negative freedom," a term that defines freedom as the right of an individual to be free from government intervention in one's personal life. Negative freedom assumes that a free individual is driven by his or her own self-interests.

In response, Green offered the concept of "positive freedom" as the fairest and most productive way to achieve the common good.[12] Green's definition of freedom was similar to Rousseau's concept of the General Will (*see* Chapter 2).[13] Freedom, in Green's view, could only be achieved in a society in which the collective interests of all within the community were promoted and protected. "If the ideal of true freedom is the maximum of powers for all members of human society alike to make the best of themselves, we are right in refusing to ascribe the glory of freedom to a state in which the apparent elevation of the few is founded on the degradation of the many."[14]

In practical terms, positive freedom requires that government play a more active role in protecting the less fortunate and in leveling the playing field so that all members of society may truly have an equal chance to be successful and to contribute to the common good. The impact of this revised notion of freedom can be seen in certain policies that were adopted in the industrializing countries during the late 19th century and stretching into the 20th century, including laws dealing with such issues as child labor, food safety, and the rights of workers to form unions.

In the United States, the momentum for social reform picked up steam with the election of Roosevelt in 1932, following the onset of the Great Depression in 1929. FDR sought to expand the authority of the federal government as a tool for lessening the economic hardships experienced by the masses as a result of the economic crisis. His New Deal package featured a number of social welfare programs, including the creation of the social security system, the passage of laws designed to protect the rights of workers, and the creation of several programs designed to provide employment to the jobless.

The New Deal was not without its critics. Some on the far-right criticized it for expanding the scope of the federal government's authority over activities that had traditionally been either unregulated or had fallen under the jurisdiction of the individual states. Meanwhile, some on the far-left argued that the New Deal was simply a thinly-veiled effort by a failing capitalist state to forestall full-scale revolution and to preserve the long-term viability of capitalism through the implementation of reforms. Yet, most Americans believed the New Deal had staved off a complete economic catastrophe, and in fact that they had benefited from the programs that FDR created.

The New Deal kicked off an era in American political history in which modern liberalism was ascendant. The high-water mark for the modern liberal movement in America occurred in the 1960s when President Lyndon Johnson announced his "Great Society" program. Against the backdrop of a booming American economy, Johnson argued that the country could afford to fight a sustained battle against the tenacious problem of poverty in sections of America's urban centers and rural countryside.

In 1963, an astonishing 22.2% of the American population still lived below the poverty line.[15] Lyndon Johnson sought to take advantage of the political momentum created by his landslide victory over Republican Barry Goldwater in the 1964 election to declare war on poverty in the United States. Johnson crafted policies intended to promote better educational outcomes among poor children (the Head Start Program), to extend health care assistance to the elderly (Medicare) and the poor (Medicaid), to offer job training to the poor, and to provide greater levels of protection to American consumers against fraud and unsafe products. Johnson's administration was also responsible for the passage of a series of civil rights acts designed to guarantee the voting rights of African-Americans and to outlaw discrimination in employment and housing.

The record of Johnson's ambitious program was mixed. Clearly, some impressive gains were made in the War on Poverty. The overall poverty rate in America declined to 12.6% by 1970.[16] The number of black Americans living in poverty was halved between 1960 and 1968, falling from 55% to 27%. Infant mortality among the poor fell by one-third between 1965 and 1975.[17] Many of the key programs that were at the core Johnson's Great Society—for example, Head Start, Medicare, and Medicaid—have become widely accepted pillars of the US government's social welfare network.

Despite these advances, even before the decade of the 1960s ended a growing number of Americans were questioning the effectiveness of Johnson's Great Society. Tens of billions of dollars were spent on the War on Poverty. Although the poverty rate declined, it remained stubbornly high, especially in the African-American and Native-American communities. There was growing frustration, particularly among some white Americans, over the sense that Johnson's programs were really not delivering enough "bang for the buck" when it came to spending tax dollars on reducing poverty.

The late 1960s in America saw the beginning of a backlash against Johnson's version of modern liberalism. Increasing numbers of Americans felt under siege at home from the combination of urban riots and anti-war protests. Critics on the right felt that too much taxpayers' money was being spent on wasteful big government programs that were producing modest improvements at best. Critics on the left charged that the Johnson administration's building commitment to the war in Vietnam undermined the ability of the federal government to fully fund its anti-poverty programs. Still others, as represented by critics such as the Democratic Senator Robert Kennedy, argued that Johnson's programs needed to be dramatically reshaped in a way that would emphasize job training and education as a better alternative to welfare, while also shifting responsibility for implementing government programs away from the federal government and toward local communities. Clearly, the political base of support for Johnson's Great Society was rapidly eroding.

In a dramatic reversal, the modern liberal ideology, which had seemingly reached its peak of influence and popularity with Johnson's overwhelming victory in 1964, faltered so badly within 4 years time that Republican Richard Nixon captured the presidency in 1968. Modern Liberalism's age of political dominance was drawing to a close; conservatism's rise to prominence was underway, although it would be a brand of conservatism that was fundamentally different from the original version of that ideology.

Conservative Ideology: Traditional Conservatism

In the last quarter of the 18ᵗʰ century classical liberalism seemed to be on the march. In France, revolutionaries, spurred by classical liberal notions of universal, natural rights as expressed in the slogan "Liberty, Equality, and Fraternity," destroyed the absolutist monarchy of Louis XVI. Meanwhile, in America, revolutionary colonists proclaimed in 1776 in the Declaration of Independence that "all men are created equal," and secured their independence from Britain.

These events, and in particular the revolution in France, sent shock waves across Europe. Long-held assumptions regarding the legitimate role of traditional institutions ranging from the monarchy to the church to the landed elite class seemed under assault. The threat that the masses would be shaken from centuries of slumber caused fear and consternation among *status quo* oriented elites.

One of those who sensed this threat was the British writer Edmund Burke. For Burke, the most important lesson of the French Revolution was that the authority vacuum that exists when traditional institutions of power are destroyed creates a breeding ground for unrestrained chaos and violence. In France, the classical liberal dreams of democratic governance under the banner of "Liberty, Equality, and Fraternity" were quickly replaced by a Reign of Terror in which radical revolutionaries executed tens of thousands of their fellow citizens for being "enemies of the revolution." If this was the typical outcome of classical liberalism's call for equality and liberty, Burke wanted nothing to do with it.

Burke's critique of the French revolutionary experience laid the groundwork for what became the first organized ideological alternative to classical liberalism: traditional conservatism. Burke fretted over the effects of empowering average citizens with the belief that they are fully equal with traditional elites. "The effect of liberty to individuals is that they may do what they please; we ought to see what it will please them to do, before we risk congratulations which may be soon turned into complaints."[18] Moreover, Burke viewed the preservation of dominant roles for traditional institutions of power—and most particularly the hereditary monarchy and the church—as being essential for maintaining stability and morality in society.

At the core of Burke's worldview was his belief that inequality, not equality, was the natural state of things. The philosophical roots of Burke's assumptions regarding inequality within society can be traced back to Plato. Recall from our discussion in Chapter 2 that Plato believed that the best type of political system—an Aristocracy—is comprised of three horizontal, descending layers of citizens: leaders, soldiers, and workers. From Burke's perspective, the preservation of class distinctions across society was essential for the maintenance of order and stability. As one late 20ᵗʰ century scholar observed: "Burke holds that the legitimate and natural social inequalities, such as those found in class distinctions within society, are conducive to the common good."[19]

It is important to recognize that Burke was not inalterably opposed to political, economic, and social change. However, he did support the preservation of traditional institutions of power until such time as they proved inadequate for dealing with evolving conditions within society. At that point, Burke believed, gradual reforms should be implemented, with the goal being to enact just enough reforms to reestablish stability, without going so far as to bring about radical change or revolution.

Interestingly, the traditional conservative's support for gradual reform as a way to address building social problems, while also dampening the possibility of radical revolution, meant that the first impulse toward social welfare programs came not from the liberal school (recall that classical liberals argued for a "hands-off" approach by the government to the economy), but from traditional conservatives. Philosophically, the traditional conservatives support for social welfare programs was linked to the feudal concept of *Noblesse Oblige*, under which it was understood that lords had the responsibility to provide a basic quality of life, including security, to their serfs.

Beyond moral considerations, the traditional conservatives sought to use social welfare programs as a means to manage change in society. One important early example of such laws being implemented by traditional conservatives were the Poor Laws that were put in place in England, highlighted by the Speenhamland Laws, which guaranteed a minimum wage to rural workers, pegged to the price of bread and size of the family.[20] The purpose of the Speenhamland Laws extended beyond moral concern for the plight of the rural poor: it was also intended to slow the migration of peasant workers from the countryside to the cities, and in the broadest sense to dampen the possibility of revolution in England against the backdrop of breathtakingly rapid social and economic change. On that final point—reducing revolutionary pressure inside of Britain—Speenhamland was a success.[21]

By the 1830s, however, opposition to the Speenhamland Laws in particular, and to the concept of government-mandated social welfare for the poor in general, was building. The newly empowered middle class in Britain opposed the Speenhamland Laws because they saw it as creating an impediment to a fully competitive labor market, which was viewed as being an essential component of an efficient and productive capitalist economy.[22] The gutting of the social welfare system in Britain that began in the 1830s ushered in a period characterized by the operation of a nearly pure version of *laissez faire* economics, and signaled the decline of traditional conservatism.

Conservative Ideology: Contemporary Conservatism

The process by which ideologies develop and evolve over time has been described as a "discourse."[23] Ideologies are created and change in response to the arguments being put forward by advocates of competing ideologies, as well as in reaction to events that are occurring within society. The development of contemporary conservatism is an excellent example of this process.

During the period of time stretching from the 1930s through the 1960s, conservatism was on the defensive and in decline, at least partially because it did not provide a clear, persuasive ideological alternative to modern liberalism. In America, the seeds of the comeback of conservatism were actually sewn in the crushing defeat that Barry Goldwater suffered in the 1964 presidential election. Goldwater was an unapologetic champion of a new brand of conservatism, one that emphasized a strong defense, defeating communism around the world, and a broad suspicion regarding the expanding size and role of the federal government, including in the area of civil rights. Although Lyndon Johnson won in a landslide in 1964—capturing 61% of the popular vote, and 486 popular Electoral College votes to just 52 for Goldwater-Goldwater's platform captured the imagination of a new generation of conservative activists and politicians.

Among the hallmarks of the emerging contemporary conservatism was a faith in free market economics as the best engine for creating economic growth and prosperity. Contemporary conservatives resented the national government's active intervention in economic affairs. In that sense, Goldwater's brand of conservatism remains little changed since the 1960s.

It is in the area of social policy that a crucial turn took place, one that brought contemporary conservatism back to its classical roots. Goldwater was a social *libertarian*, believing that just as the government should avoid interfering in economic affairs, so the government should steer clear of intervening in the right of individuals to make decisions that affect their private lives. For example, he favored the right of a woman to choose for herself whether or not to have an abortion. Ironically, Goldwater's combination of *laissez faire* economics and social libertarianism mirrors the views of the original version of classical liberalism. By the 1960s, what it meant to be "conservative" or "liberal" had been turned inside out.

A key shift in contemporary conservatism took place in the 1970s and 1980s. Goldwater's libertarianism lost ground within the conservative movement, and was replaced by a reemphasis on the importance of traditional moral values. Led by Christian fundamentalist pastors such as Jerry Falwell and his Moral Majority group, conservatism became equated with the belief that the state had a right and obligation to intervene when necessary in order to preserve traditional values. With the ascendancy of the Christian right as an important constituency of conservative Republicans, contemporary conservatism became firmly anchored in three pillars: an emphasis on strong defense and defeating the threat from Soviet communism; support for the free market, unencumbered as much as possible from government interference; and support for government intervention in defense of traditional moral values on issues ranging from abortion to gay rights.

The election of Margaret Thatcher as prime minister of Great Britain in 1979, followed by the election of Ronald Reagan to the presidency in the US in 1980, highlighted the growing power and popularity of the contemporary conservative ideology, in America and elsewhere. Contemporary conservatism's emphasis on smaller government, tax cuts, increased military spending and defense of traditional values has resonated with a significant number of voters. At the same time, since the 1980s conservatives have done an effective job of convincing the voting public that modern liberals, by definition, support high taxes and big government, and are weak on defense.

Many observers—including some on the right-wing of the American political spectrum—have argued that the Republican Party during the presidency of George W. Bush lost touch with some of its conservative roots. Specifically, government spending increased during the decade of the 2000s, and the federal budget deficit and national debt sky-rocketed. In response to these developments, the Tea Party movement was born. Tea Party activists advocate reduced taxes and smaller government. While the Tea Party movement has reenergized contemporary conservatism in the United States, whether the Tea Party is a permanent fixture on the American political scene that will come to dominate and define a new form of conservatism, or a temporary phenomenon that will fairly quickly fade away, remains to be seen.

Marxist Ideology: Classical Marxism

The development of free market capitalism caused dramatic social and economic changes. As we have discussed in this chapter, the concept of social welfare emerged in response to these changes. Whereas the traditional conservatives supported welfare measures as a means of attempting to protect the economic, social, and political *status quo* in the face of the classical liberal onslaught, modern liberals prescribed regulation and reform as the best way to address some of the economic and social problems that erupted within a capitalist system based on pure classical liberalism, while at the same time preserving and even promoting the progress of a more benign form of capitalism.

Modern liberalism was—and is—most attractive to moderates within society. Moderates by definition "are fundamentally satisfied with society . . . although they agree that there is room for improvement and recognize several specific areas in need of modification. However, they insist that changes should be made gradually and that no change should be so extreme as to disrupt the society."[24]

Radicals, on the other hand, advocate rapid, fundamental change within society. Rejecting the usefulness of reforms, radicals support revolution as the necessary means by which the basic foundations of society can be transformed. The most important and influential revolutionary ideology to emerge in the industrial era was Marxism.

Karl Marx (1818–1883), was born in Germany. During Marx's lifetime much of Europe was experiencing dramatic social and economic change and disruption as a result of the Industrial Revolution. Working closely with his friend and benefactor Friedrich Engels, Marx fostered a theory of revolution in which the urban working class (the *proletariat*) would unite to overthrow the urban capitalist elite (the *bourgeoisie*).

Marxist ideology is based on the belief that economic conditions are the driving force in history. According to Marx, history inevitably unfolds in a series of stages, each of which is characterized by a clash between economic classes. "The history of all societies hitherto," argued Marx and Engels in *The Communist*

Manifesto, "is the history of class struggle."[25] The triumph of one economic class over another in society lays the groundwork for the next stage in history.

Under Marx's model, the first stage of history was characterized by primitive communism; the second was marked by slavery; the third stage of history was dominated by feudalism; the fourth stage of history—and the one which was current during Marx's lifetime—was capitalism; the fifth stage would be socialism, when the state, under the authority of the working class, would centralize control over the means of production; and the final, utopian stage of history, would be advanced communism, when all property would be communally-owned, equality would prevail, and the state would no longer need to exist as an instrument of authority and coercion.

Marxism is very specific about the conditions that must be present for the workers' revolution to take place, and the precise reasons why the working class will inevitably revolt against the capitalist class. Marx contended that a revolution by the proletariat—the urban factory workers—would occur when capitalist societies achieved the advanced industrialized stage of capitalism. It was only under the conditions of advanced industrialized capitalism that the proletariat would feel so exploited by their capitalist bosses who sought to wring from them the highest levels of productivity while paying the lowest possible wages, and alienated from their labor due to the mind-numbing tedium of factory work, that they would unite in common cause to overthrow the capitalist system.

In 1848, much of Europe was convulsed by a series of uprisings that shook the foundations of many traditional European monarchies to the core. It is inaccurate to see the revolutions of 1848 as springing forth from Marxism, which was then still in its early stages of development. However, Marx and his colleague Engels were correct in their view that the spark for revolutionary change in 1848 could be traced to objective economic circumstances that severely hurt the working class. A number of negative economic developments, including widespread unemployment, intolerable working conditions for many of the urban workers who were employed, and massive food shortages in rural areas of the continent combined to create a "perfect storm" of catalysts for discontent. Because the European monarchies denied the masses any ability to make their grievances heard and shape the policies of the state through peaceful means, revolution was the only means available for alleviating the pain they were suffering from the economic conditions of the day.

Ultimately, the revolutions of 1848 were effectively suppressed by the governments of Europe. Still, in the working-class uprisings across Europe in 1848 one finds echoes of the famous call to revolution issued by Marx and Engels in the final sentence of *The Communist Manifesto*: "Let the ruling classes tremble at a Communistic revolution. The proletarians have nothing to lose but their chains. They have a world to win. Workingmen of all countries, unite!"[26] The fact that the first efforts at mobilizing mass working-class revolution had been defeated did not deter Marx and his followers from believing that, inevitably, irreversibly, history was on their side. Just as the previous stages of history had dissolved, Marxists believed that so too would capitalism crumble, to be replaced by a socialist state, and then finally by the communist utopia.

Marx never lived to see a successful revolution in his name. Nearly 30 years after his death, Czarist Russia collapsed under the weight of the worker's revolution. Ironically, Russia's level of development seemed to make it the least likely target among the European powers for a Marxist revolt. Russia in the early 20th century lagged significantly behind the more developed European states in terms of industrialization, and certainly had come nowhere close to achieving the advanced stage of industrialized capitalism that was supposed to create the conditions under which the proletariat would rise up. The stubborn persistence of capitalism across the rest of developed Europe in the face of objective conditions that Marx predicted should have brought capitalism's downfall, and the growing impatience of revolutionary elites, led to the first important modification to classical Marxism: Leninism.

Marxist Ideology: Marxism-Leninism

Marx had great faith in the ability of workers to develop the class consciousness necessary to mobilize and carry out the great proletarian revolution. For Marx, revolution was the inevitable outcome of the working class educating itself about its plight and mobilizing itself for successful revolutionary action. Essentially, the workers were capable of guiding themselves toward Marx's utopian vision.

The Russian revolutionary Vladimir Lenin, while adhering to many of the basic principles of Marxism, nevertheless questioned several key precepts of Marxist ideology. Principally, Lenin did not believe that the workers were capable of organizing themselves for revolution. Although Marx himself believed that a "vanguard of the proletariat" would play a modest role in educating the urban masses as to their plight, he had believed in the ability of the masses to seize control of their own destiny through revolutionary action.

Lenin, on the other hand, thought that the "vanguard of the proletariat" had **the** crucial role to play in organizing, conducting, and winning the revolutionary fight. Under Lenin's version of Marxism, the revolution against capitalism would be won or lost by this elite vanguard. Thus, the capitalist state would be overthrown even before the proletariat had achieved complete class consciousness. The vanguard would then rule the new socialist state while continuing the process of educating the masses and preparing them for their eventual role in ruling the state under the "dictatorship of the proletariat."

In his writings, Lenin also offered a new interpretation of the history of the capitalist state. In attempting to explain the persistence of the capitalist state into the 20th century, Lenin argued that the final stage of the modern capitalist state was not advanced industrialization, but rather imperialism. Under imperialism, advanced capitalist states competed with each other to maximize their control over colonial resources. Once the supply of untapped colonial territories was exhausted, the advanced capitalist states would then turn on each other in a desperate effort to cannibalize the markets and resources of other advanced capitalist states. In fact, Lenin claimed that World War I was the final showdown between the capitalist powers, and that in its wake socialist movements would seize control over weakened states all across the capitalist world.[27]

Lenin also sought to explain the perplexing issue of why Russia, the most backward, feudalistic, and under-industrialized of European powers was the first capitalist state to be overthrown, thereby laying the groundwork for the Soviet Union. Lenin once more underscored the impact of the cutthroat competition between capitalist states for market shares. In the case of Russia, argued Lenin, the fact that the Czarist monarchy was not in a position to exploit foreign colonies for cheap labor and resources meant that it had to deeply exploit Russia's own workforce in order to compete with the more advanced capitalist colonial powers. According to Lenin's theory, this deeper level of domestic exploitation explained why it was in Russia that the working class, led by the vanguard, rose up to destroy the state.

The changes that Lenin introduced to classical Marxism illustrate once again the close interaction between the "purity" of ideological frameworks and the practical realities of the political world. Lenin refashioned Marxism in an effort to address the ideology's failure to provide a persuasive account or accurate prediction of actual historical developments in the capitalist states. In doing so, he began the process of making Marxism more relevant to the masses of people around the world who toiled in misery in societies that had not yet achieved full levels of industrial development.

Marxist Ideology: Maoism

In its purest form, Marxism stated that society must achieve the advanced industrialized stage of capitalist development for the proletarian revolution to occur. As we discussed in the previous section, Lenin attempted to explain why Russia, a fairly backward country by developed Western standards, had experienced revolution by the proletariat. In Lenin's view, Czarist Russia's efforts to keep up with the more advanced capitalist powers caused the Russian state to brutally exploit its domestic working class, which became the spark for revolutionary action. Out of the ashes of that revolution was born the socialist state, in the Soviet Union.

In aftermath of the Russian Revolution, Marxists in China worked to organize a communist uprising. Led by Mao Tse-tung, the Chinese revolutionaries followed Marx's prescription by attempting to mobilize the urban proletariat. Mao and his followers quickly discovered, however, that the number of factory workers in China's cities was far too small to launch a successful revolution against the nationalist state in China. Mao's early efforts at fostering revolution were easily crushed by the Chinese government.

Bloodied but not bowed, Mao and his supporters retreated to the countryside. There, Mao set about the task of reworking Marxism. Much as Lenin had done in Russia, Mao responded to the practical challenges and pragmatic realities of China's socioeconomic system by offering a revised version of Marxism that was designed to appeal specifically to the teaming masses of peasants. He knew that in a country in which the large majority of individuals were landless peasants and where most of the land was owned by a small number of wealthy elites the peasant class in the countryside was the segment of society best positioned to carry out a revolution against the capitalist state. Thus, Mao made the case that, whereas in advanced states the urban working class would rise up against the factory owners to break the shackles of exploitation, the exploitation that the peasant classes in China suffered at the hand of the landed elites created conditions that were ripe for a rural-based, working-class revolution.

Hounded by the Nationalist army of Chinese leader Chiang Kai-shek, Mao and his forces were forced to retreat further into the hinterlands. In 1934, they embarked on The Long March, an epic, year-long 6,000 mile journey into the mountains of northern China. Over 100,000 supporters of Mao set out on The Long March; only 35,000 survived. Mobilizing a peasant-based army, Mao launched his revolution against the Nationalist government. After setting aside their differences in order to resist the Japanese occupation during World War Two, the Maoists and Nationalists turned on each other once again after the war. In 1949, Mao and his followers defeated the nationalists, and proclaimed the Peoples Republic of China to be a communist state.

At home in China, Mao's program of "continuous revolution" resulted in a series of cataclysmic policy failures, highlighted between 1956 and 1960 by the "Great Leap Forward," a development strategy under which poorly planned efforts at industrialization and ill-conceived agricultural policies left China's economy reeling, and caused tens of millions to die from starvation. In 1966, Mao organized the disastrous "Cultural Revolution," during which time young radical believers in Mao turned on all those who were suspected of being counter-revolutionaries." By 1969, China was experiencing full-blown chaos and teetering on the brink of civil war; only then did Mao begin to reign in the young radicals.

Despite the domestic chaos inside China caused by Mao's radical policies, his ideological vision of peasant-based revolution struck a cord around the lesser-developed world. Mao's success in converting the enormous sense of frustration among China's rural peasant class into revolutionary action made Maoism, as it became known, tremendously popular among Third World radicals. Maoism told the lower classes in societies that had yet to achieve advanced industrialization that they too had the right to throw off the shackles of exploitation.

Ironically, the popularity of Maoism caused tension between China and the Soviet Union, as each of the world's great socialist powers attempted to export its brand of revolutionary fervor around the world. This tension created a schism within the socialist bloc that the United States was able to exploit. By the 1970s, American President Richard Nixon was able use his policy of *detente* to pursue a strategy in which the US had warmer relations with the USSR and China than the two socialist states had with each other.

In the aftermath of the collapse of the Soviet Union in 1991, old-style Soviet Marxist-Leninism was largely discredited. Meanwhile, China began to pursue a policy of "Market Stalinism," in which the government in Beijing moved toward greater economic freedom while still maintaining a tight control over the political system. Still, Maoism remains a popular tool for mobilizing peasants to revolutionary action, particularly in some lesser-developed parts of Asia.

Marxist Ideology Diluted: Democratic Socialism

In the abstract, Marxist ideology seems to reflect the democratic ideal of equality among all individuals within the community. In practice, however, many self-proclaimed socialist states have been characterized by totalitarian regimes in which all power was centered in the hands of a single ruling party. Democratic socialism emerged in Western societies during the 20th century as a sort of middle group option between what many leftists saw as capitalism's inherent tendencies toward exploitation and socioeconomic inequality, and the dictatorial, totalitarian nature of a number of socialist states.

Unlike Marxists, democratic socialists believe that some economic activities need not be nationalized, although they do believe that the state should own the most critical sectors of the economy, including key industries. The underlying principles of democratic socialism include economic and political equality, support for a robust welfare state, communal ownership of critical economic sectors by the state, protecting the environment, the provision of free public education as an essential pillar of a democratic society, and the achievement of political change through the democratic political process—that is, free, fair, open, and competitive elections.[28] Perhaps more than any other element the commitment to change through the ballot box distinguishes democratic socialism from more traditional versions of socialism. Whereas Marxists believe that change can only be achieved through revolution (which is likely to be a violent and bloody affair) democratic socialists believe that effective change can take place via the peaceful process of voting. For Marxists, change relies on bullets not ballots; for democratic socialists, change should be achieved through ballots not bullets.

Democratic socialism has been an influential political ideology in Europe. For example the Labour Party in Great Britain has long defined itself as a democratic socialist party. Clause 4 of the Labour Party constitution states: "The Labour Party is a democratic socialist party. It believes that by the strength of our common endeavour we achieve more than we achieve alone . . . ."[29] It is important to note, however, that beginning in the 1990s the Labour Party moved to the center in terms of its support of free market principles.

On the other hand, despite charges from some on the right in the United States that the Democratic Party is "socialist" or "democratic socialist" in its ideology, it is clear that, judging by the objective, scholarly definitions of those words, the Democratic Party, while moderate to left-leaning by American standards, in no way fits the definition of either socialism or democratic socialism. The Democrats generally do not support direct government ownership of the means of production in any sector of the economy. Nor do the health care reforms that were passed in 2010 mandate a government-run health care system. Thus, Democrats in the US are neither "communists," nor "socialists," nor "democratic socialists," just as it is incorrect for Democrats and those farther on the left of the American political spectrum to label the Republicans as "fascists."

Fascism

As a political ideology, fascism developed much later in history than liberalism, conservatism, or Marxism. Although it is clear that concepts such as Darwin's 19th century theory of Survival of the Fittest helped foster fascist thought, it was not until the 20th century that fascism burst on the international arena as an alternative to the three existing major ideologies. Gaining footing first in Italy in the 1920s and then spreading to Germany in the 1930s, by the 1940s and World War II, fascism was engaged in a life-and-death struggle for global ideological dominance, primarily with liberalism and Marxism.

Fascism differs from the other ideologies we've discussed in some very crucial ways. Most importantly, fascism is more an *ad hoc* compilation of quasi-scientific and culturally specific claims than it is a coherent political ideology. As we have seen, liberalism, conservatism, and Marxism were based on clear, objective, assumptions about certain universal truths. For classical liberals, the universal truth was that all humans are created equal and have the natural right to as much freedom of choice in their lives as possible. For traditional conservatives, the universal truth was that humans are inherently unequal, and that those who are born superior have the right and responsibility to govern in the name of stability and the public good. For the original Marxists, the universal truth was that the urban proletariat will be so exploited and alienated under advanced industrialized capitalism that they will organize and pull-off a successful revolution against the capitalist state.

Fascists, on the other hand, tend to avoid universal assumptions, preferring instead to cobble together particularistic arguments that are specific to their national context. For example, classical liberals believed that all people everywhere are born equal and blessed with inalienable rights of freedom. Traditional conservatives believed inequality was the natural state of things in every society. Traditional Marxists believed that the proletarian revolution would occur in any society that had achieved the conditions that foster revolution. Fascism, on the other hand, was designed to fit the conditions, fears, and goals of a particular national community of people within the boundaries of a specific state. Looked at in another way, liberalism, conservatism, and Marxism make theoretical assumptions about politics and society that cut across national boundaries and therefore at least in theory have universal applicability; fascism by its very nature makes the nation and/or state the primary unit of identity and analysis.

For example, Italian fascism assumed the superiority of the Italian nation and state and German fascism assumed the superiority of the German nation and state. In fact, it is interesting to ponder what would have happened if the Axis powers—Italy and Germany, along with Japan in the Asian Pacific—had been victorious in World War II. It seems likely that Italy and Germany would have turned on one another in the name of settling their respective claims of national superiority. (For its part, Imperial Japan of the 1930s and 1940s, while possessing an emphasis on militarism and regional supremacy that echoed the fascist states of Germany and Italy, also lacked certain critical elements that one tends to find in a fascist state, including domestic rule by a single, well-organized, mass-based totalitarian party led by fascist elites).[30]

It is important to note that, like the other three major ideologies, the content of fascist ideology reflects the historical conditions of its birth. In countries such as Italy and Germany, fascism took hold against the backdrop of social and political instability, which the fascists blamed on democratic and socialist forces within their societies. For example, Italy's fascist leader Benito Mussolini presented national unity to the Italian people as the only alternative to the chaos of democracy and the threat of socialist revolution. After spending his early life as a self-professed socialist, Mussolini seized power in 1922. Only later would Mussolini admit that he had no clear ideological vision in mind when he came to power; his sole focus was on seizing control of Italy. Once in power, Mussolini then made up the content of Italian fascism—its emphasis on the threat from liberal individualism and Soviet-style socialism—on the fly. Only later would he add a professed belief in the racial superiority of the Italian nation.

Adolf Hitler's fascist vision for Germany had its origins in Hitler's bitterness over Germany's surrender at the end of World War I. Like many Germans, Hitler, who was wounded during the war, believed that Germany had not so much lost the war as it had its interests and power undercut by incompetent political leaders and Jewish financiers. Hitler burned with the desire to reassert Germany's rightful place (as he saw it) at the top of the international system, and to punish those whom he perceived as being responsible for Germany's embarrassing defeat in World War I—primarily, in his mind, the Jews.

As Germany sunk into economic ruin and political crisis during the 1920s, the Nazi Party began to gain support among the weary and frightened German public. The Nazis made increasing gains through the democratic electoral process during the 1920s and early 30s. In 1933, the Nazi Party won a clear majority in the German parliament, and Hitler was asked to form a government. Once in power, Hitler moved rapidly to destroy the institutions of German democracy, and to assert his personal control—and that of the Nazi Party—over all the levers of power in Germany.

Over time Hitler developed a clearer set of ideological claims as a means to pursue his political ends. These included proclaiming the nation as being the only legitimate source of identity; positing the racial and cultural superiority of the Aryan nation and German *volk* (people); supporting elitist assumptions that rejected the liberal assertion that all humans are created equal; glorifying military conquest and the use of violence as the only legitimate and useful means for achieving necessary change; and, rejecting the notion of objective scientific knowledge (the Nazis believed that the "truth" was a relative concept that could be rightly manipulated through the use of myths, legends, stereotypes, and the twisting of science for political ends). Thus, for example, the Nazis borrowed liberally from theories such as Social Darwinism and Racial Eugenics to justify a strategy of promoting the purification and advancement of the Aryan race through intermarriage among "pure Aryans" and elimination of non-Aryans through a policy of mass genocide directed against such communities as the Jews, Gypsies, homosexuals, and the mentally and physically challenged.

As the three-cornered ideological fight between democracy, socialism, and fascism played out during World War II, the socialist camp (as represented by the Soviet Union) first aligned with the fascists, only to see Hitler break Germany's non-aggression pact with the Soviet Union in 1941. Thereafter, the Soviet Union had little choice but to join the Western, democratic Allies in their war effort against the fascists in Germany and Italy, and against the militarist, ultranationalists in Japan. The victory by the Allies in 1945 signaled the death knell for fascism as a powerful force in the international system. Although so-called neo-fascists (e.g., Skin Heads in Europe and the United States, and the Ku Klux Klan in America) have been active in some Western countries, fascism no longer represents a major competitor for global ideological domination.

Within the context of ideological discourse, fascism has lost much of its international weight and influence. However, in the aftermath of the 9/11 terrorist attacks the label "fascism" was reintroduced into the contemporary political lexicon. The term "Islamo-fascism" was coined and used, particularly by some on the right-wing of the American political spectrum, who sought to foster an image of an emerging international conflict between the forces of liberty and freedom (as represented by the United States) and the forces of oppression and evil (as represented by radical Islamist militants).

The attempt to equate the Al Qaeda terrorists responsible for 9/11 with fascism is fraught with conceptual pitfalls. For example, fascism as we have seen generally glorifies the superiority of a particular nation of people. Moreover, fascists rely on the organization of a single mass-based party as their primary tool for mobilizing the nation. In the case of Al Qaeda, the "nation" it claims to represent is deeply divided by religious schisms (the major divisions within Islam is between the Sunni majority and the Shi'a minority), as well as by ethnic differences and geographic dispersal (Muslims live in large numbers in the Middle East, Africa, and Asia). Moreover, Al Qaeda is a small terrorist organization, not a mass-based political party. In short, it simply does not fit the conceptual criteria to be accurately labeled a fascist entity.

PUZZLE: IS MARXISM DEAD?

The collapse of the Soviet Union in 1991 represented a critical turning point in history. In the view of many observers, the crumbling of the bipolar distribution of power created a special "unipolar moment" in the international system.[31] Due to the shift toward a unipolar system, the United States would be "significantly unconstrained and enjoy(s) wide discretion in its statecraft."[32] In theory, the rest of the states in the international system had the choice to either "bandwagon" with the United States by forging tighter ties with America, or to "balance" against its power by forging a countervailing alliance. Not surprisingly, in the initial aftermath of the Cold War most states chose to bandwagon—to hitch their wagon to the American star. The widespread preference for this policy first came into sharp focus during the Gulf War crisis of 1990–1991, when dozens of states across the system aligned with the US in its efforts to evict Iraq's army from Kuwait.

On an ideological level, many scholars and pundits believed that the end of the Cold War signaled the inevitable, irreversible triumph of democratic capitalism over the forces of Soviet Marxism. In the words of the scholar Francis Fukuyama, the conclusion of the Cold War marked the "End of History." According to Fukuyama, "The triumph of the West, of the Western *idea* (italics in original), is evident first of all in the total exhaustion of viable systematic alternatives to Western liberalism."[33]

After the demise of the Soviet Union, the death of Marxism was widely acclaimed as both a historical fact and a morally positive development. As one critic of Marxism wrote in 1993: "Marxism is quite simply *wrong*, and thankfully, *dead* (emphasis in original). It is not a viable economic, social, or political theory. Marxism has been repudiated by nearly every country that ever entertained it."[34] Many defenders of Marxism seemed almost apologetic in expressing their views after the collapse of the Soviet Union. Writing in 2000, one proponent of Marxism admitted that he continued to espouse Marxism with "apprehension because we live in a period that is suspicious of visions of alternative futures, skeptical of grand historical narrative, dismissive of materialist explanations, rejecting of class analysis while tolerating capitalism's defects and pathologies as unavoidable and natural."[35]

Is there any reason to question the assumption that Marxism is dead and buried as a viable ideology? Three developments come to mind that at least potentially reassert the continued relevance of some form of Marxism in the contemporary political and economic system. First, several states—including China, Cuba, and North Korea—have clung to key elements of their communist ideological roots even as the tide of history seemed to turn so heavily against them. Of these, the most important and influential in terms of the global stage is China. Clearly, the People's Republic of China has adopted substantial market reforms that have helped to spur impressive rates of economic growth in recent years. At the same time, however, the Chinese Communist Party (CCP) has maintained tight control over the domestic political system in China. And, in reality, the state in China still exercises substantial control over the Chinese economy through a policy that has been branded "mixed-market socialism."[36]

Second, in a number of democratic countries around the international system leftist parties have reasserted themselves in recent years. To be sure, the majority of the new generation of leftist leaders support milder forms of socialism in place of Soviet-style Marxist-Leninism or Chinese Maoism. And, their performance at the ballot box has been uneven, particularly in Europe where strong electoral performances by leftist parties in several elections have been followed by swings back to the right. On the other hand, leftist politicians in several Latin American states came to power in recent years through democratic elections, and have managed to hold on to power for extended periods of time. These left-wing political leaders—including the firebrand president of Venezuela, Hugo Chavez—have gained political support at home by tapping into the growing frustration among the poorer classes in their countries over the perceived failure of the free market system to spread the benefits of economic growth evenly across societies.

Finally, to some pundits and critics of capitalism, the sudden collapse of the economies of the developed capitalist world in 2007–2008 revealed yet again the pain that can be inflicted on average citizens when free market capitalism is permitted to operate without sufficient regulation by the state. On the other hand, it must be noted that it is not at all clear that Marxism—or even mild democratic socialism—will be the preferred elixir for state leaders or the masses in addressing the problems caused by the recent economic collapse. In fact, it is interesting to note that in a number of developed states hardest hit by the global recession, the political pendulum has largely swung back to the right since the onset of the most recent economic crisis. Thus, while Marxists and other leftists may be able to take some comfort in the knowledge that their ideological framework seems to provide a telling critique of the recurring ills of unrestrained free market capitalism, the prescription they offer for those ills may not engender much enthusiasm among the voting publics of the hardest hit Western economies.

On the question of whether Marxism is dead, where do you stand?

Notes

1 Donald E. Ingersoll, Richard K. Matthews, and Andrew Davison, *The Philosophic Roots of Modern Ideology: Liberalism, Conservatism, Fascism, Islamism*, 3rd ed. (Upper Saddle River, NJ: Prentice Hall, 2001), 4.

2 Brigid C. Harrison and Thomas R. Dye, *Power and Society: An Introduction to the Social Sciences*, 11th ed. (Boston: Thomson Wadsworth, 2008), 42–43.

3 Adam Smith, *The Wealth of Nations*, Book I–III (London: Penguin Group, 1999), 119.

4 Smith, *The Wealth of Nations*, 513.

5 Smith, *The Wealth of Nations*, 152.

6 Karl Polanyi, *The Great Transformation* (Boston: Beacon Press, 1957), 140.

7 Smith, *The Wealth of Nations*, Book V.

8 Ibid., 102.

9 Ibid., 113.

10 Ibid., 93.

11 Ibid., 102.

12 T.H. Green, *Lectures on the Principles of Political Obligation and Other Writings* (Cambridge, UK: Cambridge University Press, 1986), 200.

13 Stanford Encyclopedia of Philosophy, "Positive and Negative Liberty," http://plato.stanford.edu/entries/liberty-positive-negative/ (accessed July 28, 2010).

14 Green, *Lectures on the Principles of Political Obligation*, 200.

15 Joseph A. Califano, Jr., "What Was Really Great about the Great Society," *The Washington Monthly Online*, (October 1999), http://www.washingtonmonthly.com/features/1999/9910.califano.html (accessed July 28, 2010).

16 Ibid.

17 Digital History, "The Great Society and the Drive For Black Equality," http://www.digitalhistory.uh.edu/database/article_display_printable.cfm?HHID=372 (accessed July 28, 2010).

18 Edmund Burke, *Reflections on the Revolution in France*, http://www.constitution.org/eb/rev_fran.htm (accessed July 26, 2010).

19 Joseph L. Pappin, III, *The Metaphysics of Edmund Burke* (New York: Fordham University Press, 1993), 133.

20 Polanyi, *The Great Transformation*.

21 Ibid., 93.

22 "Polanyi and the Definition of Capitalism," in *Theory in Economic Anthropology*, ed. J. Ensminger, (Walnut Creek: AltaMira Press, 2001). http://www.anthrobase.com/Links/cache/Polanyi%20and%20the%20definition%20of%20 capitalism.htm (accessed July 27, 2010).

23 Monsoor Moaddel, "Ideology as Episodic Discourse: The Case of the Iranian Revolution," *American Sociological Review* 57 (1992): 360. http://www.jstor.org (accessed July 27, 2010).

24 Leon P. Baradat, *Political Ideologies: Their Origins and Impact*, 8th ed. (Upper Saddle River, NJ: Prentice Hall, 2003), 22–23.

25 Karl Marx and Friedrich Engels, *The Communist Manifesto* (New York: Pocket Books, 1964), 57.

26 Ibid., 116.

27 Baradat, *Political Ideologies*, 197–200.

28 The Socialist Party of Wisconsin, "What is Democratic Socialism," http://expandyourmind.tripod.com/ whatisdemocraticsocialism.htm (accessed August 9, 2010).

29 "Labor Party, Clause IV," http://www.telfordlabourparty.org.uk/site/constitution.htm (accessed August 9, 2010).

30 George M. Wilson, "A New Look at the Problem of Japanese Fascism," *Comparative Studies in Society and History* (1968): 406. http://www.jstor.org/stable/177637?seq=6 (accessed August 11, 2010).

31 Charles Krauthammer, "The Unipolar Moment," *Foreign Affairs* 70 (1990/91): 23–24. http://www.jstor.org (accessed August 11, 2010).

32 Michael Mastanduno, "Preserving the Unipolar Moment," *International Security* 21 (1997): 55. http://www.jstor. org (accessed August 11, 2010).

33 Francis Fukuyama, "The End of History?" in *The New Shape of World Politics*, Rev. ed. (New York: Foreign Affairs, 1999), 1–2.

34 Terry F. Buss, "Marxism is Wrong, and Thankfully, Dead," *The Academy of Management Review* 18 (1993): 10. http://www.jstor.org (accessed August 13, 2010).

35 Michael Burawoy, "Marxism after Communism," *Theory and Society* 29 (2000): 151. http://www.jstor.org (accessed August 13, 2010).

36 Shue Tuck Wong and Sun Sheng Han, "Wither China's Market Economy? The Case of Lijin Zhen," *Geographical Review* 88 (1998): 29.

Part II
POLITICAL INSTITUTIONS

Democratic Governments

THE DEFINITION OF DEMOCRACY

Among the institutions, events, beliefs, and individuals in which many Americans take pride, it may very well be that they are most proud of our political invention, presidential democracy. If you think about it, it is truly amazing how all this came into being. When our Founding Fathers wrote the Constitution, creating the democracy, they engaged in a series of lengthy and contentious debates largely because they were literally creating an unprecedented form of government. About two and a half centuries later, this US-made form of democracy has been exported to many countries in the world with a respectful success in countries such as Brazil and South Korea.

For those who have developed democracy as we have in the US and as they did across the Atlantic Ocean in Western Europe, democracy is one side of coin that we call the Western civilization while capitalism is the other. Not only do many of us have a strong emotional attachment to it, but we take it for granted. Few, if any, will challenge the legitimacy and the virtue of democracy. When was the last time we had a *coup d'etat* proposing an alternative form of government? The fact that a *coup d'etat* is not even a viable option shows us how deeply democracy is rooted in our country. Now, ask yourself if you like democracy. The answer may come easily and promptly. Now ask yourself another question, "What is democracy?"

What is democracy? Some may recall President Lincoln's famous quote from his Gettysburg address, "government of the people, by the people, for the people." Many students use this phrase to discuss the nature of democracy because this is very intuitive. According to this, democracy is different from monarchy because the sovereignty belongs not to monarchs, but to the people. It also addresses the fact that democracy allows the people to participate. For this, we may assume Lincoln meant to say election. Finally, democracy has a purpose, the welfare of the people, not king or God. This is a good start, but are we ready to discuss the definition of democracy now? Not yet? Well then, let's begin with a classical book of political science to explore its definition.

In his classic work, *Capitalism, Socialism, and Democracy*, Joseph Schumpeter begins with his introduction of a traditional definition of democracy. According to him, the 18th century philosophy generally defines democracy as "institutional arrangement for arriving at political decisions which realizes the common good by making the people itself decide issues through the election of individuals who are to assemble in order to carry out its will."[1] There are two major elements in this definition: general will and election. The first seems to be a part that resonates well with Lincoln's definition, "for the people" and again makes for intuitive sense. It is likely that many of the readers will accept this notion of the common good. Now, if you think about the common good of our democracy, what would that be? International peace or citizen's welfare would come up and many will agree. Schumpeter, however, does not. He points out that such common good cannot be uniquely determined by the public. Many readers may find this hard to believe. How can we not find a public good in our democracy? Don't we have a few, at least, that we all agree to as an important goal of our democracy? Let's talk about international peace for a while. At a glance, international peace seems to be a good candidate for such public good. Who would like a war in a democracy? In 2003, the US military began its invasion into Iraq under the name of "Shock and Awe" and this war has killed many people: about 100,000 Iraqi civilians[2]; many thousands of Iraqi forces, and about 5,000 invading forces, including 4,418 American soldiers,[3] as of September 2010. The decision to start this war was of course supported by the majority of the American public and legally made by the American leaders. If you think about war, however it is justified, it is by definition not peaceful. (War for peace is simply an oxymoron.) The question is, then, how can we reconcile the international peace that we thought the public were longing for in democracy and the war that democracy blessed? In fact, there has been a large opposition to the war here in the US as well as abroad. In 2003 about 32% of public opposed the war, and the figure had steadily risen to 60% in 2008.[4] In other words, if we think about democracy as something for public good, we are further in confusion than in a clear understanding because its purpose may not be so obvious (peace or something else?) and the public are always divided.

Therefore, Schumpeter argues, our discussion of democracy should narrowly focus on how we select our leaders, leaving the entire notion of its purposes out. Following this, Schumpeter defines democracy as a political system "for arriving at political decisions in which individuals acquire the power to decide by means of a competitive struggle for the people's vote."[5] As you can see, this definition does not entertain any notion of the purpose of the polity and the like. Instead, his definition is largely about one element and one element only: election. Because of this narrow scope of the definition, Schumpeter's approach toward democracy is known as a minimalist approach.

The advocates of minimalism emphasize the fact that elections allow people to fight in a peaceful manner and that is the most important virtue of democracy. For example, Przeworski saw ballots as "paper stones" by which people peacefully fight.[6] To him, democracy does not have to be perfect. "This is not consensus, yet not mayhem either. Just limited conflict; conflict without killing."[7] Thus, elections are critical not only as a major component of the definition of democracy but also as a vital mechanism to maintain the peace in a society. One way that this mechanism works is by providing information. The loser of an election learns that "Here is the distribution of force: if you disobey the instructions conveyed by the results of the election, I will be more likely to beat you than you will be able to beat me in a violent confrontation." On the other hand, the winner hears that "If you do not hold elections again or if you grab too much, I will be able to put up a forbidding resistance."[8] Given this information, political actors, winners, and losers alike find merits in following democratic rules, rather than following a very costly route of nondemocracy.

While minimalists narrowly focused on election as the key component of democracy, others have raised questions about this approach. Is the presence of a competitive election sufficient for a country to be called a democracy? The critics of the minimalist approach often come up with a case where elections are quite competitive and regular but the system and society are not truly and wholly democratic. Let's imagine Country X where competitive elections are regular and common. However, in Country X such political competitions are controlled, but not overtly rigged. In addition, there is no apparent and violent repression toward opposition parties or their leaders, but their activities are nonetheless deterred or discouraged by the authorities: a famous opposition group gets a letter from the tax authority notifying it that the tax for their office is overdue and demanding a stiff penalty; the court freezes the group's account for no apparent reason; the members are followed by suspicious people; independent journalists find it impossible to renew their passport or they receive a pink slip out of the blue. Is this country really a democracy?

According to the minimalist approach, Country X may be a democracy or at least a borderline case. However, to its critics, the country cannot be democratic. For one, the opposition is under political pressure. Worse still, the freedom of the press is being challenged. Without basic civil liberty, no country can have a healthy democracy. Hence, those who share this type of criticism take a more aggressive approach toward democracy, known as the maximalist approach. The maximalist approach is aggressive because their definition of democracy is much more inclusive and has a higher expectation of the quality of democracy than the minimalist approach. So, what does such a broad definition of democracy include? For that let's turn to a longtime advocate of the maximalist approach, Robert Dahl.[9] Dahl introduces a list of necessary conditions for democracy.

> Control of governmental decisions is vested in elected officials;
> Elected official are chosen in frequent and fair elections;
> Universal suffrage;
> Any adult can run for office;
> Free expression without danger of being punished;
> Alternative sources of information protected by the law; and
> Freedom of association

Let's review a few of these. First on the list may sound too mundane to be significant. After all, elections bring power to the elected, don't they? Not necessarily. Thailand is an interesting example of this point. This country has fair and free elections. The problem is that there are many unelected leaders with a powerful political influence. For example, the king of the country is supposedly a symbolic figure; however, his popularity has brought him undeniable and substantial political weight. However, more than anybody else, it is the military who have exercised the political authority with no electoral legitimacy. Their military *coup d'état* have been quite numerous. The most recent one in 2004 ousted the democratically elected Thaksin government out of power for its alleged corruption. The allegation is one thing, but military occupation of the capital city while the prime minister was in New York City was quite another. Many opponents of Thaksin, largely in cities, welcomed the rolling tanks and armed troops who were restoring democracy, but many of his supporters, largely in the rural area, resented the military intervention destroying democracy. Even though the army returned the power to civilians in about a year, the legitimacy of the following governments has been repeatedly challenged since then. Is Thailand really democratic? Maybe or maybe not (or should we say sometimes but not always?). However, what is clear to us is that the control of governmental decisions must be in the hands of elected officials, and no one else.

Universal suffrage may seem an important condition for democracy. Behind this notion we believe that excluding a group of people for their common, often physical, character is not what the idea of democracy stands for. Therefore, universal suffrage may also seem to some readers as given in any democracy. However, it is anything but a given. If we look back at our own history, it will become clear. The US has a long history of democracy since the day of independence. However, throughout the history, the majority of the population had been excluded from democratic processes until very recently. For example, women had little voting right until the 19th Amendment in 1920 guaranteed it. The large number of African Americans lacked the voting right until the Congress finally passed the Voting Rights Act in 1965. This expansion of suffrage came only after a long marathon of political struggle. During the fight, many people suffered: lost time for their daily routine, harassed by their neighbors, beaten by mobs, arrested by the police, or killed by the KKK. Here we should confront a perplexing question, "when have we begun to have democracy in the US?" In 1776? In 1920? In 1965? One could say that we have had a democracy from the beginning and it has evolved to be more and more inclusive. Or one could argue that our society became democratic only after 1965. Either way, all the arguments acknowledge the importance of universal suffrage in democracy and our democracy was not complete until recently. How about now?

You may think such practices of disenfranchisement long gone and that now the American democracy is complete. However, a similar problem persists. For example, in the US prisoners are disenfranchised. So are many people on probation or parole. This is not a particularly serious problem or unique to the US since most democratic countries have restricted voting rights to similar kinds of their citizens. What distinguishes our situation is the sheer size of imprisonment and racial disparity of the inmate population. According to the Pew Center, "more than 1 in 100 adults is now locked up in America. With 1,596,127 in state or federal prison custody, and another 723,131 in local jails, the total adult inmate count at the beginning of 2008 stood at 2,319,258. With the number of adults just shy of 230 million, the actual incarceration rate is 1 in every 99.1 adults."[10] If you add adults on probation or parole, more than 1% of adults are disenfranchised. This becomes more troubling considering racial discrepancy. The same study shows that 1 in 106 white men of age 18 or older is behind bars while 1 in 15 black men of age 18 or older is imprisoned.[11] This legal practice may have its justification; however it is certain that it renders millions of potential voters, especially members of minority, unable to be full citizens.[12] Is the universal suffrage a norm here in the US? The answer is yes if we can tolerate the fact that 1 in 100 adults can't vote.

Then, is the US not a democratic country? You may find it hard to say it is not even though we just discussed a couple of problems that could seriously challenge the basic meaning of democracy. Or one could argue that it is not fair because compared to countries such as Russia, the American democracy is healthy and strong. One would say that there would be no democracy left in the real world if all these elements were meticulously evaluated. Therefore Dahl once proposed not to use the very word, democracy.[13] It may be hard to believe (may be not so much now), but the debates on the definition of democracy relentlessly continues among scholars even now. However, we do not want to, and cannot, introduce all the debates and arguments on this issue (haven't you had enough already?). Rather it is our hope that you have a better idea of the compound and complicated nature of the concept, democracy, now than before. This is especially important to the American students who have rarely had a chance to give second thoughts to democracy, wondering what it is, pondering about its alternative, or criticizing its problems. Many of us here in the US regard democracy as a virtuous given. However, that is not the case in many other countries. Rather, many countries have struggled, until very recently, to adopt democracy and many more countries still do not have a democratic political system.

A BRIEF HISTORY OF DEMOCRATIC DEVELOPMENT: THE THREE WAVES OF DEMOCRACY

Look around the world. Now democracy is common. Most countries in the West have healthy democracies while many new born countries in the former Soviet bloc have adopted democracy. Many countries in Asia and Africa also have democracy. Some have more stable democracy than others, but many do have democracy. Or at least many countries hold competitive election, which is of course the hallmark of democracy. If even that is not the case, countries at least claim to have a democracy. All these tell us that democracy has become an international norm. Not many countries claim that they do not have a democracy. On the contrary, nondemocratic countries either avoid the discussion of democracy (like Saudi Arabia) or claim to have a modified form of democracy (like North Korea). In spite of this popularity of democracy on the global scale, democracy is a quite a recent invention. It is only in the 19th Century that democracy began to take off as a important form of government.

Huntington documents this rise of democracy in a very interesting way.[14] According to him, the world has experienced waves of democratization and the reverse of democratization back and forth throughout modern history. He observed that there have been groups of "transitions from nondemocratic to democratic regimes that occur within a specified period of time and that significantly outnumber transitions in the opposite direction during that period of time"[15] and called them a wave of democratization. There were three waves of democratization and two reversals of waves in between them, and thus the "democratization waves and the reverse waves suggest a two-step-forward, one-step-backward pattern."[16] We are now on the third wave of democratization according to him. Let's review how Huntington's account of history that brought us here.

First, a long wave of democratization (1828–1926) began with the rise of a limited, but meaningful democracy. It was still the 19th century when democracy was in its infancy, and thus, democracy looked different and less mature compared to today's form. Thus, it would be unfair to apply current standards to evaluate the democracy of the early days. Nevertheless, there was a noticeable development of its quality. "US abolished property qualifications in the older states and the admission of new states with universal manhood suffrage boosted to well over 50% the proportion of white males actually voting in the 1828 presidential election."[17] Comparable progress followed in the West: expansion of suffrage, introduction of secret ballot, responsible prime ministers and cabinet system in countries such as Switzerland, France, Great Britain, Italy, Argentina, Ireland, and Iceland.[18] The first wave of democratization was countered by an opposite tide, the first reverse wave (1922–1942). It began with Mussolini's victory in Italy in 1922 and similar dictatorial regimes grew in Lithuania, Poland, Latvia, and Estonia. Most remarkably during this era, the Nazi party brought down the democratic government, engulfing Germany in 1933. The downfall of democracy was not limited to these countries. Democracies fell in Greece, Portugal, Brazil, Argentina, and Spain at the hands of military coups in this era.[19]

The Second World War destroyed much of the world, and from the ashes of destruction democracy was given a chance to bud. In this time of the second wave of democratization (1943–1962) the Allies built democracy in their occupied territories such as West Germany, Italy, Austria, Japan, and South Korea.[20] In addition to the end of the war, the end of Western colonial rules also gave opportunities for the rise of democracy in newly created countries such as Malaysia, India, Sri Lanka, the Philippines, and Israel.[21] However, this renewed wave of democratization was short-lived. Soon, many states all over the world went through the second reverse waves (1958–1975). Authoritarian regimes spread in Latin America. Military intervention toppled the government in countries such as Peru, Brazil, Bolivia, Argentina, Ecuador, Uruguay, and Chile.[22] In Asia, democracies were losing ground to authoritarian dictatorships: Pakistan, South Korea, Indonesia, the Philippines, and India. Huntington mentions how strong this wave was: "By an estimate one-third of 32 working democracies in the world had become authoritarian by the mid-1970s."[23]

The third wave of democratization finally began in 1974. It started with the end of Portuguese dictatorship, followed by similar regime changes in Greece and Spain. Latin American military regimes also fell: Ecuador, Peru, Bolivia, Argentina, Uruguay, Brazil, Honduras, El Salvador, and Guatemala. The sign of democracy's recovery was also obvious in Asia: authoritarian regimes unraveled in India, Turkey, South Korea, the Philippines, and Taiwan. The most dramatic event of this time was the sudden collapse of the Soviet Union and its ally regimes in Eastern Europe. Beginning in the late 1980s, the communist regimes began to fall in Hungary, Poland, East Germany, Czechoslovakia, and with Romania, Bulgaria, and Mongolia embracing democracy as an alternative.[24]

Is the third wave still marching strong? There are many different opinions, but it would be safe to say that the consensus is that the current status of democracy is promising, but challenging. On one hand, democracy is still collecting new members. "During a five-year span in the early 1990s, the number of democracies increased by over fifty percent (from 48 in 1989 to 77 in 1994). . . . At the same time, the number of autocracies continues to plummet: from the peak of eighty-nine (89) in 1977 to just twenty-three (23) in late 2009. There are ninety-two (92) countries classified as democracies in late 2009. Countries that have transitioned to, or returned to, democratic governance since 2000 include Bangladesh, Burundi, Comoros, Ghana, Guinea-Bissau, Kenya, Lebanon, Liberia, Peru, Serbia, Sri Lanka, and the newly independent states of East Timor and Montenegro."[25] On the other hand, some worry that the expansion itself is not as rigorous as it used to be, and some even lament that "Liberal democracy has stopped expanding in the world . . . the third wave . . . has come to a halt, and probably to an end."[26]

There are signs indicating the autocratic tradition will not subside easily. The Cuban communist regime has endured the US economic and political sanctions while it has successfully silenced the domestic opposition. North Korea has probably the most interesting story of maintaining its stability. The North Korean communist regime was founded by Kim Il-sung who passed his throne to a son, Kim Jung-il. Recently, Kim Jung-un, the grandson of the founder, was anointed as a future leader. In spite of their poverty and famine that are all too common, the country is still united under the flags of the Kims and communism. We may want to treat these cases of communism as an insignificant testimony for communism due to the small size of the population and country. Well, then how about China? Even though China has a strong market economy and vibrant international trade, it is being ruled by a communist dictatorship. Hence, we have one-sixths of the entire human population living in a communist country. Unlike the other examples, communist China is neither largely isolated nor chronically underdeveloped. Its economy became the second largest economy, passing Japan in 2010, and continues to be the world's factory exporting a variety of goods to the rest of the world. Moreover, the public support for the regime remains strong. In a sense, these cases show that nondemocracies also adapt to the challenges to the regime and some did quite successfully.

The resilience and development of nondemocracies must be quite astonishing to many readers; however, it is equally perplexing to many to observe the deterioration of established democracy. Many countries with a seemingly stable democracy have fallen back to the side of nondemocracies, if not experienced collapse into outright authoritarian regimes, and these countries often took the path through the military's intervention in political or social problems. A good, but sad, example would be a series of political scandals, the political tensions, and discontent among the urban population of Thailand, which resulted in yet another military coup in 2006. The Prime Minister Thaksin, and at the same time one of the most successful and richest businessman of the country, helplessly watched as the military led by the army chief, General Sonthi, took over the capital while he was visiting the UN at New York. This purge was a final attempt of a series of similar attempts by the opposition to oust him. The opposition, including not only opposition parties but also urbanites and professionals, had waged protests, occupied the capital city, and manipulated an election only to realize that they could not remove the elected incumbent prime minister. At last, the military took over the country for a year and returned the power back to the civilian politicians. However, the damage was already done, and it was serious. The opponents of Thaksin and his supporters repeatedly clashed against each other and they were not always peaceful. Violent confrontations in 2008 followed another lockdown of the capital, Bangkok, removing another pro-Thaksin prime minister. In the following year another wave of mass protests by Thaksin supporters swept the country. In 2010, they renewed their resistance against the government by occupying part of central Bangkok for a couple of months, demanding the current prime minister resign.[27] This series of events have challenged the legitimacy of the democratic political institution itself. Both sides have turned to any means possible for their political goals and the means were often not legitimate elections. Without any clear end in sight, political instability goes on and its democracy still lacks the necessary legitimacy.

Democracy is still an international norm to which most countries subscribe or at least claim to do so. However, challenges for democracy are abundant in many parts of the world, as briefly seen. Some countries such as those in Western Europe have been enjoying the fruit of their democracies for more than a century now while many countries lag behind to varying degrees. Then, the question that we should ask must be what explains this variation. Why are some countries ahead of others in democratization, while still others seem to be in a political abyss?

THEORIES OF DEMOCRATIZATION: ECONOMIC DEVELOPMENT; EDUCATION AND URBANIZATION; POLITICAL CULTURE AND CIVIL SOCIETY; FOREIGN INFLUENCE; ELITE PACTS

Some countries have maintained a vibrant democracy, but in other countries authoritarian regimes have persisted. All Western European and Northern American countries have strengthened and maintained their democratic system over the last century while many countries in Africa (Congo, Algeria, and Sudan) have failed to do so. Many countries in South America (Argentina, Brazil, and Chile) and Asia (Indonesia, Taiwan, and South Korea) ended an authoritarian era after a long political struggle, but at the same time many (Cuba, China, and Myanmar) still have not adopted democracy. Former communist countries have experienced different paths as well: while the communism in many Eastern European countries (Czech Republic, Hungary, and Poland) has collapsed and yielded to democracy, many former Soviet republics (Kazakhstan, Turkmenistan, and Uzbekistan) have continued their authoritarian tradition. This gap in democratic development has generated wide and rigorous research among political scientists: why do some countries have democracy while others don't? Even though the discussions among scholars continue, the research has found some interesting patterns.

Economic Development

Seymour M. Lipset famously found that national wealth is a critical condition for the rise of democracy: "The more well-to-do a nation, the greater the chances that it will sustain democracy,"[28] and since then many studies have confirmed this judgment. To many readers, this finding may not be so surprising. Rather, it may seem too obvious to be studied, analyzed, and debated by scholars. After all, all the Western European countries have a strong tradition of democracy following their great success of industrialization and its global expansion. However, the causal link between economic development and democratization is not so obvious, at least as much as it seems. For example, China's economy is exploding through its huge trade surplus over the years, real estate boom, technological innovation, and unstoppable foreign direct investment.

Democratization in China still seems to be only just a dream. Then, maybe the relationship between the two is not so linear. Przeworski and Limongi actually observed such a nonlinear link between economic development and democratization.[29] According to their study, wealthy authoritarian states as well as wealthy democracies remain stable as in the case of China; however, democratic countries with a per capita income of $6,000 or more are extremely unlikely to turn nondemocratic. According to this, wealth, above a certain level, is a critical element for democratization, but certainly not a panacea. Even the very notion that economic development is a precondition for democracy was challenged since, according to these critics, economic development could be a curse for democracy. O'Donnell points out that economic development actually increased the need for an authoritarian order in order to maintain the prosperity for the rich.[30] Many countries in South America during the 1960s and 1970s experienced this rise of "bureaucratic-authoritarian" regimes. According to this analysis, economic development is actually harmful to the development of democracy, not its precondition.

Education and Urbanization

As economic wealth is identified as a positive factor for the development of democracy, so are other socioeconomic factors such as education and urbanization. Education is widely expected to be a major precondition for the rise of democracy. Democracy needs citizens who understand public affairs so that they can be active in participation, or at least can afford to do so. Of course, education allows such development in the civic society. Moreover, education encourages a necessary change of attitudes among the citizens. According to Lipset, "[e]ducation ... broadens man's outlook, enables him to understand the need for norms of tolerance, restrains him from adhering to extremist doctrines, and increases his capacity to make rational electoral choices."[31] In a similar vein, urbanization is also a link to the democratization of a society since it tends to create a population that demands more open society and rejects an authoritarian political order, spurring political changes toward democracy.[32] The examples include urban developments in the ancient Greek states and modern Western society.

Political Culture and Civil Society

Another major correlate of democracy is the political culture favoring democracy over the other forms of government. Assuming that we define political culture as political beliefs and judgments shared largely by members of a group, it would be logical to expect that democracy-friendly political culture should help a country to develop a democratic government compared to a country with no such political culture. Then, the question is which political culture is democracy-friendly. Many scholars have studied and identified such political cultures that promote democracy and hinder democratization. One of such positive political culture has been civic culture. As we already discussed in a previous chapter on political culture, there is a long and persistent tradition within political science that analyzes the link between a present civic culture and the country's strong democracy.[33] This tradition claims that a society largely made of people who care about public affairs or engage in discussions is more likely to have a higher degree of democratic government than a society of people who lack such public spirits. The scholars of this tradition often use survey data to measure the level of civic culture and claim that such civic culture is common in the Western European countries, hence proving the link between the civic culture and democracy.

Foreign Influence

A country's democratization can be helped by foreign countries. After the end of the Second World War, Japan decisively severed its long tradition of authoritarian rule by military leaders or shogun, and later the emperor. However, their embrace of democracy was forced by the occupying US forces led by General McArthur. The US authority dictated the terms of its new constitution, creating liberal democracy almost overnight. The US occupation broke another ground for democracy in Iraq after its successful military campaign that toppled the long lasting dictatorship by Saddam Hussein in 2003. It should be noted that the process of democratization under military occupation by a foreign power is not as smooth as it may sound. Political struggles were fierce and accompanied violent confrontations between political rivals. Many citizens of the occupied countries did not even understand, let alone want, democracy. As a result, democracies of these countries, in early days, often failed to function as effectively as expected.

Aid to democracy often occurs in many forms beyond military intervention. The Western countries have provided various financial supports to assist electoral processes in developing countries. For example, in 1994 Mozambique's election cost $64.5 million, close to 4.5% of the country's GDP and the country heavily relied on foreign donors to finance this.[34] Beside this financial help, foreign intervention can be in the format of technical and logistic support. For example, the United Nations works to "design electoral assistance projects and the electoral components of peacekeeping operation,"[35] often in postconflict countries. Many NGOs provide similar assistance. The Carter Center is well known for its pioneering efforts to send monitoring teams to emerging democracies so that elections in the countries can be more legitimate and fairer than without such a presence by a neutral party. The foreign presence could be unexpectedly decisive. For example, in 2010 Ivory Cost held a long delayed presidential election and the result was, to say the least, controversial. President Gbagbo declared his victory after the runoff election as the electoral authority sealed the verdict. However, foreign observers, including the Carter Center that spent months monitoring not only the election itself but also the political progress toward it, declared the challenger, Ouattara, the winner. This foreign intervention boosted the morale among the challenger's supporters and encouraged them to create a *de facto* government recognized by all but the incumbent president and his loyal members of armed forces.

Foreign intervention can be less direct but more consequential. The membership of the EU has been a major strategic goal for many developing countries in Eastern Europe since the membership promises rewarding economic possibilities with open access to a huge market of labor, goods, and services. Therefore, the countries in the region tried to consolidate their democracies in order to meet the EU standard. "Efforts to meet the EU's membership criteria have significantly accelerated the modernization of institutions, the introduction of the rule of law, and the building of a transparent market economy."[36] In other words, the EU's emphasis on liberal democracy that was not really meant to encorage democratization in the Eastern Europe made a substantial contribution to the major political changes in the region.

Elite Pacts

If you review what we have discussed thus far, democratization is possible for economic, social, cultural, and international factors. Then, you might begin to wonder if there is any political aspect to democratization (especially when this course is about politics!). After all, it is political leaders who initiate or fight the process of democratization. The process is not as easy as it may sound here in the US where the political and military struggles toward democracy were largely over centuries ago. However, if you think about the process of democratic transition it is extremely difficult. Imagine you were the dictator who has maintained a firm control over the armed forces for the last two decades. Now add mass street protests demanding the immediate adaptation of a free and competitive presidential election that, you think, would cost your seat for sure. What would you do? Would you give up overnight not only the presidency but also all the political and financial privileges that you and your family members have enjoyed? Would you do that even when you know you would undoubtedly go to jail for what you have done as a dictator? Well, I'm not so sure about you, but I wouldn't, especially when the army is behind me.

Authoritarian leaders typically concede to the demand for democratization only when they are convinced that they will continue to enjoy safety and power. The opposition tries to convince them through a series of negotiations and promises, often called elite pacts. Since the government often has the upper hand, it is the opposition that makes more significant concessions during the pacts. For example, as discussed by Przeworski, in the 1982 Brazilian elections the authoritarian government "allowed the formation of additional parties, with the aim of splitting the opposition ... created obstacles that made it difficult for parties that were popular . . . to register . . . made it more difficult for illiterates to cast their ballots, as they were expected to vote against the government."[37] As a result its party, the Democratic Social Party could manage to gain the most seats in the Chamber of Deputies.

CONCLUSION

Democracy is an important theoretical and political subject, but many issues about democracy are still subject to debate. What is democracy? Many students might have thought that they know what it is. However, as you see now, the concept still means different things to different people depending on their theoretical perspectives and where you live. Nevertheless, the form of political system that is based on the competitive election has evolved over many years in many parts of the world. The development was not always promising or linear. Rather, there were many setbacks and holdouts, but various political, cultural, and socioeconomic factors help many countries overcome these and move the countries to develop this very popular form of political system.

Notes

1 Joseph Schumpeter, *Capitalism, Socialism, and Democracy* (New York: Allen & Unwin, 1976); Robert A. Dahl, Ian Shapiro, and Jose A. Cheibub, eds., *The Democracy Sourcebook* (Cambridge, MA: The MIT Press, 2003), 5.

2 Iraq Body Count website, http://www.iraqbodycount.org/.

3 icasualties.org website http://icasualties.org/.

4 Jeffrey M. Jones, "Opposition to Iraq War Reaches New High," April 24, 2008, http://www.gallup.com/poll/106783/opposition-iraq-war-reaches-new-high.aspx. (accessed November 6, 2011).

5 Joseph Schumpeter, *Capitalism, Socialism, and Democracy*, 9.

6 Adam Przeworski, "Minimalist Concept of Democracy: A Defense," in *Democracy's Value*, Ian Shapiro and Casiano Hacker-Cordon, eds. (Cambridge: Cambridge University Press, 1999) from Robert A. Dahl, Ian Shapiro, and Jose A. Cheibub, eds., *The Democracy Sourcebook* (Cambridge, MA: MIT Press), 17.

7 Ibid., 17.

8 Ibid., 15.

9 Robert A. Dahl, *Democracy and Its Critics* (New Haven: Yale University Press, 1989), 233.

10 Pew Center on the States, "One in 100: Behind Bars in America" a report by the Pew Center on the States, February 2008, 5. http://www.pewcenteronthestates.org/uploadedFiles/8015PCTS_Prison08_FINAL_2-1-1_FORWEB.pdf. (accessed November 6, 2011).

11 Pew Center on the States, "One in 100: Behind Bars in America" a report by the Pew Center on the States, 6.

12 David Cole, "Can Our Shameful Prisons Be Reformed?" *The New York Review of Book*, November 19, 2009.

13 Robert A. Dahl, *Polyarchy* (New Haven: Yale University Press, 1972).

14 Samuel P. Huntington, *The Third Wave: Democratization in the Late Twentieth Century* (Norman and London: University of Oklahoma Press, 1991).

15 Ibid., 15.

16 Ibid., 25.

17 Ibid., 16.

18 Ibid., 16–17.

19 Ibid., 17–18.

20 Ibid., 18.

21 Ibid., 19.

22 Ibid., 19.

23 Ibid., 21.

24 Ibid., 23–25.

25 Monty G. Marshall and Benjamin R. Cole, *Global Report 2009: Conflict, Governance, and State Fragility* (Arlington, VA: Center for Global Policy, George Mason University), 11. http://www.systemicpeace.org/Global%20Report%202009.pdf. (accessed November 6, 2011).

26 Larry Diamond, "Is The Third Wave Over?" *Journal of Democracy* 7, no. 3 (1996): 31.

27 BBC "Timeline: Thailand," http://news.bbc.co.uk/2/hi/asia-pacific/country_profiles/1243059.stm. (accessed November 6, 2011).

28 Seymour M. Lipset, "Some Social Requisites of Democracy: Economic Development and Political Legitimacy," *American Political Science Review* 53 (1959): 75.

29 Fernando P. Limongi and Adam Przeworski, "What Makes Democracies Endure?" *Journal of Democracy* 7, no. 1 (1997): 39–55.

30 Guillermo O'Donnell, *Modernization and Bureaucratic-Authoritarianism: Studies in South American Politics* (Berkeley: University of California, Institute of International Studies, 1973).

31 Seymour M. Lipset, *Political Man: The Social Base of Politics* (Baltimore: The Johns Hopkins University Press) from Robert A. Dahl, Ian Shapiro, and Jose Antonio Cheibub, eds., *The Democracy Sourcebook* (Cambridge, MA: MIT Press, 2003), 58.

32 Lipset, Political Man, 57; Tatu Vanhanen, *Democratization: A comparative analysis of 170 countries* (London: Routledge, 2003).

33 See Gabriel A. Almond and Sidney Verba, *The Civic Culture: Political Attitudes and Democracy in Five Nations* (Princeton, NJ: Princeton University Press, 1963); Ronald Inglehart, "Culture Shift," in *Advanced Industrial Society* (Princeton: Princeton University Press, 1990); Robert D. Putnam, *Making Democracy Work: Civic Traditions in Modern Italy* (Princeton: Princeton University Press, 1993).

34 George Sorensen, Democracy and Democratization: Processes and Prospects in a Changing World, 3rd ed. (Philadelphia: Westview Press, 2008).

35 The United Nations, http://www.un.org/Depts/dpa/ead/overview.html#TrustFund (accessed January 6, 2011).

36 Jiri Pehe, "Consolidating Free Government in the New EU," *Journal of Democracy* 15, no. 1 (2004): 36–47.

37 George Sorensen, Democracy and Democratization: Processes and Prospects in a Changing World, 3rd ed. (Philadelphia: Westview Press, 2008), 35.

Nondemocratic Governments

THE TWO FORMS OF NONDEMOCRATIC REGIMES: AUTHORITARIANISM AND TOTALITARIANISM DEFINED, COMPARED, AND CONTRASTED

In the previous chapter, we had discussed the meaning of democracy. As discussed, there are still various debates on its definition. However, the consensus is that free and fair election is the central part of democracy. Inversely speaking then, nondemocratic regime can be characterized by the absence of such free and fair elections. Therefore, a wide range of regimes can be characterized as nondemocratic, and they share some similarities. However, they are actually quite different from each other. Since these nondemocratic regimes may be new to many of you, it is important to understand how these regimes function. Let's begin with a brief discussion on various types of regimes.[1]

There are a few ways to categorize political regimes, and we would like to suggest two. First, we could look at the size of leadership as in Table 8.1. In ancient Athens, the leadership was shared by almost all qualified male citizens, and they rule on their own. Necessary officials were selected by lot. There, citizens had the power and direct say on their lives. It was a rare case of direct democracy with all qualified citizens as rulers. In representative democracies, the size of leadership is much smaller since citizens do not rule, but delegate their powers to their representatives. However, there are still many leaders in representative democracies. For example, here in the US, Mr. Obama is a major leader as the president of the country. However, he is hardly the only leader. The political power is shared with leaders of the Congress led by the Speaker, judges of federal courts like Chief Justice Roberts of the Supreme Court, opinion leaders such as Rush Limbaugh, a radio host, and much more. Unlike democracy, in oligarchy, the leadership is limited only to a few. Today, in China, about two dozen high-ranked members of the CCP collectively rule not only the party but also the entire country. They are immune to any public scrutiny and insulated from any meaningful political challenge. However,

TABLE 8.1 Political regimes by the size of political leadership.

All	Many	Few	One
Direct democracy	Representative democracy	Oligarchy	Monarchy/Dictatorship
Democracy		Autocracy	

TABLE 8.2 Political regimes by the degree of government control over society.

Limited	Oppressive	Total
Democracy	Authoritarian	Totalitarian

there have been political regimes such that even oligarchy was the envy of the people as they were under the rule of a single person. Countries under absolute monarchs, such as Louis XIV of France, are good examples. More recently, we witnessed dictators such as Mao Zedong or Hitler whimsically ruled their countries with virtually no restraint from anybody. Hence, we can more broadly group direct democracy and representative democracy together and call them democracy in which political leadership is made of a large number of people while oligarchy and monarchy/dictatorship can be put together under a category called autocracy in which only a small number of people exercise political power.

Another dimension to categorize political regimes is the degree to which the government exerts control over society as shown in Table 8.2. In democracy, the government controls the society, but the control is limited. Rather, the citizens enjoy a high level of liberty in most private and public sectors and their liberty is actively and legally protected by the government. Here in the US, like most democratic states, citizens can say anything without fear of the government's retaliation as long as they remain within the legal boundary. In that sense, there are some limits. Nevertheless, the limits are subject to reviews, debates, and modification, which the citizens can influence. That is not the case in authoritarian states where the government's control can be oppressive and pervasive. Citizens are given typically limited civil liberty that the government refuses to provide an active protection of. The authoritarian government often ignores legal codes regarding the civil liberty of its citizens or arbitrarily interprets and follows them. Criticisms of the government are not tolerated and the critiques often face retaliation in various forms such as surveillance, harassment, loss of income, jail terms, violence, or death. Totalitarian governments take additional steps by acquiring near total control over the society. They not only disallow any opposition but also control or at least greatly influence the citizens' private lives, including the way they think, whom to marry, which crops to grow, or kinds of arts they create and enjoy.

In modern days, authoritarian systems have been typically observed in monarchy, one-party system, personal dictatorship, military rules, and theocracy. Totalitarian systems were seen most noticeably in the form of communist one-party systems and fascist one-party systems. The nondemocratic regimes that we focus on in this book include military dictatorship, theocracy, one-party rule, and a totalitarian state. In these regimes, elections are only a formality or are strictly controlled by the political authority. Dissent is discouraged, and repression is commonly applied. However, the regimes draw the political power from different sources. Military dictatorship basically relies on the physical forces while theocracy uses a religious entity. One-party rule develops an extensive reach of a political party all over the society, and totalitarianism cultivates the idea that the entire society is unified for common goals.

Before we begin our discussion of nondemocratic regimes, it should be noted that even a democratic regime may experience a shift in its democratic quality. In other words, the degree of democracy of a democratic regime could deteriorate even though its democratic institutions remain largely intact. This is possible whenever the state leader feels tempted to use his or her power over the state apparatus in order to fight political opponents, and democratic leaders are not immune to this temptation. Even if such an attempt to abuse the political power is legal, this should be treated as being quite serious because such deterioration could be a canary in a coal mine. In this regard, South Korea's democratic regime is an interesting example.

In 2009, a petition signed by scholars in North America accused President Lee Myung-bak, who was elected through a free and fair election and whose administration oversaw competitive elections since, of compromising democratic principles. According to the document,[2] during mass protests in 2008 against the administration's decision to open the domestic market to US beef, peaceful protests were violently suppressed. Journalists who filed reports critical of the government were harassed by the Public Prosecutor's Office. For example, "In March 2009, four journalists and union activists from Yonhap Television Network (YTN), a 24-hour news channel, were arrested for 'interfering with business'. The journalists had been calling for guarantees of editorial independence after the appointment of Ku Bon-hong, formerly an aide to President Lee Myung-bak, as YTN president."[3] In addition, major broadcasting networks' executives were replaced with pro-government figures. Unfortunately for Korean democracy, breaches of democratic principle continued. For example, it became public that the Prime Minister's office illegally spied on citizens. The subjects included not only anti-government activities but also the Congressmen of the president's own political party, the Grand National Party. Even a TV anchorman and a show host were robbed of their airtime due to their opinion against Lee's rule. According to the Amnesty International, in 2009 "blogger Park Dae-sung or 'Minerva' was arrested for violating the Framework Act on Telecommunications after he posted gloomy economic forecasts. He was accused of spreading malicious rumors to destabilize the economy."[4]

In summary, Lee's administration has been actively disparaging the principle of free association and free speech, but doing so largely within a legal boundary. Therefore, few people would say that Lee had no legitimacy as a democratic leader, but it is also clear that Lee was pushing the envelope in protecting his political power more than he should. Is South Korea a democratic state? The answer should be probably a yes, but its quality has been certainly deteriorated over the years under Lee's watch. Now, let's look at the various types of nondemocratic regimes.

Authoritarianism

Authoritarian regimes lack genuine democratic mechanisms such as competitive and regular elections and free press, which allows political leaders to set and control political agenda, manipulate the public opinion, and create the appearance of legitimacy. However, their controls usually remain in the domain of politics and important economic decisions. Political oppositions are repressed but usually tolerated as long as they are not so dangerous. However, social and cultural activities, such as music, arts, and commerce, are watched, but left to the hands of civil society unless they become the sources of political headache. In other words, their controls do not reach every aspects of life of the citizens.

Military Dictatorship A military dictatorship is a political regime whose survival depends on military support and the ruler is a leader of the military. The military is powerful due to its monopolistic control over armed forces and its vast and resourceful organization. The power of the military often fails to remain in the matter of national security. Due to the violent nature of its power, the military is typically very influential in the realm of politics. Mao once famously said "political power grows out of the barrel of a gun." This is the case even in democratic countries such as the US where the military's budget soared to $720 billion in 2011 from $432 billion in 2001.[5] For example, the military leaders' decision to buy or stop buying a certain weapon affects the economy of the state that hosts the manufacturer. Therefore, the political leaders often give in to the military's demand for its evermore large budget year after year, which translates to less money for numberless civilian projects. However, the military's influence is far beyond this in a military dictatorship. Military leaders gain power usually through a *coup d'état* that can be defined as a sudden and violent overthrow of the government, replacing the national leadership with a new group of military leaders. These new leaders are often still in the military uniform. The military leaders often believe that they are better qualified to run a country than civilian leaders, and they have good reasons to do so. As a group, officers often make up one of the most educated groups in the country. Moreover, the military has various functions such as gathering intelligence, procurement, recruiting and training, finance and planning, construction, providing health care, as well as combat. Therefore, the military produces leaders with experience necessary to govern a country. Such experience might be valuable if the country lacks civilian leaders with similar qualities. However, the military's culture is influenced by its vertical relationships, largely characterized by giving an order and following it. This is not really the case with civilian politics where endless compromises are being forged among equal partners. This is one of the reasons why the military dictatorship often relies on violent repression.

Augusto Pinochet was such a military dictator, in Chile. General Pinochet gained power in a violent and bloody *coup d'état* in 1973, toppling the socialist regime led by Allende who died during the military's attack on the presidential place.[6] The coup followed a month-long social unrest in the country where hyperinflation, recession, labor strife, and middle-class protests eroded the public support for the socialist regime.[7] Once in power, Pinochet replaced mayors and university leaders with military officers or retired military members.

The mass media was censored while any opposition was brutally repressed. The National Intelligence Directorate, or DINA, conducted repression by means of extra-judicial killing or torture: "more than 3,200 people were executed or disappeared, and scores of thousands more were detained and tortured or exiled."[8] He received some credit for steering the country away from economic problems into a market-oriented, successful economy at the cost of a violently suppressed labor movement. Feeling confident, Pinochet allowed political reforms including writing a new constitution in 1980 and free presidential elections. However, not only was his own bid for another 8 years as a president rejected in 1988 but his hand-picked presidential candidate was defeated in the presidential election in 1989. Nevertheless, the armed forces stayed as "guarantors of institutionality" or a political arbiter while Pinochet himself remained as a senator for life and continued to hold his military leadership as the chief of army until 1998.

Theocracy A theocracy is a ruling regime based on religion. Actually, it is the political prominence of a religion's text and of the authority to interpret the book that distinguishes theocracy from other forms of government. In a theocracy, the religious power triumphs the secular authority and shapes politics. For example, as early as 1971, while in exile, Ayatollah Khomeini, the paramount leader of Iranian Revolution of 1978, declared that "all secular government was illegitimate"[9] and "Muslims should not wait for [the twelfth Imam] to reveal himself but try to establish Islamic government even in his absence."[10] The Iranian Revolution of 1978–1979 toppled the West-backed authoritarian monarchy, and Khomeini created the first Islamic Revolution. In the new republic, there was no the separation of religion and politics; state and church were joined while the ayollah as supreme religious leader oveaw the work of all branches of government.[11] Even though he's long gone today, the institutionalized merger between the mosque and the state lingers. For example, the head of state or Supreme Leader should be an Islamic cleric, and this appointment is decided by yet another layer of the religious authority known as Assembly of Experts, an advisory body of elected religious scholars.[12] The constitution gave this religious leader paramount influence over a wide range of politics: power to supervise "the proper execution of the general policies," to issue "decrees for national referendum," to assume "supreme command of armed forces," to finalize the result of presidential election, dismiss the president of the republic, and to fill and vacate important governmental positions including religious men on the Guardian Council, the chief of joint staff, the supreme commanders of armed forces, among others. The Guardian Council, made of six "religious men" and six jurists, is responsible for ensuring that all "civil, penal financial, economic, administrative, cultural, military, political, and other laws and regulations must be based on Islamic criteria,"[13] and the constitution allows the council to force other bodies of the government to adhere to Islamic principles. For example, the council reviews legislations for their compatibility with Islamic law and customs and can bar candidates from elections for their political or religious views. As you can notice, these political and religious authorities are exercised by people who have virtually no accountability to the voters of the country. People can elect the president and the members of the legislature called the Islamic Consultative Assembly; however, these elected officials are obligated to follow the guidance of the religious leaders.

In addition to the governmental structure, Iran has developed other institutions to maintain the religious ideology and order. For example, Iran maintains an armed force, the Islamic Revolution Guards Corps that is committed to the Islamic ideology as well as the regular army. Legally, Iran has religious courts following Sharia laws, especially regarding the principle of retribution. In school, Islamic ideology became a school subject, creating generations of citizens exposed to their religious doctrine.[14] On streets, so-called morality police enforce a conservative and religious code of social customs, such as against revealing clothing. All these social and political institutions are meant to increase the religious authority and, in turn, the political clout of religious leaders who are not accountable to the people.

Iran is not the only example of theocracy. Until its downfall after the US invasion, Taliban rule of Afghanistan was a harsh form of theocracy. After its military victory in the civil war, the Taliban built a repressive regime based on a fundamentalist interpretation of Islam, known as "Wahhabism," which has its roots in Saudi Arabia. The country was largely ruled by the Taliban leader, Mullah Omur and his close advisors. Any form of modern government that is not compatible with Sharia was abandoned, including constitution and elections. Taliban's legal authorities declared that the "Constitution is the Sharia so we don't need a constitution"[15] and its legal codes reflected its religious disdain toward any anti-Islamic aspect of society, including drugs and alcohol, gambling, moneylending, music and dance, Western hairstyles, the shaving of men's beards, photographs, paintings, television, and sports.[16] The Ministry for the Promotion of Virtue and the Suppression of Vice was the major governmental body that vigorously maintained and exploited the religious fervor of the society. One of the most notorious repressions of the Taliban regime targeted women of the country. Women were encouraged to stay home as much as possible while the opportunity to education and employment was robbed. The religion police forced women to wear full body-covering *burqas*. Their social and economic status abruptly collapsed.

The theocracies of Iran and Afghanistan are based on their particular interpretations of Islam; however, theocracies are not only found in the Islamic world. Even though not as repressive as the theocracy of these countries, the Vatican is another theocratic country where the Pope is the head of the state, as the paramount religious authority elected not by the people.

One-party Rule A one-party rule regime is largely characterized by, well, one-party rule. Not only is there only one political party in this type of regime but also the political power of the party often exceeds that of government institutions. Or to be more precise, the members of the political party largely control the state apparatus. Moreover, the party is likely to control large parts of the national economy and shapes social and cultural trends of the country. The party, not necessarily the state, maintains a monopolistic control over the armed forces. To manage all these tasks, the party is well-developed, with an extensive and complicated organization staffed with a huge number of talented people. Therefore, the party could be used by a charismatic leader for his personal political ambition. With no such individual leader, the party itself can exert a substantial influence, so much so that even a dictator cannot whimsically rule the country. The institutionalized strength of the political party might have also negated the reliance on the military leadership as in the military dictatorship or the need for an absolute ideology as in the case of theocracy.

One-party regimes were common during the Cold War among communist countries. Now, however, most of them have abandoned communism and also one-party rule. Nevertheless, there are a few countries, such as China and Cuba, that still maintain one-party rule. The rule of the CCP has proved to be the most interesting example in part because of its successful evolution for more than a half century. The political dominance of the CCP stems from its historical background in which the party succeeded in overthrowing not only its political rival, a nationalist party or the Kuomintang, but also the state itself under the Kuomintang's rule. The CCP was formed in 1921 and went through a decades-long struggle to survive the Kuomintang's military and political onslaught. Finally, in 1949, it was the CCP that defeated the corrupt Kuomintang even thought it was strongly supported and assisted by the US. The CCP's historical memory of the struggle and of coming so close to defeat at the hands of the Kuomintang created the political system where a political party monopolizes the whole political authority of the country.

Every political force, including the state itself, is subject to the party's control. China's military still follows the leadership of the party, and all major state agencies, such as the legislature and the executive bodies, are directly led by party leaders. The party dominance is possible through the interlocking directory of the state-party leadership. For example, the leaders of the party who regularly and frequently meet to discuss the state's affairs actually head state apparatus. President Hu Jintao's authority rises from his party leadership as a chair of the Central Military Commission (CMC) of the CCP, as Party Secretary, and as a member of the standing committee of the CCP's Politburo. Similarly, Xi Jinping is widely believed to succeed Hu as the next leader of China after he was given the seat in the Politburo and later the position as the vice chair of the CMC in 2010. In addition to this informal control of the CCP over the state, the party has an institutionalized control over the state through its power to fill a wide range of positions, or *nomenclatura*, in various organizations such as university, state-owned enterprises, newspapers, judicial bodies, mass media companies, or research bodies as well as the state and the CCP, allowing the party's tight grip on mass media, education, culture, and economy.

The CCP leaders are not selected by the party members, much less the people. Even though the party reform of 1995 allowed competitive elections at the lowest level of the party hierarchy, the selection of party representatives is far from genuine competition. Prior to the election, the CCP is the only party that can form meetings to plan and wage election campaigns. Of course, the CCP can remove any potential rival to its candidate away from position or even worse from the area using its nomenclatura. Therefore, the local elections of the party officials are often tightly controled with an appearance of contestation. Moreover, any competition, if there is any, is limited to the lowest level of the party hierarchy. Thus, as the party level goes up, it becomes increasingly difficult to see party backed candidates lose the election. At the end, it is all the party's favorites that fill the party leadership positions almost at all the levels, and in turn, these are the nuts and bolts of the Chinese political regime.

Totalitarianism

Look at this list of regimes: Nazi Germany, Fascist Italy, Stalinist USSR, Maoist China, and Juche North Korea. Even though you may not be thoroughly familiar with all of these regimes, you may sense that these are quite different from other dictatorships. Your sense is right. These are often distinguished from the others for their common attributes not found in other types of nondemocratic regimes, and this type of regime is called totalitarianism. Totalitarianism is different for its extreme level of control over the society. It is extreme in a sense that the totalitarian states always took a much more destructive and murderous path than the rest. The Nazi Germany and the Fascist Italy together started the Second World War while Germany systematically slaughtered millions of its own citizens. The Stalinist Soviets, the Maoist China, and the Juche North Korea conducted similar campaigns of fear toward their citizens by exposing them to repeated occurrences of starvation, hard labor, and torture, which resulted in the death of millions after millions. Totalitarianism is also unique because the regimes pursue a total control over every aspect of the society. It has not been about enriching a dictator's secret account in a Swiss bank or controlling diamond mines, but, it went much further.

What defines this special regime type? A major element is a total control over every aspect of society. Some authoritarian states have come close but not quite like totalitarian states. On one hand, some military regimes maintain a total control, typically using force, but the society lacks uniformity that is a typical product of totalitarianism. For example, in Burma the military regime maintained a total control until 2010, but the control is absolute largely in politics. The society is divided: an ethnic group, Karens, has been fighting the Burmese government and it is only one of many such ethnic groups fighting the Burmese regime; political opposition had remained persistent and, occasionally threatening. On the other hand, some theocratic societies have a totality based on the religion, but they do not have regimes with total control. For example, almost all Iranian citizens are Shiite Muslim, and moreover, the idea of Shiite Islam is the social and political force allowing no challenge. However, the political regime shares the ruling power with the religious establishment that is often more influential than the secular leaders who nominally rule the state. On top of these, there are signs of the growing power of the armed forces. Unlike these, in a totalitarian regime most citizens enjoy a symbiotic relationship in which the regime successfully convinced its people of their presumed, virtuous destiny, and the public enthusiastically supported or utterly depended on the regime. The creation of this kind of tie begins with the regime's successful mobilization of the large "masses"[17] encompassing different class interests. In other words, the totalitarian regimes were able to appeal to people with no regard to their political affiliation or economic status. Scholars point out that people were ready to accept a new form of regime, since the public developed "serious apathy toward bourgeoisie-led politics".[18] For example, after the First World War, Germans were devastated by repeated collapses of their government and worsening economic woes, such as the hyperinflation and the Great Depression. Germans were losing their confidence in their political leaders. The people were ready for a radical change: "the first signs of the breakdown of the [old] party system were not the desertion of old party members, but the failure to recruit members from the younger generation, and the loss of the silent consent and support of the unorganized masses."[19] Hence, people give themselves up to a set of new ideas summarized in an ideology with a great emphasis on their bright future in an almost messianic fashion.

Their set of ideas or the official ideology rests "in part on the rejection of traditional values and a demonstrative abhorrence of the past, in part on the conjuring up of chiliastic expectations of the future."[20] "Unless their power is exercised in the name of an ideology guided to a greater or lesser degree by some central ideas . . . and unless they use some form of mass organization and participation of members of the society beyond the armed forces and a police to impose their rules, we cannot speak of a totalitarian system, but . . . of authoritarian regimes."[21] In a totalitarian ideology, the sense of historical change toward betterment is common, and the development is always in the direction of totality, giving up individual liberty. For example, Mussolini, the Italian fascist leader, preached that the future comes along with the new human of Fascism who would be bonded together through the State. Here, propaganda played a major role and it was a key feature of the totalitarian regime, exploiting the masses' preference to consistent messages, as clearly demonstrated by the Nazi's exploitation of German bias against Jews.[22] The totality of a society is completed by the demonstration of blunt force, and it often aims at creating the environment where individuals have no place to turn to but to the state for their survival. For this purpose, the regime destroyed, in varying degrees, the social structure, leaving individuals totally atomized or individualized as in Bolshevik Russia where millions of the middle and peasant classes were killed or purged in the 1930s.[23] According to Hannah Arendt, such violence completely destroyed any shred of social connection, creating "the permanent domination of each single individual in each and every sphere of life."[24]

A Modern Totalitarian State The days of Nazi Germany are long gone, but there is now a state where totalitarianism survived six decades: the Democratic People's Republic of Korea, often known as North Korea. As a start, the society of North Korea is totally dependent on the state. For example, government activities account for most of the national economy: the government expenditure to gross national product (GNP) was "71.9 percent in 1990 compared with 34 percent in pre-reform China in 1979" while "its state owned manufacturing industries employ more than 56 percent of the work force, as against the USSR's 46 and Poland's 37 percent in the late 1980s."[25] The people rely on the food rationing, and the private market is limited or strictly under the control of the government. For example, in 2009 the government abruptly announced its currency reform that practically confiscated the wealth of the citizens overnight, by allowing only a small amount of money to be exchanged into the new currency, after tolerating limited market economy. They are not dependent only in the realm of economy. The people are allowed to watch and hear only the government sanctioned media, where political propaganda is the major part. Those who seek alternative sources of information risk severe government punishment: the security forces recently increased "their efforts to crack down on illicit video-viewing. North Korean law provides for a four-year sentence to labor camp for those who are found guilty of this offense."[26] Even their domestic travels require the government approval as was the case in China in 1950s.

Like the classic totalitarian states, the North Korean regime has used legalized violence against anyone with any form of challenge, however insignificant, to the regime, making fear a permanent feature of the society. The North Korean legal code specifies various crimes that are strange to the eyes of outsiders, including not reporting to the work, "anti-state, anti-people crime," "crimes injurious to socialist economy," or "importing and spreading depraved culture."[27] To punish and isolate violators, the state has built an extensive set of facilities. The notorious National Security Agency (NSA) runs about 14 labor camps (one of which is 31 miles long and 25 miles wide and houses 50,000 inmates),[28] and the agency has the power to pretty much eliminate anyone who deems to be a threat to the regime with no due legal process or by using its own court known as the Central Court in Pyungyang. The NSA's facilities are often located at the far northern part of the country where the weather is cold and brutal. Inmates suffer the harsh weather, maltreatment, hard labor, disease and starvation, which often results in death.[29] There are separate penitentiaries, collection centers, and labor training centres.

The central feature of this totalitarian regime is its unique political ideology, called Juche or "self-reliance." Kim Il-sung, the founder of North Korea, promulgated Juche in 1960s, emphasizing political, economic, and military independence, and it remains as the only ideology allowed by the state.[30] Its adherence to Juche made the country exceptional even among communist countries. It has refused to allow the Soviet or Chinese troops to be stationed on its soil even though they were the major military and political allies. Furthermore, North Korea denounced the countries for abandoning a pure version of Marxist-Leninism. Juche also served as a military guideline, allowing the country to develop nuclear weapons on its own and fostering a series of aggressive military actions toward South Korea and the US. Moreover, Juche has greatly contributed to the justification of the country's mayhems as well as the rule of the regime. The North Koreans accept the argument that the country's difficulties, including even the murderous famine in the 1990s, have resulted from the country's commitment to "self-reliance" defying the evil scheme of its enemy. Therefore, patience and endurance have become a proud part of the people while the blame and responsibility rarely reaches the regime. In short, the idea of Juche made the regime almost infallible.

Nondemocratic Regimes Reconsidered

By now, you might regard nondemocratic regimes as illegitimate or immoral. As we have seen, some are actually quite disastrous to the citizens. However, we should also remember democracy is a recent invention. Democracy spread all over the world beginning only in the 19th Century. According to Huntington, a long wave of democratization began in 1828 and lasted until 1926.[31] Even then, democracy was rather limited: democratic elements such as expansion of suffrage, introduction of secret ballot, responsible prime ministers, and a cabinet system were being embraced in largely western countries such as Switzerland, France, Great Britain, Italy, Argentina, Ireland, and Iceland. Prior to this, nondemocratic forms of government were the global norm. In a small political unit, elders collectively led the society, as still seen among native populations in remote and isolated areas of South America, Australia, and Africa. As small political units merged and became more complicated, a state was born and monarchy was a popular form of political system.

Monarchy, not in all countries with the system though, evolved to a political system with authoritative monarchs backed by a centralized and efficient bureaucracy as in Europe in the 17th and 18th centuries and China for the most part of its long history. Throughout the history of monarchy, there were many illegitimate and immoral monarchs such as a Roman Emperor, Nero who enjoyed mass executions and persecuted Christians. However, countless benign monarchs also existed as in the case of beloved King Sejong of Yi Dynasty of Korea whose achievements include defeating foreign enemies, strengthening a legal system, and inventing Hangul, the Korean alphabet. Thus, it should be remembered that nondemocratic regimes were actually legitimate and popular depending on how they ruled.

Persistence of Nondemocratic Regimes

A puzzle regarding authoritarian regimes is their sustainability in the era of democracy. It is possible that citizens were satisfied with nondemocratic political systems when there was no alternative form of government until recently. In such a situation, even a revolution typically replaced old monarch with new ones or brought about a new dynasty, at best. However, it is puzzling to see similar authoritarian regimes lasting in the era when a democratic form of government is present and democracies perform a state's basic functions much better than nondemocracies. Do citizens of nondemocracies not want to have democracy? What sustains nondemocracies?

The puzzle of resilience of nondemocracies deepens when we think about modern monarchies. The government that is ruling through rigged elections or not so fair ones is one thing, but the government ruled by a family over generations is quite another in the 21st century when information flow at the speed of light and cultural exchanges across borders are easy. It is also interesting to note that most modern monarchies are in one area, the Middle East. For example, Saudi Arabia has been under the rule of Saud family since 1932 when Abdul Aziz founded the Kingdom of Saudi Arabia. Ever since, all the kings have been his sons, including the current monarch, King Abdullah who ascended the throne in 2005.[32] Saudi Arabia is only one of many monarchic countries in the region, and the list includes Bahrain, Jordan, Kuwait, Oman, and Qatar. What sustains these monarchies?

A cultural argument asserts that the traditional patriarchic order is reflected in the political system. Extended families have been the social and economic basis in the region, and the monarchy is simply the political extension of the tradition. For example, Saudi monarchs have often addressed their subjects as children. Such a patriarchical system successfully adapted to modern political development and hence it is flourishing in the region.[33] However, the fact that all the monarchies in the region are a modern phenomenon requires another explanation. For that, one could provide an account based on the colonial past in the region. As Western colonial powers, including France, Italy, and Great Britain were busy with dividing the land of the Ottoman Empire, the monarchy model was, especially for the British, familiar from their own experiences and a convenient one for them to install and control.[34] Once created, the tradition of monarchy has stayed. It did, in part, because the monarchs were the founding fathers of the countries and in a position to create a political and social system favoring their rules. For example, the Saud family crushed all religious as well as political opposition in the early 1930s, and the family forged and strengthened its grip on the religious movement known in the West as the Wahhabis. As the religious movement became the most prominent force of the country, this ideological monopoly strengthened the legitimacy of the Saud family's rule. In addition, these countries have maintained security apparatuses that are typically ubiquitous and effective in dealing with the opposition. For example, *mubahith*, the Saudi secret police is above the laws when they deal with any challenge to the regime. This domestic intelligence agency runs its own prisons, detains thousands of citizens suspected of being terrorists, as well as peaceful political dissenters, and prevents any meaningful judicial oversight.[35] Similar police forces, *mukhabarat* in Arabic, are common in the region's monarchic systems, as in Jordan.[36]

There is also the international context where the monarchs were able to thrive. Middle East monarchies have served the interests of the foreign powers well, even after the days of colonialism were over. This created an international context where monarchs gain important and crucial foreign support needed for the longevity of the monarchy. During the Cold War both the communist camp and the capitalist alliance sought friendly relationships with the countries in this area for strategic and economic reasons, and they relentlessly competed against each other.[37] As a result, the monarchs were showered with gifts in many forms, including weapons. Arms sales to the monarchs in the region of course continue even today. For example, in 2010 the Obama administration revealed that it would sell $60 billions worth of weapons to Saudi Arabia, and the items include 84 new F-15s and upgrades to Saudi Arabia's existing fleet of 70 F-15s, as well as new helicopters and a wide array of missiles, bombs and delivery systems, night-vision goggles, and radar warning systems.[38] This sale is expected to boost the political and military influence of the country in the region, especially regarding the rising power of Iran.

As the opposite of democracy, nondemocracy means the political regime with no real free and fair election that allows the people to reflect their voice in governing processes. However, the common element stops right there. As you have seen, there are a variety of nondemocratic regimes in the world today. Some leaders exploit democratic political institutions to the extent that the line between the democratic regime and actual democratic governing gets blurred while some ignore entire civilian laws, using sheer force. Some use religious ideology to silence the opposition while some rely on an effective political machine based on the rule of a political party. We have seen regimes that master all of these tactics in a way, creating a total control over the entire society. These are not things of the past, but rather current and actually evolving events in some cases, just as democracy has been developing over the years.

Notes

1 The following discussion on regime types largely depends on the insight of our colleague Greg Cashman of Salisbury University.
2 Asian Human Rights Commission, "Statement from Professors in North America Concerned about Korean Democracy," June 10, 2009. http://sites.google.com/site/koreandemocracywatch/home/2009-statement. (accessed November 6, 2011).
3 Amnesty International, "South Korea – Amnesty International Report 2010," http://www.amnesty.org/en/region/south-korea/report-2010. (accessed November 6, 2011).
4 Ibid.
5 The Center for Arms Control and Non-Proliferation, http://armscontrolcenter.org/policy/securityspending/articles/fy11_growth_since_2001/. (accessed November 6, 2011).
6 Jonathan Kandell, "Augusto Pinochet, Dictator Who Ruled by Terror in Chile, Dies at 91," *The New York Times*, December 11, 2006, http://www.nytimes.com/2006/12/11/world/americas/11pinochet.html?_r=1&pagewanted=all. (accessed November 6, 2011).
7 Ibid.
8 Ibid.
9 H.E. Chehabi, "Religion and Politics in Iran: How Theocratic is the Islamic Republic?" *Religion and Politics* 120 (1991): 73.
10 Ibid.
11 Chehabi, "Religion and Politics in Iran: How Theocratic is the Islamic Republic?" 76.
12 The Iranian Constitution, http://confinder.richmond.edu/. (accessed November 6, 2011).
13 Article 4, The Iranian Constitution, http://confinder.richmond.edu/. (accessed November 6, 2011).

14 Chehabi, "Religion and Politics in Iran: How Theocratic is the Islamic Republic?" 79.

15 Hannibal Travis, "Freedom or Theocracy?" *Northwestern University Journal of International Human Rights* 3 (2005): 1–52. http://www.law.northwestern.edu/journals/jihr/v3/4/Travis.pdf. (accessed November 6, 2011).

16 Travis, "Freedom or Theocracy?" 13.

17 Hannah Arendt, *The Origins of Totalitarianism* (Cleveland, OH: The World Publishing Company, 1951, 1958), 308.

18 Arendt, *The Origins of Totalitarianism*, 311–313.

19 Arendt, *The Origins of Totalitarianism*, 315.

20 Karl D. Bracher, "The Disputed Concept of Totalitarianism: Experience and Actuality," in *Totalitarianism Reconsidered*, ed. Ernest A. Menze (Port Washington, NY, London: National University Publication, 1981), 19.

21 Juan J. Jinz, *Totalitarian and Authoritarian Regimes* (Bounder and London: Lynne Rienner Publisher, 2000), 67.

22 Arendt, *The Origins of Totalitarianism*, 351, 355–356. To see actual propaganda pieces, go to a website called Nazi and East Germany Propaganda Guide Page. http://www.calvin.edu/academic/cas/gpa/. (accessed November 6, 2011).

23 Arendt, *The Origins of Totalitarianism*, 320.

24 Arendt, *The Origins of Totalitarianism*, 326.

25 Kim Junki, "North Korea's Economy, Once Freed, Will Need Shock Therapy," (World Bank, 2001).

26 Christian Caryl, "North Korea: The Crisis of Faith" *The New York Review of Books*, 2010, http://www.nybooks.com/articles/archives/2010/jul/15/north-korea-crisis-faith/?pagination=false. (accessed November 6, 2011).

27 Steven Haggard and Marcus Noland, "Repression and Punishment in North Korea," East-West Center Working Papers 20, 2009, 33, http://www.eastwestcenter.org/fileadmin/stored/pdfs/pswp020.pdf. (accessed November 6, 2011).

28 Haggard and Noland, "Repression and Punishment in North Korea," 7.

29 Haggard and Noland, "Repression and Punishment in North Korea," 8–9.

30 Grace Lee, "The Political Philosophy of Juche," *Stanford Journal of East Asian Affairs* 3, no. 1 (2003): 105–112.

31 Samuel P. Huntington, *The Third Wave: Democratization in the Late Twentieth Century* (Norman and London: University of Oklahoma Press, 1991).

32 PBS, Frontline: The House of Saud, http://www.pbs.org/wgbh/pages/frontline/shows/saud/tree/. (accessed November 6, 2011).

33 Lisa Anderson, "Absolutism and the Resilience of the Monarchy in the Middle East," *Political Science Quarterly* 106 (1991): 1–15.

34 Lisa Anderson, "Absolutism and the Resilience of the Monarchy in the Middle East," 5–6.

35 Human Rights Watch, "Saudi Arabia: Counterterrorism Efforts Violate Rights," http://www.hrw.org/en/news/2009/08/04/saudi-arabia-counterterrorism-efforts-violate-rights. (accessed November 6, 2011).

36 Neil MacFarquhar, "Heaby Hand of the Secret Police Impeding Reform in Arab World," *The New York Times,* November 14, 2005. http://www.nytimes.com/2005/11/14/international/middleeast/14jordan.html?_r=1. (accessed November 6, 2011).

37 Simon Head, "Monarchs of the Persian Gulf," *The New York Review of Books*, March 21, 1974, http://www.nybooks.com/articles/archives/1974/mar/21/the-monarchs-of-the-persian-gulf/?pagination=false. (accessed November 6, 2011).

38 Ewen MacAskill, "US Congress Notified over \$60bn Arms Sale to Saudi Arabia" The Guardian, October 21, 2010, http://www.guardian.co.uk/world/2010/oct/21/us-congress-notified-arms-sale-saudi-arabia. (accessed November 6, 2011).

CHAPTER 9

Political Parties, Elections and Voting Behavior

POLITICAL PARTIES DEFINED

For well over a century politics in the United States has been dominated by two main parties: the Democratic Party and the Republican Party. Their British equivalents are the Labour Party, the Conservative Party, and the Liberal Democrats. In Japan, the main political parties are the Liberal Democratic Party and the Democratic Party of Japan. Political parties are also common in nondemocratic countries. Under Hosni Mubarak's authoritarian rule in Egypt, the National Democratic Party dominated the Parliament for about 30 years while the CCP has kept its political monopoly ever since the founding of People's Republic of China in 1949. In other words, without understanding political parties and their roles, it is almost impossible to understand modern politics. So, we will discuss the issue of political parties and their most relevant function, election.

A political party is a formal association of people who share 1) a similar set of evaluations of public problems; 2) general policy solutions; and 3) a strong desire to obtain seats in the governing body such as the government and the legislature. Let's take a look at the Democratic Party in the United States. First, it is a formal organization. The Democratic Party's national committee (DNC) has its building in Washington, DC. The party leadership is made of the DNC Chairman, a few vice chairs, secretary, treasurer, and staff members with specific and professional titles such as Marketing Assistant, Analytic Engineer, or Web Developer.[1] Under the DNC, there are various organizations, such as the Democratic Governors' Association, the Democratic Senatorial Campaign Committee, the Democratic Legislative Campaign Committee, the Association of State Democratic Chairs, as well as state organizations in all 50 states. In short, the Democratic Party is not an ad hoc group, but one with a well-established physical and institutional structure.

Second, the party members and supporters largely share a set of ideas regarding the problems which face the country and how they should be addressed. For example, civil rights are important for many Democrats and the party is expected to address this issue seriously (this issue was the first item on the DNC website as of February 15, 2011). The party suggests that we assure civil rights via "strengthening the Justice Department's Civil Rights Division to better protect voting rights; . . . Ensuring civil unions and equal federal rights for LGBT couples, as well as fully repealing the Defense of Marriage Act; Ending racial, ethnic, and religious profiling."[2] A quick review shows stark differences with the party's major rival, the Republican Party. Civil rights are not on the list of the party's major issues as of the same date. Instead, the first on the list is national defense, requiring "a strong ballistic missile defense . . . and a capable intelligence community . . . ."[3]

The political parties need and create such differences because they would like to appeal to people whose ideas are more aligned to their own party rather than the other party. By increasing popular support their goal is, in the end, to increase their seats in the Congress and gain the control over the White House. Electoral successes are the most fundamental goal of any political party and the major difference with similar groups such as lobbying firms that do not seek offices. Of course, political parties inherently have public goals, such as civil rights and national defense, to pursue. So, you might think that these should be a political party's important objectives. They are, but secondary to the electoral successes because without the latter, the former cannot be effectively pursued to begin with. In other words, you have to be elected first in order to implement the ideas and proposals you believe will move the country forward.

THE FUNCTION OF POLITICAL PARTIES

Interest Articulation

Two of the most important functions of political parties are interest articulation and election campaign. The first major function, interest articulation is to articulate people's interests and turn them into policies. There are various actors in a typical democratic society that do similar tasks. Scholars, lobbyists, and various non-governmental organizations also write policies. However, political parties have serious interests in writing policies based on the public opinion because it is their major job to actually write policies and to execute them as public servants. Therefore, when other actors generate policy proposals and ideas, they often flow to the members of political parties. In addition, interest articulation is critical because the members' success and the party's popularity depend on how well they conduct this function. If a political party fails to demonstrate its ability to articulate the public's interest well, the party would be punished by losing seats in the legislative body in future elections, which could eventually bring an end to the party as an effective political entity.

It is critical, therefore, for political parties to gauge the public's interests, and this task can be done in various ways. The citizens are sometimes given opportunities to directly hear and talk to the representatives of the party in public meetings such as a hearing or a town hall meeting. Public meetings allow residents to express their concerns over certain issues in their neighborhood. For example, in 2009, Maryland Senator Cardin held such a meeting to discuss issues regarding health care programs at a concert hall at Towson University, Maryland.[4] The hall with 500 seats was packed and people who could not get seats rallied outside. It was more than a town meeting. Supporters of the reform bill gathered to listen to the senator while the opponent came to protest the bill. The two sides clashed and engaged in heated debates and even shouting matches. It was a strong demonstration of, if nothing else, deep interests of the public and the political importance of the issue. However, this kind of direct contact is relatively rare. Most often, citizens can get in touch with their representatives through indirect contact, such as letters, phone calls, faxes, and emails. In the US, law makers receive thousands of messages from constituents each week, making these a major source of input from the public.

Another way to read the public's interest is through opinion polls. Parties and elected officials hire professional pollsters or rely on polling companies to learn public opinion on various issues. President Clinton was well known for his fondness of polling and his trust of his pollsters.[5] He was the first one to read the reports of polls, and held weekly polling meetings in his residence in the White House. Polls were taken to gauge the public opinion on various issues including "supporting school uniforms . . . reforming welfare, balancing the budget, and putting 100,000 new police office on the streets,"[6] and for this Clinton's White House spent close two million dollars only in the first year in the office. Such enthusiastic following of polls affected how he handled major issues. Early in his first term Clinton attempted to tackle the controversial issue of health care reform, and the result in the midterm election in 1994 was disastrous. Clinton formed a new polling team and responded better to the wishes of median voters by moving toward the center of the political spectrum. All politicians cannot afford polling as much as Clinton did; however, his example is a good illustration of what political parties do to learn public opinion.

Elections

By definition, political parties compete, and they do so in elections. Obviously political parties hope to be successful in elections. In the US, there are many electoral positions to be filled, including chief executive officer, lawmakers, prosecutors, and judges. For example, in Maryland, there were 11 positions to be filled in the 2010 election. The positions included a judge of the Circuit Court and a judge at the Court of Special Appeal.[7] From political parties' perspective elections allow many opportunities to compete for the control over all three branches of the US government. Hence to be successful, the parties need candidates who are both appealing to the voters and in harmony with the party ideology. In this way, the parties can bring the country closer to their vision. Political parties' nomination is somewhat formal in the US where the party's candidates are mostly elected by the party members and the public in primary elections. However, such formality is not always the case in other countries. It is fairly common that party candidates are chosen behind the door for their political connection, rather than their appeal to the public or their ability to do the job, and such a practice could be politically costly. For example, in the 2008 election, the Grand National Party (GNP), the majority party of South Korea that also controls the presidency, nominated its candidates in many electoral districts based on their loyalty to President Lee Myung-bak. Many who lost the party nomination belonged to another major faction that is loyal to Park Geun-Hye, the daughter of the former dictator Park Jung-Hee. They departed the party and forged their own with an appropriate name, Pro-Park Geun-Hye Alliance. Many of them actually ended up defeating the GNP's candidates in the election.

Once nominated the candidates largely run their election campaigns by themselves, but still, political parties' roles remain substantial. For one, there is fundraising. Especially here in the US, winning elections is becoming more and more expensive and individual candidates often cannot raise enough money on their own. Therefore, political parties' financial contribution has become more important. Before we examine this function, let's first see how costly electoral victory is. The 61st Speaker of the US House of Representative, John Boehner spent $13,074,250 for the 2009–2010 electoral cycle to win the 8th congressional district in Ohio.[8] That's a lot of money. Let's just put this in a perspective. In a middle size, strong state university in the city of Salisbury, MD, the total cost for an out-of-state undergraduate student's education and living on campus was roughly $25,000 during the 2010–2011 academic year.[9] With the amount of money he spent for his election campaign, about 523 students could have all the expenses covered for a year. Boehner not only spent a huge amount of money, but also did so much more than his rivals did. He has continuously outspent his competitors by substantial ratios. For example, in the 2010 election he spent 40 times as much as Coussoule did. In the 2008 election, he spent 346.5 times more than his rival did.[10]

Boehner's spending is certainly above the norm; however, unfortunately, his case is not so rare. If we look at a few expensive senate races of 2010, The amounts of money spent in some elections are simply astronomical. For example, in a 2010 race for a U.S. Senate seat in Connecticut, candidates spent a staggering $59,214,824.[13] In all, the price tag of the 2010 midterm election was about four billion dollars, including "all federal election spending over the two-year election cycle by political parties and congressional candidates, as well as independent groups who spent big money to influence voters."[11] Again, putting this in perspective, $4 billion is "roughly equal to the amount that the Department of State has requested for assistance to Afghanistan in FY 2011 . . . [or] . . . larger than the GDPs of 55 nations worldwide, including Greenland ($2 billion), Kosovo ($3.2 billion), and Somalia ($2.7 billion)."[12]

Financing such expensive election campaigns is hard without organized help from political parties. Boehner is not an exception. In the 2009–2010 election cycle, he received more than three millions dollars from "Grand Old Party" (GOP) through the Leadership Political Action Committee.[14] In fact, in this era in which financing is a consequential factor of electoral victory, political parties's role as fund-raiser is ever more important. For the 2009-2010 election cycle, the Democratic Party raised $255,753,575 and spent $232,049,988 while the GOP raised $227,357,862 and spent $174,504,755.[15] Top contributors to the Democratic Party were political action committees such as Friends of Schumer ($4,710,000), Hoyer for Congress ($2,599,600), and Nancy Pelosi for Congress ($1,714,000). If we look at the contribution by industry, the retirees ($34,194,631), lawyer and law firms ($28,300,445), and securities & investment industry ($17,056,206) top the list.[16] The fund that the Democratic Party raised was used for various services needed to run electoral campaigns. For example, the party paid a company called Action Mailers $3,918,797 for postage, shipping, and direct mail services, a law firm, Perkins Coie $1,524,103 for the company's legal services, Allied Printing Resources $1,209,291 for design and printing, $5 to Starbucks at Salt Lake City International Airport, $2 to a parking meter at Chicago, and so on.[17]

Political Ideology

Another major function of political parties to formulate and maintain political ideologies. Discussed in detail in Chapter 6 of this text, political ideology can be defined as a verbalized image of a good society and the idea about the way toward the goal, according to Anthony Downs.[18] Political ideologies are critically important for political parties to signal where they stand given the complexity and magnitude of issues of politics. Consider that they include export of beefs, selling jet fighters, importation of oil, taxing imported steels, putting economic sanctions on Libya, cutting nuclear weapons, allowing people to carry guns on the campus of universities, barring women to seek abortion, reforming medical insurance, cutting federal government's deficits, to name only a few issues here in the US. Since there are so many issues, it is impossible for any voter to have good ideas on every single one even if they all have effects on her. Furthermore, let's say this voter has followed the issue of federal deficits and is herself familiar with this important issue. But, how much could she really know? Be mindful of the size of the federal deficit, about $1.3 trillion in 2010,[19] and there are dozens of federal agencies with various tasks.[20] Can she really be knowledgeable enough to understand the nature of the deficit and evaluate its short-term and long-term effects? Really? If not, how can she have a stance on this issue, much less vote for a political party based on her opinion on it? Now enter one more complication that she is a single mother with twin sons working three part-time jobs. Does she even have the time needed to study federal deficit and be opinionated or even dogmatic about this issue? Not so likely. But then, what can explain such an attitude shared by many people who supported the budget cut to reduce the federal deficits while many economists, including a Nobel laureate Paul Krugman, a professor of economics at Princeton University, have repeatedly warned the cut as dangerous and harmful?[21] Not everyone has been so lucky like Dr. Krugman who studied at Yale and MIT and spent the last 30 years or so studying economics. Moreover, our daily routine does not allow enough time, forcing us to be content with a very brief summary for an understanding. Actually, the more concise, the better.

Political ideologies come in handy when voters need such brief and concise explanations. People often decide on issues without serious contemplation. Instead, they usually make a decision following their political ideologies. Let's hear the justification for budget cut proposals in the middle of the Great Recession. Why do we have to cut spending while the economy is still significantly weak and the US unemployment rate is historically high? According to Republican Paul Ryan's response to the 2011 State of Union by the President, the "reason is simple . . . We face a crushing burden of debt. The debt will soon eclipse our entire economy, and grow to catastrophic levels in the years ahead. On this current path, when my three children—who are now 6, 7, and 8 years old—are raising their own children, the Federal government will double in size, and so will the taxes they pay . . . The next generation will inherit a stagnant economy and a diminished country."[22] This may sound easy enough to accept, but it leaves out all the more complicated and theoretical debates and factual information such as the fact that the government's stimulus program got us out of the financial crisis that began in 2007. Unfortunately, people often turn to even more simple explanations such as the following: "We oppose interventionist policies that put the federal government in control of industry and allow it to pick winners and losers in the marketplace"[23] or even like this: "Obama's Secular-Socialist Machine."[24] They are easy enough to understand (socialism is bad!) and brief enough to pay attention to (socialism, one word). Thus, people often become content with simple sentences or even a few nouns when the issue is worthy of several books in order to understand its causes, potential effects, and alternative views.

This desire for a brief summary provides a major opportunity for political parties. Therefore, it is important for political parties to sharpen their political ideologies that distinguish them from other political parties so that they can attract the sympathetic voters' support.

TYPES OF POLITICAL PARTIES

There are various types of political parties. Depending on who leads the party, they can be divided into cadre parties and mass parties.[25] Cadre parties are political parties largely made of the political elite who run the party for themselves and by themselves. Mass parties rely on people for the financial contribution and support, seeking as many members as possible, and they grew first in Western Europe during the early 20th century.

Nowadays, the political parties that we typically see are the hybrid parties in which the political elite lead the party while the masses contribute to their cause by paying the membership fees, giving campaign donation for the party candidates, and giving the needed allegiance to the party.

We can also categorize political parties depending on their issues. First, there are political parties, covering a wide range of major issues of the entire society. Such parties include the Republican Party and the Democratic Party of the US, the Conservative Party and the Liberal Party of Canada. They deal with almost every aspect of the entire population, or at least claim to do so. The second group of parties covers a variety of issues but with a limited or focused regional reach. The Bloc Québécois of Canada represents the interest of the French-speaking population in Quebec, often defying the interests of the entire population of Canada, and gains seats mostly in the state of Quebec. Likewise, the Scottish National Party and Plaid Cymru represent the voice of the Scotts and the Welsh, respectively, in the British parliament. The last group is issue-oriented parties. They typically have one major issue on their agenda and narrowly pursue it. Green parties are a good example. They are largely concerned with environmental issues and focus on policies regarding this theme. They often have a small size of followers, but occasionally grow to be a significant political force as in the case of the Alliance '90/The Greens of Germany that was a junior partner of the government from 1998–2005.

POLICY

Political parties forge collective wills. The members of a political party largely share similar ideas and such an ideological similarity ties them together as a political unit. In other words, political parties tie individual members, most noticeably lawmakers, together under their brand names. Had it not been for such a political boundary, it might be really difficult to pass any bill on the floor of the legislative body. Imagine forming a group, hopefully the majority, of lawmakers each and every time there is a bill. It would be hard to find whom you might want to talk to, not knowing what to expect and difficult to convince them to join your cause only with empty promises of your future cooperation. If anything, it would become an impossibly slow process of law-making. The political boundary helps the processes proceed. In addition, should there be any difference among the members of the same party, the party leaders entice or cajole the members of the party into finding common ground, either by promising favors or threatening punishment.

The political parties are not always cohesive. In fact, members of the same party do have differences: they are from different cities and states; some went to law school while some were farmers. They often do have different policy ideas, reflecting dissimilar interests, and lawmakers occasionally vote on their own, defying the party lines. Party members with a similar idea tend to flock together and sometimes form their own faction within the party. As we saw in the case of the GNP of South Korea, factions could be formed following a party leader. For example, the GNP notably comprises of members who follow the president (Lee Myung-bak faction) and those who follow Park Geun-Hye (Park Geun-Hye faction). Likewise, the Liberal Democratic Party of Japan is notorious for its powerful factions such as Michimura faction, Tsushima faction, or Koga faction.[27] Japanese elections that allowed multiple candidates from a single party to compete against each other prior to the 1994 reform enhanced the importance of factions. They provided candidates with support and finance and functioned as a major route for the ministerial positions.

American political parties are no exception even though factions are formed much more based on political ideas than loyalty to leaders. For example, within the Democratic Party, there are progressives, centralists, the Blue Dog Coalition among others. As the popularity of Obama dwindled after the first year in the Oval Office, so did progressive ideas' appeal to the public. Especially toward the midterm elections in 2010 when voters felt increasingly frustrated with the Obama administration, the Blue Dogs, who are more conservative on some issues than is the case with most Democrats, sang a different tune from the party as they became major targets of the Republican Party. As fiscal conservatives, they worry the health care reform, the flagship program of President Obama and Speaker Pelosi, would increase the cost for business owners and did their best to impede the party's efforts to dramatically change the system.[28] As a result, the attempts to reform the programe were partially stunted, lacking meaningful changes needed to cut the costs for the consumers and the country alike. One political consequence of this division within the Democratic Party was to alienate many of the core supporters of the party who had desired a substantial reform of the program.

The division and competition of factions of political parties can harm their unity and consequently confuse or disappoint their supporters as we saw in the case of the health care reform bill. They could drain the political resources, such as time and publicity, which could have been used in a more productive manner. They could significantly weaken political parties if a faction leaves the party or leaders defect to form their own political party as occasionally occurs in Japan.

By now the reader may assume that party factions are inherently bad. However, the division within a political party is not always harmful to the party. The presence of factions within a political party allows people with different ideas to stay under one roof so that they can help each other by rallying under their party's flag, but at the same time pursue the interests and goals of their own faction. Without such wiggle room, it would be difficult for the political parties to maintain enough members and for power to be significant.

ELECTIONS: FUNCTIONS AND FORMATS

Political parties compete and want to win in elections, which is the key element of democracy. Nowadays, elections are actually the most important political mechanism in most countries, including many nondemocratic countries as well. Elections create and maintain the consensus about a state's political leadership, or in other words, give them political legitimacy. They legitimize the political regime, and they do so for three important actors. First, it is the political leaders who are given the legitimacy or at least the appearance of it. Through the victory of elections, rulers claim the mandate for their political authority: people vote and their electoral system determines the winner; then, the people just decided whom they would like to follow. So, until the next election, people should follow the winner, as promised. Even Mubarak, the former leader of Egypt who ruled the country from 1981–2011, bothered to go through elections to renew his mandate. Thus, he argued that the protesters during the 2011 Revolution were seeking "to violate the constitutional legitimacy and to attack it."[29] However, the corrupt nature of the elections in Egypt was so obvious that the government needed more than elections, such as repression, to maintain the rule of Mubarak. Inversely speaking, free and fair elections are usually good enough to give the needed legitimacy to the rulers. Therefore, these leaders can avoid the debates over their legitimacy and the waste of the time and energy for political, and sometimes violent, controversies.

Second, in a similar vein, elections allow political oppositions to survive and challenge the regime in safety. The Liberal Democratic Party (LDP) of Japan lost a historical election in 2003 to the Democratic Party of Japan. It was historical because the LDP was never out of power since 1955 except for a brief 11-month period between 1993 and 1994. The 2003 election was the LDP's first actual and significant political defeat. However, the LDP remains an influential political force vying for the victory in the next election. Their members were not punished or killed as they would have been in the days of Samurai warfare. Moreover, regular elections offer the hope that losers would be given the chance to be victorious in the future. This hope would convince the losers that it is cheaper and more practical to prepare for the next election than to grab AK-47s, sharpen samurai swords, or train suicide bombers. Finally, the citizens can enjoy the opportunity to give political legitimacy to the party that appears to have done a good job while it was in power. If not, the citizens can fire the incumbent leadership and replace it with an alternative political force. Thus, elections empower citizens in an unprecedented manner. Never in human history have governments allowed such a large number of the members of a political entity the power to decide their leaders on a scale that modern democratic states have allowed. Given such opportunities, citizens can largely remain content with the current set of political leaders, or at least put up with them until the next election.

Electoral Systems

Elections select the winners by counting the votes. This may sound simple, but in fact this process of turning the votes into seats is anything but simple. So, let's review several ways to translate the number of votes to the number of seats, more formally called the electoral system. The simplest type of electoral system is the plurality system. In this system, the candidate with the most votes wins the seat. Simple, isn't it? This system can be even simpler by allowing only one candidate to win and only one vote to be cast by each voter. This is called first-past-the-post (FPP). This is widely popular for its simplicity including here in the US, the UK, and South Korea. In the 1987 presidential election, the candidate of the ruling party, Roh Tae-woo, gained 36.6% followed by Kim Youngsam (28.0%), Kim Daejung (27%), Kim Jongpil (8.1%), and Shin Jungil (0.2%).[30] The winner was, of course, Roh who gained the most votes. However, does this look right to you? The president with only 36.6% of the votes? Did he really gain the legitimacy from the people? The majority actually oppose his presidency, right? This is still a problem even when the candidate gained the majority of the vote as in the case of the Senate race in North Carolina during the 2010 midterm election. The first one who went past the pole was the Republican Richard Burr with 54.9% of the votes followed by the Democrat Elaine Marshall who gained 42.9%.[31] The winner was, of course, Burr. Can we really say Burr represent the entire state of Illinois even when his major opponent gain almost a half of the total votes? The answer must be a yes, but to be such a definite yes, the majority seems to be a little shaky.

The FPP system often generates results of which legitimacy appears to be weak, and there is another layer of problem with this system. Not only could there be a winner who captures a relatively modest level of support from the voters, but small parties tend to go extinct under this electoral system. Why? Let's review the situation here in the US. Say you were a wholehearted supporter of the environmental movement. Would you vote for the Green Party? (Yes, there is a Green Party and The Green Party actually nominated their candidates for the 2008 presidential election and ended up with no electoral vote.) Seriously. Would you? The Green Party? Can you even name their candidate under this electrol system? Why not? You don't want to waste your vote when you know that The Green Party has no chance of winning the presidency of the US. Then, what would you or did you do? You would pick the next best (in this case " the next best" meaning the mainstream party which comes closest to matching the ideology and policy prescriptions of the Green Party) among the parties with a real chance of victory, such as the Democratic Party, or don't vote at all. It is almost the same with people on the far-right who typically settle with the Republican Party. Either you vote for the party in the middle or choose not to vote; the result is the same: the two parties in the middle suck the air in, leaving no breathing room for small parties. And we end up with two-party system as we have here in the US. So, the FPP typically produces a two-party system. This idea is called Duverger's law.

Even though this system is easy to understand and cheap to run, it is problematic enough to come up with a remedy. One way to fix this problem is to generate a majority (50% and one vote or more), not just a plurality, under the two round system (TRS). For example, according to Article 7 of the French Constitution of 1958, the "President of the Republic shall be elected by an absolute majority of votes cast. If such a majority is not obtained on the first ballot, a second ballot shall take place on the fourteenth day thereafter. Only the two candidates polling the greatest number of votes in the first ballot, after any withdrawal of better placed candidates, may stand in the second ballot." In other words the French electoral system always generates the candidate with an absolute majority of votes even though the majority of the public did not necessarily support the candidate. The 2002 presidential election was especially interesting because of the person who made the second ballot. The candidate who surprised everyone was Jean-Marie Le Pen who gained 16.86% of votes in the first round of the election. That put Le Pen behind the conservative candidate Jacques Chirac (19.88%), but in front of the Socialist candidate Lionel Jospin (16.18%).[32] Le Pen was not a typical politician in a sense that he did not belong to either conservative or leftist parties. He was far too conservative to be called the mainstream. He joined the Foreign Legion in 1954 and fought in Algeria. As the leader of the National Front, he caused many heated political and cultural debates. For example, once he said in an interview "[m]assive immigration has only just begun. It is the biggest problem facing France, Europe and probably the world. We risk being submerged."[33] The French republic reacted to the election result with fury and shame that they put a racist like Le Pen on the second place. The solidarity built on the feelings created a clear and overwhelming majority: Chirac with 82.2% of votes in the second round of election. However, Chirac was not that popular to begin with. In the first round, he garnered votes only slightly more than Le Pen did. In the second round, he was forged as the victor with more than an absolute majority by the TRS.

The TRS is only one way to produce the winner with a majority of votes. The alternative vote (AV) also ends up with the winner gaining the majority. The AV is also called instant-runoff voting because of the simultaneous runoff as the voters cast their ballot, unlike in France where the runoff is called following the first round of election and the voters vote yet again in the second round. How? People vote and do so by demonstrating their preference over the entire candidates. So, you mark "1" for your favorite candidate, "2" for your second, and so on. The candidate with an absolute majority becomes the winner. Should there be no such candidate, the candidate with the least number of "1" votes is eliminated, and his or her votes are transferred to the others according to the voters' preferences.[34] Confusing? Here is an example.

Table 9.1 shows the preferences of voters in the town called Superherovillage. 40% of voters have the following preference: Superman-Batman-Storm-Spiderman. 25% of them prefer Batman to Storm to Spiderman to Superman. 15% of them like Storm the most followed by Spiderman, Batman, and Superman. The rest's first choice is Spiderman followed by Storm, Batman, and Superman. Now let's say there is an election for their sole leader using the AV system and they all vote according to these preferences. Table 9.2 illustrates the results. They all vote as assumed, and then Superman tops the list (remember 40% of voters like him the most). He could have been declared as the winner under FPP, but not here. Likewise, under TRS, Superman and Batman will go the second round, but not here. So, what then? Since there is no one with a majority, the candidate with the least "1" votes is eliminated, and it is Storm. If you see Table 9.1, you can tell that her votes will be then transferred to Spiderman who was the second most popular among Storm supporters. As a result, in the second round, Spiderman surged as the candidate with the second most votes (35% = his votes from the first round [20%] + votes for Storm [15%]). But, there is still no candidate with a majority. Then who is at the bottom now? Batman! The candidate who could have gone to the second round under TRS! Let's see whom his votes should be transferred to. Storm is the second choice among his supporters, but she is already eliminated. Then who is the next in line? It is Spiderman. Then, Spiderman gets the votes originally cast for Batman. Adding Batman's votes (25%) to his votes (35%), Spiderman gains the needed majority (60%) and becomes the winner. Voters cast their ballots once and are done with voting. However, there were two runoffs, which produced a candidate with an absolute majority. This system is used most famously for the Australian House of Representatives.

There is a totally different electoral system, called proportional representation (PR). The major difference is that voters typically vote for a political party and the party greatly affects who will get seats in the legislative body. The idea behind this system is that the electoral system should allow a high level of similarity between the distribution of political forces in the society, the number of votes that they gain, and the number of seats as a result of the elections. A good example can be found in Israel where the major political cleavages include

TABLE 9.1 Preference of voters in the Superherovillage

40% of voter	25% of voters	20% of voters	15% of voters
Superman	Batman	Spiderman	Storm
Batman	Storm	Storm	Spiderman
Storm	Spiderman	Batman	Batman
Spiderman	Superman	Superman	Superman

TABLE 9.2 Election in the Superherovillage using AV system

Superhero	Round 1	Round 2	Round 3
Superman	40%	40%	40%
Spiderman	20%	35%	60%
Batman	25%	25%	—
Storm	15%	—	—

religious ideas as well as political ideologies. These cleavages are represented by responding political parties, and various parties have seats in the Israeli parliament, Knesset, representing their ideas. In the 2009 elections, the following parties gain significant seats in the parliament: Kadima (28 seats), Likud (27 seats), Yisrael Beiteinu (15 seats), Labour (13 seats), Shas (11 seats), and United Torah Judaism (5 seats).[35] Kadima, Likud, and Labor parties have been relatively more ideological than being religious. Kadima is central while Labor is leaning left and Likud is heavily conservative. Yisrael Beiteinu is strongly nationalist while Shas and United Torah Judaism are religiously conservatives. Moreover, all of these parties except for Labor sit in the cabinet, creating a coalition government with a wide range of ideologies. This kind of representation is not possible in a country that uses plurality elections as in the case of the US where a party represents the entire electoral district and the party of power is mostly one of the two major ones. Going back to the 2010 senate race of North Carolina, the winner was the Republican Party that gained 54.9% of the votes. Such a result is contrary to a the principles of proportional representation. Is it not proportional. In other words, if a political party gained about 54.9% of votes, it deserves about 54.9% of seats, not 100%.

The question is then how you could enhance the level of proportionality.

To understand the system, let's review a hypothetical election held in District Z of Fruitland as shown in Table 9.3. If it were an election that is typical here in the US, an FPP in a single member district, the winner should be the candidate from Apple, winning 100% seats (1 out of 1) only with 36% of total votes. Again, the problem is that the winner is hardly representative of the preferences of the majority of the electorate. However, it is inevitable in any plurality election. The PR system tries to amend this problem first by multiple seats in a district so that they can be divided according to the support that the political parties gain. In this election, let's assume District Z has five seats. People vote for their favorite party, not an individual candidate, and parties divide seats according to the size of votes. Let's imagine that Apple Party gained 60% of the votes, Banana Party, 20%, Cherry Party, 20% while the others gain no seats. Please guess how many seats each party will get. Think about it. Think. Ok. Yes, of course! Apple Party with 3 seats, Banana Party 1 seat, and Cherry Party 1 seat. Apple Party gained 60% of votes and thus deserves 60% of seats (3 seats) while parties with 20% of votes should be awarded with 20% of seats (1 seat). Intuitively, you will see that the price for a seat in this case is 20% of votes. In other words, political parties that failed to receive less than 20% of votes don't deserve any seat. Then, you see there is a perfect proportionality between the number of seats and the amount of votes. So far so good? The trouble is that this perfect scenario never occurs in reality. The reality resembles what you see in Table 9.3.

Now, let's go over Table 9.3. The following discussion is based on PR using a formula known as "largest remainder." The first thing that we need to figure out is the price for one seat or quota. There are various ways to calculate them, and we will use the Hare quota. As in the previous example, this quota can be gained by

TABLE 9.3 Fruitland's Parliamentary Election in District Z using Largest Remaind

Largest Remainder							
Name of Party	Number of valid votes (A)	% of total votes (B)	(A) / Hare Quota (votes/seats = 4840) (C)	Remainder (D)	(E)	Total seats (C) + (E) = (F)	% of total seats (G)
Apple	8700	36.0	1	3860	1	2	40
Banana	6800	28.1	1	1960		1	20
Cherry	5200	21.5	1	360		1	20
Dewberry	3300	13.6	0	3300	1	1	20
Eggplant	200	0.8	0	200		0	0
Total	24,200	100	3		2	5	100

dividing the total number of votes by the total number of seats. In this case, it is 4,840 (24,200 divided by 5). Then, we would like to know how much of the quota each of the political parties has met. This is shown in Column C. For example, Apple Party got 8,700 votes (Column A) and if you divide this by the quota you get 1 with a reminder of 3,860 (shown in Column D). The result of this step for all the parties is shown in Column C. Now all the top three parties gain one seat each. Remember there are five seats to fill and thus we have two more seats to give away. Which party deserves them? Can you guess? A hint: what's the name of this formula? That's right! The parties with the largest remainders get the extra seats. See Column D and look which parties have the largest reminders. Apple Party and Dewberry Party have the largest remainder and each get an extra seat. Then, that's it! We just distributed five seats. Look at Column F. Apple Party gained two seats while the rest of the parties, except Eggplant Party, receive one seat. Is this result proportional? Compare Column B and Column G. Aren't they something or what?

Largest remainder is, of course, one of many, many ways to run a PR system. Let us introduce only (!) a couple of more ways. A formula known as D'Hondt Hagenbach-Bischoff is demonstrated in Table 9.4 using the same election results as in Table 9.3. All you do is to give a seat to the party with the most votes and halve the number of votes and repeat this process until all seats are distributed. Look at the number of votes and it is Apple Party that gained the most votes. So, in this first step (1st Seat Division) Apple Party gains a seat and loses a half of its votes (8,700 ⟶ 4,350). In the 2nd Seat Division, which party is the victor now (hint: look for a star)? Yes, it is Banana Party. Banana Party gains a seat, but loses a half of its votes (6,800 ⟶ 3,400). And you go on. Another way is known as D'Hondt formula. It is rather simple. As you can see in Table 9.5, all you do is to halve the number of votes of all the parties and simply award seats to the largest numbers as indicated by stars in the table.

Please notice that results vary depending on the formula that each used. As shown in Table 9.6, Apple Party fares well with two seats or 40% of seats with 36% of votes in all formulas. Banana Party did not do so well in the largest remainder. It gained 28% of votes, but ended up with only 20% of seats. However, in the other cases, it ended up with 40% of seats. The experience of Dewberry Party is the most dramatic because it gained 20% of seats with 13.6% of votes in largest remainder election, but gained 0 seats in the others.

There is one more thing to mention here. Look at Eggplant Party. It gained only 0.8% of votes, that is, seemingly too small to be significant. However, it is always possible that small parties like this might gain a seat depending on various factors, including electoral formula. One could argue that such a party has only a very small size of support and its agenda is too extreme to be part of the national politics. In order to prevent such parties gaining any seats, states using the PR system typically have a mechanism called a threshold. It is usually 5% of national votes. In other words, political parties that gained less than 5% of votes nationwide are dropped from the calculation and votes for these parties become invalid. As you can guess, the higher the threshold gets, the more difficult it is for small parties to gain seats.

TABLE 9.4 Fruitland's Parliamentary Election in District Z using D'Hondt Hagenbach-Bischoff

D'Hondt Hagenbach-Bischoff								
Name of Party	Number of valid votes	1st Seat Division	2nd Seat Division	3rd Seat Division	4th Seat Division	5th Seat Division	Total	% of total seats (G)
Apple	8700	*8700	4350	4350	*4350	2225	2	40
Banana	6800	6800	*6800	3400	3400	*3400	2	40
Cherry	5200	5200	5200	*5200	2600	2600	1	20
Dewberry	3350	3350	3350	3350	3350	3350	0	
Eggplant	200	200	200	200	200	200	0	
Total	24,200							

TABLE 9.5 Fruitland's Parliamentary Election in District Z using D'Hondt

D'Hondt								
Name of Party	Number of valid votes	1st Seat Division	2nd Seat Division	3rd Seat Division	4th Seat Division	5th Seat Division	Total	% of total seats (G)
Apple	8700	*8700	*4350	2900	2175	1740	2	40
Banana	6800	*6800	*3400	2266.667	1700	1360	2	40
Cherry	5200	*5200	2600	1733.333	1300	1040	1	20
Dewberry	3350	3350	1650	1100	825	660	0	
Eggplant	200	200	100	66.66667	50	40	0	
Total	24,200							

TABLE 9.6 Comparison of PR Elections

Name of Party	Number of valid votes	% of total votes	Number of seats using Largest Remainder	Number of seats using D'Hondt Hagenbach-Bischoff	Number of seats using D'Hondt
Apple	8700	36.0	2	2	2
Banana	6800	28.1	1	2	2
Cherry	5200	21.5	1	1	1
Dewberry	3300	13.6	1	0	0
Eggplant	200	0.8	0	0	0
Total	24,200	100	5	5	5

VOTER'S CHOICE

*What affects voters' choice? It is not easy to tell because there are so many factors to be considered and elections are held in unique contexts in history. Nevertheless, there are a few factors to be noticed. For now let's focus on the US elections, particularly presidential elections. First of all, there is the economy. When the economy is good, people tend to support the incumbent and his or her party. There are jobs and money, and people usually like it and want to continue the trend by supporting the political leaders who they think have created such economic prosperity. For example, a study finds that "A [presidential] candidate from the president's party running in a year when real GDP grows at an annual rate of 5 percentage points during the second quarter can expect to receive an additional 3% of the vote compared with a candidate from the president's party running in a year when there is no growth in real GDP during the second quarter."[36] Another major factor is job approval ratings. The higher the approval rating the more likely that voter would vote for the candidate of the incumbent party. There is evidence with a study finding that "for every 1 percentage point increase in the president's net approval rating, the candidate of the president's party can expect an increase of just over 0.1% of the major-party vote."[37]

There is no doubt as to how the political leaders have a major impact on how people vote. It is also important to note that the attributes of voters themselves affects how they vote. In the 2008 presidential election, the voter's ethnic background played a major role: the blacks and the Latinos backed Obama. The youth, particularly the youth among the blacks, showed strong support for Obama while the married went the other way. The wealthy, especially the white wealthy, voted for McCain. The ideology and religion matter, too. The more liberal, the more likely they were to support Obama. Religious conservatives went with McCain while the Jewish voted for Obama.[39]

BEYOND CANDIDATE SELECTION: REFERENDA, INITIATIVES, RECALLS

Selecting representatives is a major goal of elections and the most obvious attention-attractor. However, there are other types of elections that are also important regarding the principles of democracy as well as significance regarding its impact on our daily lives. A major challenge of democracy is the lack of a direct institutionalized voice of the citizens. They elect their representatives who are then given the authority to do whatever they think suits the public. Therefore, the will of the public is good only as far as is reflected by the elected official. This could be a problem for democracy in which the rule of masses is *raison d'etre* or the reason for existence. To ensure the presence of direct input from the people, modern democracies typically allow three mechanisms: referendum, initiative, and recall.

A referendum is a vote on policy, which allows the public to write or oppose policy on their own. In 2011, Egyptians erupted with rage against the long-serving president, Mubarak, and ended his 30-year long regime (1981–2011). As soon as Mubarak was removed, the temporary governing body, the military council, suspended the constitution and began to prepare a new constitution to meet the public's demand for a democratic society. In the meantime, amendments were proposed to allow presidents to serve two 4-year terms, instead of unlimited 6-year periods.[40] The referendum was called to vote on reforming amendments, and the overwhelming majority (77.2%) voted in favor on March 17, 2011.

An initiative is an opportunity where voters can put a measure on the ballot by gaining enough signatures. For example, in 2008, the Supreme Court of California ruled that the state's ban on same sex marriage was discriminatory, and thus illegal. Opponents of the same sex marriage quickly acted by launching the Proposition 8 campaign to rewrite the definition of marriage as the union of men and women. The organizers of the initiative gathered 1,120,801 signatures, enough to put the measure on the ballots of the November election of 2008. The measure passed with 52% of yes votes.[41]

A recall is a device empowering the voters by giving them the opportunity to remove elected officials from their seats before their terms end. Therefore, voters do not have to wait until the next election before they can fire their representatives. Ousting elected officials does not occur frequently, but they occasionally do. For example, when people of a small city of 200,000, Spokane, Washington learned that their mayor Jim West was soliciting sex from young men, they were shocked. He was a major figure with a strong anti-gay record. His critics gathered the needed signatures, which triggered a citywide recall vote. The recall vote kicked him out of office with 65% in favor in December 2005.[42]

These measures of direct democracy are not the most popular mechanisms because they cost time and money for ordinary people who are busy with their own daily routine lives. However, they provide a rare but important opportunity to engage actively in politics and to have the sense of empowerment.

VOTING: RATIONAL TO VOTE?

Elections are the key to democracy. But, is voting rational to individual voters? The discussion of rationality of voting has two sides: costs and benefits. Let's begin with costs. Are there any costs for individual voters in participating in elections? Intuitively, you might think there is no cost with voting. After all, you do not have to purchase a ticket to get to the ballot booth. However, a quick rethinking will tell you otherwise. To be informed about issues that you care about, you have to turn to various sources, such as conversations with your colleagues, readings newspapers, watching TV, or listening to radio. On top of this, you might also need to know about candidates and their platforms. You might turn to pamphlets, TV advertisements, or online sources provided by political parties and candidates. Your research costs lots of time and in some cases a little bit of money. If not so much, it still takes away time and money that you could have used in something else such as preparing for your exams or uploading your pictures on Facebook. In other words, you have to give up something to do the necessary research to be an informed voter. In a similar vein, voting itself is costly as well. You have to register prior to election day, which takes time (figuring out how to do it, getting answers for your questions about the form, or filling and sending the form) and money. After all these, you have to spend more time and money to get to the ballet booth (gasoline, parking fees, subway ticket, or lost wages). If you still think that dropping your ballet is not so costly, image that you live in a ranch in the middle of nowhere in New Mexico and the nearest town is 15 miles away. Now you get the picture.

How about the benefits? There are a few potential benefits typically expected by voters. The most important benefit is "making a difference." You vote and expect your vote to make a critical difference in the election or at least to have some effect on the electoral result. But, did it? In other words, did your vote ever become decisive in any election? Did your vote ever create a tie or break a tie? In the US presidential elections, voters have a good idea of which party will get their electoral votes. For example, the electoral votes of Texas typically go to the candidate of the Republican Party. It has been the case since the last Democratic victory of 1976 by Jimmy Carter. In the 2008 presidential election, the Republican candidate McCain received 55.5% of Texan votes, adding 34 electoral votes from the state to his race to the White House. Even if you were in Travis County, that includes Austin, where 64.1% of the votes went in favor of Obama, you, as a Democrat supporter, just knew that your vote would not swing the state in favor of the Democratic Party. It is the same with Maryland except that the state goes in the opposite direction—it almost always fall in the Democratic column in presidential elections. Actually, according to a study, there is about one in 10 million chance that a single vote is decisive in a presidential election.[43] Putting in some perspective, there is a one in eight chance of getting into a car accident and one in 2.5 million chance of being struck and killed by lightning. In other words, most of the time, probably always in your life time, the electoral result would be the same with or without your vote. In other words, your vote does not create a tie or break a tie, and thus, your vote doesn't matter in determining the electoral result. Therefore, the expected benefit of "making a difference" is slim to none.

There is another benefit to the voters, and that is the sense of public service. People vote and feel good about it for some reasons. They feel that they did the civic obligation necessary to maintain a democratic system. Setting aside the validity of the argument, it is important to acknowledge such a sense is significant to people. It is most noticeable in a country that just adopted democracy such as in Iraq where democratic elections attracted so many people who cheered and celebrated the occasion after enduring a long dictatorship of Saddam Hussein. This kind of sentiment is a key factor driving people to the ballot booth here in the US. Therefore, this sense of civic engagement is a major reason why people do vote.

Democracy is largely characterized by political competitions that are peaceful and regulated. In democracies don't involve guns and violence. Instead, they are prepared and fought by political parties (after all, they are called election campaigns, like air campaign during war). Therefore, it is important to have healthy and legitimate parties and the population supporting them. The success and the longevity of democracy largely depend on how well the political parties reflect what most people like in their policies. However, the will of people is not automatically translated into the political leadership. Instead, the election itself plays a major role. Some electoral systems generate a two-party system while others promise a high level of proportionality. In other words, the will of people is shaped in part by what kind of electoral system the country has.

Notes

1 Democratic Party Website, http://www.democrats.org/contact/about_jobs. (accessed November 18, 2011).

2 Democratic Party Website, http://www.democrats.org/issues/civil_rights. (accessed November 18, 2011).

3 Republican Party Website, http://www.gop.com/index.php/issues/issues/. (accessed November 18, 2011).

4 David Montgomer, "Going to the Mat on Health-Care Bill,." *The Washington Post*, (August 12, 2009), http://www.washingtonpost.com/wp-dyn/content/article/2009/08/11/AR2009081102071_pf.html. (accessed November 18, 2011).

5 Joshua Green, "The Other War Room: President Bush Doesn't Believe in Polling—Just Ask His Pollsters," *The Washington Monthly*., (April 2002,) . http://www.washingtonmonthly.com/features/2001/0204.green.html. (accessed November 18, 2011).

6 Green, "The Other War Room: President Bush Doesn't Believe in Polling—Just Ask His Pollsters."

7 Maryland State Board of Elections, "2010 Gubernatorial General Election," http://www.elections.state.md.us/elections/2010/candidates/2010_general_state_candlist.pdf. (accessed November 18, 2011).

8 OpenSecrets.org http://www.opensecrets.org/politicians/summary.php?cycle=2010&cid=N00003675&type=C. (accessed November 18, 2011).

9 Salisbury University http://www.salisbury.edu/intled/iss/finainfo/default.html. (accessed November 18, 2011).

10 Opensecrets.org http://www.opensecrets.org/politicians/elections.php?chart=S&cid=N00003675&newMem=&cycle=2010. (accessed November 18, 2011).

11 Daniel Kurtzleben, "$4 Billion in Election Spending a Drop in Bucket," The US News and World Report Website (Posted November 9, 2010), http://www.usnews.com/news/articles/2010/11/09/4-billion-in-election-spending-a-drop-in-the-bucket. (accessed November 18, 2011).

12 Kurtzleben, "$4 Billion in Election Spending a Drop in Bucket."

13 Center for Responsive Politics http://www.opensecrets.org/overview/topraces.php [Feel free to distribute or cite this material, but please credit the Center for Responsive Politics. For permission to reprint for commercial uses, such as textbooks, contact the Center.] (accessed November 18, 2011).

14 Center for Responsive Politics http://www.opensecrets.org/parties/index.php [Feel free to distribute or cite this material, but please credit the Center for Responsive Politics. For permission to reprint for commercial uses, such as textbooks, contact the Center.] (accessed November 18, 2011).

15 Center for Responsive Politics http://www.opensecrets.org/parties/indus.php?cycle=2010&cmte=RPC [Feel free to distribute or cite this material, but please credit the Center for Responsive Politics. For permission to reprint for commercial uses, such as textbooks, contact the Center.] (accessed November 18, 2011).

16 Center for Responsive Politics http://www.opensecrets.org/parties/expend.php?cycle=2010&cmte=DPC.

17 Anthony Downs, *An Economic Theory of Democracy* (New York: Harper & Row, 1957).

18 Congressional Budget Office http://cboblog.cbo.gov/?p=1457. (accessed November 18, 2011).

19 To understand the complexity of this issue, play with an on-line simulation prepared by *The New York Times* at http://www.nytimes.com/interactive/2010/11/13/weekinreview/deficits-graphic.html. (accessed November 18, 2011).

20 Paul Krugman, "Willie Sutton Wept," *The New York Times*, February 17, 2011, http://www.nytimes.com/2011/02/18/opinion/18krugman.html. (accessed November 18, 2011).

21 Congressman Paul Ryan "Republican Response to 2011 State of the Union" http://www.pbs.org/newshour/interactive/speeches/5/republican-response-2011-state-union/. (accessed November 18, 2011).

22 The Republican Party website http://www.gop.com/index.php/issues/issues/ (accessed February 28, 2011).

23 Newt Gingrich, To Save America: Stopping Obama's Secular-Socialist Machine (Washington, DC: Regnery Publishing, 2010).

24 Maurice Duverger, *Party Politics and Pressure Groups* (New York: Thomas Y. Crowell, 1972).

25 The graphic shows the percentage of partisan votes taken in the House and Senate. A roll call vote is considered partisan if a majority of Democrats votes against a majority of Republicans. http://www.npr.org/templates/story/story.php?storyId=122441095. ANDREA SEABROOK "CQ: 2009 Was The Most Partisan Year Ever" National Public Radio January 11, 2010 (accessed November 18, 2011).

26 Masami Ito, "LDP Factions," *The Japanese Times*, Wednesday, October 15, 2008. http://search.japantimes.co.jp/cgi-bin/nn20081015i1.html. (accessed November 18, 2011) See also Gary W. Cox, "Factional competition for the party endorsement: The case of Japan's Liberal Democratic Party," *The British Journal of Political Science* 26 (1996): 256–269.

27 David Von Drehle, "Why the Blue Dogs Are Slowing Health-Care Reform," *The Times*, July 24, 2009, http://www.time.com/time/nation/article/0,8599,1912343,00.html. (accessed November 18, 2011).

28 Al Jazeera, "Full Text of Mubarak's Speech," http://english.aljazeera.net/news/middleeast/2011/02/20112221313603381.html (accessed March 6, 2011).

29 National Election Commission http://www.nec.go.kr/sinfo/index.html (accessed November 18, 2011).

30 The Washington Post, "Beyond the Result: Senate," http://www.washingtonpost.com/wp-srv/special/politics/2010-race-maps/senate/ (accessed March 7, 2011).

31 The BBC, "Results at a glance" http://news.bbc.co.uk/2/hi/europe/1946937.stm (accessed March 8, 2011).

32 The BBC, "Profile: Jean-Marie Le Pen" http://news.bbc.co.uk/2/hi/europe/1943193.stm. (accessed November 18, 2011).

33 ACE Project http://aceproject.org/ace-en/topics/es/esd/esd01/esd01d/default. (accessed November 18, 2011).

34 The BBC, "Q&A: Israel's General Election," http://news.bbc.co.uk/2/hi/middle_east/7613137.stm (accessed March 9, 2011).

35 Alan I. Abramowitz, "Forecasting the 2008 Presidential Election with the Time-for-Change Model," *PS: Political Science & Politics* (2008): 691–695, the quote from page 695.

36 Ibid., quote from page 694.

37 Ibid., quote from page 695.

38 Matt A. Barreto and Gary M. Segura, "Estimating the Effects of Traditional Predictors, Group Specific Forces, and Anti-Black Affect on 2008 Presidential Vote among Latinos and Non Hispanic Whites" Prepared for presentation at the Ohio State University Conference on the 2008 Election, Columbus, OH, October 2–3, 2009.

39 The BBC, "Q&A Egypt's Constitutional Referendum," http://www.bbc.co.uk/news/world-middle-east-12763313 (accessed March 25, 2011).

40 "California's Proposition 8 (Same-Sex Marriage)," *The New York Times*, http://topics.nytimes.com/top/reference/timestopics/subjects/c/californias_proposition_8_samesex_marriage/index.html?s=oldest& (accessed March 25, 2011).

41 Timothy Egan "Spokan Mayor, Caught in Gay Sex Sting, Is Ousted in Vote That May Advance Gay Rights," *The New York Times*, December 8, 2005, http://www.nytimes.com/2005/12/08/national/08west.html?pagewanted=print (accessed March 25, 2011).

42 Andrew Gelman, Gary King, and John Boscardin, "Estimating the Probability of Events That Have Never Occurred: When Is Your Vote Decisive?" *Journal of the American Statistical Association* 93, no. 441 (1998): 1–9; Andrew Gelman, Nate Silver, and Aaron Edlin, "What is the probability your vote will make a difference?" NBER Working Paper no 15220, issued in August 2009 http://www.nber.org/papers/w15220. (accessed November 18, 2011).

Interest Groups

Barack Obama was swept into the presidency in 2008 on the tide of an impressive electoral victory, securing 365 Electoral College votes to just 173 for his opponent, John McCain. One of the key elements of Obama's platform for the 2008 campaign was his belief that "Every American has the right to affordable, comprehensive, and portable heath care."[1] The health care plan that Obama proposed during his successful campaign for the White House touted universal health care for all American citizens, based on a combination of the existing health insurance options to which many Americans already had access through their employers or private health care providers, and a new public health care program administered by the federal government or states. Under Obama's plan Americans would have the right to choose to stay with their existing plans, or to switch to the new public option.

The health care reform bill that became law in 2010 differed in important ways from that which President Obama had proposed during his campaign. One of the central pillars of Obama's plan—the government-run public health insurance option—was not included in the final bill. Although the bill that Obama signed into law in 2010 did aim to extend health care to 31 million uninsured Americans, that still left millions of Americans without health coverage.[2] Clearly, the president was forced to compromise on major components of his original proposal to get the watered-down version of the bill passed by Congress.

What explains the fact that a Democratic president whose party was in control of both houses of Congress would have to make concessions on crucial elements of his first major legislative initiative after coming to office? Answering this question requires that we take into account the role that certain key organized forces in American society played in shaping the outcome of the debate over health care. Large, well financed and highly-motivated organizations such at the American Association of Retired People (AARP), the American Medical Association (AMA), the AFL-CIO labor union, the Pharmaceutical Research and Manufacturers of America (PhRMA), and America's Health Insurance Plans (the most influential group representing the interests of insurance companies) spent thousands of hours and hundreds of millions of dollars trying to shape public opinion on the issue as well as the opinions of key members of Congress.[3]

The example of the debate over health care underscores the influential role that interest groups often play within the policy-making arena, particularly in a democracy such as the United States. In this chapter we will examine the functions of interest groups and the strategies they employ in pursuit of their objectives. We will also distinguish interest groups according to their level of organization and the types of interest group systems that can exist within a society. This chapter concludes by asking you to think about the legitimate role of interest groups in politics, including the underlying question of whether interest groups strengthen or undermine a democratic system and society.

INTEREST GROUPS DEFINED

An interest group is "an organized body of individuals who share some goals and who try to influence public policy."[4] Like political parties, interest groups in a democratic system bring like-minded people together in pursuit of a common objective. However, whereas the main goal of a political party in a democracy is to capture as much power as possible through the process of competitive elections, interest groups are designed to promote or achieve a specific set of interests or goals. By definition, political parties focus on dozens of issues and must broaden their political tenet at least to some degree in order to maximize their appeal to voters. Interest groups on the other hand focus on one issue, or perhaps a category of issues. Supporters are attracted to a particular interest group both because they believe that group shares their view on a specific issue or set of issues and because they believe that group may be well-positioned to shape public policy in accordance with their issue preferences.

In the US, interest groups play several crucial functions. These include:

1. Representing the interests of their constituents, thereby providing a channel through which the wishes of members are expressed to the government.
2. An opportunity to participate in the political process on a more sustained and focused basis than is provided by elections alone.
3. Educating the public and government officials about issues that are of interest to the interest group.
4. Highlighting problems that have previously gone unnoticed or been largely ignored. In this process of agenda building, problems become issues that require a response from the government.
5. Monitoring existing government programs that affect the constituents of an interest group and calling attention to any shortcomings in how those programs are being plemented.[5]

What are the types of interest groups that exist? One way of answering this question is by describing these groups according to the interests they represent and goals they pursue. Another approach to analyzing interest groups is to distinguish them according to their level of organization. We begin by categorizing interest groups according to the sets of interests and concerns they are designed to represent.

DESCRIPTIVE MODEL OF INTEREST GROUPS

Economic Interest Groups

It is clear that the protection and promotion of a set of shared economic interests is one of the most important catalysts in promoting the organization and mobilization of interest group activity. More than any other set of concerns, economic interests serve to bind sub-sets of people within a society together in common cause. By organizing around economic goals, like-minded citizens seek to promote their own economic interests while fending off perceived threats to those interests by other organized interest groups within society.

In the modern era, the sharpest dividing line in western capitalist societies such as the United States has been between management and labor. Corporations, both as individual entities and acting in concert through professional organizations such as the US Chamber of Commerce, have acted to protect their shared interest in keeping wages low and reducing government regulation over their business activities. These companies argue that by controlling wages and decreasing regulation they will be more competitive and expand their shares of markets, which in the long-run they say means lower costs for consumers, higher profits for the companies, and more employment opportunities for workers. In response, labor unions such as the United Autoworkers and United Mine Workers have pushed for higher wages and benefits and greater workplace safety for their members. The unions argue that the firms for whom their members work are focused almost solely on the bottom line, and that the companies would drive down wages for workers, reduce their benefits, and ignore safety issues if not for the actions of the unions.

Research shows that the percentage of workers in the US who are members of unions has declined drastically in recent decades as many union jobs in the manufacturing sector have been lost to advanced technology or have been shipped overseas. A report issued by the Bureau of Labor Statistics in January 2011 revealed that 11.9% of wage and salary workers were union members in 2010, a decline from 12.3% the year before, and down from 20.1% in 1983, the first year for which data was available. Although 36.2% of public sector workers were members of unions in 2010, just 6.9% of private sector workers were union members.[6] These numbers, combined with the efforts by governors in states such as Wisconsin to sharply reduce the bargaining rights of public employees, are strong indicators that unions appear to be losing substantial ground in the tug of war between competing organized economic interests in the United States.

Professional Associations

Some of the largest and most influential interest groups in the US represent specific professions and occupations. Examples of well-known professional associations include the American Medical Association (AMA) and American Bar Association (ABA). These groups have very large memberships and can tap into huge amounts of resources. Because of the highly specialized knowledge of the professions they represent, professional associations are seen as important sources of expertise on issues within their fields, and the views these organizations express may carry special weight within policy debates.

In addition, in some nondemocratic states, professional associations have served as a kind of outlet for a form of democratic, political competition. In these states, elections to positions of authority in professional associations can be highly politicized and ideologically-driven affairs. Using the Middle Eastern country of Jordan as an example, in April 2011 the Jordan Medical Association (JMA) held elections for the position of president and for the nine-member council. The posts were heavily contested, with self-professed leftists, Islamists, and independents running for office.[7] In the end, the incumbent president, a leftist, held off challenges from his Islamist and independent rivals.[8]

The political relevance of professional associations such as the JMA has been strengthened by the "Arab Spring." phenomenon, a term that has been widely used to describe the political upheavals that led to the overthrow of long-entrenched authoritarian regimes in Tunisia and Egypt in early 2011, and to the eruption of mass-based efforts at regime change in several other countries. In Jordan, where the demands of most protesters seem oriented more toward political and economic reform than to full-scale revolution, professional associations have acted as crucial channels through which grievances have been passed along to the government. These associations have been at the forefront of organizing the largely peaceful protests calling for reform in Jordan. In the process, they promote the interests of their own members (in this case, the demand for higher wages for public sector doctors), while also providing an organizational structure through which wider sets of demand by the general population can be articulated in the form of street protests. It is fair to say that without professional organizations such as the JMA acting as the vanguard to organize protests, the reform movement in Jordan would be haphazard and poorly organized.

Identity-Based Interest Groups: Age, Race, Gender, or Religion

Some of the most important and influential interest groups in US history have been organized to protect the interests of a particular sector of society—for example, an age group, race of people, gender, or religious group. Examples of such groups include the American Association of Retired Persons (AARP), the National Association for the Advancement of Colored People (NAACP), the National Organization of Women (NOW), and the American-Israel Public Affairs Committee (AIPAC).

One of the most powerful interest groups in the United States is AARP. Long one of the most politically active interest groups in America, AARP's draws on the fact that it claims to represent a portion of the population (those who are retired or close to retirement) that is both growing in size and traditionally votes in large numbers to wield significant influence on issues ranging from health care reform to the debate over the future of social security and Medicare.

AARP also offers a superb example of how interest groups grow by attracting new members. One of the questions that has long puzzled social scientists is the following: why should an individual become active in an interest group if that individual figures to benefit from any gains that are achieved by the group on issues that are of concern to the individual, regardless of whether the individual invested any of his or her own time and energy to achieving those gains? For example, what incentive is there for an individual to join AARP if that individual will benefit anyway from the hard work of AARP executives and lobbyists on the issue of preserving social security? Isn't it rational for an individual to choose to "free-ride" on the hard work of others, thereby enjoying the benefits of their work without actually having to expend her or his time, effort, and money? How can organizations overcome this rational tendency on the part of individuals to "free-ride?"

Economist Mancur Olson has suggested that organizations overcome the problem of free-riding by offering material incentives to people to become active in the organization.[9] For example, in return for becoming a dues-paying member AARP offers a host of material incentives, including discounts on items ranging from travel and lodging to consumer goods to financial services. These material incentives entice senior citizens who otherwise might be tempted to free-ride on the work of AARP to contribute to the organization's efforts by paying annual dues. By 2011, the organization's membership ranks had grown to 37 million. In fact, some critics began to charge that AARP had become so large, and its policy agenda so diffused, that it was in danger of losing sight of its founding purpose—to protect the interests of retired Americans.[10]

Single-Issue Interest Groups

The categories of interest groups we have discussed thus far tend to have far-reaching policy agendas. Economic groups attempt to shape public policy on any economic issue that might affect the interests of their members. Those groups that are mobilized around shared characteristics such as age, race, gender, or religion typically seek to protect the interests of their members on a wide array of issues. On the other hand, some groups are created specifically to promote a particular policy toward one specific issue.

Single-issue interest groups attract support from individuals who feel quite strongly about one particular issue. They provide an organized outlet through which the preferences of citizens who share a particularly strong sentiment on a specific issue can be channeled to government officials. For example, Mothers Against Drunk Driving (MADD) is a 3 million-plus strong organization devoted to educating young drivers about the dangers of drinking and driving, and to passing stronger penalties for drunk-driving offenses. On the abortion issue, a number of single-issue groups have emerged, including the National Association for the Repeal of Abortion Laws, which is a pro-choice group, and the National Right to Life organization, which opposes abortion. On the issue of gun control, the National Rifle Association (NRA) wields substantial influence as it advocates for the right to keep and bear arms in the United States.[11]

One advantage that single-issue interest groups have over the other types of groups we have discussed is that the issues they address tend to spark a great deal of emotion within the interested public. For example, members of MADD are often drawn to the organization because they have had a family member or friend who was injured or killed as a result of drunk driving. The abortion issue generates extreme emotions on both sides of the debate, with both pro-choice and pro-life advocates believing that they are morally and legally right on the issue. NRA supporters are very staunch in their belief that the US Constitution guarantees the right to keep and bear arms. Because of these strong emotions, single-issue interest groups do not have to worry as much about providing incentives to people to get them to participate in the group's activities.

Public Interest Groups

The interest group categories we have discussed to this point all describe types of groups that are designed to protect the interests of a specific sub-set of the overall population. By comparison, public interest groups promote policies that they specifically claim to be in the interest of all of society. By definition then, public interest groups focus on outcomes which, if achieved, will be universally available. For example, as we saw previously in this chapter, AARP is focused on "delivering the goods" for its specific constituent base—Americans who are at or near retirement age. By comparison, if a group such as Greenpeace is successful in achieving its objective of a cleaner environment, everyone will benefit from such an outcome, including those who contributed nothing to the fight for that outcome, and those who in fact may have opposed the efforts of Greenpeace on ideological grounds.

One of the best known public interest groups in the US is the Public Interest Research Group (PIRG). According to its website, PIRG "stands up to powerful special interests on behalf of the American public, working to win concrete results for our health and our well-being."[12] In operational terms, PIRG's structure is typical of many public interest groups. These groups tend to rely on large numbers of "foot-soldiers," including students and social activists, in pursuit of their objectives. The structure of PIRG is fairly decentralized, with active chapters in a number of individual states as well as college campuses. PIRG is focused primarily on grassroots activities, including educating the public and raising contributions by going door-to-door. The strength of these types of groups lies not in their ability to lobby government officials directly. Although public interest groups such as PIRG do on occasion attempt to make their voices heard through typical interest group strategies such as lobbying, they often lack the resources to compete consistently and effectively with better-financed interest groups in the these efforts. The effectiveness of public interest groups depends primarily on their ability to mobilize large numbers of voters, through strategies such as petition-drives, to put pressure on their elected officials to adopt policies that are supported by the organization.

ORGANIZATIONAL MODEL OF INTEREST GROUPS

In the previous section we offered a descriptive typology that divided interest groups according to their interest and goals. Another way to analyze and distinguish among interest groups involves examining the level of organization of different types of interest groups. Gabriel Almond and G. Bingham Powell, Jr, are generally credited with developing this organizational model of interest groups, which is summarized below.[13]

Anomic Interest Groups

Although we generally think of interest groups as resting on the foundations of prolonged, cohesive sets of shared interests, there are occasions in which a group of like-minded people with a shared set of values and interests come together rapidly, and without much if any organizational forethought, in pursuit of their common goals. These are known as anomic interest groups. Typically, an anomic interest group expresses its members' grievances and goals through such actions as street protests and riots. Once the inspiration that sparked the spontaneous mass action peters out, or the members of the group come to believe that the issue that the action was designed to call attention to has been adequately addressed, an anomic interest group disappears as quickly as it appeared.

In recent history some of the most famous examples of anomic interest groups are the spontaneous street protest movements that erupted in a number of Arab states in the spring of 2011. A single incident in Tunisia provided the impetus for these movements. Mohammed Bouazizi, a street vendor, was fined for selling vegetables without a license. When he tried to pay the fine the policewoman who had fined Bouazizi slapped his face, spat on him, and cursed his dead father. After officials at the local municipal office refused to meet with him to hear his complaints, Bouazizi had reached his breaking point. Feeling humiliated and frustrated with the lack of economic opportunity and rampant corruption in Tunisia, he set fire to himself in the street.[14]

Bouaziz's isolated act of protest struck a broader chord, both in Tunisia and across the region. Almost overnight, spontaneous street movements calling for the overthrow of corrupt, authoritarian rulers sprung up in multiple states, including Egypt, Syria, Jordan, Yemen, and Bahrain, and a violent civil war erupted in Libya. Within the span of 2 months or so the autocratic governments in Tunisia and Egypt had been toppled.

The process of interest group formation, disintegration, and reemergence in Tunisia and Egypt fit the classic pattern of anomic interest groups. Just as the protest movements coalesced with breathtaking speed in those two countries, they dissipated rapidly following the overthrow of the authoritarian regimes as those who participated in the successful protests sought to construct new political systems based on stable political parties and democracy, only to reemerge again in the summer of 2011 when the pace of change was judged to be too slow by protesters.

Before moving on from our discussion of anomic interest groups, it is interesting and important to consider the impact of technology upon anomic interest groups. Clearly, in states such as Tunisia and Egypt the availability of technologies such as twitter, Facebook and Youtube were critical tools in bringing protesters together and in conveying sympathetic images and messages to the broader international community.

The widespread use of these new forms of communication technology should make it easier for anomic interest groups to play a more frequent and influential role in political life in the future.

Non-associational Interest Groups

There are examples, particularly in lesser-developed countries, of groups of people who are not regularly and consistently organized for political action, despite the fact they share a clearly definable, continuing set of characteristics that distinguish them from other groups in society. Such groups, which Almond and Powell labeled non-associational interest groups, share features such as ethnicity, race, class, or tribe. However the members of non-associational groups fail to use their shared identity as a tool to mobilize for collective political action. Social scientists refer to such characteristics as "latent," which means they exist but do not yet have a sustained impact on politics, although they might at some point in the future.

Although by definition non-associational interest groups are poorly organized and only infrequently articulate a set of group interests, political leaders may still choose to treat them as an organized interest group. For example, in a multiethnic, multi-tribal, multi-religious society leaders may see playing to the latent interests of non-associational groups as a way to practice a divide-and-rule strategy. Meeting with key tribal, ethnic, or religious elites is a useful mechanism for signaling to the communities that the tribal, ethnic, or religious elites represent that the political leader is sensitive to, and concerned about, the interests of those communities. In return, the political leader hopes that those communities that have traditionally been favored by the state will support the ruling government and, if necessary, come to its defense in the event of threat to its rule.

This policy of cooptation of non-associational groups has been used by leaders in a number of states where rulers have been especially sensitive to the needs of key religious communities (e.g., Syria and Iraq), tribes (e.g., Libya and Yemen), and race (e.g., South Africa). For example, in South Africa during the apartheid era the ruling National Party attempted to play to tribal identities in an effort to undermine a cohesive racial identity among the black majority in South Africa. In that instance, the state's strategy failed, and the white minority was eventually forced to surrender its political control in 1994 through the conduct of free and fair democratic elections.

Institutional Interest Groups

Many entities in society are well organized and possess extensive resources, and yet are not designed specifically to act as interest groups as we have defined that term in this chapter (see above). Still, these entities find it necessary to behave like an interest group at certain times in order to protect their interests. Institutional interest groups (e.g., corporations, churches, universities) were created to serve some specific functions. At the same time, their advanced level of organization and access to resources allows them to engage in strategies that are typical of classic interest groups.

An example of institutional interest groups that you may be particularly familiar with are public universities. Of course the primary function of public universities is to act as institutions of higher education. However, in carrying out their core mission these institutions often find it necessary to also wear the hat of an interest group.

Most public universities have a person or office whose purpose is to serve as the legislative liaison between the school and elected officials. Ideally, public universities are interested in increasing their slice of the state government's budget pie. This goal became both harder to achieve and all the more vital as a result of the fiscal crisis that swamped many states, beginning around 2007. Within the context of the economic recession universities must fight harder than ever to protect their interests in the face of shrinking budgets at the state level. In this context, universities become interest groups, vying with other actors for financial support from cash-strapped governments during lean economic times.

Associational Interest Groups

Some organizations are specifically designed to act as structures for articulating the interests of a particular group. Several of the groups that we described in the previous section—organizations such as the NRA, the NAACP, and PIRG—fit this category. These associational interest groups are well-organized, highly-structured entities that feature a clear distribution of roles and responsibilities within the organization.

As noted by Almond and Powell, "associational interest groups are often organized either around a social group base or around a special policy interest."[15] Among the interest groups we have described in this chapter, the NAACP, NOW, and AARP would be classic examples of associational interest groups based on a social group base. In the case of the NAACP, the social group base is racial identity; in the case of NOW, the social group base is gender; in the case of AARP, it is age. The NRA is a good example of an associational group based on a particular policy interest. Not surprisingly, given their size, level of organization, and focus associational interest groups are often more consistently successful in achieving their goals than are groups that fall in the category of anomic, non-associational, or institutional group.

INTEREST GROUP STRATEGIES

How do interest groups attempt to achieve their policy objectives in a democratic system? There are a number of strategies and tactics that interest groups utilize in pursuit of their goals. What follows is a list of some of the most important strategies utilized by interest groups in a democracy such as the United States.

Lobbying

When most Americans think of interest groups, the first tactic that comes to mind is that of lobbying. Lobbyists represent interest groups by seeking direct contact with government officials (in the US, usually members of Congress). Their goal is to persuade those elected representatives to back the policy preferences of the interest group that the lobbyists represent.

Lobbying may occur in two forms. First, lobbyists may connect with elected officials through informal meetings, either with a single politician or small group of politicians. These small-scale meetings give the lobbyist the opportunity to makes his or her case for why those politicians should support the views of the interest group that the lobbyist represents. In 2009 alone, more than 4500 lobbyists were hired by companies and professional organizations who wished to shape the debate over President Obama's health care reform package.[16]

Second, lobbying may take the form of an appearance before a congressional committee. Interestingly, while most interest groups have a clear agenda and thus may be seen as a biased source of information, it is also the case that some interest groups are recognized as possessing a tremendous amount of knowledge on the issues upon which they focus. Thus, lobbyists may be invited to appear before a congressional committee to share their expertise. Among those organizations that were invited to testify before the Senate Health Committee during the debate over health care reform were the American Academy of Pediatrics, the Federation of American Hospitals and the American Association of Colleges of Nursing.[17]

There is an old political maxim that goes "Knowledge is power." An interest group that possesses scarce knowledge is in a powerful position to exert influence over public policy. For example, in 2006 it came to light that the US government was relying exclusively on self-reporting by oil companies to keep track of the amount of drilling occurring on public lands. Incredibly, the government had no independent source of information on the amount of drilling, and thus had to trust oil companies to be honest in their reports. The exclusive knowledge that the oil companies possessed gave them tremendous power over the issue of drilling on public lands.[18]

Campaign Contributions

One well-known—and controversial—strategy used by interest groups is to provide campaign contributions to candidates for elected office. Many people assume that campaign contributions amount to a "pay-off" of sorts between the interest groups making the contributions and the candidates who receive them. Candidates, it is assumed, will propose laws and promote policies that meet the needs of those groups that contributed to their campaigns. In short, campaign contributions open the door to corruption.

In recent history, perhaps the most infamous example of the link between money and corruption in politics was the case of Rod Blagojevich, the former governor of Illinois. Blagojevich was convicted in June 2011 on 17 counts of fraud, attempted extortion, and soliciting bribes. Among the crimes for which he was convicted were attempting to secure campaign contributions in return for political favors.[19]

The perceived corrosive effect of campaign contributions on the democratic process is potentially worsened by the huge amounts of money spent on political campaigns in the US today. A staggering $5.3 billion was spent on the presidential campaign of 2008, with much of that money coming from campaign contributions. The fear is that this level of spending opens the door for large corporations and powerful interest groups to ihi-jacki the process of democratic elections.

A review of the figures from 2007–2008 underscores the prominence of big donors. Interestingly, the top donor was ActBlue, a political action committee (PAC) designed to raise and funnel contribution to Democratic candidates around the country.[20] PACs are groups, put together by corporations, unions, or associations, that are organized to distribute campaign contributions from donors to favored candidates. ActBlue distributed nearly $24 million in campaign contributions to Democrats in 2007–2008. Some of the other top 10 donors in 2007–2008 included well-known corporations and professional associations such as Goldman Sachs, JP Morgan, and the National Association of Realtors. Cynics would argue that we should not be surprised that banks, investment institutions, and realtors would be among the top contributors given the fact that this was during the period of time when the federal government was designing large-scale bail-out programs to assist those ailing sectors of the economy.

On the other hand, technology—and in particular the ability to raise money via the internet—has created new avenues for individuals to participate by making campaign contributions. During his successful 2008 campaign, Barack Obama raised $337 million from individual contributors, of which 34% came from individuals who donated $200 or less.[21] Still, a note of caution is warranted. Although it is true that Obama raised a huge amount of money from small donors, it is also true that he raised substantially more—approximately 48% of all donations to his primary and general election campaigns—from those who contributed $1000 or more.[22]

The question of what—if anything—should be done about campaign financing is an extremely contentious issue. The effort to control the flow of campaign contributions and spending reached its zenith in 2002 with the passage of the Campaign Finance Act. The new law banned national political parties from raising and spending so-called "soft money," a term that refers to contributions that are given to a party for reasons other than supporting a particular candidate, but which often ends up being spent in ways that support the candidacy of the party's candidates for office. In addition, the new law prohibited parties at the state level from spending money on television ads that mention candidates for federal office, and made it illegal for large-scale interest groups such as corporations and labor unions to pay for "issue ads" (many of which are actually thinly-veiled ads in support of, or opposition to, a particular candidate) in the weeks leading up to an election. Finally, the Campaign Finance Act increased the amount of money that individuals are allowed to contribute to campaigns from $1000 to $2000.[23]

The debate over the legality of laws designed to control campaign financing has been quite heated. In a series of closely-watched decisions, the US Supreme Court struck down campaign finance laws at both the federal and state levels, declaring those laws to be unconstitutional restrictions on free speech. In the most famous of those cases (Citizens United versus Federal Elections Commission) in January 2010 the court ruled in a 5-4 decision that laws that ban political spending by corporations violate the free speech rights of those corporations. This decision struck down key elements of the Campaign Reform Act of 2002. The dissenting justices complained bitterly that the majority was mistaken in treating corporate entities as if they have the same constitutional rights as individual citizens, and warned that removing these limits would create new opportunities for companies to buy access to candidates through their large corporate contributions.[24]

In June 2011, the Supreme Court struck down an Arizona law that provided for matching funds to any candidate who accepts public financing for their campaign. Under the law, any candidate who agreed to a certain set of provisions—limiting personal spending on the campaign to $500, participating in at least one debate, and returning any unused funds—would receive funds from the government that would match the amount of money raised by another candidate in the same race through private fundraising efforts. As in the Citizens United case of 2010, the majority found that the Arizona law resulted in an unconstitutional limitation on the right of free speech. Specifically, the majority argued that the matching public funds provision might discourage a candidate who relied on private fundraising efforts from spending money out of fear that in doing so his or her opponent would benefit from the matching funds provision.[25] As long as the Supreme

Court continues to view campaign finance reform through the prism of free speech, it is highly unlikely that substantial chaes to the current system of finance can survive any court test.

Influencing Public Opinion

In a representative democracy, the most effective way for an interest group to achieve its goals is by persuading politicians to support the objectives of the group's members. We have already seen that interest groups can use the strategies of lobbying and campaign contributions to acquire direct access to politicians. Another, more indirect method by which an interest group can apply pressure on elected leaders is by influencing public opinion.

The most efficient method available to interest groups for influencing public opinion is advertising. Specifically, recent history shows that the effective use of television advertising can be a powerful tool for interest groups to use in educating the masses on the group's position regarding a particular issue. Such ads are used to explain to the public why the interest group's preference on that issue is also in the best interest of the viewer.

One of the more famous examples of a television advertisement playing a critical role in shaping public opinion on an important issue was a series of ads featuring a fictional couple, "Harry and Louise," which ran during the debate over President Bill Clinton's health care reform proposal in 1993 and 1994. In the ads, which were sponsored by the private insurance industry, Harry and Louise fretted over the possibility that the quality of their health care would suffer if Clinton's reform proposal becomes law. As they sat around their kitchen table sifting through medical bills, the couple noted that certain items covered in the past by their private insurance plan would not be covered under the Clinton plan, and ended with the warning "If we let the government choose, we lose."[26]

The Harry and Louise ad campaign proved to be tremendously successful in swaying public opinion against Clinton's proposal. In fact, in an ironic twist the Harry and Louise characters were brought back to life during the debate over President Obama's health care policy, but this time Harry and Louise, played by the same actors who had portrayed them in the original slate of commercials during the Clinton administration, advocated *for* health care reform. Sitting again around their kitchen table, the couple noted with concern the rising costs of health care, the reduction in health benefits offered by small companies, and the fact that "too many people are falling through the cracks." The ad, which was sponsored by several powerful groups, including the American Hospital Association, ended with the statement that heath care reform is needed and a plea that the next president bring "everyone to the table and make it happen."[27]

While no one would claim that the Harry and Louise commercials were the determining factor in the health care debates under the Clinton and Obama administrations, it is interesting that the characters in the ads advocated for the sides that ended up winning the policy fights over health care reform, first in 1994 (when Clinton's health care plan was blocked), and then in 2010 (when health care reform, albeit in a watered-down form, was enacted). If nothing else, this example underscores the fact that a well-financed ad campaign, backed by powerful inrest groups, can have an impact on the debate over crucial policy issues.

Litigation

We typically think of courts as being judicial institutions designed to apply the laws that have been passed by legislative bodies (Congress at the federal level in the United States; state assemblies at the state level) and signed into law by political executives (the president at the federal level; governors at the state level). According to this view, courts usually do not make public policy. The primary exception to this traditional role of the court system is in the area of constitutional law, although even here there is a sharp disagreement between judicial activists, who believe that courts, and most especially the US Supreme Court, have the right to interpret laws in the light of changing social norms, and strict constructionists, who believe it is the job of the court to view any question brought before it through the narrow prism of what the framers of the US Constitution originally intended.

The large majority of cases that courts hear involve crimes (in the case of criminal law) and disputes (in the case of civil law) in which existing law can be applied without setting broader legal precedents. On occasion however, courts decide cases that fundamentally alter the policies and laws of the state. For example, in a string of famous decisions rendered by the Supreme Court over the period of nearly a decade, the court went from defining a black slave as a piece of property who lacked any of the rights of citizenship (the Dred Scott case of 1857) to declaring that racial segregation under the policy of "Separate but Equal" was constitutional (Plessey v. Ferguson, 1896) to declaring in Brown v. Board of Education (1954) that "Separate but Equal" in fact was unconstitutional because in practice it preserved inequality for blacks in the name of racial segregation.

Often in high profile cases interest groups may play an important role in bringing the case before the court. One such example was Brown v. Board of Education, in which the NAACP provided the funds required to take the case through the court system. The organization was approached by Oliver Brown, the father of third-grader Linda Brown, an African-American student who was forced to walk over a mile to school instead of being allowed to attend a much closer school reserved for white students. With the legal and financial assistance of the NAACP Brown carried the case all the way to the Supreme Court, which ruled that the "Separate but Equal" doctrine that served as the basis for school segregation, not just in Kansas, but in much of the country, was unconstitutional.[28] Although it would take a while for Brown v. Board of Education to come into full effect, as a result of the litigation efforts of the NAACP, integration and racial equality in America's school systems became the law of the land.

Demonstrations, Protests, and Strikes

One technique available to interest groups for voicing their demands is through organized actions such as demonstrations, protests, and strikes. These activities can be effective tools for shining a spotlight on a group's grievances. In the process, the group may generate public support for its position while also bringing public pressure to bear on those with the power to meet the group's demand.

In this chapter we have already used the Arab Spring of 2011 as an example of the successful use of mass protest. In the United States, one of the most famous examples of the power of protest to effect change is the Montgomery Bus Boycott. On December 1, 1955 a single act of defiance by Rosa Parks—her refusal to give up her seat on a Montgomery, Alabama transit bus to a white man—sparked a movement that eventually led to the end of the policy of racial segregation on Montgomery busses.[29] Within 24 hours of Parks' arrest, a movement began to launch a general boycott by African-American riders of the bus system in Montgomery. The boycott lasted 381 days, and was actively supported by many of the giants of the civil rights movement in the United States, most notably Dr. Martin Luther King, Jr. and Rev. Ralph Abernathy.

The successful bus boycott provided a template for future action by civil rights activists in the late 1950s and 1960s. The use of mass civil disobedience through nonviolent means became the bell-weather strategy of the civil rights movement in the US. The Montgomery bus boycott was an important early victory in the fight for racial equality in America. It illustrates that demonstrations, protests, and strikes, when properly organized and managed, can be extremely effective tools for interest groups to employ in the pursuit of their goals.

INTEREST GROUP SYSTEMS

America has long been viewed as a country in which interests groups are both large in number and important in influence. In his classic 19th century study of political life in the United States, Alexis de Tocqueville observed "In no country in the world has the principle of association been more successfully used or applied to a greater multitude of objects than in America."[30] Tocqueville argued that the ability to freely associate, and in particular the ability for those who hold a minority view to create associations that both express their interests and attempt to sway others within society in a peaceful way to their side, is a crowning characteristic of American democracy and distinguishes the US from European countries.

It could be argued that Tocqueville presented a highly idealized version of American political life and of the role of interest groups in American politics. Yet, the image he projects of a society in which people join forces in countless associations to protect their interests and jostle for influence reflects a powerful strain of thought in the study of interest groups. This concept of a pluralist system in which multiple interest groups compete on an even playing field with each other can be compared and contrasted to two other types of interest group systems: elitism and corporatism.

Pluralism

In his famous treatise *Federalist Papers Number 10* James Madison warns of the dangers that factionalism poses to stable democratic government.[31] Madison defines a faction, or what we have labeled here as interest groups, as "a number of citizens, whether amounting to a majority or a minority of the whole, who are united and actuated by some common impulse of passion, or of interest, adverse to the rights of other citizens, or to the permanent and aggregate interests of the community." In Madison's view, the causes of faction are . . . sown into the nature of man . . . ."[32] Factions are dangerous, according to Madison, not simply because they cause deep divisions with society, but also because they are instruments through which a well-organized majority can exercise its tyranny over the minority.

What are the solutions for addressing the threats that factions pose to democracy? Madison identifies two general approaches. The first would be to eliminate factions by removing the liberties that allow citizens to organize themselves into groups; the second would be for the government to attempt to infuse every citizen with the same interests and opinions. Neither solution is practical or desirable, says Madison, because the cure (denial of liberty) is worse than the disease (factionalism). Instead, Madison proposes the idea that the best way to avoid the threat of the tyranny of the majority is by permitting the emergence of as many factions as possible across a large territory with a republican form of democracy, thereby lessening the influence of any one faction.[33]

Madison's prescription for controlling factions provided the intellectual basis for what later became known as pluralism. According to the pluralist model, interest groups flourish in a democratic society, providing institutional channels through which the preferences and interests of large numbers of citizens can be heard and taken into account by the government. In this way most people can have their voices heard, and no one faction has the size and influence to dominate the levers of power.

In 1951, David Truman made the theoretical case for pluralism in his book *The Governmental Process*.[34] Truman asserts politics is basically the stuff of the interaction and competition between groups in society. In fact, Truman believes that the influence of groups over the political behavior of individuals trumps the influence of the entire society over that behavior, asserting "the individual is less affected directly by the society as a whole than differentially through various of its subdivisions, or groups."

One of the things that distinguishes Truman's argument from the original version of pluralism is the concern he expresses over the possibility that competition between multiple competing factions within society might tear the political system apart. How can democracy operate efficiently and effectively if interest groups are focused only on achieving their own group-specific goals while being oblivious to, and perhaps even antagonistic toward, the interests of other groups? Truman's solution to this threat was his faith that, in the end, interest groups will be willing to compromise on their goals and that they will acknowledge that there exists a system of broader interests "that is not accounted for by the 'sum' of the organized interest groups in society"[35]

One of the early case studies that seemed to lend credence to the pluralist model was Robert Dahl's book *Who Governs?*[36] Based on research he conducted in the city of New Haven, Connecticut, Dahl concludes that the power to influence public policy in New Haven is diffused across a number of interest groups. According to Dahl, although many citizens tend to be apathetic when it comes to local politics, they do become involved in a particular issue when they calculate that their interests are at stake, and the way they become involved is often through participation in interest groups. In this way, the preferences of average people are said to carry a great deal of weight.

Authors such as Truman and Dahl believe that pluralism—a system in which countless interest groups provide countless opportunities for citizens to become involved in political life and to make their preferences heard—is the best cure for the mischief of factions. But what if the pluralists are incorrect in their assumptions? What if the system is organized around, and serves the interest of, the wealthy and powerful, rather than the masses? This is the question raised by the elitist school of thought.

Elitism

The central pillar of pluralism is the belief that average citizens are able to make their voices heard on issues that matter to them through the creation and operation of interest groups. However, a number of scholars have called in to question this core assertion of the pluralists. Instead, according to the elitist model interest groups are formed primarily by those with an advantage in resources and power. Thus, the main result of interest group activity is to protect and advance the interests of the privileged strata in society.

One of the most influential early critiques of pluralist was provided by the sociologist C Wright Mills, in his book *The Power Elite*.[37] Mills notes that it is common for Americans almost subconsciously to subscribe to the "theory of balance," which reflects the "assumptions of independent, relatively equal, and conflicting groups of the balanced society."[38] Mills rejects the "balance of power" as a false claim put forward by those who benefit from the *status quo* system and who seek to disguise a system of gross inequality by presenting it in the guise of a system in which all groups have a fair and equal opportunity to organize and protect their interests.

Along the same lines, Theodore Lowi blasts pluralism for its inaccurate portrayal of the outcomes of interest group competition.[39] Lowi argues that, given the inequality that exists between interest groups, the outcomes of the battle between interest groups over policy are tilted heavily in favor of certain groups. In particular, given the history of economic, social, and political development in the US, "classes of wealth (have) emerge(d), and power centers organize(d)" around the protection and promotion of capitalism. Over time, the interests of the government and the interest of powerful private sector classes have come to coincide. Far from providing an even playing field upon which competing interests expressing different opinions are legitimized, Lowi believes that the interest group system in the United States operates to support the *status quo* interests of the dominant capitalist classes in America.

Critics of the pluralist model often point to the failure of those who are disadvantaged by their economic status (the poor) or race (minority communities) to organize effectively as evidence to support their claims about the inequalities that they believe are inherent in the real-world operation of a "pluralist" system. In the view of the critics, if the interest group system was truly an arena in which all groups, regardless of their economic or social standing, had an equal chance to carry the day in public policy debates, victories for those groups that promote morally superior arguments in defense of the disadvantaged in society over the forces of the elite *status quo* would be more frequent. The fact that policy victories for those with built-in disadvantages are so rare is proof-positive according to the elitist critique that most successful interest groups are those formed by, and to serve the interests of the power elite in society.

Corporatism

In the US system interest groups are largely thought of as being private sector actors making competing demands on the government. In a number of European democracies, however, the interest group system is organized in such a way that the state and interest groups forge a policy-making alliance. This interest group system, known as democratic corporatism, favors cooperation and compromise over competition and conflict.

The democratic corporatist model is found primarily in parts of Europe. In states such as Germany, Austria, the Netherlands, Norway, Sweden, and Denmark the governments have formally designated specific interest groups as partners in the policy-making and policy-implementation processes.[40] This arrangement guarantees that the interests and concerns of key socioeconomic sectors are addressed in the policies of the state, thereby greatly reducing the friction that might lead to labor actions such as strikes or management actions such as lock-outs.

A version of corporatism is also employed is some nondemocratic states.[41] Under state corporatism, the government divides society along functional lines by sanctioning the creation and operation of interest groups for each sector of the economy. For example, the state may sanction one interest group for peasants, a different interest group for industrial workers, etc. As part of this arrangement, the state may offer certain incentives (a minimum wage, benefits, etc.) in exchange for which the workers in those sectors are expected to accept the authority of the state.

In the most extreme cases of state corporatism, the state may call upon one or more of its functional interest groups to defend the government during times of domestic unrest. One classic example of this took place in the late 1970s and early 1980s in Syria, when the embattled leftist regime of President Hafez al-Asad faced an internal revolt led by the Muslim Brotherhood. With his regime teetering on the verge of collapse, Asad first mobilized the Peasants' Union in street demonstrations meant to shore up his rule, and later armed members of the Peasants' Union and called on them to defend the government. Over 25,000 peasants heeded

Asad's call to arms in 1980 alone, and in doing so assisted the regime in thwarting the attempted overthrow of Asad.[42] The Syrian example illustrates how authoritarian rulers use interest group corporatism as a way to bind critical sectors of society to their regime in a mutually beneficial fashion.

PUZZLE: DO INTEREST GROUPS CONTRIBUTE TO OR UNDERMINE DEMOCRACY IN AMERICA?

It is typically assumed by most Americans that the higher the level of political participation, the healthier the state of American democracy. In fact, as we have seen, Tocqueville believed that one of the strengths of America's particular form of democracy is to be found in the propensity for Americans to organize and participate in associations as a means for protecting and furthering their interests.

Also, in this chapter we examined the work of 20th century political scientists such as David Truman and Robert Dahl, both of whom advanced the claim that pluralism not only accurately described the American interest group system but was also a core pillar of democracy in the United States. Truman and Dahl believed that pluralism in both theory and practice represents a system in which all points of view may be heard through the competition between interest groups.

Later in the 20th century, the political scientist Robert Putnam fretted over what he believed was the decline in the propensity for Americans to come together in group associations. In his seminal work "Bowling Alone," Putnam argues that a robust system of private sector associations (what Putnam and others refer to as "civil society") enhances the opportunities available to citizens to engage in productive civic, political, and economic activities.[43] Moreover, Putnam asserts that these activities are important in promoting a collective sense of "us" within a society among individuals who might otherwise focus solely on their own narrow self-interests.

Agreeing with Tocqueville's findings regarding Americans' love of associations early in the country's history, Putnam reviews several measures of group activity in the contemporary United States and comes to the conclusion that the number of Americans participating in collective activities is in steep decline. From organized church-related activities to union membership to membership in youth groups such as the Boy Scouts to volunteering for charity organizations to membership in fraternal clubs like the Elks, Americans participate substantially less in organized group activities than used to be the case. In the most famous example examined by Putnam, participation in bowling leagues between 1980 and 1993 decreased by 40%, despite the fact that the total number of bowlers increased by nearly 10%.[44]

One interesting trend that Putnam uncovered was the booming growth in organizations such as the Sierra Club and AARP. However, from Putnam's perspective these types of organizations don't really provide a counter to the worrisome trend that he sees in declining participation rates in group activities because the participation of most of their members is limited to the act of writing a check for membership dues. In Putnam's words, the bond between members of these types of groups is similar to the bond between two people who happen to root for the same baseball team; they may be aware of their affiliation with and affinity for the same team, but other than that they have no real connection with each other.[45]

Putnam's concern over the decline in participation rates in collective organized activity in the United States reflects the pluralists' faith in the positive role played by interest groups in politics, and stands in stark contrast with the concerns expressed by those who believe that pluralism in practice undermines democracy. Earlier in this chapter we discussed the works of authors such as Mills and Lowi, both of whom argued that interest group politics in the United States represented the elitist wolf in the pluralist sheep's clothing. According to this view, under the guise of fair competition between interest groups the interests of elite segments of society actually hold sway. As EE Schattschneider eloquently phrased this argument in his book *The Semi-Sovereign People*, "The flaw in the pluralist heaven is that that the heavenly chorus sings with a strong upper-class accent."[46]

Consider for a moment one of the most famous studies every conducted on the prerequisites for a stable democratic system. In their book *The Civic Culture*, Gabriel Almond and Sydney Verba distinguish between three types of political culture. The first type is labeled participant political culture, and is characterized by citizens who are both well-informed and active in the political life of their community. The people in this category of political culture possess a high degree of efficacy—a belief that they have right and responsibility to participate in politics, and that if they do so they can make a real difference. The second type is labeled subject political culture, and includes those citizens who are dimly aware of the political life of their community but are generally rather uninvolved. These people possess a much lower sense of efficacy. The third type is parochial political culture, a category in which people possess little, if any, efficacy. They are detached from and disinterested in politics, particularly at the national level.

Which type of political culture is most conducive to nurturing a stable democracy? Is it better to have a culture in which people are highly involved in an array of political behaviors, including forming or joining interest groups? Or is better to have a society in which most people are relatively passive or even relatively disinterested in politics?

Most Americans would assume that a culture characterized by high rates of participation would be most conducive to supporting a healthy democracy. However, Almond and Verba argue that while it is important that there be a substantial degree of participation, too much participation will overwhelm the government with demands. Thus, in both theory and practice (Almond and Verba studied several countries in their research, including the US and Great Britain), having a mix of participant, subject, and parochial political culture is best.

The findings put forward by Almond and Verba return us once again to the debate between the pluralist and elitist schools of thought. If in fact the pluralists are right that all interests in America have the equal opportunity to organize into groups and thus that all preferences can be heard, having a mix of participant, subject, and parochial political cultures seems to be a workable formula for the maintenance of a fair and stable democracy. If on the other hand, however, the elitists are correct in their argument that the American system of political representation—including interest groups politics—is tilted heavily in favor of the wealthy and powerful, Almond and Verba's recipe for a healthy democracy would in fact reinforce the privileges of the elite classes because it is they who would be most likely to fall into the category of participant political culture.

Ultimately, the debate over the impact of interest groups on American democracy rests on the question of whether, as the pluralists argue, interest groups empower a broad cross-section of citizens, or, as the elitists argue, interest groups empower the privileged few. On the issue of whether interest groups strengthen or weaken the American democracy, where do you stand?

Notes

1   The Washington Post, "Barack Obama," *The Washington Post*, http://projects.washingtonpost.com/2008-presidential-candidates/issues/candidates/barack-obama/ (accessed June 22, 2011).

2   CNN Politics, "White House Unveils Compromise Health Care Bill," *CNN Politics*, http://articles.cnn.com/2010-02-22/politics/obama.health.care_1_health-insurance-medicare-advantage-program-white-house?_s=PM:POLITICS (accessed June 22, 2011).

3   Dan Egan, "Expecting Final Push on Health Care Reform, Interest Groups Rally for Big Finish," *The Washington Post*, February 28, 2010, http://www.washingtonpost.com/wp-dyn/content/article/2010/02/27/AR2010022703253.html (accessed June 22, 2011).

4   Jeffrey M. Berry, *The Interest Group Society*, 2nd ed. (New York: Harper-Collins Publishers, 1989), 3.

5   Ibid., 6–8.

6   Bureau of Labor Statistics—US Department of Labor, "News Release: Union Membership 2010," January 21, 2011, http://www.bls.gov/news.release/pdf/union2.pdf (accessed June 24, 2011).

7   Mohammad Ben Hussein, "Candidates Step Up Election Campaigning," *The Jordan Times*, April 8, 2011, http://www.jordantimes.com/?news=36306 (accessed June 29, 2011).

8   Mohammad Ben Hussein, "Armouti Reelected President of Medical Association," *The Jordan Times*, April 17, 2011, http://jordantimes.com/index.php?news=36589 (accessed June 29, 2011).

9   Mancur Olson, *The Logic of Collection Action* (Cambridge, MA: Harvard University Press, 1971).

10 Frederick R. Lynch, "How AARP Can Get Its Groove Back," *The New York Times*, June 24, 2011, A 23.

11 Edward Sidlow and Beth Enschen, *America at Odds*, 6th ed. (Belmont, CA: Wadworth, Cengage 2009), 136.

12 "US PIRG," http://www.uspirg.org/about-us (accessed June 28, 2011).

13 Gabriel A. Almond and G. Bingham Powell, Jr., *Comparative Politics: System, Process, and Policy*, 2nd ed. (Boston: Little, Brown and Company, 1978).

14 Rania Abouzeid, "Bouazizi: The Man Who Set Himself and Tunisia on Fire," *Time*, January 21, 2011, http://www.time.com/time/world/article/0,8599,2043557,00.html (June 30, 2011).

15 Almond and Powell, *Comparative Politics*, 176.

16 Egan, "Expecting Final Push on Health Care Reform, Interest Groups Rally for Big Finish."

17 Katie Wright, "Lobbyists Played a Critical Role in Health Care Reform," *The Times-Gazette* (Hillsboro, OH), April 7, 2011, http://www.timesgazette.com/main.asp?SectionID=1&SubSectionID=382&ArticleID=178917 (accessed June 24, 2011).

18 W. Phillips Shively, *Power and Choice*, 12th ed. (New York: McGraw-Hill, 2011), 294.

19 Monica Davey and Emma G. Fitzsimmons, "Ex-Governor Found Guilty of Corruption," *The New York Times*, June 28, 2011, A 1.

20 ActBlue, "Frequently Asked Questions," https://secure.actblue.com/faq (accessed July 17, 2011).

21 Campaign Finance Institute, "All CFI Funding Statistics Revised and Updated for the 2008 Presidential Primary and General Election Candidates," January 8, 2010, http://www.cfinst.org/Press/Releases_tags/10-01-08/Revised_and_Updated_2008_Presidential_Statistics.aspx (accessed June 28, 2011).

22 Ibid.

23 Almanac of Policy Issues, "Summary of the Shay-Meehan Campaign Finance Reform Law," February 14, 2002, http://www.policyalmanac.org/government/archive/2002-02-14_shays-meehan_summary.shtml (accessed June 29, 2011).

24 Adam Liptak, "Justices, 5-4, Reject Corporate Spending Limits," *The New York Times*, January 21, 2010, http://www.nytimes.com/2010/01/22/us/politics/22scotus.html?hp (accessed June 29, 2011).

25 Adam Liptak, "Justices Reject another Campaign Finance Law," *The New York Times*, June 28, 2011, A 15.

26 "Harry and Louise on Clinton Health Care," http://www.youtube.com/watch?v=Dt31nhleeCg (accessed June 29, 2011).

27 "Harry and Louise Return," http://www.youtube.com/watch?v=RGvkZszS21Y (accessed June 29, 2011).

28 Lisa Cozzens, "Brown v. Board of Education," http://www.watson.org/~lisa/blackhistory/early-civilrights/brown.html (accessed June 29, 2011).

29 For a useful summary of the events surrounding the Montgomery Bus Boycott, including first hand accounts, see "They Changed the World: The Story of the Montgomery Bus Boycott," http://www.montgomeryboycott.com/frontpage.htm (July 5, 2011).

30 Alexis de Tocqueville, *Democracy in America*, vol. I http://xroads.virginia.edu/~HYPER/DETOC/1_ch12.htm (accessed July 1, 2011).

31 Alexander Hamilton, John Jay and James Madison, *The Federalist Papers*, http://www.foundingfathers.info/federalistpapers/ (accessed July 2, 2011).

32 James Madison, *The Federalist Papers Number 10*, http://www.foundingfathers.info/federalistpapers/fed10.htm (accessed July 2, 2011).

33 Ibid.

34 David Truman, *The Governmental Process*, 2nd ed. (New York: Alfred A Knopf, 1971), 15, cited in Donald Brand, "Three Generations of Pluralism," http://www.mmisi.org/pr/15_01/brand.pdf (July 2, 2011).

35 Truman, *The Governmental Process*, 51, in Brand.

36 Robert Dahl, *Who Governs?* (New York, Yale University Press, 1961), cited in Berry, *The Interest Group Society*, 9–11.

37 C. Wright Mills, *The Power Elite* (New York: Oxford University Press, 1956).

38 Ibid. 243.

39 Theodore Lowi, *The End of Liberalism*, 2nd ed. (New York: WW Norton & Co., 1979), cited in Brand, *Three Generations of Pluralism*.

40 Ellen Grigsby, *Analyzing Politics*, 12th ed. (Belmont, CA: Wadsworth Cengage Learning, 2012), 201.

41 Ibid., 204.

42 Hanna Batatu, *Syria's Peasantry: the Descendents of Its Lesser-Notables and Their Politics* (Princeton, NJ: Princeton University Press 1999), 255. It should be noted that the single event most often credited with ending the Islamist uprising in Syria in 1982 was the Asad regime's brutal crackdown in the city of Hama, where somewhere between 10,000 and 25,000 people—most of them civilians—were killed by state security forces in February 1982.

43 Robert Putnam, "Bowling Alone: America's Declining Social Capital," *Journal of Democracy 6* (1995): 65–78, http://canonsociaalwerk.be/1995_Putnam/1995,%20Putnam,%20bowling%20alone.pdf (accessed July 4, 2011).

44 Ibid.

45 Ibid.

46 E.E. Schattschneider, *The Semi-Sovereign People: A Realist's View of Democracy in America* (New York: Holt, Reinhart and Winston, 1960), 35.

Political Executives, Legislatures and Courts

A Political institution is a set of structures, rules and processes created and implemented to govern a country. The American political system is made of many parts, including the President, the Senate, the House, and so on. Not only are they in different forms (there is only one seat in the presidency while 435 in the House), but they also have their own distinctive functions. If we compare political institutions in the US to those in other countries, the variation of political institutions becomes even clearer. At the same time, there are crucial common aspects of these various elements of political institutions in different countries. What is most important of all is that political institutions matter not only as an abstract concept but also as a matter of our daily lives. Did you wake up in the morning NOT hearing the garbage truck on the garbage day? It might have to do with the government's shutdown that was in turn caused by the political conflict between your governor and the state legislature, which have more or less the same amount of power. Had either one have an overwhelming power over the other, the government might have continued to function somehow. This seemingly mundane episode tells us that political institutions shape the political arena where political leaders compete for their political interests and power. In this sense, the political institution is not just a political theater but an important and active political actor with its own influence. Of course, that's why we want to study political institutions.

Modern political institutions vary in different countries, and they are typically made of three specialized entities, namely the legislature, the executive, and the judiciary. In this chapter, we will review these different entities and their functions, but largely the executive and the legislature because they are the most influential in the realm of the politics. For the sake of a more precise understanding than a wider one, we will largely discuss political institutions in democracies. In our discussion, we will compare them across countries to broaden our understanding. Later, we will review two most popular forms of the democratic governmental institution: the presidential system and the parliamentary system.

THE LEGISLATURE

The legislative body is called by many names: the Congress (US), the National Assembly (South Korea), the Parliament (many European countries), and so on. The members are generally elected by popular vote in electoral districts and accountable to the general public. When they are not elected, for example, in the upper house of the British parliament, they typically have less power than their counterpart in the lower house. The structure of legislatures vary: in some countries the body is huge. The US Congress* is made of 535 members. It is really not big compared to the legislature of Mexico* with 628 members, the German*, 691, the Indian*, 790, the French*, 920, and the British*, 1,436. On the smaller side, there are the Bangladesh legislature with 345, the Dutch*, 225, the Chilean, 158, and Iceland's*, 63.[1]

---

* bicameral legislature

Another important point of distinction hinges on the number of houses or "chambers" within a legislative branch. In many countries such as South Korea and Sweden, the legislature has only one chamber—unicameral legislature. However, what is more typical, especially among well-established democracies, is that the legislature is made of two chambers—bicameral. The bicameral legislature is typically comprised of two chambers based on different principals: one to represent the citizen; the other, subnational units. For example, the House of Representatives, the lower house of the US Congress is made of members who were elected in their local electoral districts. The number of seats in any given state is determined by the population of that state; the larger the population, the greater the number of seats that state has in the House of Representatives. This means, for example, that some states will lose seats over time in the House as their populations dwindle. Thus, in 2010 both New York and Ohio lost two seats. Meanwhile, Texas added four seats, and Florida two.[1] However, since all states have the same number of seats in the Senate (two) regardless of population, no such changes were made in that body.

Bicameralism in the American system is unique in many ways: the members of the Senate are popularly elected; have exclusive authority such as approving treaties with foreign countries and executive appointments made by the president and at the same time share other authority with the House; and confront the lower house in conference committees. This is of course a result of the Founding Fathers' constitutional design, ensuring division of power. However, in most other countries the upper house is typically dominated by the lower house. Unlike in the US, the upper house members of most countries are not elected by the electorate, but are chosen by the regional governments (as in Russia and Germany). Furthermore, most upper houses do not have power equal to their counterparts, and many often lack any real political power at all.

Almost all legislatures have committees because the members cannot master all the issues in the legislature and because it is not practical for all of them to sit, discuss, and vote. In the US Congress, there are about 50 committees that are filled with members of Congress helped by specialized staff. Most of the Congress' work occurs in committees with specific areas of responsibility. For example, regarding agricultural issues, there are the Senate Agriculture, Nutrition and Forestry Committee, and the House Agriculture Committee. Such a division of labor largely matches the division of the executive branch (US Department of Agriculture). They hold hearings regarding the government policy and legislation, have the members of the executive testify, and bring in witnesses and experts. They have the power to investigate the executive branch's operations. In addition, there are numerous subcommittees with even more specialized interests. Therefore, they wield strong and institutionalized power. However, this is not necessarily the case everywhere. The committees in the British House are typically assigned small staffs. Since political parties are much more powerful than parties in the US, committee members vote strictly along the party line and rarely deviate from the party leaders' instruction. As a result, committees are dominated by the political party with a majority. Moreover, since committee members are appointed to discuss just one bill after another, they do not have the opportunity to develop expertise in a specific area of competence that their US counterparts have by serving in a committee for many years. Compounded by their lack of enough financial resources and time, the British committees are much weaker than their American counterparts.

The major function of the legislature is, of course, to enact laws. The members deliberate, debate and vote on bills and upon the approval of the president, the bills become laws. Among the most important bills considered by legislatures are those having to do with the government's budget. By allocating the financial resources, the legislature can emphasize one program over another, which gives a tremendous amount of influence and responsibility to the members of the legislature. However, it should be pointed out that the bills are often written not by the members of the legislature but by the high ranked members of the executive or the bureaucracy whose experiences and expertise are usually deeper and lengthier than the members of the legislatures. As an example of an extreme case, there is the Japanese case in which the dominance of the bureaucracy was strong that many observers of Japanese politics perceive that the bureaucrats actually rule the country.[2] The Japanese bureaucracy has attracted brightest college graduates and filled its ranks with the most promising and ambitious of the elite. The competent and confident bureaucrats lead the policy debates, especially regarding economic development. The opposite case would be the US legislature where members of the Congress play a very active role in overall legislation, including the budget bill. However, in any case, the legislature is the center of law-making.

The legislature also plays an important role in monitoring and approving appointments by the chief executive. The US Senate holds hearings of the president's appointment of judges at high courts. Federal Supreme Court appointments are highly publicized events. Such power allows the Senate to express their view on the presidency itself, as well as the candidates. In some cases, the legislature even has the power to give consent to the appointment of the head of the government as we will see when we discuss the parliamentary system. In countries such as France, Russia, and South Korea, the prime minister is appointed by the president but this appointment requires the support of the legislature. Regarding its influence on who controls the government, the legislature is also a crucial recruitment tool. In the UK and many other European countries, national leaders usually debut in the national political scene as a member of the legislature. The current British Prime Minister, David Cameron, first appeared as a junior member of the parliament in 2001 as his predecessor, Gordon Brown, who was first elected in the parliament in 1983 and served as the prime minister from 2007 to 2010. As a member of the parliament, they accumulate their leadership skills and knowledge on key issues, and they learn how to govern as they become more senior members and eventually gain the seats in the cabinet and the party leadership. It is also the case in the US as is the case with Barack Obama who began his political career in the Illinois state legislature in 1997 and later served as the US Senator until 2008.

The legislature wields oversight powers vis-a-vis the executive and its programs. Committees can hold inquiries and hearings where ministers are summoned into the floor of the legislature and are expected to answer and explain to the lawmakers. In 1973, the US Senate voted to form a committee to investigate the Watergate scandal and the hearings were aired live on TV delivering serious blows to President Nixon including the revelation of the existence of the secret White House audio tapes. In some cases the legislature can even censure the head of government. In the famous case of Bill Clinton's sex scandal with a female intern at the White House in 1998, House impeachment proceeded and invoked subsequent Senate trials where he was acquitted. Nevertheless, the damage was done to Clinton. Studies by congressional committees and congressional agencies such as the Congressional Budget Office can be also effective in affecting the executive. The legislature also has the function to check the power of the executive by maintaining the exclusive right to declare war, forcing the executive to be cautious with using the military. It could also have the power to approve the emergency measures such as martial laws, without which the measure would be nullified within a certain time period.

Some legislatures have more power than others. One study compares the legislatures of 16 Western democracies regarding their power,[3] and according to the study, Germany comes at the top of the list with the most powerful legislature, and it is followed by Denmark, Belgium, Luxembourg, and Spain. The legislatures in Italy, Austria, Norway, Portugal, and Netherlands are also powerful, while the legislatures of Iceland, Greece, Ireland, and Sweden are relatively weak. According to this study, the legislature of France and Cyprus are quite weak. The French legislature is particularly interesting since, given the size of the country and the long history of democracy, you would expect to see its legislature holding formidable power. In the French parliament, the executive has the power to block the introduction of bills and amendments if they are considered to bring financial burden on the public (Article 40).[4] Knowing this, the legislature would tailor bills more to the executive's liking, than without it. Moreover, the executive is given the power to object to "the consideration of any amendment [by the parliament] which has not previously been referred to committee" (Article 44), thereby reducing the opportunity for the legislature to give their input.

THE EXECUTIVE

The executive branch is typically complex, large, and powerful in modern states as the society gets more developed. At the top of this increasingly important body, there is the head of the government, being called by different names: the president (also the head of the state), the prime minister, the chancellor, the premiers, and the like. However, their major task is almost the same: they are responsible for executing the governmental program and following through the legal mandate, including carrying out the budget.

The structure of the chief executive is slightly different from one country to another. Here in the US and many Latin American countries, the president is the sole person as the chief executive who leads the government and represents the country. The president presides over cabinet meetings, serves as the chief military commander, and has the last word on most governmental policies. When the president visits foreign countries, he represents not just his government, but the entire USA to the people of hosting countries. The entire power of the executive branch is directly and indirectly under the president's control. Such a unified executive body, as in the US, is only one sort. In other countries with different political systems, the power of the executive is shared by multiple leaders.

There are countries such as the UK, Japan, and Germany where the chief executive office, such as the prime minister, heads the government while a symbolic figure, such as Queen Elizabeth II, Emperor Akihito, and President Wulff, respectfully, represent their countries as heads of state. These heads of state typically do not have real political power. They usually serve as a cultural icon unifying their nation and continuing their historical linage in the minds of the people. The British monarch bestows honors or peerages with her wand and formally appoints a new prime minister. She appears in national celebrations such as royal weddings—most recently one between Kate Middleton and Prince William in 2011—or Wimbledon Tennis Championship games. There are a few exceptions to a monarch's powerlessness. For example, the Thai monarch is, legally speaking, a symbolic figure according to their constitution. However, King Adulyadej is immensely popular in part because of the long history of his reign—since 1946—and his persona. This public support gives him political clout that even the prime minister does not want to challenge. The king rarely exercises his power, but when he does, he does so in a very covert manner. His opinion is usually well received by the public and the political elite alike.

Beside these countries with a symbolic head of state, there are some countries allowing a formal and real division of power within the executive branch. Among democratic countries, the most obvious example is France where the president is popularly elected and given real, not symbolic, power—as in the US—but at the same time, the president appoints the prime minister who is accountable to the legislature. When the president and the prime minister are from the same party, the governing is relatively smooth, and the president is the driving force. However, the candidate of Party A could win the presidential election while Party B wins the parliamentary election, which could split the control over the executive branch since Party B will support its member as the prime minister. When these positions are occupied by two different and competing parties—often called cohabitation[5]—there could be a major problem. In Russia, the president still has the authority to push his agenda by dissolving the parliament or forcing his nomination of the prime minister despite the majority's opposition in the parliament. However, presidents of other countries do not enjoy such overwhelming power and then are forced to either share the executive power or give up much of their power regarding domestic politics to the prime minister, largely leaving foreign policy issues as the president's major responsibility.

The chief executive, such as the president in the presidential system and the prime minister in the parliamentary system, has a range of important functions. He or she is responsible for overseeing policy implementation and has the power to hold officials accountable for their acts. By appointing governmental officials who share the president or prime minister's ideas and political ideology, the chief executive can shape or adjust the governmental policies and programs in a certain direction. For example, the Environmental Protection Agency was seriously weakened and various environmental protection measures were dismantled under President Bush, but this trend was reversed or at least modified by his successor, Mr. Obama.[6] Legislation is the executive branch's major function even though the legislative branch has the major power in this task. The executive often initiates new policies by writing a bill or helps lawmakers write one. When it does not actually initiate the bill, the executive branch still assists and affects the legislation by providing information and ideas to the legislature. In some cases, the executive can legitimately bypass the legislature by using the executive orders or decrees. In Russia, presidential decrees were frequently used. Especially during the Yeltsin era, presidential decrees largely substituted laws written by the Russian Parliament. According to data, from 1992–2002, the annual number of decrees exceeded 1,500 with the exception of 1995 and 1997 while the annual number of laws remained under 200 except in 1995 and 1999.[7] Yeltsin who saw himself as the national hero and a fighter against the remnants of Communism, took the liberty of turning to ruling with decrees, freeing himself from the challenges of the legislature. If decree power is not enough, the head of the government is usually given power to veto the bill by the legislature, forcing the latter to accommodate to the former's wish in their legislation.

The chief executive has the authority to appoint and dismiss high-ranking officials in a range of governmental positions. They typically include senior civil servants in the governmental agencies, ambassadors, military leaders, executive officers in the government owned enterprises, the state-run universities, and judges as well.

As discussed, this function of appointment and dismissal is an important tool for the chief executive to move the country into one direction over another. He or she also functions as the country's commander-in-chief. The military leaders report to the chief executive who set the agenda and priority for the military. President Bush ordered the military to invade Afghanistan in 2001 and Iraq in 2003. Prime Minister Blair sent British troops to join these war efforts. President Obama's choice to implement a military "surge" in Afghanistan resulted in an increase of the US troops in the country by 30,000 in 2009. In short, primary responsibility for crucial decisions on the use of military force and other critical aspects of US foreign and defense policy rest largely in the hands of the president.

The President's Legislative Power in the Presidential Democratic States

Let's review the legislative power of the president in more detail because this power can explain the link between the executive and the legislature that is unique in the US and countries with similar political institutions. First of all, there is the presidential veto power—the power to stop the bill passed by the legislature from becoming a law—and there are two types of vetoes to review: partial veto (called item veto in the US) and pocket veto.[8] Partial vetoes allow the president to target specific elements or parts of a bill for veto, allowing the rest to be promulgated. This power substantially increases the president legislative power because the legislature cannot package a bill that includes an element that the president dislikes. Partial vetoes are common in most Latin American presidential systems,[9] but not allowed in the US system.

Another form of veto strengthening the president's power is pocket veto. It is the power to put the bill in his or her "pocket", not signing the bill within a certain time period as described by the constitution. When the president refuses to sign the passed bill into the law or, in other words promulgate it, it would be difficult for the legislature to override the veto, which typically requires two-thirds of the votes in the legislature—because the president never actually vetoed the bill. This measure becomes more effective when the legislature goes to the recess and the president alone can call for the special session. Then, the legislature would have no means to counter this move but have to wait until the next session. That is exactly what happened at the end of December, 2007. President Bush pocket vetoed a defense bill that approved $696 billion in spending, including $189 billion for the wars in Iraq and Afghanistan and a 3.5% pay raise for uniformed service personnel. In the bill, however, there was a provision that could have exposed the Iraqi government to lawsuits seeking damages from the Saddam Hussein era, which could have hampered the government's efforts to rebuild the country. Bush argued that this provision could "imperil billions of dollars of Iraqi assets at a crucial juncture in that nation's reconstruction efforts."[10] The Congress rewrote the bill in the next month, addressing the president's concern.[11]

Beyond the veto power, the president usually has the power to introduce bills to the legislature. This is very important for several reasons.[12] This authority puts the president out of a passive position where the president has to react to the initiatives from the legislature. This power becomes even more important when the president has exclusive power to initiate certain bills, such as a budget proposal, as in Brazil, Chile, Colombia, and Uruguay. Without the president's initiative in these cases, there would be nothing to be done by the legislature, which puts the latter in a very passive position in legislation. In some cases such as Chile, the president's proposal in certain areas cannot be modified. It is usually a budget bill and this places the bill in a take-it or leave-it position. The legislature has not a lot of options in this situation because rejecting a budget bill is too big a risk to take. In addition to these legislative powers, some presidents are given the power to issue decrees. The legislature should pass it in some cases such as Brazil and Iceland. In some cases, the decree stands unless the legislatures reject it, as in Chile.[13]

The legislative power given to presidents are hardly the same: some have more than others. Shugart and Carey measured the legislative power of the president in democracies on a numeric scale of 0 to 15.[14] According to this framework, Chilean president of the 1969 constitution comes at the top with 12 points, followed by the Brazilian president of the 1988 constitution with 9 points. There are a few with 8 points such as the Colombian president in the pre-1991 constitution and the Chilean one in the pre-1969 constitution. On the weak side, there are presidents of Austria and Bulgaria with zero points, followed by Costa Rica (1), Portugal (1.5), and the US (2). Notice the US president is quite weak in this measure, which would surprise many readers. After all, we have a president who is typically dominant in politics. This discrepancy comes from the fact that this measure is only for the legislative power. Of course, the president has more power beyond the realm of legislation, such as power to form and lead the cabinet, to dissolve the legislature, and so on. Shugart and Carey called this the president's nonlegislative power and they measure this as well. According to their data, the power of the US president scored 13 points, with significantly more nonlegislative power than legislative power.

This discussion of the legislative power of the president illustrates an important aspect of political institutions. To be precise, an important absence in the discussion is critical: the prime minister. The preceding discussion of president's legislative power is based on a simple assumption that the president and the legislature compete for the legislative power. However, such discussion is almost meaningless in a political system where the prime minister is the head of the government because the prime minister usually does not compete with the legislature. Rather, he or she dominates the legislation, and the legislature typically follows the direction of the prime minister and the cabinet. Is it because the prime minister is too strong? An answer to this question could be yes, and there is more to this issue. And that is our next topic.

The Presidential System versus the Parliamentary System

The political system that American readers are familiar with is called the presidential system. This is most familiar to us and many people in Latin America because this political institution has been the basis of the government for many, many years and it must have been probably the only form of the government that the countries have had. However, on the other side of the Atlantic Ocean, the story is the opposite. Most Western European countries have had the government that is called the parliamentary system. To them, the presidential system is totally foreign. So, let's compare these two.

Presidential System The presidential system is mainly characterized by the president being elected by popular vote and holding significant power. Since the members of the legislature are all elected by popular vote in a democracy, this additional election adds a set of special features to the presidential system (after all, it was invented by those who rejected the European political system). The president is given a separate mandate in the individual election in the presidential system. Here in the US, the presidents serves 4-year terms and could be reelected only once more. The president serves the term with no regard to the elections of the legislature. Voters may cast the ballots for the presidential candidate of Party X while they vote for the candidate of Party Y in the legislative election for whatever reasons.

In a presidential system the chief executive has powers and responsibilities that are largely different from the legislature, and each branch has means to check the other's power. This institutional setting is called as separation of powers. This separation comes with mechanisms for them to balance each other's powers. As already discussed, the presidents have veto power and the power to appoint high-ranking judges. The legislatures have the power to disapprove top-level presidential appointments and override the presidential veto. The legislatures are typically given the power to remove the president or to initiate such processes even though actual expulsion is extremely difficult. In the US, the Supreme Court has the power of judicial review, allowing the court to declare any act of the president, Congress, or even state and local governments to be unconstitutional.

The separation of powers between the three branches of the government was created to divide the political power to prevent a dictator from dominating the country. However, as a result, effective policymaking can be complicated by the challenge of this division. In short, it can be very difficult for the government to deal with urgent issues quickly when two different parties control two different branches of the government. For example, in 2011 the most urgent issue has been the slow economy. However, the characterization of the crisis and suggested solutions were different from the President and the Congress. Liberal democrats—the backbone of the President's political base—saw unemployment (9.1% as of May 2011 according to the US Bureau of Labor Statistics) as the most urgent issue and thus they proposed that the government should support the battered economy while it recovers from a severe recession. In other words, the government should keep spending money to boost the economy and hopefully create jobs even at the risk of an increase of government debts.

On the other hand, Republicans who controlled the House have argued that the most serious problem of the county is the ever mounting federal deficit ($973 billion for the first 9 months of fiscal year 2011 as of July 2011), and especially Tea Party members have been adamant about any suggestion of an increase of governmental spending. The President and the GOP leaders have tried to reach an agreement, but the efforts were repeatedly hampered by the difference between two parties. Of course, the political struggles between two governmental branches has delayed and hindered the government's efforts to react to the sluggish economic situations of the country.

Parliamentary System In countries with the parliamentary system, the head of state is either elected, usually by the parliament (in case of the Dutch president), or ascends to the post through hereditary lineage (in case of the British monarch). In this system, however, there is no popular election for the head of the government. The people elect the members of the parliament via voting often for the list of candidates written by their political party (in the UK people vote for the candidate as in the US). Once the election is over, the parliament forms the government, including its head, typically called the prime minister. The selection is done like any other vote in the parliament. In other words, the prime minister is elected typically by the majority, and he or she is almost always the leader of the political party with the most seats after the election. The prime minister practically appoints the members of the cabinet, mostly from the elected members of the legislature. Therefore the government is accountable to the lower house of the legislature, not directly to the people. Since the government is backed by the majority of the parliament, the government's decisions and policy proposals are usually passed by the parliament. Therefore, there is no strong sense of the separation of power in this system. Rather there is the fusion of power.

A challenge rises when there is no party with majority seats after the election. Remember that to form the government, it needs the majority's votes. What if there is no such majority? In a parliamentary election, it is actually quite rare for a political party to pull the majority seats in the lower house after an election. To make the necessary majority, the political parties form alliances, sometimes even before the election, but usually after the election. Of course, the party with the most seats is practically in an advantageous position to form such a coalition government and is typically the first one given the chance to form a government by the head of the state. To lure the support from other parties, the leader usually makes policy compromises to accommodate the demands from potential partners and promises them seats in the cabinet. As a result, the cabinet is typically made of leaders of several political parties. For example, as of July 2011, the Dutch government is made of four parties: People's Party for Freedom and Democracy (VVD), Christian Democratic Appeal (CDA), Labor Party (PvdA), and Socialist Party (SP). The German government is a center-right coalition of the Christian Democratic Union (CDU), Christian Social Union of Bavaria (CSU), and the Free Democratic Party (FDP). Therefore, these governments cannot sustain themselves in power without the cooperation of their coalition partners. In a situation like this, the prime minister is only one of equals, even though a more powerful one than his or her peers. Occasionally, the coalition partners pull out their support for the government, and the government then loses the majority votes in the parliament. Similarly, if the parliament passes a motion of "no confidence", the government collapses, which could prompt a new parliamentary election.

The Presidential system versus the Parliamentary system: Which one is better? The presidential and parliamentary systems are the two major models of the democratic government. When a new state is created or a state is adopting democracy, it typically turns to these to find one that suits their situation. For example, South Sudan, the country most recently born, in July 9, 2011, picked the presidential system. Were you given the power to choose one, which one would you like? Let's review the pros and cons of these institutions.

Since most readers of this book are familiar with the presidential system and would prefer it over the parliamentary system, why don't we begin with the case against the presidential system and compare it to the parliamentary system? We have already discussed the major disadvantage of the presidential system, the gridlock. When two different and competing parties divide the control of the government, it is often extremely difficult to bridge their differences. In 1995, such deadlock over the budget issue pushed the Democratic Party, then controlling the presidency through Clinton, and the Republican Party, led by the Speaker Gingrich, over the cliff. The President's budget proposal was opposed by the Republican-controlled Congress that demanded deep spending cuts. No compromises were made and without the approved budget, the government suspended its various services including the national parks, the supply of health care for veterans, and issuing the US passport and visas among other things. Since there is no such separation of power in the parliamentary system—remember that the prime minister will usually have the support of the majority in the lower house—this gridlock of the presidential system is not an issue for most Western European countries. What the executive decides usually goes smoothly in the legislature since its majority backs the government.

There is also an argument regarding the presidential system's temporal rigidity.[15] The president's term in the office is guaranteed by the constitution: 4 years in the US; 5 years in Korea, 6 years in Mexico, and 7 years in Rwanda. Now imagine a hypothetical situation in which the president cheated on his wife, started an unjustifiable war and quickly lost it, proposed an outrageous budget bill, closed all national parks, stopped funding the science research while taxing religious institutions, and often appeared drunken and disoriented in public events. And let's just say he managed to do all these in the first year in office. Can you imagine how unpopular he could be? However unpopular and incompetent the president is, it is almost impossible to remove the person from the office unless he violates laws as specified by the constitution. Even when there is an obvious wrong-doing by the president, it could take a long time to replace him with a new one. A case in point: the Watergate Scandal. Five men who broke into the Democratic National Committee's office were arrested in June 17, 1972. The involvement of the White House was investigated by major newspapers. Congressional hearings followed in 1973, which revealed the presence of tape recordings within the White House among other things. The release of the tapes, including ones showing the president's order to cover up the event, was ordered by the Supreme Court on July 24, 1974. Only after all these, Nixon finally resigned in August 9, 1974.

Inversely, let's just say there were a president who was immensely popular because of his skillful management of politics and national economy. As a result, the business was booming all over the country while the workers experienced a better life. Moreover, let's assume that he were from a very humble background with a warm personality. He could very well be reelected for another term. But, what if the constitution bars another term for him? Then, even though virtually every citizen wants to give another term to that person, he cannot run for another term. This is similar to the situation faced by the former president of Brazil, Lula da Silva who served from 2003 to 2010. His last years as the president was marked by an astonishing approving rate—over 80%(!), first reached in late 2008. However, he had to resign, which he did. The temporal rigidity is less of an issue in the parliamentary system. The prime minister can enjoy the executive leadership as long as he or she can manage the support from the parliament. Therefore, a successful prime minister can enjoy quite a lengthy tenure. In the UK, both Margaret Thatcher and Tony Blair led three parliamentary victories and served three terms. In Canada Jean Chrétien did the same. If not so popular, the prime minister can be fired by the legislature like Kiichi Miyazawa who lost the vote of no confidence after being the prime minister only about 9 months.

Along with the gridlock and the temporal rigidity of the presidential system, its majoritarian tendency is pointed out as a major problem.[16] As discussed, the parliamentary system forces the political parties to create a kind of consensus in order to make and maintain a political alliance. Therefore, the coalition government represents various voices within the executive. Such consensus-building mechanism does not exist in the presidential system. Since the presidential system is based on the winner-takes-it-all principle—there is only one seat at stake; nothing to share—there is no place for the loser of the presidential election or no need to compromise with the opposition party within the executive. The dominance by one party could be hardly helpful with resolving issues regarding various social divisions. Moreover, there are not really strong and urgent needs for political parties to cooperate when one party dominates the executive and the other does the same in the legislature. It is also tricky to determine who has an upper hand when two branches are both popularly elected and thus can claim a popular mandate.

These disadvantages of the presidential system could be view in the light of the advantages of the parliamentary system as we saw. However, the presidential system has, of course, plenty of merits. For one, it has a high level of accountability to the public. The president is elected and forms his or her own cabinet and they are subject to the punishment or award from the public in the next election. If the president did a good job, it is very likely that he or she would keep the job. Inversely, a poor performance as the president would likely result in electoral defeat. It is not always the case in the parliamentary system since the prime minister can change before the election. For example, Tony Blair lost his leadership as the Labour Party leader and thus had to resign as the prime minister in 2007. The new Labour leader Gordon Brown became the prime minister without ever asking the public. In such cases, the continuity of the policies and programs would be lost, and when the election comes it would be not so clear which leadership the public should evaluate in the next election.

In a similar vein, the link between the chief executive and the public is strong in the presidential system since voters cast their ballot directly to the presidential candidates. In the US, when people vote for the president, they know who they are voting for. In 2008, many people voted for Obama and many other people voted for McCain. Their support for the candidate was in part based on their political party affiliation, but it was not the only factor. The candidates' personalities, characters, and policies mattered as well to their decision to vote. Many people even built an emotional tie with the candidate and cheered for them. This is not as common in the parliamentary system. In the parliamentary system, people vote for the party in the parliamentary election, and the legislature elects the prime minister. In other words, people have no chance to vote for the head of their own government. Of course, people could have a pretty good idea of who would lead the cabinet, especially in the UK where usually two parties, the Labour and the Conservative, compete for the majority. However, if there were a dozen or so parties and the party with largest seats gained only about 20% of seats, it could be hard for the public as well as the politicians to know who would lead the government even long after the election is over.

Another major advantage of the presidential system is its stability that its critiques would call the "temporal rigidity". Once in the office, the president is hard to remove. Because of this, the president can resist social and political pressures to cave into special interests without worrying about the collapse of the government. The collapse of the government? Most of you would wonder what that is because it is so foreign to the US public. However, it is not so uncommon in countries with a parliamentary system. Since 2006 Japanese prime ministers and their governments have not lasted long. The following list is the recent prime ministers and the date they became prime minister: Abe Shinzō (September 2006), Fukuda Yasuo (September 2007), Asō Tarō (September 2008), Hatoyama Yukio (September 2009), Kan Naoto (June 2010), and Noda Yoshihiko (September 2011). For one reason or another such as dismal approving rates among the public, scandals, or electoral defeat, the government had lasted about a year. It is hardly an ideal political environment for the country with decades long recession as well as other problems to solve. But, no such worry in the countries with the presidential system.

So, which one is better? This is a hard question to answer, and scholars and politicians are still debating on this issue. For us, the better question is what we should learn from this comparison. As citizen of the country born with the presidential system, we have to understand that some of the political problems stem from the very nature of our political system. In addition, by learning other political systems, we could discuss alternative political institutions and might come up with an institutional remedy for our political problems.

THE JUDICIARY

The third institution is the judiciary, whose responsibility it is to render fair and just judgement on matters having to do with law and the constitution. Both in presidential and parliamentary systems, the judiciary is relatively independent of the political powers of the other branches. It sometimes has the legal ability to challenge or limit what the other branches do. However, such powers of the judiciary vary widely from country to country. On one hand there are countries such as China or Egypt (prior to the revolution in 2011) where the judiciary largely serves the political leaders' interests. Political opponents such as the members of the Muslim Brotherhood of Egypt or Democratic Party of China as well as regular citizens who expressed their social grievances were often jailed in the name of national security or national harmony. In these countries, the judiciary rarely challenges the political leaders, and it is hardly independent from them.

On the other hand, there are countries such as the US and Germany where the high courts have wide latitude to interpret the laws of the country and the strong power to invalidate laws and policies as unconstitutional, a power known as judicial review. The high courts in these countries have a significant power to shape and reshape the political course of the country, most noticeably in the US. For example, the Supreme Court's decision to legalize the practice of abortion in 1973, instead of ending the issue, resulted in heated political debates over this issue and has galvanized political movements on both sides until today. More recently in 2010, the Supreme Court practically allowed unlimited political funding by corporations and unions, deepening their political influence. The Federal Constitutional Court of Germany started both jeers and cheers in 1994 when it ruled that the possession of small amounts of marijuana and hashish should no longer be subject to criminal penalties.

However, not all democratic countries have a strong tradition of judicial review. According to Arend Lijphart's categorization, only four of the 36 democratic countries have strong judicial reviews (the US, Germany, India, and Canada after 1982).[17] Medium-strength judicial reviews were observed in 12 cases, and weak ones, in 21. In nine cases, there was no judicial review. In some parliamentary democracies, such as the UK, the parliament is the ultimate guarantor of the constitution. It is based on the notion that important decisions such as regarding constitutionality should be made by the representatives elected by the public, not by the appointed judges.[18]

Political institutions are important because their impact is so wide and pervasive across society. There is hardly any sphere of citizen's lives that is not affected by politics, and a country's politics is unfolded on the map written by its political institutions. Even when there are several major types of political institutions, it is hard to tell which one is better because they all have their own pros and cons. However, we would like to point out that it is very important to understand them so that you can understand the link between the political situation and the nature of political institution and we can hopefully improve our political institution based on such knowledge.

Notes

1 Sabrina Tavernise and *Jeff* Zeleny, "South and West See Large Gains in Latest Census," *The New York Times*, December 21, 2010.

2 Chalmers Johnson, "Japan: Who Governs? An Essay on Official Bureaucracy," *Journal of Japanese Studies* 2.1 (1975): 1–28.

3 Taehyun Nam, "Rough Days in Democracies: Comparing Protests in Democracies," *European Journal of Political Research* 46 (2007): 97–120.

4 It should be noted that the presidents in many democratic countries have the power to propose the budget as well as in France.

5 Most recently the conservative President Chirac of and the socialist Prime Minister Jospin experienced this from 1997 to 2002.

6 Eric Lipton, "With Obama, Regulations Are Back in Fashion," *The New York Times*, May 12, 2010.

7 Oleh Protsyk, "Ruling with Decrees: Presidential Decree Making in Russia and Ukraine," *Europe-Asia Studies* 56, no. 5 (2004): 637–660.

8 Matthew S. Shugart and John M. Carey, *Presidents and Assemblies: Constitutional Design and Electoral Dynamics* (Cambridge: Cambridge University Press, 1992), 134.

9 Shugart and Carey, *Presidents and Assemblies*, 135.

10 Ben Feller, "Bush to reject defense bill with 'pocket veto'," *The Associate Press, December* 28, 2007.

11 David M. Herszenhorn, "After Veto, House Passes a Revised Military Policy Measure," *The New York Times*, January 17, 2008.

12 Shugart and Carey, *Presidents and Assemblies*, 139–140.

13 Shugart and Carey, *Presidents and Assemblies*, 140–141.

14 Shugart and Carey, *Presidents and Assemblies*, 155.

15 Shugart and Carey, *Presidents and Assemblies*, 28–30.

16 Shugart and Carey, *Presidents and Assemblies*, 30–32.

17 ArendLijphart, *Patterns of Democracy: Government Forms and Performance in Thirty-Six Countries* (New Haven and London: Yale University Press, 1999), 226.

18 Ibid.

Part III
GLOBAL POLITICS

International Relations | 12

During the 20th century the world was wracked by a series of cataclysmic international conflicts and crises. The devastating destruction of World War I was followed by the global Great Depression, and then by World War II, an epic struggle for global domination featuring the three great ideological forces of the day—fascism, Marxism, and democracy. Following quickly on the heels of the Second World War, the United States and Soviet Union were locked for four decades in the Cold War competition for supremacy in the international system. With both superpowers armed with thousands of nuclear weapons, the fate of the world literally hung in the balance.

Given the warfare, destruction, and deadly competition that characterized the international system throughout most of the 20th century, it was not surprising that there was a strong inclination in the United States to return to a focus on domestic issues in the aftermath of the Cold War. One study conducted in 1993 revealed that the large majority of respondents wanted the United States government to focus on domestic issues. In fact, only 10% of Americans polled for the 1993 survey supported the notion that the US should play the role of the sole global leader in the post-Cold War era.[1]

The terrorist attacks of September 11, 2001 shook Americans from their post-Cold War foreign policy stupor. The sense that the American homeland was effectively insulated from international threats was dramatically shattered. International relations reemerged from the shadows of the collapse of the Soviet Union and the end of the Cold War, and became a core concern one again for policymakers and citizens alike.

INTERNATIONAL RELATIONS DEFINED

We define international relations as the military, political, economic, social, and cultural interactions between actors in the global system. As we discussed in Chapter 4, there are several types of actors that play an important role today. In addition to states, about which more will be said in the next paragraph, the other categories of actors that we identified in Chapter 4 as having an impact on contemporary international politics include: IGOs such as the UN, whose members are states; NGOs such as Amnesty International and Greenpeace, whose members are private individuals from around the world; transnational corporations (TNCs) such as Wal-Mart, which have operations in multiple countries; influential individuals, ranging from the leader of India's nonviolent movement for independence Mohandas Gandhi to the terrorist leader Osama Bin Laden, and quasi-states that aspire to statehood, such as Palestine.

The most important of these actors in the modern international system is the state. In Chapter 4, we defined the state as a political unit that features a government that exercises jurisdiction over a specific territory and the population living within that territory, and whose existence as a sovereign state is recognized by the international community. States began to emerge as the dominant territorial and political units in the international system following the Treaty of Westphalia in 1648, which ended the Thirty Years' War. The Treaty of Westphalia signaled the decline of religion as the source of political identity and territorial boundaries, and the rise of the secular state. Currently there are nearly 200 sovereign independent states in the international system.

States operate in a world in which they must balance their internal interests, which typically include goals such as political support at home for the ruling government and a growing domestic economy, with their external objectives, and in particular securing their territory from foreign threats. It is important to recognize that, while scholars may find it useful at times to treat domestic politics and international relations as if they are completely distinct and separate arenas, in fact they are closely intertwined. Domestic considerations and crises can have a major impact on the decisions a political leader makes regarding his or her state's foreign policy. For example, many people believed that Bill Clinton ordered bombing raids in 1998 on targets inside Afghanistan and Sudan in an effort to distract attention from the scandal unfolding in America regarding Clinton's improper relationship with White House intern Monica Lewinsky.[2]

In a variation on this theme, domestic conditions in one state may influence the foreign policy of other states. For example, in 1971 India saw an opportunity to strike a debilitating military blow against its regional enemy Pakistan. At the time, Pakistan was experiencing a severe internal crisis in the form of a civil war, as East Pakistan (what is today know as Bangladesh) sought to break away from the rest of the country. India supported the independence drive by East Pakistan because its leaders believed that a divided Pakistan would leave India as the unquestioned power in the region. As recounted by former US Secretary of State and National Security Advisor Henry Kissinger, India resisted the US demand not to use the unrest in Pakistan as a pretext to intervene in Pakistan's internal conflict.[3]

On the other side of the coin, external crises can have dire domestic implications. Continuing with the example of the 1971 Indo-Pakistani War, Pakistan's humiliating defeat in that war sparked a domestic political crisis inside Pakistan. Not only had a large chunk of Pakistan's territory been shorn away to create the newly independent state of Bangladesh, the citizens of Pakistan were shocked by the swift and total nature of their country's loss to India. Most Pakistanis blamed their leader, Yahya Khan, for the defeat. Within days, Yahya Khan was forced to resign his post. Pakistan's external crisis had shaken the country's domestic system to its core.[4]

As the examples discussed above illustrated, there are important linkages between politics at the domestic and international levels. At the same time, it is also true that the differences between the two realms of politics are profound. Let us now turn our attention to the key concepts and characteristics that distinguish and define international relations as a distinct and unique realm of political action.

KEY CONCEPTS IN THE STUDY OF INTERNATIONAL RELATIONS

Anarchy

The central function and characteristic of a state is the ability, through effective institutions of governance, to exercise authority over its population and territory. In a few states in the international system—Somalia being a classic recent example—the central government is weak or nonexistent. In such failed states, instability is the norm and disputes between contending factions are often resolved through the use of violent force.

The international system is similar to a failed state in the sense that the global arena is characterized by anarchy, which refers to the absence of an overarching governing authority. Thinking back to our discussion of political philosophers in Chapter 2, Thomas Hobbes addressed the condition of anarchy in domestic systems. Recall that in Hobbes' view humans by their nature are insecure, greedy, and violent. Hobbes argued that the best way to control these impulses was through the creation of a Leviathan—an all-powerful central government whose job it is to create stability where chaos would otherwise be the norm.[5]

Does a "Leviathan" exist in the international system? Despite the hand-wringing from some people over the supposed "power" which the UN has to enforce its will on the international system, in reality the UN does not come close to operating as a true world government. As an IGO, the most important decisions made by the UN are actually made by its member states. Therefore, when someone asks, for example, "Why didn't the UN do something to stop the genocide in the Darfur region of Sudan?" what he or she should really ask is "Why didn't the member states of the UN, and in particular the five permanent members of the Security Council (the US, Great Britain, France, Russia, and China) do something to stop the genocide in Darfur?"

As even a cursory review of the history of the debate on the Darfur issue reveals, China was quite proactive in blocking efforts at international intervention in that crisis. China's policy on the issue was shaped both by its economic ties with Sudan as well as by its long-standing commitment to the norm of negative sovereignty, which asserts that states have the right to govern their domestic affairs free from external intervention. Because China as one of the five permanent members of the Security Council has the unilateral right to veto any resolution brought before the Council, the Chinese were able to block efforts to crack down on their Sudanese allies. Thus, it was not the UN as an autonomous institution that failed to protect innocent Sudanese civilians; it was its member states and one member state in particular that caused that failure.

Again, in the absence of a government such as that which exists in stable domestic systems, the international system is said to be characterized by anarchy. However, the term "anarchy," as used in the study of international relations, can be misleading. When we think of the word anarchy in its more everyday usage, we tend to think of a condition characterized by unending chaos and violence. If that were true, however, then war and instability would be occurring everywhere all the time in the international system. The fact that this is not the case leads us to consider those strategies and structures that states employ to increase their security in and enhance the stability of an anarchic system.

Self-Help

In the absence of a world government with the power to enact and enforce laws that effectively regulate the behavior of the members of the international system, states must be concerned with protecting themselves. There is no permanent global police force or army with the authority to protect states that might be the victims of aggression by states or other actors in the system. Each state is responsible for ensuring its own security and survival.

How does self-help work? In theory, the most obvious way for a state to engage in self-help in the international system is by increasing its ability to defend itself by increasing its own power. The basic recipe for engaging in self-help is for a state to seek to build a large army, supplied with sophisticated weapons and supported by a modern, robust economy. The goal is for the state to make itself so powerful that its enemies dare not threaten it.

In reality, however, the effect of self-help behavior is more complicated than might first appear to be the case. International relations scholars have noted that self-help behavior is often counter-productive in the long-run. It can leave a state less, rather than more, secure. How is this possible? In order to understand the hidden contradictions of the self-help strategy, we must examine the concept of a security dilemma.

Security Dilemma

In the previous section we suggested that the basic goal of a state in a self-help system is to make itself more powerful than its potential enemies. And yet, those who seek to strengthen themselves by increasing their own military capabilities often find that doing so does not necessarily make them more secure. What explains this phenomenon?

The answer lies in the fact that states do not operate in a vacuum. What one state does to enhance its own security will have implications for other states in the system. Specifically, measures taken to increase the security of one state in the name of self-help will decrease the security of other states in the system. It is only natural that other states, feeling threatened by their own growing insecurity, will respond with measures intended to make themselves feel secure again. To use the simple metaphor of a sling-shot, one state's decision to build a bigger sling-shot will motivate other states to respond by pursuing the acquisition of a sling-shot of equal or greater power. This is the epitome of the security dilemma.

In more specific terms, a state that tries to bolster its security through a build-up of its military capabilities may find itself less secure in the long-run because such efforts may trigger an arms race with others in the system. Other states that feel threatened will endeavor to catch up with or surpass the state that initially engaged in an arms build-up. Assuming those states achieve their objectives, the state that initiated the arms race in the first place will once more feel less secure, and thereby calculate that it must seek yet again to increase its military capability. And so, the cycle of security and insecurity continues.

Deterrence and Compellence

We have noted that states are responsible for ensuring their own security in a self-help system. The concept of state security incorporates a number of factors, including preserving the territorial integrity of the state, protecting its political stability from external threats, and defending the state's allies and interests abroad. In Chapter 3 we identified coercion as being one of the two main techniques of power available to states (persuasion being the other). To repeat, coercion relies on the threat or use of force to bring about a desired result in the behavior of an actor. Under a strategy of coercion, one actor tells another actor: "do what I demand of you, or you will experience a pain or loss."

What conditions must be in place for deterrence to be effective? Several requirements are most critical. First, the state must specifically define its willingness to use force, if necessary. Second, the state must clearly communicate its readiness to employ force as well as delineating clearly to the target state what it must do to avoid having force used against it. Third, the state that is attempting to employ deterrence must possess a level of military capability sufficient to carry out its threat effectively, and to make the costs of resisting the demands of the deterring state outweigh the benefits. Finally, the target state must believe that the threat to use force is credible.[6] The issue of credibility takes us back to another point that we made in Chapter 3: the will to use force is an important characteristic of power.

To a significant degree, the logic of deterrence assumes that both the leaders of the state attempting to use deterrence and the leaders of the state that is the target of deterrence are rational. On the one hand, the leaders of the state seeking to employ deterrence must be able to clearly identify the interests that are at stake in a crisis, rationally calculate whether they have both the capability and will to use deterrence effectively, and must be able to convey the threat to use force to the leaders of the target state. On the other hand, the leaders of the target state must be rational enough to understand the threat of force that is being conveyed to them, as well as the costs they will suffer if they resist the demands that are being placed against them.

In Chapter 3, we used the case of the Desert Shield military operation in the fall of 1990 as an example of deterrence. In that instance one act of aggression (Iraq's invasion and occupation of Kuwait) had already taken place in August 1990. By placing hundreds of thousands of troops in Saudi Arabia the United States and its allies set out to deter the Iraqi regime of Saddam Hussein from extending its aggression to surrounding states in the region. At the same time the US-led coalition received the backing of the UN to use military force to drive the Iraqis out of Kuwait if they failed to withdraw by January 15, 1991. It was hoped that the threat of the use of force would be enough to deter Saddam from invading Saudi Arabia, and convince him to withdraw from Kuwait, all without the actual use of force by the US and its allies.

Desert Shield was successful in terms of securing Saudi Arabia from an Iraqi invasion (although that assumes that Saddam ever intended in the first place to use Iraq's occupation of Kuwait as a launching point for an invasion of Saudi Arabia). Clearly, however, Desert Shield was a failure in the sense that it did not convince Saddam to reverse the initial act (Iraq's invasion of Kuwait), which triggered America's effort at deterrence.

The failure to convince Saddam to withdraw from Kuwait forced the US and its allies to transition from a strategy of deterrence to one of compellence. Under the strategy of compellence, one actor employs the threat or actual use of force against another actor in order to convince the second actor to retract actions it has already taken. In short, whereas deterrence is utilized as a strategy to prevent an unwelcome action not yet taken, compellence is employed to reverse an unwelcome action already taken.

It is fair to assume that most states most of the time would prefer to achieve their objectives through the threat rather than the actual use of force. After all, the use of force can be quite costly in terms of lives, money, infrastructure, and equipment, and the outcome and effects of war are difficult to predict with precision. In that sense, the US threat, backed by UN resolutions, to resort to military action against Iraq should Saddam not choose to withdraw on his own from Iraq, was a failure. In the end, the anti-Iraq coalition launched Desert Storm, a military operation that liberated Kuwait.

What explains the failure of the US to achieve compellence—to convince Iraq to end its occupation of Kuwait—solely through the threat of the use of force? One problem had to do with the credibility of the US threat. The Iraqis calculated—incorrectly it turned out—that America would not lead a military attack intended to drive the Iraqis out of Kuwait. As President George HW Bush would later recall, Turkish leader Turgut Ozal relayed to Bush a conversation he had with a diplomatic representative from Iraq early in the crisis in which the Iraqi envoy dismissed the US threats as a bluff.[7] Put simply, the Iraqis did not believe that the United States had the political will to follow through on its threat to use military force.

A second impediment to the successful application of compellence in the case of Iraq's occupation of Kuwait had to do with the US administration's misunderstanding of what it was rational for Saddam Hussein to do under the circumstances. On the most basic level, the degree to which Saddam was truly capable of rational decision making was open to question. For example, Saddam miscalculated badly when he launched Iraq's attack against Iran in 1980, an offensive that led to a bloody 8-year stalemate that devastated Iraq's economy and infrastructure, and greatly weakened Saddam's hold on power.

Beyond that, the administration of George HW Bush misapplied the concept of rationality by failing to take into account political considerations that might drive Saddam to resist US efforts at deterrence. American officials hoped that Saddam would understand how heavily the military balance of power was stacked against him and thus choose to withdraw Iraqi forces from Kuwait in order to avoid the possibility of military annihilation. What they failed to fully grasp was that given Saddam's tenuous hold on his domestic political system, as well as his long-standing dream of becoming the leader and hero of the Arab world, it was in fact rational for Saddam to risk military defeat if in doing so he could solidify his political position at home and in the Arab world. In retrospect, it is clear that the effort by the US to compel Saddam Hussein to change his policy course without having to resort to the actual use of force against Iraq was doomed to fail from the start.

Security Arrangements: Collective Security and Collective Defense

Throughout history alliance-building has been a popular strategy for enhancing the security of partner states. One general alliance strategy has been collective security. The logic of collective security is simple: all member states to the collective security pact pledge nonaggression toward one another, and at the same time agree to come to the defense of any member state that faces aggression from another member state. If collective security works as intended, the likelihood of war is greatly reduced within the pact because any member state that is contemplating aggression knows it will meet with overwhelming opposition—including the use of force—from the other member states.

Collective security pacts may be small in membership (e.g., the 19th century Concert of Europe, which incorporated the several great European powers of that period—Britain, France, Russia, Austria, and Prussia), or very large in membership (e.g., the League of Nations and the UN). Regardless of the size of a collective security organization, the goal is the same—to avoid war among the member states. Moreover, for collective security arrangements to be as effective in practice as they are intended to be in theory, member states must place their commitments to collective security above any other alliances. If the primary purpose of collective security is to reduce the likelihood of war breaking out between members of the pact, each member state must believe that all other member states—including those with whom they normally enjoy warm, friendly relations—will oppose them should they be contemplating an act of aggression. In that way, member states are deterred from going to war with each other.

The requirement that member states to a collective security pact put aside their natural alliances in the name of the universal interest of maintaining peace is the biggest challenge to the effective operation of collective security. In the real world of international affairs, states are rarely willing to sacrifice their strategic self-interests, which often include the forging of exclusive pacts with other states that divide the international system into competing security arrangements (see the discussion of collective defense below). For example, the Concert of Europe did not prevent the outbreak of World War I, at least partially due to the formation of alliances within the Concert that, over time, divided Europe into two competing camps of Great Powers. This development reflected the shifting self-interests of the European powers. Throughout much of the 19th century the Great Powers of Europe shared a mutual economic and political interest in avoiding warfare with each other. By the dawn of the 20th century this was not the case, and the collective security arrangement frayed and then collapsed.[8]

One is hard-pressed to find examples of effective collective security. One case this is sometimes pointed to is the Korean War. In that instance, the United States led a UN-sanctioned military effort to halt North Korean forces after they invaded South Korea in June 1950. The UN coalition against North Korea could be justified under the terms of collective security, a strategy that is one of the cornerstones of the UN's approach to maintaining peace and security in the international system.

However, the Korean War is a weak example at best of collective security. Remember, collective security rests on the assumption that all states will come to the defense of any state that faces the threat or use of military force against it. In the case of the Korean War, it is highly doubtful that, if the roles had been reversed and South Korea (an American ally) had invaded communist North Korea, the United States would have been willing to come to the defense of the North Koreans.

In fact, the Korean War is probably a better example of the second general approach to organizing security in the international system. This approach, known as collective defense, involves the forging of a mutual pact in which the member states agree to come to each other's defense in the event of an aggressive threat or act by a nonmember of the pact. For example, during the Cold War both the United States and Soviet Union arranged and supported collective defense pacts with key allies in Europe. In the case of the US, the North Atlantic Treaty Organization (NATO) served as a collective defense instrument to protect American interests and allies, particularly in Western Europe, from possible Soviet aggression. The USSR's collective defense instrument was the Warsaw Pact, comprised of the communist regimes of Central and Eastern Europe. Both NATO and the Warsaw Pact were primarily intended to defend member states from aggression by the member states of the other pact.

One concern regarding the use of collective defense to enhance the security of member states is that such pacts may end up amplifying the security dilemma. If it is logical for a single state to feel less secure as a result of a single enemy's efforts at increasing its own security, it is also logical that the member states of a collective defense pact might feel threatened by the efforts of a rival defense pact to increase the security of its pact's members. Furthermore, collective defense can expand the scope of a conflict by dragging into a war a larger number of participants than might otherwise have been the case.

World War I, pitting the members of the Triple Entente (Russia, France, and Britain), against the members of the Triple Alliance (Austria-Hungary, Germany, and Italy), is the classic cautionary tale of the perils of collective defense. In that case, when Austria-Hungary declared war on Serbia following the assassination of Archduke Ferdinand by a young Serb, Russia responded by coming to the defense of its Serbian allies. Germany then met its treaty obligations to Austria-Hungary. France, followed by Britain, reacted to Germany's move by meeting their treaty obligations to Russia. Meanwhile, Italy refused to meet its obligations as spelled out in the Triple Alliance because of side agreements it had signed with powers from the other alliance, and because of Italy's interpretation that, since Austria-Hungary and Germany had started the war, Italy was not required to come to its "allies'" defense.

If World War I presents the pitfalls of collective defense, the Cold War seems to illustrate its strengths, and in particular for the United States, which was the superpower left standing at the end of the Cold War. Remarkably, this major struggle for global domination between two great empires was not resolved through direct warfare. Instead, as will be chronicled later in this chapter, the Soviet empire gradually eroded from within, an eventuality that was predicted with remarkable prescience by the American diplomat George Kennan as early as 1947.[9] Through the strategy of containment and collective defense, and bolstered by its nuclear arsenal, the US outlasted the Soviet Union until the USSR collapsed under the weight of its own internal economic and political contradictions and shortcomings.

Distribution of Power in the International System

The importance of power as a core focus of political scientists, and a fundamental tool in politics, has been a recurring theme throughout this text. As we noted in Chapter 3, power is a relative concept. Although we can measure the objective instruments of military, economic, and political power that an individual state possesses, in the real world of politics power is most usefully viewed in relation to other states. As we discussed in Chapter 3, at the time of the Gulf War, Iraq was more powerful than Kuwait, but much less powerful than the United States. In other words, Iraq suffered a relative power disadvantage *vis-à-vis* America as that crisis played out.

Another way to understand the role of power in political life is to examine how it is distributed across the international system. In other words, how many great powers (or "poles of power" as it is described in the international relations literature) are there within the international system at a given moment in time? How does the distribution of power create opportunities for actions or place constraints on actions by states in the international system?

In a unipolar system, there is one great power (or hegemon) that is dominant. At the height of its power, the hegemon in a unipolar system sets the "rule of the game" in terms of permissible behavior by other states in the international system. The period of time immediately following the collapse of the Soviet Union and the end of the Cold War has been branded a "unipolar moment," during which time the United States was clearly the dominant power in the system and enjoyed a great deal of freedom of action.[10] It was during this period that the US was able to organize the international effort to force Iraq out of Kuwait.

It is important to note that unipolarism is not a static condition. As is the case with all states in the international system, a unipolar state's relative power rises and falls over time. In the case of dominant powers this process is known as the hegemonic cycle. The hegemonic cycle unfolds in several stages. First, a new hegemon rises as the existing hegemon declines. Eventually the new hegemon seizes dominance in the system. Second, the new hegemon consolidates its control over the system. During this period the hegemon creates and enforces norms of acceptable behavior by states in the international system. Third, the hegemon begins its decline. This relative power descent is typically linked to what has been called imperial overstretch.[11] Put simply, the foreign responsibilities and activities of the hegemon begin to outpace its domestic capacity to fund those external actions. In the final stage, a new hegemon ascends, and eventually eclipses the existing hegemon's power in relative power. If we assume that in fact the conditions in the post-Cold War system created a "unipolar moment," it is interesting to consider where the United States stands right now in the hegemonic cycle. That question will be addressed in more detail at the end of this chapter.

How peaceful is a system characterized by a unipolar distribution of power? The answer to this question is unclear. Many scholars assume that the dominant power in the international system inherently favors global peace and stability because it makes it easier to manage the system and to maintain the unipolar power's hegemony. Under this view, the dominant state practices benevolent hegemony in the sense that it does not seek to occupy and/or destroy all weaker states in the system.[12] On the other hand, we can find many examples throughout history of malevolent hegemony—empires and great powers that sought to press their power advantage on weaker states around the system. Recall for example Thucydides' account of the Melian Dialogue (*see* Chapter 3 in this text), in which the Athenians bluntly stated to the Melians "the strong do what they have the power to do and the weak suffer what they have to accept."[13]

In addition to the importance of the hegemon's intentions, how other states react to the unipolar hegemon will affect the nature of relations in a unipolar system. The other states have two general options available. They may align themselves with the hegemon through a process that is known as bandwagoning. Or, they may seek to band themselves together in an effort to balance against the power of the hegemon. If successful, balancing may lead to the emergence of additional poles of power in the system.

The international system may feature a bipolar distribution of power, in which two great powers dominate the international system. The Cold War stood as a classic example of a bipolar distribution of power in the international system. Between 1945 and 1991, it was clear to every other state in the system that the US and USSR were the dominant poles of power. Although the other states could theoretically choose a policy of nonalignment (and in fact some did proclaim themselves to be aligned with neither the US nor the USSR), the dominance of the two superpowers was beyond dispute.

Interestingly, prior to the Cold War it was assumed by many scholars that bipolar systems might be particularly war-prone. And yet, during the entire length of the Cold War the Americans and Soviets managed to avoid going to war. How did this come about?

During the height of the Cold War, renowned international relations scholar Kenneth Waltz argued that there were four main factors that contributed to the stability of the bipolar system.[14] First, both superpowers clearly understood that the other had strategic interests around the world, and that threatening those interests might lead to direct conflict between the two. Second, it was clear to each superpower that the other superpower was their main enemy; further, it was clear which economic, political, and military factors might affect the balance of power between them. Third, by dealing with a series of Cold War crises (e.g., the Berlin Blockade; the Korean War; the Bay of Pigs invasion; the Cuban Missile Crisis), both superpowers became adept at dealing with crises without going so far as to provoke a military response from the other. Finally, because of their clear advantages within the international system both superpowers had the capacity to deal effectively with changing circumstances and unexpected events across the system. Considered in total, Waltz's argument regarding the stability of a bipolar system rests on his assertion that each great power learns over time how to deal with the other and how to manage their conflict so as to avoid a direct war. In short, it is a system marked by predictability. Of interest is the fact that Waltz discounted the role that nuclear weapons played as a deterrent to war.

A tripolar international system features three great powers. Examples of true tripolar systems are fairly scarce. Some point to the period of time beginning in the 1960s and ending with the collapse of the Soviet Union. During this span of time a geo-political split emerged that divided the two great communist powers, the USSR and China.[15]

Others argue that the international system on the eve of World War II was tripolar in nature, with the United States, Germany, and the Soviet Union standing as the major powers, and other middle-level powers (Great Britain, France, Japan, and Italy) forging alliances based on whether they sought to preserve the *status quo* in the system (Great Britain and France saw the US as the best choice for maintaining the general contours of the international system at the time) or revise the system (Japan and Italy believed that Hitler's Germany stood as the best hope for achieving fundamental change).[16] The Soviet Union straddled the fence between the two poles, first signing a nonaggression pact with Hitler's Germany, then being forced into an alliance with the US and its allies after Hitler's forces broke the nonaggression pact and invested the USSR.

How stable and peaceful is a tripolar system? There is no clear answer to this question. On the one hand, a tripolar system diffuses power, making it harder for any single state to become powerful enough to exert its dominance. Moreover, in a tripolar system the potential exist for two of the poles to join forces to check the aggressive actions of the third pole. On the other hand, under tripolarism two powers can forge an alliance to gang up on the third power in an attempt to destroy it. Imagine, for example, the threat that would have existed (or at least would have been perceived to exist) to the United States if the Soviet Union and China had managed to forge a lasting strategic alliance during the Cold War. If nothing else, the uncertain impact of a tripolar distribution of power on security within the international system illustrates the fact that the greater the number of great powers in the system, the more complicated the calculations for the leaders of the three poles.

Finally, a multipolar system is characterized by four or more great powers. The Concert of Europe during the 19th century was an example of a multipolar system. As was noted earlier in this chapter, during that period of time Great Britain, France, Russia, Austria, and Prussia operated according to an informally agreed-upon set of principles under which no great power would pursue policies that threatened the core strategic interests of any of the great powers. In addition, Great Britain, by dint of its status as the "first among equals" in terms of its relative power, served as the "core balancer" in maintaining the stability of the system.

As is the case with the other distributions of power, there is no general agreement among international relations scholar on the question of whether multipolar systems are inherently more or less stable than the other distributions we have discussed here. Yes, it is possible that multipolarism may be inherently stable in the sense that power is widely dispersed across a number of states, thereby making it more difficult for any single state to enforce its will on the others. However, it is also possible that multipolar systems might increase instability because they can increase uncertainty. According to this view, the larger the number of great powers, the more challenging it is for leaders to understand and predict the interests, goals, and behaviors of all the other great powers in the system.

We have seen during this discussion of distribution of power that there is no broad consensus as to the precise impact of power distribution on global politics. Intuitively, it seems to make sense that the distribution of power affects the behavior of states in the international system. However, scholars disagree on the question of which distribution may be most peaceful and which may be most war-prone. In fact, despite the "common sense" view that distribution of power affects the relative amount of peace or war in the system at any given moment, much of the research suggests that the true impact of distribution of power is negligible at best in terms of increasing or decreasing the frequency of military conflict in the international system.[17]

A HISTORICAL OVERVIEW OF THE MODERN INTERNATIONAL SYSTEM

Having discussed the key concepts in the study of international relations, we now turn our attention to an examination of the historical evolution of the global system. As we shall see, although each era in international relations features a unique set of events and actors, there are certain factors that offer points of comparison and contrast between those eras. Specifically, each period may be distinguished according to a particular distribution of power (unipolar, bipolar, tripolar, or multipolar), as well as a dominant security arrangement (either collective defense or collective security). We begin with the year 1648, which launched what has been called "The Westphalian System" in international relations.

The Treaty of Westphalia and the Founding of the Modern International System

We have already touched on the crucial importance of the Treaty of Westphalia in shaping the modern international system. Signed in 1648 at the conclusion of the Thirty Years' War, the treaty signaled the demise of the Holy Roman Empire and recognized the sovereign right of the European monarchs to choose which of the two main Christian branches—Catholicism or Protestantism—would be the dominant faiths within the boundaries of the territories they governed. The Treaty of Westphalia initiated a process under which the sovereign state would gradually emerge as the dominant territorial unit in Europe, and then would be exported around the world through the experience of colonialism. As will be clear over the next several paragraphs, it was a period of time marked by a multipolar distribution of power, as well as shifting, collective defense alliances among the European powers.

Also during this period of time, much of Europe was experiencing dramatic economic changes. Feudalism—an agriculturally-based economic system that rested on the tightly interwoven relationship between lords and serfs—was challenged by the new economic system of capitalism. Particularly in Western Europe, including England, capitalism began to take root in the cities and towns, and in the process gradually undermined the dominance of the feudal elite class.

Toward the end of the 18th century Europe and the world were rocked by the French Revolution. One critical by-product of the revolution in France was the change it affected in the way that many Europeans defined their relationship with the monarchs who ruled over them. Increasingly, particularly in much of Western Europe, people began to define themselves as citizens rather than subjects. This was an important transformation in self-identification, both because the idea of citizenship carried with it the notion of inalienable rights for all, and because it also carried with it the weight and expectations of responsibility upon all, including the responsibility for citizens to defend their state's territory from military threat. The era of the mercenary army was drawing to a close in Europe; the era of nationalism in defense of the state was born.[18]

In France itself, the afterglow of revolutionary triumph quickly descended into chaos. In 1793–1794, France suffered under the infamous Reign of Terror, which included the execution of King Louis XVI and the queen, Marie Antoinette, as well as the wholesale slaughter of tens of thousands of civilians who were suspected of being antirevolutionaries. Finally, in 1799 the French military commander Napoleon Bonaparte seized political control of the state. For the next decade, Napoleon expanded France's control and influence over much of Europe. In 1815, however, the French emperor and his forces suffered a crushing defeat at the Battle of Waterloo. Napoleon was exiled to the island of Saint Helena.

In the aftermath of Napoleon's defeat, the other victorious European powers sought to remake the rules of the strategic game in Europe. After centuries of warfare, bloodshed and instability, they wanted to create a system of relations that would promote cooperation among, and reduce the likelihood of conflict between, the great powers. At the Congress of Vienna, they constructed such a system: the Concert of Europe.

The Concert of Europe

For much of the 19th century, Europe—and in particular the dominant states of Europe—enjoyed an extended period of peace and prosperity. At the Congress of Vienna in 1815, the major European powers—Britain, France, Russia, Austria, and Prussia—agreed to construct a system that promoted peace and stability. Thus, the Concert of Europe era, a multipolar system characterized by collective security, was born.

The Concert of Europe proved to be a successful arrangement for managing conflict. With the exception of the Crimean War (1854–1856), which pitted Russia against an alliance of the Ottoman Empire, Britain, France, and Sardinia (part of modern-day Italy), and the Franco-Prussian War of 1870–1871 (which resulted in a victory by Prussia and thereafter in the unification of Germany), war between the major powers was avoided. Why was the Concert of Europe generally successful in dampening the fuse of war in Europe?

First, the success of the Concert of Europe may be traced to the effective functioning of multipolarism and collective security. Power in the 19th century Europe was in fact fairly equally distributed between the five great powers. Having said that, Great Britain was the "first among equals," by dint of its economic power and military might. The British played the key role of "balancer" by making it clear that they would swing their support against any state that behaved aggressively. More generally, the collective security arrangement under the Concert of Europe worked effectively because states generally avoided entangling collective defense alliances and provocative behavior that might trigger those alliances and start a war.

Second, the Concert of Europe preserved peace precisely because, by a happy coincidence of fate and timing, the self-interests of each of the major powers were tied to stability and peace at that particular point in history. These common factors included their mutual concerns over fighting external wars that might expose their domestic systems to political instability; their desire to focus on the development of their domestic economies without the draining affects of fighting major wars, and the policy of colonialism, which permitted the powerful states of Europe to "compete" with one another through the acquisition and exploitation of foreign territories. As long as these factors held, it was rational for the major powers of Europe to abide by the principles of non-interference in each other's internal affairs and peaceful external competition with one another for new colonies.

The Concert of Europe began to crumble in the latter stages of the 19th century. One critical development was the unification of Germany. Overnight, a new power emerged on the European continent, one characterized by rapid industrial growth at home and a hunger to colonize territories abroad. Germany's demands for a place at the great power table were at least temporarily met in 1878 at the Congress of Berlin, which guaranteed Germany a colonial stake in Africa.

Other European powers, and in particular the continental states of France and Russia, felt threatened by the rapid rise of Germany. The balance of power within the multipolar system was thrown into disarray. Furthermore, the underlying requirements of collective security—and in particular the requirement to avoid collective defense alliances within the collective security arrangement—seemed increasingly obsolete and even dangerous. Increasingly, Europe was divided by collective defense agreements. One was the Triple Alliance between Germany, Austria, and Italy; the second was the Triple Entente, which brought together Britain, France, and Russia. As was chronicled in the discussion on collective defense earlier in this chapter, the assassination of Archduke Ferdinand of Austria-Hungary provided the spark that triggered the collective defense alliances to action, and plunged Europe, and eventually much of the world, into war. Fought between 1914 and 1918, World War I cost the lives of 8.5 million soldiers and 1.5 million civilians, and laid the groundwork for another great war 20 years later.[19]

The Interwar Era

The outcome of World War I fundamentally reshaped the international landscape in a number of important ways. Germany was left a greatly weakened and impoverished power. The Ottoman Empire dissolved and disappeared from the map. Italy, though part of the victorious coalition during the war, gained nothing from its outcome. The czarist regime in Russia was overthrown, to be replaced by the Marxist Soviet Union. The United

States returned to its traditional foreign policy of isolationism after the war, while the Soviet Union was isolated as well by the capitalist powers that feared the spread of Marxism-Leninism. In Asia, Japan was a rising power but still geographically on the periphery of a system long dominated by Europe. In the short-run, these factors came together to create an environment in which, despite the multipolar character of the international system at the time, Britain and France were the dominant actors by default, especially during the 1920s.

During the war, US President Woodrow Wilson had imagined that World War I indeed would be the "war to end all wars." In pursuit of that dream, the League of Nations was formed in 1919.[20] The League represented a classic collective security organization, based on the concept of joint action by member states against any aggressive state in the system.[21] In that sense, the League of Nations continued the dominant security approach that had been practiced during the Concert of Europe period.

At the same time, however, the underlying philosophical and strategic rationale for collective security during the Interwar Era differed greatly from that which existed during the Concert of Europe. The Concert of Europe rested on a classic balance of power equation, incorporating each of the great powers. On the other hand, the League of Nations was hobbled from the beginning by the fact that neither the United States nor the USSR joined the organization. In fact, the distribution of power in the international system was in a state of flux between World War I and World War II, with traditional powers such as Britain and France trying to maintain their deteriorating hegemony. This greatly weakened the effectiveness of the League of Nations.[22]

To a significant degree, collective security during the Interwar Era reflected a "utopian" belief that all human beings are rational, and that rational human beings preferred peace over war. Moreover, the utopianists assumed that the nationalist sentiments that helped stoke the fires in World War I were becoming a thing of the past. It never dawned on the proponents of this view that the policy of exacting economic revenge on Germany via reparations following World War I would inflame, rather than dampen, nationalist sentiment in Germany.

The assumption that all human beings are capable of rationality (and that all rational people prefer peace) had profound implications for how the system would respond to aggression. It became popular to assume, particularly in parts of Europe that had been ravaged by war, that the best check against aggression by a state was international public opinion.[23] After all, so the thinking went, if wars simply reflect moments of irrational behavior by normally rational people, it should be very simple to use logic and reason to convince a wayward leader of the error of his aggressive ways. The faith that many people held in the power of public opinion to stop aggression proved to be woefully misguided. International public opinion was not enough to stop states such as Germany, Italy, and Japan from behaving aggressively.

Developments during the 1930s showed just how naïve the idealists had been. Not only was nationalism alive and well, a particularly dangerous brand of hyper-nationalism emerged. Drawing their ideological inspiration from Darwin's concept of Survival of the Fittest, hyper-nationalist leaders in countries such as Germany, Italy, and Japan felt fully justified in targeting for domination or annihilation those peoples and states whom they judged to be the "weaker of the species."[24] Nationalism also played out in the economic sphere, as states employed protectionist strategies within the context of the Great Depression.

The idealists were also wrong when they assumed that all states inherently preferred peace over war. A system that delegitimizes war without providing for any sort of peaceful mechanism by which rising powers can have their needs and demands met is bound to increase the frustration and resentment of the rising powers. Ideally, the best way to preserve the existing system in the face of a threat from a rising power is to try to give the new power a stake in the current arrangement. For example, during the Concert of Europe the other powers at least attempted to recognize the rise of Germany by granting it the right to seize colonies in Africa. During the Interwar Period, however, the League of Nations provided no such mechanism. With no stake in the *status quo* system, states such as Germany, Italy, and Japan perceived that it was in their best interest to try to remake that system.

World War II pitted the forces of totalitarianism and imperialism on one hand (the Axis powers of Germany, Italy, and Japan) against the alliance of Western democratic states and the Marxist-Leninist Soviet Union. In 1945, the Allies achieved final victory in Europe over Germany and Italy and in the Pacific, over Japan. The stage was set for the Cold War, pitting the United States and the Soviet Union in a titanic struggle for global supremacy.

The Cold War

Even more so than had been the case with World War I, the Second World War fundamentally remade the international system. Germany, Japan, and Italy were defeated shells of their former great power selves. Britain and France were almost as weakened in victory as the Axis powers had been by defeat. The two superpowers left standing after the war were the United States and the Soviet Union. The bipolar Cold War system was born.[25]

In theory, international peace and security after World War II was supposed to rest once more on collective security. The Charter of the UN, newly-built on the ashes of the failed League of Nations, called for a variety of collective security measures to control aggression, including economic sanctions, diplomatic isolation, and joint military action.[26] In reality, the bipolar competition between the United States and the Soviet Union rendered collective security an empty promise. Instead, international stability was based on collective defense, with the Western bloc led by the US and institutionalized in NATO aligned against the Eastern Bloc, organized around the USSR's Warsaw Pact.

Peace between the superpowers during the Cold War rested on the strategy of deterrence. According to the doctrine of Mutual Assured Destruction (MAD), leaders in both the United States and the Soviet Union were rational in the sense that they understood that a provocation by either state against the other could result in a war that might threaten the very existence of the human race.[27] With each side armed with thousands of nuclear weapons, MAD assumed that neither state would risk starting a war in which both had everything to lose.

Instead of engaging in direct military conflict with each other, the superpower competition for dominance took place primarily through proxy wars, fought between allies of the US and USSR, usually on the so-called periphery on the international system. Europe was divided by what Winston Churchill called the "Iron Curtain," with American-led NATO forces aligned in Western Europe against Soviet-led Warsaw Pact forces that were stationed in Eastern Europe. Anxious to avoid a direct war with each other in Europe, the Americans and Soviets exported their conflict to lesser-developed regions such as Asia, the Middle East, Africa, and Latin America, where each superpower sought to spread its own influence while restricting the influence of the other.

Beginning in the early stages of the Cold War US military and foreign policy rested primarily on the strategy of containment. As we noted earlier in this chapter, containment was the brainchild of George Kennan, a US diplomat who had served for a period of time in the Soviet Union.[28] Kennan believed that the US could win the Cold War simply by controlling the spread of Soviet influence around the world. Eventually, in Kennan's view, the USSR would collapse from within due to inherent flaws in the Soviet Union's Marxist-Leninist economic model.

US adherence to the Kennan's view of the superpower competition greatly affected specific policies that American leaders adopted during the Cold War. For example, in the late 1940s the United States under President Harry Truman adopted the Truman Doctrine, according to which the US promised to support any state that was threatened with the expansion of Soviet influence. In the immediate term, the Truman Doctrine aimed at supporting the pro-American governments in Greece and Turkey, both of which faced threats from pro-Soviet forces at the time.[29]

Meanwhile, in Asia a new threat loomed on the horizon for the United States. In 1949, forces led by Mao Tse-tung seized power from the pro-Western nationalist government. Strategic and ideological disagreements plagued the relationship between the Soviet Union and China from the start. The erstwhile "global communist movement" was in fact divided between those who aligned themselves with the USSR and those who aligned themselves with China. However, at the time that Mao came to power, the image of another large socialist state emerging in the East, one which might cooperate with the Soviet Union to erode America's power and threaten its interests around the world, was cause for substantial concern among US policymakers. In fact, just one year after seizing power, China and the United States became involved in the Korean War, with China intervening on the side of communist North Korea, and the US intervening on the side of anti-communist South Korea.[30] As was noted earlier in this chapter, although the Korean War gave the appearance of being a collective security operation (the UN authorized military action to halt aggression by North Korea against South Korea), in reality the US intervention was a collective defense operation, with America coming to the defense of an ally that was being threatened by states that were not allies.

During the 1960s the global struggle between the US and USSR was centered primarily in two places: Cuba and Southeast Asia. In Cuba, Fidel Castro had come to power in the late 1950s and aligned his country with the Soviet Union. The United States considered the establishment of a pro-Soviet socialist state 90 miles off the coast of Florida as posing a threat to US national security. The fear of the spread of Soviet influence in America's backyard drove the US to carry out the ill-planned and poorly executed Bay of Pigs invasion.[31] The US recruited, armed, and trained an "army" made up of Cuban exiles who were living in the United States. This anti-Castro militia launched an invasion of Cuba in April 1961, but was cut to ribbons by Castro's forces. While the Bay of Pigs fiasco reinforced Castro's image and popularity at home in Cuba, it was a major embarrassment to the administration of President John Kennedy.

A year and a half later, in October 1962, the Cuban Missile Crisis brought the world the closest it had ever been to the brink of a nuclear holocaust. In the fall of 1962 the United States discovered that the Soviet Union was erecting missile systems in Cuba that would be capable of delivering attacks on US territory. A tense stand-off followed, with the Americans demanding that the Soviets dismantle and withdraw the missile systems. Finally, after 13 wrenching days the Soviets agreed to the US demands. In exchange, the Kennedy administration quietly agreed to withdraw American missile systems from Turkey. With the whole world watching, the superpowers managed to step back from the nuclear abyss.

Meanwhile, as the crisis in Cuba was cooling down, the conflict in Southeast Asia was heating up. As an extension of the doctrine of containment, US policymakers applied the domino theory to Southeast Asia. Specifically, the United States feared that if anti-communist South Vietnam fell to communist North Vietnam, this would create a domino effect, with one country after another in the region falling to Soviet and Chinese influence. Beginning in the early 1960s with just a few thousand military advisors, by late 1960s, under the leadership of President Lyndon Johnson, the United States had over 500,000 troops fighting in the Vietnam War. As the Vietnam War dragged on it caused deep divisions inside the US, with many Americans opposing the war and others supporting it.

In 1968, Richard Nixon was elected to president with the promise that he had a "secret plan" for ending the war in Vietnam. In fact, Nixon had no such plan, and the war dragged on through Nixon's first term in office and into his second term, until a peace treaty was finally signed in Paris in 1973 (although the fighting quickly erupted again once US forces had withdrawn, and South Vietnam fell to North Vietnam in 1975). In total, over 58,000 American service personnel lost their lives in the Vietnam War.[32] The war left deep scars on the psyche of the American people. For many Americans, including a number of military commanders, the lessons of Vietnam were clear: war should be an instrument of last resort; the goals of a military operation should be clearly defined, and overwhelming force should be brought to bear on the battlefield in order to win the war as quickly as possible.

Against the backdrop of America's draw-down in Vietnam, the Nixon administration adopted the foreign policy strategy of détente.[33] Under *détente*, the US and USSR would seek to establish friendlier relations, although against the backdrop of their continuing Cold War competition. Through such mechanisms as diplomacy (US President Richard Nixon and Soviet President Leonid Brezhnev met several times for face-to-face meetings in the early 1970s) and cultural exchanges between the peoples of the two superpowers, the goal of *détente* was not to resolve the underlying causes of the Cold War, but simply to lessen the tensions between the US and USSR. One key objective was to reduce the likelihood that a regional conflict between allies of the superpowers might trigger a direct military confrontation between the Americans and Soviets. This goal was put to the test during the 1973 Arab-Israeli War, when both the United States (which was aligned with Israel) and the Soviet Union (which was aligned with Egypt and Syria) moved up the ladder of military preparedness for war, but then managed to avoid a direct military exchange.

It was also during this period of time that the United States first "played the China card."[34] The US recognized the divisions that existed at the time between the great socialist powers in the system, the Soviet Union and China. By reaching out to both the Chinese and Soviets at the same time, the United States sought better relations with both states, even as disagreements continued to divide the USSR and China. In a sense, the United States played one socialist power against the other.

Following the Watergate scandal and Nixon's resignation in 1974, the policy of *détente* was continued, first by President Gerald Ford, and then by President Jimmy Carter. However, a series of events, culminating with the Soviet invasion of Afghanistan in 1979, signaled an end to the era of *détente*. Ronald Reagan was elected to presidency in 1980 on a platform of rigid anti-communism. Reagan considered the Soviet Union to be the "Evil Empire." In Reagan's view, either the US or Soviets would prevail in the Cold War. He believed that *détente*, which marked an effort at compromise, was a flawed strategy that must be replaced.[35]

In the first half of the 1980s, the United States undertook a substantial build-up of its military arsenal. In addition, under Reagan the US became much more proactive in using the military option to deal with foreign crises than it had been in the years immediately following the Vietnam War. In 1982, US forces intervened in the civil war in Lebanon (where in 1983 American marines would become the target of the first major suicide bombing against American interests) and in 1983 America invaded Grenada, toppling the socialist regime which held power there.

Meanwhile, Kennan's theory that the Soviet Union would collapse due to flaws in its domestic system was beginning to come to fruition. Contrary to the widely-held perception in the West at the time that the Soviet Union had equaled or surpassed the power of the United States, in reality the Soviet economy was in steep decline. The economic system in the USSR was plagued by inefficiencies. The state decided what would be produced, where it would be produced, how many things would be produced, where they would be sold, and at what cost. With market forces completely removed from the economic equation, productivity declined and the quality of goods available to Soviet consumers suffered greatly.

Against the backdrop of its growing economic crisis, the USSR was bogged down in an expensive and inconclusive war in Afghanistan that was unpopular at home. Furthermore it was hard-pressed to try to match the US arms build-up, while also dealing with increasing unrest within a number of pro-Soviet socialist states in Eastern Europe. Increasingly, it appeared that the Soviet Union was in the position of a declining hegemon, with its growing external responsibilities outpacing its shrinking domestic economic capacity.[36]

Faced with this emerging "perfect storm" of foreign and domestic crises, Mikhail Gorbachev came to power in the Soviet Union in 1985. Gorbachev's approach to dealing with the multiple crises that threatened to destroy the USSR involved several policy initiatives. At home, the Soviet leader implemented *glasnost*, a package of political reforms designed to allow Soviet citizens to vent their frustration while maintaining Communist Party control over the system, and *perestroika*, a series of economic reforms intended to jump-start the Soviet economy mainly by reducing the role of state bureaucrats in making economic decisions.[37] Abroad, Gorbachev undertook a substantial reduction in military support for the unstable socialist regimes in Eastern Europe and explored a path toward the eventual withdrawal of Soviet forces from Afghanistan, all the while seeking better relations with America.

Ultimately, Gorbachev's effort to save the Soviet system through reforms failed. The Soviet leader's attempts to create a more efficient and productive economy met with significant resistance from the bureaucrats who ran the socialist economy. When Soviet citizens came to realize that the promised benefits of economic reform were not materializing, they moved beyond venting their frustrations over the slow pace of economic change to demanding a fundamental transformation in the system.[38] Although the relationship between the US and USSR improved to the point that the Soviets did not block resolutions before the UN Security Council during the Gulf War crisis calling for the use of force against Moscow's traditional ally Iraq, the Soviets never reaped the hoped-for economic benefits of warmer relations with Washington. Meanwhile, in Eastern Europe one Soviet satellite state after another began to fall to the forces of democratic change.

By the beginning of the 1990s, it was clear that reform had become an untenable option in the Soviet Union. At that point, the USSR faced a stark choice: to move back toward the days of totalitarian one-party rule, or forward toward democracy and capitalism. In August 1991, pro-communist military commanders attempted to stop the march toward change, only to be met by stiff resistance from citizens, other elements of the military, and political elites led my Boris Yeltsin. The forces of revolutionary change carried the day, and on December 25, 1991 the Soviet Union officially disbanded. The Cold War was over. The United States had prevailed.

The Post-Cold War Era

As we noted earlier in this chapter, the years immediately following the end of the Cold War were widely heralded as a "unipolar moment" in the international system. America's emerging hegemony over the world affairs became obvious even before the Soviet Union collapsed. The fact that the Soviets acquiesced to the use of force against Iraq, and further that a traditional Soviet ally such as Syria supplied forces to the US-led coalition, illustrated the extent to which states were eager to bandwagon with the United States.

The Gulf War also seemed to signal an effort by the US to organize a new collective security framework. President George HW Bush coined the phrase "New World Order" to describe a global security arrangement in which aggression by one state against another would no longer be tolerated. The New World Order concept provided a sort of underlying philosophical justification for the American-led coalition to end Iraq's occupation of Kuwait. It was intended to signal that the war against Iraq in 1991 was based on universal moral principles, not the narrow self-interests of the United States.

In reality, after the Gulf War the US never again applied the principles of the New World Order to justify using military force to stop interstate aggression in the global system. In fact, rather than collective security a system of selective security has emerged, one in which the United States organizes *ad hoc* coalitions to carry out military actions against actors who threaten US interests. The Gulf War, the invasion of Afghanistan, and the invasion of Iraq are each examples of selective security in action.

The end of the Cold War triggered a sort of ideological euphoria in the West. It was widely believed that the collapse of the Soviet Union and the demise of Soviet satellite states proved the superiority of the ideologies of democracy and capitalism. The scholar Francis Fukuyama even went so far as to declare that end of the Cold War really marked "the end of history" as far as the development of new ideologies was concerned. From that moment forward, said Fukuyama, there would only be one viable ideological path for states around the system—the path of democratic capitalism.[39]

Ironically, some pundits and policymaker in the US seem to long for "the good old days" of the Cold War.[40] At least during the Cold War it was clear which country posed the major threat to US security interests (the Soviet Union). As Waltz had stated in presenting his scholarly argument for the stability of a bipolar system, a bipolar distribution is stable because each side over time comes to understand the interests of the other. As long as both poles behave rationally, a bipolar system is fairly stable and predictable.

By contrast, the post-Cold War system has been messier and more complicated. In the years following the Cold War there was a growing debate as to whether in fact the system was gravitating toward multipolarism. Those who supported this view based their thesis on the argument that military might was increasingly irrelevant as the main measure of state power. In its place, economic wealth would become the primary determinant of power. By that measure, the system was multipolar, with the US vying with the European Union, Japan, and increasingly China for economic supremacy.

Others argued that military conflict would continue, but in a crucially altered way. Samuel Huntington predicted that the end of the Cold War signaled the end of an era that he branded the "Clash of Ideologies." Increasingly, said Huntington, the world was dividing into blocs of civilizations. Conflict was most likely in those areas of the international system where civilizations came into friction with one other. Most importantly, Huntington warned of an emerging "Clash of Civilizations" pitting the Islamic and Confucian civilizations in an alliance against the West.[41]

Some people believed that the 9/11 terrorist attacks proved the accuracy of Huntington's predictions. In reality, there are many problems with Huntington's thesis in general, and in its accuracy as an explanation for the 9/11 attacks and the events that followed. If there is a cohesive Islamic civilization bloc, how can we explain the fact that Al Qaeda has targeted fellow Muslims much more often than it has the West? Furthermore, if the West is a solid civilization bloc, why did so many Western European states—traditional allies of the US—oppose the 2003 invasion of Iraq? As for the purported alliance between the Islamic states and the Confucian states, that relationship is based mainly on traditional strategic calculations—the demand for advanced weaponry on the part of some of the states of the Muslim world (e.g., Syria, Iran, Iraq, Libya), and the desire by states such as China and North Korea to reap the economic benefits of sales to those Muslim countries that are hungry to acquire sophisticated arms. Moreover, with its rapidly growing economy China needs access to the oil that flows from certain Arab and Muslim states, and oil-producing states are only too happy to have China as a customer.

The rapid rise of China as an economic power underscores the possibility that the very economic ideas and forces said to symbolize the irreversible triumph of the West have done more to undermine the security and confidence of the US and the EU states than Al Qaeda managed to do with the attacks of 9/11. Through the process of globalization, states such as China and India have been able to take advantage of trade and investment opportunities to grow their economies at astounding rates. In the United States and part of Europe, however, globalization has had a decidedly more mixed impact. Many corporations have benefited because of the relative ease through which they can relocate their facilities abroad where the costs of production are substantially lower, and consumers have benefited by paying less for goods than they would if those same goods were produced at home. At the same time, globalization has taken a toll on the American workforce, with many manufacturing jobs and other positions being outsourced overseas.

At home, an absence of sufficient oversight and regulation of domestic markets—and in particular over the banking and financial sectors—laid the groundwork for the economic collapse of 2007. The challenge for policymakers at any given moment in a capitalist economy is to find the perfect balance between economic freedom and regulatory oversight. On the one hand, history shows that overregulation is a break on growth in the economy. On the other hand, an absence of regulation inevitably creates bubbles—investment patterns that drive up the value of things such as houses, securities, and currency—to artificially high levels. When the bubble bursts (usually due to a crisis of some sort), an entire sector of the economy is negatively affected. If that sector is an important enough pillar—as the housing and financial sectors are in the US—it can trigger a dramatic decline in the overall economy—as happened to the US in 2007. The impact of the crisis that began in 2007 is still being felt in the US today at the time of the writing of this text. Unemployment rates remain stubbornly high, and the country faces mounting public debt and a huge budget deficit. These conditions have given rise to a debate over the status of America's role as unquestioned leader in the international system. We shall address that question below in our puzzle question on American hegemony.

PUZZLE: IS AMERICA A DECLINING HEGEMON?

As discussed in the previous section, at the time of the collapse of the Soviet Union and the end of the Cold War it was widely agreed that the United States was the unquestioned unipolar hegemon. Few doubted that America possessed an overwhelming superiority in its combination of vast military superiority, economic wealth, and political influence. Although as the 1990s unfolded there was a school of thought that claimed that the international system was taking on more of a multipolar character because of the rise in the importance of economic measures of powers, the centrality of military power was highlighted once again by the crucial role the United States played in organizing NATO's air campaign in Kosovo.

With the 9/11 attacks, the focus shifted in international relations back to the role of military forces in shaping events. On the one hand, the relative ease with which the US was able to topple the Taliban regime in Afghanistan and Saddam Hussein's regime in Iraq seemed to reinforce both America's hegemonic status as well as the core role military power plays in determining international outcomes. On the other hand, the very fact that the United States could be hit so hard by Al Qaeda in the first place, the problems America had in attempting to stabilize Afghanistan and Iraq after overthrowing the previous regimes in those countries, and the difficulty that the US encountered in tracking down and killing Osama Bin Laden (a goal which the US finally achieved in the spring of 2011) illustrated the changing security landscape of the Post-Cold War system. During the Cold War America's security rested on its ability to deter Soviet aggression. MAD worked because it was easy to identify and target America's main enemy—the Soviet Union. Moreover, the US was able to assume with some degree of confidence that Soviet leaders fully understood and abided by the logic of deterrence.

By comparison, it much more difficult to deter aggression by a nonstate actor such as Al Qaeda.[42] Such organizations are "slippery" in the sense that they are not bound to defend any particular piece of territory. During the Cold War, the US knew where to aim its missiles—at the territory of the Soviet Union. In the case of Al Qaeda, the organization has cells in dozens of countries, and its leadership hides among the local population. It took nearly a decade for the American military to finally pin down the location of Bin Laden and carry out the military operation that resulted in his death.

In addition, nonstate actors may be much harder to deter, depending upon their ideology. In the case of jihadist groups such as Al Qaeda its members have been trained to believe that their just rewards wait for them in heaven if they die for the cause. Deterrence hinges on the ability to signal clearly to your enemy "Do what we want you to do or you will experience pain." However, it is extremely difficult to deter an enemy that considers death to be the ultimate reward rather than the ultimate pain.

Given the questionable utility of deterrence under these circumstances, American policymakers have resorted increasingly to the use of military force in an effort to destroy its enemies. The administration of George W. Bush employed the strategy of compellence to achieve its objectives in Afghanistan and Iraq. However, although the ruling regimes in Afghanistan and Iraq crumbled quickly, in both instances the United States found itself bogged down for years in an expensive, complicated effort to construct stable, pro-American states on the ashes of the former regimes. The tens of thousands of American and other coalition forces that were left on the ground in these countries became inviting targets for insurgents.

The financial costs of the occupations of Afghanistan and Iraq have been staggering. According to a report issued by the non-partisan Congressional Research Service in March 2011, the US government had spent $1.250 trillion since the 9/11 attacks on the wars in Afghanistan and Iraq.[43] Meanwhile, under the Bush administration tax cuts were implemented and overall rates of spending rose. The United States government was forced to borrow ever larger sums of money, much of it from abroad (and in particular China) to meet its financial obligations. The federal budget deficit widened, and the national debt grew.

Recall our discussion of the hegemonic cycle. Typically speaking, the relative power of the hegemon begins to decline during a period of imperial overstretch, when its external obligations outpace its domestic capacity to meet those obligations. There are those who believe that this is what is happening to America today. For example, in their book *Imperial Overstretch: George W Bush and the Hubris of Empire*, Roger Burbach and Jim Tarbell bluntly charged the Bush administration with "engaging in a reckless policy of imperial overstretch."[44] According to this view, America's relative power is sliding in the international system, with countries such as China, India and Brazil experiencing robust rates of economic growth while the US is burdened with the costs of paying for two wars during a time of shrinking government revenues and, beginning in 2007, a severe economic downturn. Moreover, it is argued that the political image of the United States has taken a hit in recent years, with some people around the world coming to see America as an adventurist great power that is too quick to resort to military force around the international system.

Others believe that pundits and naysayers are too quick to consign the United States to the category of a declining hegemon. In terms of the military instrument of power, few can doubt the supremacy of the United States. America possesses a unique combination of objective military capability and the will to use that capability that puts it head and shoulders above any other state or plausible combination of states in the international system today.

As for the economic realm, some observers see the very fact that foreign investors were willing to pump money into the US even as its budget deficit mushroomed and national debt boomed as proof that the rest of the world maintains its faith in the long-term strength of the American economy. In the words of one commentator in 2008, "American consumer and capital markets are still the primary engine of global economic growth."[45] The same commentator wryly noted that the hand-wringing over the emergence of China as a "rising power" in the international system has a familiar ring to it. Similar distress was expressed in the 1980s over America's purported relative decline, but at that time it was Japan that many "experts' believed was poised to supplant the US as the global economic hegemon.[46]

In terms of political influence, an argument can be made that the popular revolts that rocked the Middle East in 2011 underscored the hunger for democratic freedoms that the United States claims to stand for around the international system. America's commitment to democratic reforms was put to the test, particularly in Egypt, where an authoritarian leader, President Hosni Mubarak, had long enjoyed a cozy relationship with the United States. Although the decision by the US to turn its back on Mubarak was not the deciding factor in his regime's collapse, it did send an important signal that America was willing to place its political values above traditional strategic ties. To the extent that democracy in the international system is linked to the United States and its values, it is possible to argue that the greater the number of democracies in the system, the greater the opportunity for the US to exercise political influence within the system.

On the question of whether America is a declining hegemon, where do you stand?

Notes

1 Ronald Steel, "The Domestic Core of Foreign Policy," *The Atlantic*, June 1995. http://www.theatlantic.com/past/politics/foreign/dcore.htm (accessed July 22, 2011).

2 BBC News Online, "World: Africa—Clinton Defends Military Strikes," http://news.bbc.co.uk/2/hi/africa/155252.stm (accessed August 15, 2011).

3 Henry Kissinger, *White House Years* (Boston: Little Brown, 1979), http://www.globalwebpost.com/genocide1971/chaps/kiss_71.htm (accessed July 21, 2011).

4 Greg Cashman and Leonard C. Robinson, *An Introduction to the Causes of War: Patterns of Interstate Conflict From World War I to Iraq* (Lanham, MD: Rowman & Littlefield, 2007).

5 Thomas Hobbes, *Leviathan* (New York: Barnes and Noble, 2004).

6 Greg Cashman, *What Causes War? An Introduction to Theories of International Conflict* (New York: Lexington, 1993), cited in Cashman and Robinson, *An Introduction to the Causes of War*, 15.

7 George Bush and Brent Scowcroft, *A World Transformed* (New York: Vintage Books, 1999), 332.

8 Cashman and Robinson, *An Introduction to the Causes of War*, 27–87.

9 George Kennan, "The Sources of Soviet Conduct, *The History Guide: Lessons of Twentieth Century History*," http://www.historyguide.org/europe/kennan.html (July 29, 2011).

10 Charles Krauthammer, "The Unipolar Moment," *Foreign Affairs* 70 (1990/91): 22–33.

11 Paul Kennedy, *The Rise and Fall of the Great Powers* (New York: Random House, 1987).

12 E.H. Carr, *The Twenty Years Crisis* (New York: Palgrave, 2001).

13 Thucydides, "The Peloponnesian War and the Melian Debate," in *Classic Readings and Contemporary Debates in International Relations*, Phil Williams, Donald M. Goldstein, Jay M. Shafritz, ed., 3rd ed. (Belmont, CA: Thomson/Wadsworth, 2006), 43.

14 Kenneth Waltz, "The Stability of the Bipolar World," *Daedalus* 83 (1964): 881–909. http://www.jstor.org (accessed August 14, 2011).

15 Gerald Segal, "China and the Great Power Triangle," *The China Quarterly* 83 (1980): 490–509. http://www.jstor.org (accessed August 14, 2011).

16 Randall L. Scweller, "Tripolarity and the Second World War," *International Studies Quarterly* 37 (1993): 73–103. http://www.jstor.org (accessed August 14, 2011).

17 Cashman and Robinson, *An Introduction to the Causes of War*, 18.

18 Samuel P. Huntington, "The Clash of Civilizations?" *Foreign Affairs* 72 (1993): 23.

19 Karen MIngst, *Essentials of International Relations* (New York: WW Norton, 1999), 27–39.

20 George A. Finch, "The Covenant of the League of Nations," *The American Journal of International Law* 15 (1921): 4–13. http://www.jstor.org (accessed August 14, 2011).

21 PBS, "Wilson—A Portrait/League of Nations," http://www.pbs.org/wgbh/amex/wilson/portrait/wp_league.html (accessed August 14, 2011).

22 Ruba Zinati, "International Relations in the 21st Century," *World Security Network*, http://www.worldsecuritynetwork.com/showArticle3.cfm?article_id=18431 (accessed August 14, 2011).

23 Carr, *The Twenty Years' Crisis*, 32.

24 Ibid, 150.

25 "Cold War," GlobalSecurity.org, http://www.globalsecurity.org/military/ops/cold_war.htm (accessed August 14, 2011).

26 United Nations, "United Nations: Charter of the United Nations," *The American Journal of International Law* 39 (1945): 190–229, http://www.jstor.org (accessed August 14, 2011).

27 Henry D. Sokolski, ed., *Getting MAD: Mutual Assured Destruction, Its Origins and Practice* (Carlisle, PA: Strategic Studies Institute), http://www.strategicstudiesinstitute.army.mil/pdffiles/pub585.pdf (accessed August 14, 2011).

28 Kennan, "The Sources of Soviet Conduct."

29 US Department of State, Office of the Historian, "The Truman Doctrine, 1947." http://history.state.gov/milestones/1945-1952/TrumanDoctrine (accessed August 14, 2011).

30 Ibid, "The Korean War, 1950–1953." http://history.state.gov/milestones/1945-1952/KoreanWar2 (accessed August 14, 2011).

31 Ibid, "The Bay of Pigs, and the Cuban Missile Crisis, 1961–1962. http://history.state.gov/milestones/1961-1968/CubanMissile (accessed August 14, 2011).

32 Digital History, "Learn About the Vietnam War," http://www.digitalhistory.uh.edu/modules/vietnam/index.cfm (accessed August 14, 2011).

33 Raymond Garthoff, *Détente and Confrontation: American-Soviet Relations from Nixon to Reagan*, rev. ed. (Washington, DC: The Brookings Institute, 1994).

34 Ibid.

35 John L. Gaddis, "Ronald Reagan's Cold War Victory," in *Major Problems in American History Since 1945*, Robert Griffith, ed. (Lexington, Massachusetts, 1992), 705–710. http://us.history.wisc.edu/hist102/readings/Gaddis_ColdWarVictory.pdf (accessed August 14, 2011).

36 Ibid.

37 The Cold War Museum, "Fall of the Soviet Union," http://www.coldwar.org/articles/90s/fall_of_the_soviet_union.asp (accessed August 14, 2011).

38 Ibid.

39 Francis Fukuyama, "The End of History?" in *The New Shape of World Politics*, rev. ed. (New York: Foreign Affairs, 1999), 1–2.

40 Paul Kennedy, "The Good Old Days of the Cold War," *Los Angeles Times*, February 18, 2007, http://www.latimes.com/news/printedition/opinion/la-op-kennedy18feb18,0,813222.story (accessed August 14, 2011).

41 Huntington, "Clash of Civilizations," 45.

42 Robert Jervis, "Mutual Assured Destruction," *Foreign Policy* 133 (2002): 40–42. http://www.jstor.org (accessed August 12, 2011).

43 Amy Belasco, "The Cost of Iraq, Afghanistan, and other War on Terror Operations Since 9/11," Congressional Research Service, March 29, 2011, http://www.fas.org/sgp/crs/natsec/RL33110.pdf (accessed August 12, 2011).

44 Roger Burback and Jim Tarbell, *Imperial Overstretch: George W Bush and the Hubris of Empire* (London: Zed Books, 2004), 26.

45 Daniel W. Drezner, "The Eagle Still Soars," *Newsweek*, February 19, 2008, found online at *The Daily Beast* website. http://www.thedailybeast.com/newsweek/2008/02/19/the-eagle-still-soars.html (accessed August 12, 2011).

46 Ibid.

The Global South: Dilemmas of Development

THE SOUTH: A NEW LABEL FOR AN OLD PROBLEM

Can you imagine selling your own daughter who is just 11-years-old to be a second wife to a man who is decades older than her just to pay back a $16 loan that was used to feed your family?[1] However horrible it may sound, events like this are not really rare in many parts of the world. Often, families live in a hut in a village where paved roads and tap water are unthinkable. Poor families eat one or two meals a day when there is anything to eat at all. Schooling is cut short, especially for girls, and jobs are rare. With no infrastructure, their livelihood and agriculture are extremely vulnerable to droughts and floods. Now, if you enter civil war or ethnic conflict into this picture, you can imagine the difficulties of people in the developing world.

Why don't we look at some data to have a real sense of this lack of development? Graph 13.1 illustrates the GDP per capita of six countries. The first three countries on the left, Sierra Leone, Congo, and Niger are one of the poorest countries in the world. Their GDP per capita are all under $800: $518, $658, and

GRAPH 13.1 GDP per capita ($). Graph created by the authors.

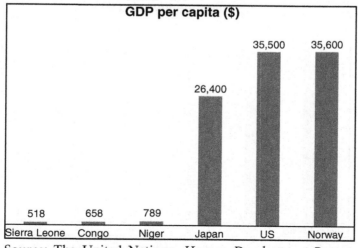

Source: The United Nations, *Human Development Report*, 2005.[2]

$789, respectively. Compare these numbers to the three on the right: $26,400, $35,500, and $35,600 for Japan, the US, and Norway, respectively. The gap between the two groups of countries is truly astronomical as you can see. For example, Sierra Leone's GDP per capita is just 1.5% of Norway's. Graph 13.2 shows these countries' child mortality rates—percentage of children who died before the age of five. Again, the three figures on the left contrast the ones on the right. From the right, the figures are 0.4%, 0.8%, and 0.4 for Norway, the US, and Japan, respectively. In other words, only 0.4% of children in Norway die before their 5th birthday. One death, especially of a child, is one too many, but this measure tells us that Norway is doing a marvelous job in providing health care for women and children. The same can be said of the US and Japan. In contrast, the three figures on the left are troubling. Sierra Leone's figure reaches 28%. It is 26% in Niger and 21% in Congo. In other words, about a quarter of children in Sierra Leone and Niger do not see their 5th birthday. This may sound hardly real, but they are painful facts in the many poor countries. These gaps between the countries on the left and the ones on the right are striking, as you can see, but it is more troubling if you think about the bigger picture.

The bigger picture is this: such gaps are not limited to a region, but global. If we look at any economic indicator, such as GDP per capita, it is easy to see that there is a group of rich countries in North America and Western Europe. In their surrounding regions, such as Eastern Europe including Russia and South America, people in these areas earn far less than their counterparts in the West, but make a decent amount of income. However, to the south of Russia, countries begin to become poorer and people are largely worse off than their counterparts in the north. When it comes to Africa and Southern parts of Asia, countries are largely quite poor. There are a few obvious exceptions to this pattern of clustering such as South Korea, Japan, Australia and New Zealand. However, the bifurcation between rich countries in the north and poor countries in the south is clear enough to render the terms such as North, referring to the rich, and South, the poor.

The gap between the North and the South is not just economic, but involves multidimensional aspects of development. One of them is health. Please take a look at Graph 13.3. The graph's horizontal axis shows regional GDP per capita in US dollars and the vertical, child mortality rate. The reason why we come back to this measure again and again is that it is a good indicator of the overall condition of a country's socioeconomic status. For example, when there is a war or a severe drought, damaging the food supply, young children often go to the bottom of the distribution of available food. They are also physically the weakest of all and easily become the victims to enduring such hardships, and without medical attention.

GRAPH 13.2 Child Mortality Rate (%). Graph created by the authors.

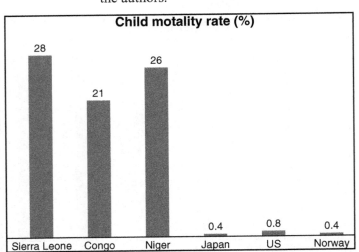

Source: The United Nations, *Human Development Report,* 2005.[3]

GRAPH 13.3   Regional GDP per capita ($) & Child Mortality rate (%). Graph created by the authors.

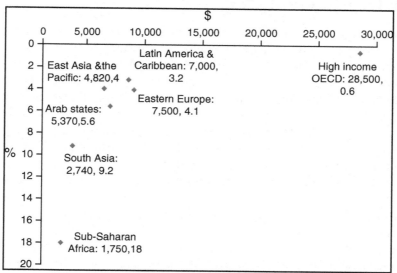

Source: The United Nations, Human Development Report, 2005.[3]

When the state fails to provide the necessary safety nets for the young children, it is often their mothers who are left as their last protectors. However, mothers typically lack basic, essential necessities, such as access to food, clean water, and housing. As a result, in some parts of the world, children often die for simple reasons such as diarrhea. Inversely, countries that are stable and wealthy can now afford to take care of the weak, including young children and women. Therefore, the child mortality rate is, again, a good measure of the wellbeing of the society in general.

In Graph 13.3, the child mortality rates are shown upside down because as this figure gets lower, it indicates a more positive development. The member states of the OECD—made of wealthy, largely Western, countries—are located on far top-right corner (and of course they are geographically located in the north), marking high scores in both economic development and health. This group's GDP per capita reaches $28,500 and child mortality rate is only about 0.6%, meaning that only 0.6% of children die before their 5th birthday. The total opposite is the group on the lower-left corner, and this are, as you can guess, the Sub-Saharan states where both economic development and health care are far, far behind their OECD counterparts. This region's GDP per capita hovers only at $1,750, that is, roughly 6% of the OECD's. The child mortality rate is as high as 18%, and that is thirty times higher than the OECD's. According to this graph, South Asia is another noticeable region that is poor in both dimensions: GDP per capita, $2,740: child mortality 9.2%.

However we look at this developmental gap, it is strikingly wide. A more troubling aspect of this is the persistency of the gap. When the Second World War ended in 1945, the Western countries were devastated by the war with the exception of the US, but they quickly recovered their industrial might and have kept their economic and political dominance in the world. However, many countries in Africa and Southern Asia that gained their independence after the end of the war have been busy with maintaining political and social stability much less developing national economy and health care systems. Not many new born countries narrowed the gap with Western countries, and their hopes to achieve sufficient development has remained as just hopes for so many years.

This chapter will include various discussions on this issue of development or the lack of it. What is development? Is it an appropriate term? How do we measure it? Why is it so hard for some countries to achieve and maintain development? Is there anyone to blame? Is there any way to exit this vicious cycle of poverty and chaos?

DEVELOPMENT DEFINED: ECONOMIC, POLITICAL, AND SOCIAL DEVELOPMENT

You most probably would agree with the assertion that countries such as the US or Norway are developed while Sierra Leone or Congo are not, at least as much as the former. Many would agree especially as we have reviewed their striking differences regarding GDP per capita and child mortality rates. But precisely what do we mean by development? To get an answer to this question, why don't we use the US as a barometer since it is the most familiar case for many of you? What is the element of our society, beside economic prosperity and health care, that enriches the quality of life here in the US but that is absent or not adequate in other countries? There are a few things that immediately pop up and one of them is education. The public schools here in the US are a popular subject of political debates, often in a scornful tone; however, it is usually ignored that our public school system in general offers an inexpensive and good education virtually anyone who wishes, and this is not the case to many people in developing countries. For developing countries, providing quality education to the youth is often a major challenge, and the failure to deliver it usually results in serious consequences such as the lack of productive workforces and violent political division.

In regard to the economic sector, beyond the high GDP per capita, the US is also equipped with a large industrial infrastructure. Even during the Great Recession that began in 2008, it has been mass-producing various goods, such as cars, airplanes, computer software, sophisticated weapons, crops, meat, fuel, etc. That is not always the case with countries even with high GDP per capita. For example, the figure for Kuwait is $17,000, and that is on par with countries such as Portugal ($17,100). However, most of Kuwait's wealth comes from its oil industry with no real industrial bases beside that, which makes the country vulnerable to the global economy. In other words, the national economy of Kuwait largely depends on the international price of one commodity, oil. When the world's oil consumption increases, so does the price, which enriches its national economy. The opposite also happens: lower oil prices, the dwindled national economy. Kuwait's economic development also has a serious problem: the unavoidable future with less oil production than now. However, Portugal, with about the same GDP per capita as Kuwait, has no such issue of a single-commodity-dependent economy. Moreover, a serious gap regarding socioeconomic infrastructure exists between the two countries. For example, if we look in "port container traffic" that measures "the flow of containers from land sea transport modes and vice versa" the figure of Portugal was 1,012,845 units in 2006 while Kuwait's number was only 750,000 in the same year.[6] The situation is similar in the air. The number of "domestic takeoffs and takeoffs abroad of air carriers registered in" Kuwait was 20,673 in 2006 while Portugal had 119,668.[7] They all indicate an inadequate infrastructure in Kuwait compared to a country with a similar economic size. As you can see, GDP per capita is a good and important measure, but far from being a perfect one. In addition to social and economic elements, we may want to consider political elements as well in our discussion of development. Here, we assume that people are better off in a political system with no restriction on their political participation or no fear toward the political authority. Such a political system is typically achieved by adopting democracy. Inversely, without democracy, a country's economic and social development may not be adequate. For example, Pinochet of Chile ruled the country from 1973 to 1990 and brought about economic and social development; however, his rule was authoritarian in the nature and violent toward the citizens. On the contrary, the US has kept a lively democracy ever since the country was founded in the 18th Century. People here have no fear toward the government due to the democratic system and this allows active participation by the people in pubic as well as private sphere of life. It is, of course, a major difference from other countries with no such political system.

In our discussion, therefore, we would regard a country as being developed when it can and does provide necessary services for the people's wellbeing in a broad sense. Let's go back to Graph 13.3. As we have discussed, the OECD countries are at the top, and the rest are behind them. Latin America and Eastern Europe are behind but they are way ahead of South Asia and Sub-Saharan Africa. Development is a concept based on this continuum with the West at the peak and hence the goal of development for the rest of the world. In other words, development based on the notion that the Western European and Northern American states share common positive features and these elements are absent or in short supply in other areas. Therefore, the notion continues, the countries out of this zone of development should fill the void of the Western hallmarks.

This sense of a destination needs a note of caution. Should the US be the model for countries such as India or Venezuela for their development? Are people in the US better off or happier than those in India or Venezuela? Maybe or maybe not. Actually, polls often show the complexity of this debate. See the following global poll results from Gallup.[8] In this worldwide poll, respondents had three options to choose from: "thriving," "struggling," or "suffering" to evaluate their lives. Table 13.1 shows part of the result. The countries with the largest segment of population regarding their life as "thriving" is Denmark with 72% followed by Canada and Sweden (69%) and Australia (66%). The country at the bottom is Chad where only 1% of population would say their life was thriving. If we look at the top ten countries, there is a noticeable country. Venezuela is not a country that you would expect to see with so many happy people. According to the Western media, the country is often in political confrontations between the poor and the rich and the president Hugo Chavez is an eccentric, manipulative, and populist dictator. Moreover, their GDP per capita $12,700 is 91st largest in the world while 37.9% of population are below the poverty line.[9] And yet, a significant majority of the population seem to be happy. In addition, this is more puzzling if you consider a surprising absence of a country on this top ten list. The US is not on this list. Why is it that the largest economy with the strongest military on this planet is not on this list while a country such as Venezuela is ranked 5th? We do not have a definite answer for you, but this should remind us of the need not to forget that all the implicit assumptions of development may not be universally accepted.

MEASURING UNDERDEVELOPMENT: GDP PER CAPITA AND THE HUMAN DEVELOPMENT INDEX

How would you measure the levels of development? You may have a vague idea that the US is better off than countries such as Mexico and Afghanistan even though you have never been to the countries or researched on them. However, how can you prove that your sense is correct? Can you tell Mexico is better off than Afghanistan, too? To answer all these, and explore more about development, we should be able to measure this concept, development. Two of the most often used measurements of development are already discussed: GDP per capita and child mortality rate. GDP per capita is an average of the market value of the country, dividing

TABLE 13.1 How Happy Are They? Top Ten And Bottom Ten Countries

Top ten countries	Bottom ten countries
1. Denmark: 72%	1. Chad: 1%
2. Canada: 69%	2. Central African Republic: 2%
2. Sweden: 69%	3. Haiti: 2%
4. Australia: 66%	4. Burkina Faso: 3%
5. Finland: 64%	5. Cambodia: 3%
5. Venezuela: 64%	6. Niger: 3%
7. Israel: 63%	7. Tajikistan : 3%
7. New Zealand: 63%	8. Tanzania: 4%
9. Netherlands: 62%	9. Mali: 4%
9. Ireland: 62%	10. Comoros: 4%

From *High Wellbeing Eludes the Masses in Most Countries Worldwide*, April 19, 2011. Copyright © 2011 by Gallup, Inc.

the national value by the number of people in the country. This is a better measurement than GDP because GDP could provide a somewhat distorted picture of the country's economic wellbeing. For example, China's estimated GDP of 2010 was $10 trillion and it was the 3rd largest national wealth in the world.[10] However, even though China is a global economic engine as the world's factory, Chinese economy has a long way to go to catch up with its Western competitors, much less being a number three in the world, considering the poverty in the Western part of China and the overall economic gap. Then is it really the number three in the world or not? This confusion comes from the nature of GDP. For a fact, the Chinese economy produces a gigantic quantity of wealth as a country. However, there are so many people, 1.3 billion, that the national wealth is too small to be adequately shared by them. The amount of income for the Chinese individual on average, the Chinese GDP per capita, was only $7,600 in 2010. It was only 126th largest in the world, putting China on par with countries such as Albania ($8,000), Turkmenistan ($7,500), or Algeria ($7,300).[11]

Some may see this measurement as not entirely satisfying. Is Chinese economic really comparable to the Algerian economy? The answer is yes according to their GDP per capita, but the answer is troubling if you think about your clothes, pens, cell phones, or bags made in China and all other things made in Algeria. Do you have any product made in Algeria in your possession now? No? Well, then GDP per capita may be a good indicator but not good enough by itself to capture an accurate picture of a country's economic development since it misses something. Alternatively, you could use multiple indicators. For example, the International Monetary Fund (IMF) categorises countries as advanced and emerging and developing countries depending on not only per capita income level, but also how diversified a country's exports are and how much the economy is merged into the global financial system.[12] According to this measure, Chinese economy is by far better than the Algerian one that relies on petroleum, natural gas, and petroleum products for 97% of its exports and attracts only an insignificant amount of foreign direct investment.

As we have discussed, however, economic development is not the sole element of development. Therefore, typical measurements of development rely on various indicators for different aspects of development. For example, the UN specifies three indicators to include countries into a category called "least developed countries." The indicators include 1) low gross national income (GNI); 2) a weak human resources involving nutrition, health, and education and literacy; and 3) economic vulnerability such as unstable agricultural production or export.[13] According to this measurement, the least developed countries (LDCs) include countries such as Angola, Bangladesh, Cambodia, Sierra Leone, and Haiti.

There is a measure of development that is more widely used for various purposes: the Human Development Index (HDI) of the United Nations Development Program (UNDP). This index is based on the measurement of three dimensions of development: health, education, and living standard. Each dimension is assessed using distinct indicators. Life expectancy at birth is used to measure the general health of the population. For the level of education, years of schooling is measured. GNI per person is used to determine living standards.[14] Each measure is merged into the composite index between 0 and 1 showing where each state stands in relation to set minimum and maximum for each dimension. For example, according to the 2010 index, Zimbabwe comes at the very bottom of the index with 0.14 followed by countries such as Congo (0.239), Niger (0.262), Burundi (0.282), and Mozambique (0.284). At the top of the list there are countries like Norway (0.938), Australia (0.937), New Zealand (0.907), the US (0.902), and Ireland (0.895).

The UNDP categorizes countries into four groups according to the HDI index: very high, high, medium, and low. Western European and Northern American countries as well as Japan, Australia, New Zealand, Argentina, and Chile are shown to have achieved a very high level of human development. The countries with a "high" development include Russia, Kazakhstan, Ukraine, Belarus, Iran, Saudi Arabia, Turkey, Algeria, Mexico, Brazil, Venezuela, Columbia, Ecuador, and Peru. The countries with a "medium" development are Mongolia, China, Indonesia, Thailand, Vietnam, Laos, India, Iraq, Syria, Egypt, South Africa, Bolivia, Paraguay.[15] A number of countries made significant strides toward higher levels of human development between 1990 and 2010. China and India moved from "low" to "medium" and so did their neighboring countries such as Vietnam and Indonesia. In South America a few countries moved from "medium" to "high," including Mexico, Venezuela, Columbia, Ecuador, and Peru. Despite these positive progresses, many countries in Africa and South Asia have remained in and experience "low" human development. These are Sudan, Congo, Zimbabwe, Kenya, and Zambia in Africa and Nepal and Bangladesh in South Asia, to name only a few.[17] The North-South gap is seen yet again in this measurement. The US, Canada, and Western Europe are highly developed while Eastern Europe and South America are following. Asia is largely behind these regions with Africa at the bottom of the scale.

EXPLAINING UNDERDEVELOPMENT

The gap between the North and the South is wide and persistent. How can we explain this lasting pattern of inequality? Why do countries in the South continue to suffer low levels of development while ones in the North seem to enjoy the fruits of development as if they would do so forever? Is the development of the North related to the underdevelopment of the South? If so, how? Is development possible in the South? Can the development of the North be replicated in the South? Let us introduce a number of theories addressing these perplexing issues of development.

Modernization Theory

During the 1950s and 1960s famous American political scientists explored the issue of underdevelopment and many concluded the lack of development of the South would be eventually overcome by copying what the West did. What the Western countries achieved was summarized by one word, modernization. What's being modern? What needs to be done to be modern? The first necessary step is to adopt modern cultural values. Traditional values are irrational and unscientific—healing the sick with chanting or astrology—while modern values are rational and universal. In a society with modern values, people are evaluated by their ability and merit, not by their family ties or ethnic origin; people are encouraged to develop, not to stay with traditional norms; people believe in the values of science and technology; and people care about the public, not just their family members. Of course, such modern values spur the development of a more efficient economy and a more centralized political system, scholars argue. In traditional societies, the scholars claim, political authority is held by a few people, such as elders or healers, who monopolize various political and social institutions like the executive, legislative, judiciary, religious, and educational ones. This traditional society needs to change to a modern one: professional bureaucracies make decisions following the written rules; political leaders guide bureaucrats; well-organized political parties collect the public opinion and deliver it to the leaders; religion is separated from the state. As a result, the modern society is much more specialized and complex than traditional ones.[18] Early modernization theorists expected that such modernization would inevitably result in overall progress in the society. For example, Rostow laid out stages of economic develment and predicts "the ideas spreads not merely that economic progress is possible, but that economic progress is a necessary condition for some other purposes, judged to be good . . . [W]here the resistance to economic growth disappears, agriculture is commercialized, industry and investment expand, income increases the entrepreneurial class expands, and new technologies spread."[19] Again, cultural changes are presumed to open the path to the overall development, and then the modernization would come smoothly and comprehensively.

The optimism of the modernization theory has been seriously challenged, however. Most of all, it was clear that modernization did not come either smoothly or comprehensively in many countries as expected by the theory. Economic industrialization and cultural modernization in major industrial countries in South America, such as Argentina, Brazil, and Chile, failed to calm the political tension and unexpectedly resulted in the rise of authoritarian dictatorship in the countries during the 1970s and 1980s. A huge influx of foreign investment into countries such as Saudi Arabia and Kuwait has not brought about cultural modernization, let alone a political one. It took more than two decades for the revolutionary economic development in South Korea and Taiwan to generate corresponding modernization in the political area, and it came only after a series of long, violent, and sometimes bloody conflicts. Then what went wrong with the modernization theory? A group of scholars began to point out that the theory lacked any attention to the force of history that actually set the South apart from the North, and many critics responded to this shortfall by studying the historical background of underdevelopment and its effect on the current situation in these countries.

Dependency Theory

Offering an alternative to modernization theory, dependency scholars have identified colonialism by the West as the major contributor to the underdevelopment of the South. They discard the very idea that what the North did can be replicated in the South. Why? First of all, the world has fundamentally and forever changed. When European countries began their industrialization, the competition was limited within Europe while they were able to exploit resources and markets in the rest of the world by creating and expanding their colonies. Now, however, this option is simply not available to developing countries. The function of these countries within the global capitalist economy is to provide raw materials. This is a role first carved out for lesser-developed countries (LDCs) by the European powers during the height of the colonial era, and, according to dependency theory, it is a role or "niche" in which most LDCs have found themselves stuck in the post-colonial era. Therefore, restructuring is not easy. Any efforts to copy the Western industrialization have encountered serious and almost unwinnable competition with countries such as the US, Japan, or Germany. Second, the developed countries control the world economy and they will not give up their control, these scholars point out. These advanced industrialized countries, also called the core, maintain their dominance in the most profitable sector, such as finance, manufactured goods, and technology while the South or countries in the periphery, have been left to specialize in economic sectors that do no generate large values such as agriculture or raw materials. This situation forces the countries in the periphery to accept foreign trades on unfavorable terms. This problem of declining terms of trade is detrimental. During the early days of industrialization, commodities such as coal and iron ore made a substantially larger part of the value of goods than now. However, today's products need a less and less share of such parts. For example, look at your cell phone. Is your battery as significant a part of the product in terms of cost or technology as coal was for steamboats? How about Microsoft's Window 7? How about the banking industry? Theoretically then, developing countries must export more and more raw materials so that they can barely keep up with their basic need to import manufactured goods and sophisticated services from developed countries. As time goes by their dependency on foreign producers will only get deeper and deeper, and industrialization would become harder and harder. This does not mean that the core countries have conspired for total control over the periphery, but rather:

> [Dependency is] . . . a historical condition which shapes a certain structure of the world economy such that it favors some countries to the detriment of others and limits the development possibilities of the subordinate economies . . . a situation in which the economy of a certain group of countries is conditioned by the development and expansion of another economy, to which their own is subjected.[20]

Dependency is not only economic in the nature, but also political. The political elites in periphery states ally with their economic counterparts, and they collect a huge amount of economic benefits from the dependent economy, often at the cost of the majority of the citizens. Since this type of political arrangement serves the interests of the core, the core countries have incentives to support such political regimes in the periphery. Therefore, it is not surprising to see that the core countries back leaders in countries such as Saudi Arabia, Pakistan, Equatorial Guinea, Cuba (before Castro), and Chile (before its democratization), and they rely on such support from the core. Sometimes, political and economic support yields to direct military intervention by the core as the US occasionally did in the Central American countries such as Cuba, Nicaragua, or Panama.

As problematic was the blind optimism of the modernization theory, the pessimistic view of the dependency theory raises serious questions: if modernization is not easy and dependency is hard to shake off, then is development impossible for the developing countries? Are they doomed to fail? Were there any successful cases of development? If so, how did these states manage to end the curse of dependency as predicted by the dependency theorists? To address these issues, now we turn to a number of attempted solutions to the problems of underdevelopment.

DEVELOPMENTAL STRATEGIES

There were two major strategies used by developing countries in the second half of 20th century: import substitution industrialization (ISI) and export-oriented industrialization (EOI). There were varying degrees of success, but the countries that adopted EOI were more successful than others. Most recently, China has successfully utilized this strategy to the extreme degree using its huge size of labor forces and market, among other elements.

Import Substitution Industrialization

"Import substation industrialization" literally means producing goods that were previously being imported from abroad so that domestically produced goods can substitute for the imported ones. This strategy was largely used by countries in Latin America right after World War II as a way to break their dependent ties with former colonial masters. These countries tried to shift industrial bases from production of raw materials to producing manufactured goods that were then being imported from European countries. For this purpose, these countries provided various mechanisms of protection for domestic producers such as high tariffs, overvalued currency, and discouragement of foreign direct investment. The hope was that such protection along with vibrant domestic markets would give enough time for the domestic producers to gain expertise and capacity to compete with Western counterparts. However, the initial success of industrialization was rocked by a series of economic shocks from abroad: a hike in food prices in the 1970s, oil shocks, and debt crisis. Moreover, the initial assumptions for the strategy were also proven to be not entirely correct. Domestic producers saw few incentives to be competitive both in domestic and foreign markets when there were well protected by the state. In addition, the domestic market never grew big enough to reach the point of economies of scale to be profitable for the producers. Politically speaking, such governmental protection eventually became a prerequisite for the protected industries and they grew powerful enough to make sure the protection was permanent, not temporary as originally planned. It was increasingly difficult to remove the protection while it became a source of corruption and economic headache rather than a cure.

Export-oriented Industrialization

After World War II, a handful of countries led by Japan went in the opposite direction to the Latin American countries in terms of their development strategies. Instead of isolating themselves from the world by discouraging imports, these countries proceeded to integrate with global markets by encouraging exports. Their target was the Western markets, such as the US and Europe, unlike domestic ones as ISI emphasized. These countries, Japan, followed by South Korea, Taiwan, Hong Kong, and Singapore, also known as Asian Tigers, were able to sharpen their competitive edge by using a large pool of well-educated and cheap workers. In the beginning the exported goods were typically labor-intensive goods, such as dolls and cloth. As these countries established industrial bases by gaining skills, knowledge, and experience in producing and marketing, they began to produce increasingly more sophisticated and expensive goods such as electronics or vehicles. This transition was typically led not by the market, but by the government. The government wrote master plans for the national economy and executed them with a strong and sometimes even fearful commitment. Private companies that refused to follow the government's leadership were excluded from financial incentives of the government, punished, or even dismantled. This strategy was highly successful and brought astonishing economic development to Japan and later the Asian Tigers. Only a half century ago, the Asian Tigers were poverty-stricken and, in the case of South Korea and Taiwan, war-devastated. But now, these countries, needless to say about Japan, are major global economic powers. A few cases in point: Hyun-dae, a South Korean automaker opened its factory in Montgomery, Alabama; LG and Samsung, South Korean electronics companies have become leading producers of home electronics such as TV and cell phones; Taiwanese computer brands, such as Asus and Acer, are immensely successful in the US. Most recently, China became another example of a successful development based on this strategy.

DEBATE ON STRATEGIES

The astonishing success of the Asian Tigers was hailed as a major stamp of approval for the liberal argument that the market would do the best job in development if the government limits its intervention to the minimum. The liberals assert that the governments' intervention were limited to investing in human capital such as educated workforces and talented bureaucracy, establishing a competitive climate for private enterprises, opening the economy to trade, and maintaining macroeconomic stability.[21] Such public policies created an environment where private companies could grow strong and productive enough to compete in the global market, which in turn brought economic prosperity to the countries. This observation grew to be part of a larger body of consensus among Western policy makers such as state officials and leaders of international financial organizations who have been convinced that development would be achieved by a competitive market, free trade, and minimum intervention by the government in the economy, and this became known as the Washington consensus. This idea became even more powerful during the 1980s when the Thatcher government in the UK and the Reagan administration in the US actively pursued a series of policies based on it. The consensus has become also palpable in typical Western foreign aid and most visible in the IMF rescue packages that stipulate the liberal public policy for its loans. For example, Greece and foreign lenders, including the IMF, European Union, and European Central Bank, agreed to an austerity plan in exchange for $17 billion worth emergency aid to Greece.[22] The plan includes an additional $5.4 billion in tax increases and spending cuts, sale of about $70 billion in state assets, and allowing liberalization of the banking industry.

Is the Washington Consensus correct? Is the market a solution? Should governmental intervention be kept minimum in the economy? As powerful and popular as its argument is, there is no shortage of its criticism. According to Chang Ha-joon, an economics professor of the University of Cambridge, the very idea of a free market is only a myth because the market can exist only when the government actively protects and regulates the market.[23] In other words, the market could thrive and economy can develop only when the state has established a concrete political system. According to this idea, therefore, the market-oriented solution may never work in a state where its political institutions are still being developed. In a similar vein, it should also be emphasized that the Asian Tigers' economic development was possible not because the government took the backseat, but because the governmental intervention was intense and effective. After all, South Korea, Taiwan, and Singapore had authoritarian governments during the heydays of their economic development. These governments repressed labor movement using violence in order to keep the cost of production artificially low. Labor unions, much less labor disputes, were not allowed and practically prohibited for most years of the early stages of development. The governments also controlled the capital and channeled investments according to, not the market demand but, the government's master plan for the overall economy. The governments heavily invested in public education, guaranteeing a consistent flow of skilled and bright work force into the market. Moreover, going back further into 1950s and 60s, both South Korea and Taiwan aggressively pursued protectionist policies while the US provided the foreign market and financial aid as well as political and military assistance.

EAST ASIAN MODEL IN OTHER REGIONS

The sources of economic development in East Asia are debatable; however, what is indisputable is the level of overall development in this area. Graph 13.4 demonstrates this trend in East Asia as well as a few other countries. Successful economic development was followed in East Asian countries such as Japan, South Korea, and Hong Kong. This developmental strategy was copied by other Southeast Asian countries such as Vietnam and Indonesia and these countries have also experienced a similar developmental trend as shown in this graph. Among these countries, Japan, South Korea, and Hong Kong's levels of development are comparable even to the American one. Compared to these, Zimbabwe's score is not only the lowest, but also surprisingly plunged since 1980, due in large part to the government's poor management of economy. Political crises have never been in short supply in Zimbabwe, but the land reform that began in 2000 was too destructive to salvage. White farmers were forced to give up their land for they supported President Mugabe's rival and without them the agriculture was simply not sustainable. The country plunged into economic chaos with inflation reaching 231,000,000% in 2008.[24]

If the East Asian model is successful and was replicated in some countries in Southeast Asia, can it be also tried more broadly including sub-Saharan Africa and South Asia for a similar result? It could, but such

GRAPH 13.4 Human Development Index, 1980–2010. Graph created by the authors.

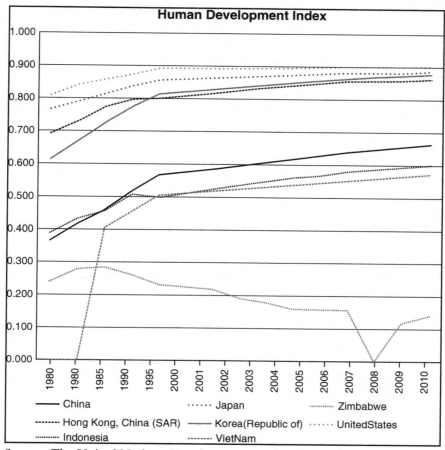

Source: The United Nations Development Program (UNDP).

replication is easier said than done. Before we discuss this issue, let us remind you of the variation both among Asian Tigers and among sub-Saharan countries. EOI strategies are not the same in all the countries. For example, Hong Kong pursued policies aiming at a *laissez-faire* economy while South Korea and Taiwan emphasized a strong presence of the government. South Korean economy was directed toward development of heavy industry sectors owned by a few conglomerates, but Taiwan did not follow this path. Sub-Saharan countries are also different to each other. There are countries such as Botswana and Uganda that continuously grew, defying the myth that all African countries are in a miserable economic condition. Therefore, be mindful that the following discussion will address general and abstracted aspects of the problems.

Remember that EOI was led by the government in East Asia. The government has been typically staffed by the elite of the country who usually went through the public education and saw their future in the governmental jobs. The government was stable enough to fulfill their expectation by giving them job security and social status in return. This tells us two important elements of development: the presence of quality education and stable government. First, unfortunately, in many developing countries in Sub-Saharan Africa and South Asia, this is not the case. It is frequently the case that opportunities for educational advancement are lower in other lesser-developed regions than has been the case in the East Asian countries. For example, in Congo 2010 average year schooling is only about 3.76 years, which results in a low level of adult literacy rate, 67.2%. The average year schooling in Bangladesh is also low with 4.77 years and its adult literacy rate hovers only at 47.9%. Compare this to South Korea where the mean schooling years reach 11.64 years with almost universal adult literacy rate.[25] Of course, a small size of well-educated population also means a small pool of quality workers that is absolutely crucial for industrialization. Without well-educated workers, it is really hard to build the manufacturing industry, much less service sectors such as banking and financing.

Second, in countries such as Congo and Somalia, governance is fragile due to various political challenges such as political violence or even ethnic and civil war. In Somalia, a series of civil war since 1991 created a virtual anarchy where the governmental authority has been limited only within Mogadishu, the capital city. Congo was also dragged into one civil war after another since 1996 until 2009. Civil wars devastated countries such as Chad, Central African Republic, Niger, Rwanda, Sierra Leone, Sudan, and Uganda, to name only a few. In another example, Kenya, which enjoyed political stability for decades, was plunged into violent ethnic confrontations when the incumbent president Kibaki won the rigged presidential election in 2007. Situations like this are hardly ideal for the government to lead any industrialization efforts, let alone development of the entire society. Therefore, for the success of EOI to be replicated, it is crucial to forge, first of all, stable and effective political leadership and build a productive educational system.

Foreign trade was crucial to the success of East Asia, but they were hard to come by in other developing countries. For one, many leaders who remembered the colonial era saw foreign trade and investment as an extended form of colonialism, which prevented these newly-independent countries from actively seeking the export-based developmental strategy. Even when these countries want to trade, it is still difficult. Many countries are landlocked, or do not have an effective transportation system, such as paved roads or big ports, or both, which increases the cost of production and lowers their competitiveness. Moreover, developing countries largely do not have the access to international capital markets as much as they would like to have (which country would you lend your money to? Zimbabwe or Singapore?). This lack of sufficient financial resources is compounded by their debt crisis. Many developing countries have continued to suffer the problem of debt service payments.

Another difficulty of replicating the success of East Asia in other regions is the international environment. When East Asian countries, especially South Korea and Taiwan, began their industrialization in the 1960s, the Cold War put these countries in the frontline in the battle against the communist camp. Thus, the West had a strong incentive to keep these countries politically stable, militarily secure, and economically developed. The financial aid and later investment from the West kept flowing in while they opened the market to the products from these Asian countries. This economic opportunity for South Korea and Taiwan became even more promising since it was the time when the global trade was exploding, encouraged by the General Agreement on Trade and Tariffs (GATT), and the European economy was rapidly recovering. Moreover, the US had a robust military presence across the region, including the presence of the 7th Fleet, consisting of 60–70 ships, 200–300 aircraft and 40,000 Navy and Marine Corps personnel.[26] This presence of the US military was the key to the security of these countries, deterring the threats from hostile neighbors such as China, North Korea, and the Soviets. In addition, the US provided substantial economic assistance to these states. However, such a favorable international environment does not exist for today's developing countries. Worse still, many developing countries, especially countries with a large agricultural sector, suffer from the developed countries' strong protection of their own agriculture. The US and the EU provide a large amount of subsidies in various forms, such as tax breaks or direct payment, to their farmers who can afford to sell their products at a price that is much lower than it should be without the government subsidies. This, in turn, lowers the global prices and reduces the revenues of many developing countries. EOI was successful in part because of noneconomic factors in and around East Asia. Therefore, in order to be successfully replicated in other regions, the countries and international community must address these other issues as well as the economic aspects of the regions.

Industrialization in any country depend on access to sufficient resources, an educated population, a stable domestic environment, and a friendly the international climate. The improvement of the quality of life using the fruits of industrialization is yet another challenge. There are obstacles everywhere: corrupt politicians, war, divided population, lack of social infrastructure, malfunctioning education system, cultural barriers, colonial experience, brutal competition with foreign industries and countries, and so on. The task seems to be almost impossible and many countries have been struggling. However, there are cases where these obstacles were overcome impressively by some and modestly by others, which give us hope.

Notes

1 Sharon LaFraniere, " Young Brides Pay the Price of African Poverty," *The New York Times*, November 27, 2005. http://www.nytimes.com/2005/11/27/world/africa/27iht-brides.html.

2 http://hdr.undp.org/external/gapminder/2005/2005.html (accessed November 18, 2011)

3 http://hdr.undp.org/external/gapminder/2005/2005.html (accessed November 18, 2011)

4 GDP (purchasing power parity) Per Capita based on 2008 IMF estimates http://upload.wikimedia.org/wikipedia/commons/f/fa/GDP_PPP_Per_Capita_IMF_2008.png. (accessed November 18, 2011)

5 http://hdr.undp.org/external/gapminder/2005/2005.html. (accessed November 18, 2011)

6 The World Bank's website: http://data.worldbank.org/indicator/IS.SHP.GOOD.TU/countries/KW--XR. (accessed November 18, 2011)

7 The World Bank"s website: http://data.worldbank.org/indicator/IS.AIR.DPRT/countries/KW--XR. (accessed November 18, 2011)

8 Erin Valois, "Survey says: Canada is second happiest country in the world" *National Post*, (April 20, 2011). http://news.nationalpost.com/2011/04/20/survey-says-canada-is-second-happiest-country-according-to-new-poll/ (accessed November 18, 2011)

9 The CIA, The World Factbook. https://www.cia.gov/library/publications/the-world-factbook/geos/ve.html. (accessed November 18, 2011)

10 The CIA, The World Factbook. https://www.cia.gov/library/publications/the-world-factbook/geos/ch.html. (accessed November 18, 2011)

11 The CIA, The World Factbook. https://www.cia.gov/library/publications/the-world-factbook/ (accessed November 18, 2011)

12 The International Monetary Fund website. http://www.imf.org/external/pubs/ft/weo/faq.htm#q4b. (accessed November 18, 2011)

13 "(1) a low-income criterion, based on a 3-year average estimate of the GNI per capita (under $750 for inclusion, above $900 for graduation); (2) a human resource weakness criterion, involving a composite Human Assets Index (HAI) based on indicators of: (a) nutrition; (b) health; (c) education; and (d) adult literacy; and (3) an economic vulnerability criterion, involving a composite Economic Vulnerability Index (EVI) based on indicators of: (a) the instability of agricultural production; (b) the instability of exports of goods and services; (c) the economic importance of nontraditional activities (share of manufacturing and modern services in GDP); (d) merchandise export concentration; and (e) the handicap of economic smallness (as measured through the population in logarithm); and the percentage of population displaced by natural disasters." The United Nations website. http://www.un.org/special-rep/ohrlls/ldc/ldc%20criteria.htm. (accessed November 18, 2011)

14 The United Nations Development Program (UNDP), http://hdr.undp.org/en/statistics/hdi/. (accessed November 18, 2011)

15 The UNDP, http://hdr.undp.org/en/data/map/. (accessed November 18, 2011)

16 Ibid.

17 Among these countries, the welfare of people in Zimbabwe is especially worrisome because the country is at the bottom of the HDI list of 2010 (the index, 0.181) and the country's situation has rapidly deteriorated since 1990, when the index was 0.336.

18 Howard Handelman, *The Challenge of Third World Development*, 5th ed. (Upper Saddle River, NJ: Pearson Prentice Hall, 2006, 2009), 13–15.

19 Wat W. Rostow, *The Stages of Economic Growth* (New York: Cambridge University Press, 1960), 6–8, Requoted from Ruth Lane, *The Art of Comparative Politics* (Allyn and Bacon, 1997), 53.

20 Theotonio Dos Santos, "The Structure of Dependence," in *Readings in U.S. Imperialism*, eds K.T. Fann and Donald C. Hodges, eds. (Boston: Porter Sargent, 1971), 226, requoted from Handelman, *The Challenge of Third World Development*, 17.

21 The World Bank, *The East Asian Economic Miracle: Economic Growth and Public Policy* (New York: Oxford University Press, 1993).

22 Rachel Donadio and Niki Kitsantonis, " Greece and Its Lenders Agree on Austerity Plan," *The New York Times*, June 23, 2011.

23 Ha-Joon Chang, *Bad Samaritans – The Myth of Free Trade and the Secret History of Capitalism* (New York: Bloomsbury Press, 2008).

24 Chris McGreal, "Zimbabwe's inflation rate surges to 231,000,000%," *The Guardian*, October 9, 2008.

25 The United Nations Development Program (UNDP) and the Central Intelligence Agency Factbook.

26 The US 7th Fleet website http://www.c7f.navy.mil/about.htm (accessed November 18, 2011).

INDEX

CPSIA information can be obtained
at www.ICGtesting.com
Printed in the USA
LVOW02s0811180117
521327LV00005B/24/P